Culture and Privilege in Capitalist Asia

The social and economic transformation of Asia has been closely associated with the rise of the new rich. These mostly successful capitalists and salaried professionals have influenced not only the economic changes in the region, but also the cultural restructuring that has accompanied these changes.

Through a range of social settings – village, factory, city, nation, diaspora and region – this book looks at the cultural changes in national, ethnic, religious and class identities. The authors employ case studies from Singapore, China, Malaysia, the Philippines, Thailand, India and Indonesia and break new ground with their documentation and analyses of privilege in capitalist Asia. The book also employs a strong theoretical component that questions the approaches to be found in other studies of the new rich.

The contributions to *Culture and Privilege in Capitalist Asia* include a variety of approaches and subject-matter. All testify not only to the powerful structural positions occupied by the new rich, but also to the contentious cultural relations through which the new rich have become a powerful social force in Asia.

Michael Pinches is Senior Lecturer in Anthropology at the University of Western Australia, Perth, and President of the Philippines Studies Association of Australia.

The New Rich in Asia series
Edited by Richard Robison

**The New Rich in Asia: Mobile Phones,
McDonald's and Middle-class Revolution**
Edited by Richard Robison and David S. G. Goodman

Political Oppositions
Edited by Gary Rodan

Gender and Power in Affluent Asia
Edited by Krishna Sen and Maila Stivens

Culture and Privilege in Capitalist Asia

Edited by Michael Pinches

 London and New York

This book is a project of the Asia Research Centre,
Murdoch University, Western Australia

First published 1999
by Routledge
11 New Fetter Lane, London EC4P 4EE

Simultaneously published in the USA and Canada
by Routledge
29 West 35th Street, New York, NY 10001

© 1999 Selection and editorial matter, Michael Pinches; individual
chapters, the contributors

Typeset in Baskerville by Routledge
Printed and bound in Great Britain by Redwood Books, Trowbridge,
Wiltshire

British Library Cataloguing in Publication Data
A catalogue record for this book is available from the British Library

Library of Congress Cataloging in Publication Data
A catalogue record for this book has been requested

ISBN 0–415–-19763–5 (hbk)
ISBN   0–415–19764–3 (pbk)

Contents

Tables   vii
Notes on contributors   ix
Preface   xi
Acknowledgements   xvii

1 Cultural relations, class and the new rich of Asia   1
   MICHAEL PINCHES

2 Consumption, social differentiation and self-definition of the
   new rich in industrialising Southeast Asia   56
   KEN YOUNG

3 From *Orang Kaya Baru* to *Melayu Baru*: cultural construction of
   the Malay 'new rich'   86
   A. B. SHAMSUL

4 The contribution of a Japanese firm to the cultural
   construction of the new rich in Malaysia   111
   WENDY A. SMITH

5 Singapore: where the new middle class sets the standard   137
   CHUA BENG HUAT AND TAN JOO EAN

6 The years of living luxuriously: identity politics of Indonesia's
   new rich   159
   ARIEL HERYANTO

7 The new rich and cultural tensions in rural Indonesia   188
   HANS ANTLÖV

8 How a revolution becomes a dinner party: stratification,
   mobility and the new rich in urban China   208
   CHRISTOPHER BUCKLEY

9 Creating the Thai middle class   230
   JIM OCKEY

10 The state, globalisation and Indian middle-class identity   251
    SALIM LAKHA

11 Entrepreneurship, consumption, ethnicity and national
    identity in the making of the Philippines' new rich   275
    MICHAEL PINCHES

    Index   302

Tables

5.1   Average proportion of expenditure spent on cooked food, by
      household size   138
5.2   Distribution of monthly household income (from all sources), 1990   140
5.3   Political attitudes of the middle and working classes   143
5.4   Political behaviour of the middle and working classes   143
5.5   Distribution of resident private household and car owners by type
      of dwelling, 1990   146
5.6   Married couples by monthly income from work and working status,
      1990   147
8.1   Occupational class classifications   212
8.2   Average monthly income by occupational class and other major
      variables for working respondents (N = 1128)   214
8.3   Inflow table of respondents' most recent occupational class by
      family head's occupational class (%)   216
8.4   Distribution of friendship ties by class (%) (N = 1168)   220
8.5   Frequency of different forms of personal help in urban Beijing
      friendship networks (%) (N = 1168)   223
9.1   Occupational groups in Thailand age 11 and up, 1960, 1970,
      1980, 1990   235
9.2   Occupations ranked by status   236
9.3   Advertising expenditures in million baht, 1979–1993   241
9.4   Advertising expenditures by category, 1994   241

Notes on contributors

Hans Antlöv is a programme officer at the Ford Foundation in Jakarta and former director of the Centre for East and Southeast Asian Studies, Göteborg University, Sweden. He has written on cultural constructions of leadership, nationalism, revolution and democracy in Indonesia and other parts of Southeast Asia. His main works include *Exemplary Centre, Administrative Periphery: Leadership and the New Order in Rural Java* (1995) and *Mosaic of Nations: Indonesia, Vietnam and Malaya, 1945–1950* (forthcoming, co-author).

Christopher Buckley is a Ph.D. student at the Contemporary China Centre, RSPAS, Australian National University, and is presently teaching at Peking University, Beijing, China.

Chua Beng Huat is currently Associate Professor in the Department of Sociology, National University of Singapore. His recent publications include *Communitarian Ideology and Democracy in Singapore* (1995) *and Political Legitimacy and Housing: Stakeholding in Singapore* (1997). His current research interest is in comparative cultural studies in Asia. He is also a frequent commentator on social and political developments in Singapore in public media.

Ariel Heryanto lectures at the Southeast Asian Studies Programme, National University of Singapore. Previously he was a lecturer in the Postgraduate Program, Development Studies at Universitas Kristen Satya Wacana, Indonesia. He is the author of *Language of Development and Development of Language* (1995), edited *Perdebatan Sastra Kontekstual* (1985), and has contributed chapters for several volumes, articles for journals, and columns for newspapers and magazines.

Salim Lakha is an honorary research fellow with the National Centre for South Asian Studies in Melbourne and he teaches in Economic History at Monash University. Prior to that he was a senior lecturer in Politics at Swinburne University of Technology. His research and teaching interests include globalisation, diasporic studies, political economy of development, and urbanisation. His regional areas of expertise are India and Pakistan. He is the author of *Capitalism and Class in Colonial India: The Case of Ahmedabad*

(1988) and co-editor of *Wage Labour and Social Change: The proletariat in Asia and the Pacific* (1987, 1992).

James Ockey is a Senior Lecturer in Politics at Canterbury University in Christchurch, New Zealand. He is currently doing research on 'Hyde Park Democracy' in 1950s Thailand.

Michael Pinches is Senior Lecturer in Anthropology at the University of Western Australia, Perth, and President of the Philippine Studies Association of Australia. He has carried out extensive research on the Philippines, mainly among workers in Manila and the Visayas. He is co-editor of *Wage Labour and Social Change: The proletariat in Asia and the Pacific* (1987, 1992) and is author of a number of articles on urbanisation, class, culture and politics in the Philippines.

A. B. Shamsul is Professor of Social Anthropology and, currently, Dean, Faculty of Social Sciences and Humanities, at The National University of Malaysia, Bangi, Malaysia. He researches, teaches and writes extensively on 'politics, culture and development' in Southeast Asia, with an empirical focus on Malaysia. His most well-known book is *From British to Bumiputera Rule* (1986). He is currently completing a volume on 'Identity Formation in Malaysia'.

Wendy Smith is a Senior Lecturer in the Department of Japanese Studies, Monash University, Melbourne, Australia. Her doctorate in anthropology focused on Japanese management and industrial relations in a Malaysian–Japanese joint venture. She has lived and researched in Japan for five years and Malaysia for nine years. Her current research projects include Japanese masculinity, the globalisation of Japanese new religions and the working lives and temple management strategies of Japanese Buddhist priests.

Tan Joo Ean is a Lecturer in the Department of Sociology at the National University of Singapore. Her current research focus is on the family in Southeast Asia.

Ken Young is Professor of Asian Studies and Director of the Asia Australia Research Centre at Swinburne University of Technology, Melbourne. His research has involved numerous periods in Indonesia, Hong Kong, Singapore and Malaysia. He is the author of *Islamic Peasants and the State* (1994), co-editor of *The Politics of Middle-Class Indonesia* (1990), and is currently preparing an edited volume on citizenship in Indonesia.

Preface

Over the three decades to the late 1990s an increasing number of countries in the Asian region experienced industrialisation and rapid economic growth. Within their populations new layers of people were accumulating wealth and enjoying material prosperity. While the recent economic crisis has severely curbed the successes of the new rich in some countries, their rise and, in some cases, their fall have left a longstanding imprint on societies in the Asian region, and indeed on the whole global order. Just who are these new rich, how have they come into being, and what place do they occupy in their societies and the Asian region at large? In the first volume in this series these questions are addressed primarily in reference to the changing political-economic structures in the region. The second and third volumes explore these questions with reference to political oppositions and gender. In this, the fourth volume, we address these questions with reference to cultural processes in the region. In particular we focus on the social and cultural identities of the new rich as they are variously constructed by themselves and by others, through ethnic stereotyping, lifestyle and consumption patterns, interpersonal conduct, moral judgements, and nationalist or class ideologies. Our analyses do not preclude an examination of structural forces in accounting for the emergence and character of the new rich, but they draw attention to the cultural arena as crucial to an understanding of these new and powerful layers of people in Asia.

Cultural accounts of Asia's new rich invariably seek either to explain their emergence in reference to alleged Oriental cultural traits, or else characterise them as global consumers whose lifestyles more or less emulate those found among the affluent in the West. In the first introductory chapter, I critically examine each of these representations, not so much as explanations or self-evident descriptions in their own right, but rather as powerful cultural constructs that themselves require interpretation and analysis. I locate these representations historically in reference to the changing configurations of class and status relations in the region, and argue that they bear out important social tensions and hegemonic shifts in much of Asia. The chapter is critical of both culturalist and narrow political economy readings of the new rich in Asia, and seeks to develop an understanding of the new rich through a cultural relations perspective on class and power. In particular, I argue that the varied identities attributed to, and sought by, Asia's new rich have developed through a series of status oppositions centred around such ideas as development, ethnicity, nationalism, merit and taste.

In the second chapter Ken Young looks at the importance of consumption as the chief means by which the new rich in Indonesia, Malaysia, Thailand and Singapore create new identities for themselves. While outlining the structural conditions that prefigure the emergence of the new rich in these four societies, Young draws attention to the new roles, social positions and lifestyles in which the new rich find themselves, and for which they are being resocialised. He argues that this takes place through the practices of everyday life at such sites as workplaces, schools, shopping malls and residential neighbourhoods, the last two of which he deals with in some detail. While the new rich may be structurally heterogeneous, they have a common capacity for discretionary spending which they use to mark themselves off from others socially. The most important unifying force among them is to be found in their new forms of consumption and public display, derived largely from international middle-class fashion. Shopping malls, in particular, present the new rich with an opportunity both to learn and display a style of life appropriate to their new material circumstances. New residential estates serve a similar function, but offer the new rich greater opportunity for social exclusivity. In developing this argument, Young expressly rejects the common cultural stereo-typing of the new rich as predominantly ethnic Chinese. While this may appear to be statistically true, Chinese ethnicity is not the pre-eminent mode of identifica-tion among the new rich, nor is its meaning uniform. In noting the commonly apolitical character of the new rich, Young also argues against the stereotype that defines them in terms of their political agency.

In Chapter 3, A. B. Shamsul examines the historical trajectory of popular, academic and official conceptualisations of the Malay new rich, in particular the shift from the popular term *Orang Kaya Baru* (new rich person) to the state-spon-sored expression *Melayu Baru* (new Malay). Though the dominant understanding is positive, there are also elements of a subaltern discourse in which both terms are rendered negatively. While acknowledging the importance of global and regional political-economic processes to the formation of the Malay new rich, Shamsul argues that their emergence also needs to be understood in terms of local cultural politics. Thus the Malay new rich are shown to have come into existence as an end product of the pursuit of Malay nationalism, first formulated in the 1920s in response to British colonialism and the presence of a large, economically powerful, Chinese immigrant community. On the one hand, the Malay new rich are neo-liberal in their economic perspectives and share close economic and professional relations with local Chinese capitalists; on the other, they have been a major force behind the resurgence of Islam in Malaysia. Thus, Shamsul argues, the emergence of the Malay new rich is as much about the pursuit of tradition as it is about the arrival of modernity.

In the fourth chapter, also on Malaysia, Wendy Smith draws attention to the importance of understanding the micro-processes through which the new rich have been shaped, and to the workplace as the arena in which many of these processes are focused. Based on a study of the Japanese company Iroha (Malaysia), Smith highlights and analyses the important distinctions that have emerged among the Malay new rich in terms of state and corporate patronage, lifestyle differences, village, ethnic and class affiliations. These differences variously centre on the impact of the Japanese system of management, and on the Mahathir regime's New Economic Policy. While all Malays working for Iroha enjoy new wealth, socio-cultural distinctions have opened up between four groups: senior managers from the old Malay middle class; veteran junior managers from peasant origins, who have risen up through the company; educated junior managers, also from peasant origins, who have benefited from state scholarships; and workers, who enjoy greater spending power than they had in their home villages. Smith documents and explains the varied ways in which these groups have assumed distinctive social and cultural identities.

Singapore has been transformed over three generations from a society that was more or less homogeneously poor to one in which nearly everyone can be described as newly rich. Relative both to their own pasts and to other peoples in the region, Singaporeans are encouraged by their politicians to see themselves as high achievers. Moreover, heavy state spending on goods of collective consumption often evokes images of a nation that is now uniformly middle-class. In Chapter 5, Chua Beng Huat and Tan Joo Ean reject this image, along with the other common representation of Singapore as a society founded on ethnic distinction. Instead, they argue that Singapore has become an increasingly stratified society, in which social distinctions and private aspirations revolve around the idea of meritocracy, measured principally through differing levels of private consumption, in particular the possession of a car and private house. According to Chua and Tan, this general preoccupation exceeds any overt concern with or involvement in political matters, and accounts for the absence of a distinctive working-class consciousness in Singapore. Yet among the middle class, they suggest, there is an important distinction between the contented and the anxiety-laden. They argue further that the richest Singaporeans are notable for their inconspicuous consumption, in part because of their 'transnationalised' identities, and because of attempts by the state to contain the potentially disruptive effects of growing wealth disparities.

In the sixth chapter, Ariel Heryanto traces the origins of the Indonesian new rich to the economic boom of the three decades to 1997, but he expressly rejects any attempt to reduce their emerging cultural identity to economic forces alone. In particular, he draws attention to the increasing preoccupation with lifestyle and consumption, both on the part of the new rich themselves, but also among the general populace. In large part this can be understood as an outcome of the need to establish a new hegemonic order for the emergent bourgeoisie, in the face of an older nationalist/populist political culture that was hostile to capitalism, foreigners and the West. This could be sustained while the rich were predominantly Caucasian or Chinese, but the growing number of rich or middle-class indigenous Indonesians, commonly allied with wealthy ethnic Chinese, created a new need to legitimate wealth. Anti-Chinese sentiments were being phased out of New Order political rhetoric and capitalism is being redefined as consistent with the state ideology of *Pancasila*. Leading business figures sought to establish their nationalist and cultural credentials through such activities as public poetry recitals and declarations of their willingness to help the needy. According to Heryanto, the legitimacy of the new rich as big-spending consumers rests heavily on the fact that Indonesian national identity is itself being redefined through the appropriation and thus subversion of things Western. Even the ascendancy of Islam among the new rich works through their consumer lifestyles. Yet there is no consensus on the meaning of national identity, and Heryanto observes that the conspicuous consumption associated with the new rich continues to arouse moral condemnation from some quarters, critical of its Western origins.

Similar points also arise in Chapter 7 where Hans Antlöv examines the contradictory character of the new rich in the west Javanese village of Sariendah. He disputes the argument that the new rich constitute an unambiguous force for modernisation, arguing that while they increasingly pursue a life of privatised consumer comfort, they choose to do so as members of a close-knit village community. In part, this choice arises because of the dependence of most new rich on state privileges, which in turn depend on their promoting state developmental programmes and political consent within the village. The contradictory character of the village new rich in part rests on the different roles they perform on behalf of the state: as political and economic brokers between state agencies and the community, and as role models of modernity, expressed in their private accumulation of wealth and consumer lifestyle. While ordinary villagers are themselves largely dependent on 'modern' factory employment and green revolution technology, they invoke a 'traditional' discourse in their criticisms of these tensions in the behaviour of the new rich.

Like Antlöv's chapter, Chris Buckley's on China (Chapter 8) traces the sources of wealth of many of Beijing's new rich to the position they occupy or occupied within the state, and to the way in which they have turned this to private material advantage. The most prominent and numerous are well-credentialled party members associated with bureaucratic authority and/or professional expertise, in particular those who have moved from such positions into business . While some have risen from small businesses and lower occupational backgrounds, an inordinate number have parents with backgrounds similar to their own. In a context of an uncertain market and capricious bureaucracy, access to capital depends crucially on the generation of, and participation in, mutual help networks made up of people from like backgrounds. The patterns of trust and reputation that are central to the operation of these networks are in turn played out through particular modes of gift-giving and status signification centred on conspicuous consumption. The literature which simply describes this conspicuous consumption, usually critically, generally ignores or trivialises the social processes that lie behind it. Furthermore, while there is an important instrumental dimension to the individual practices associated with this, what is generated too is a particular form of collective identity and sociality that offers its own rewards, and which is coming to represent a distinctive middle-class way of life.

In Chapter 9, Jim Ockey deals with the varied ways in which the Thai new rich are represented as middle-class in academic and political discourse. He argues that, both sociologically and conceptually, there is not one middle class but a number: the white-collar middle class, the educated middle class and the consumer middle class, measured respectively in terms of occupational categories, educational credentials and patterns of consumption. Ockey notes that each of these middle classes is defined according to objective structural criteria. In addition, he says, there are two other middle classes, identified according to the criteria of action or consciousness. The first, characterised in terms of a particular lifestyle constructed through commodity consumption and advertising, is most directly associated with the 'consumer middle class'. The second, characterised in terms of democratic activism and political influence, is founded on a particular interpretation of popular urban uprisings as 'middle-class'. This latter construction, which ignores working-class participation in popular uprisings, is principally the self-serving creation of educated intellectuals. In Thailand the general term 'middle-class' is applied to all of these categories and modes of behaviour. Yet Ockey argues that while there is some overlap between them, there is also significant variation. While much discursive energy has been devoted to the cultural construction of a Thai middle class, it has not produced nor converged around a clearly delineated social entity.

In India, as in Thailand and a number of other countries in the region, the new rich are popularly represented as the middle class. Over the past two decades much attention has focused on the burgeoning Indian middle class, equating it not just with increasing prosperity in India, but also with the processes of economic liberalisation and global consumerism. In Chapter 10, Salim Lakha traces the growing number of Indian capitalist entrepreneurs and educated middle-class professionals in relation to state-sponsored development programmes and the globalised movement of capital and professional labour. He argues that there has now come into being a new rich middle class whose identity is both global and, at the same time, rooted in India. He focuses, in particular, on the cultural role of diasporic Indians in the formation of this global Indian middle class, both as the bearers of outside knowledge and experience, and as the carriers of such things as Indian religious nationalism and caste or communal identities. The peculiar tension between global and local that characterises this new rich middle class is what distinguishes it from other classes in India, including other segments of a more broadly defined middle class.

In the final chapter, on the Philippines, I examine the emergence of the new rich as a social and cultural phenomenon that largely needs to be understood in a context of regional and domestic contestation over national and dominant class identities. The chapter deals with two principal representations that have developed around the new rich. The first concerns a rhetoric of entrepreneurship which variously celebrates the ideas of liberal democracy, Filipino-Chinese ethnicity and indigenous Filipino values. The second concerns a lifestyle of conspicuous consumption, which, on the one hand, denotes newly found affluence and heightened social standing, yet, on the other, is commonly the subject of denigration. These two representations constitute the cultural battleground in which the old and new rich seek ascendancy. While the social divide between new and old rich is shown to be a good deal more problematic than these representations suggest, an important conclusion is that significant hegemonic weight has shifted behind the 'new rich', and that this has as much to do with the reconstruction of Philippine nationalism as it does with the internal struggles over the accumulation of wealth.

The chapters that make up this collection do not pretend to offer an exhaustive coverage of the Asian region. Rather, they deal with a range of settings, themes and issues in such a way as to provide insight into actors and processes that are shaping the Asian region as a whole, as well as particular localities within it. As is evident from the two complementary chapters set in both Indonesia and Malaysia, there are also different insights to be drawn from studies set at the level of the nation or large city, and others set at the village or enterprise level. One of the major strengths of the collection is both its documentation of local and national differences, and its concern with broader processes of change centred on the social and cultural constructions of the new rich. Together, the eleven chapters in this volume map out an empirical and conceptual terrain that is largely new to the Asian region. While the arguments and subject-matter of individual contributors vary substantially, there is broad consensus that the new rich stand at the heart of contemporary change in Asia. There is also agreement among the contributors that an understanding of the new rich, and the social relations in which they are founded, calls for both detailed ethnography as well as an approach that draws simultaneously on cultural analysis and political economy.

Michael Pinches
1998

Acknowledgements

I would like to thank the Asia Research Centre, Murdoch University, for its generous funding and administrative support, without which this volume would not have materialised. In particular, I want to thank the Centre's past and present Publications Coordinators, Helen Bradbury and Mandy Miller, for their guidance and encouragement. I have also benefited greatly from the patient support and direction of a number of people at Routledge, especially commissioning editor Victoria Smith, copy-editor Rita Winter and production editor Lisa Carden. For the final proofreading, I was assisted by Cheryl Lange and the Department of Anthropology, University of Western Australia. I want to give special thanks to the contributors to the volume, who have made its production such an intellectually rewarding experience. Lastly, for her tolerance and good humour over the course of this project I thank my wife, Lenny.

1 Cultural relations, class and the new rich of Asia

Michael Pinches

INTRODUCTION

> Now, where Japan has succeeded is being duplicated by other East Asian coun-
> tries. South Korea, Taiwan, Hong Kong, and Singapore have amassed enormous
> trade surpluses...All five of these East Asian countries have embraced Western
> capitalism...Most of their people are dressed in Western suits; many of them
> speak English; a good portion of them travel, study, and do business abroad. In
> their outward appearance these East Asian nouveaux riches are Westernized. Yet
> behind this facade the people of these countries pursue a way of life that remains
> essentially Oriental. They prefer to eat Oriental food, observe lunar-calendar-
> based national festivities, place the family at the center of their social and
> economic relationships, practise ancestor worship, emphasize frugality in life,
> maintain a strong devotion to education, and accept Confucianism as the essence
> of their common culture.
>
> (Tai 1989b: 1–2)

Hung-chao Tai's characterisation of Asia's new rich echoes a powerful orthodoxy which is evident in the views of many business people, politicians,
journalists and academics, both within and outside the Asian region. It suggests
three things about the new rich of Asia: that they are superficially Western,
essentially Oriental, and represent the majority of the population. While
economic growth has brought material betterment and the trappings of Western
affluence, Asians, according to this view, remain fundamentally rooted in a world
of unchanging Oriental culture. Although few would accept the view that most
Asians are newly rich, there is broad agreement, among those who espouse the
sort of culturalist paradigm found in Tai's writing, that the cultures and ethnic
groups of Asia differ fundamentally from those in the West, and that they are
more or less uniform and unchanging, no matter what the social inequalities or
class structures within. The most common general assertion along these lines is
that where Western cultures are individualistic and conflict-ridden, Asian
cultures are communitarian, family-oriented and more or less harmonious.[1]

While the quotation from Tai, like much of the recent literature on economic
development in Asia, is specifically concerned with Confucianism, it reverberates

with a more general view that the region as a whole, its growth and its newly rich, must be understood primarily in terms of the uniqueness of Asian Values.[2] This book is not directly concerned with debating the source of the so-called Asian economic miracle. Rather, it is an attempt to understand the cultural constructions of its main protagonists and beneficiaries – the newly rich. The kind of culturalist account found in the above quotation from Tai is one of the most influential of these constructions. Although its explanatory merit must be seriously questioned, there is no doubt as to its wide rhetorical power.

However, there is a second popular cultural construction of Asia's new rich, partially articulated in the middle sentences of the quotation from Tai, but then effectively dismissed. This construction pictures the new rich of Asia as rampant consumers of luxury goods, caught up in the global whirl of changing fashion, at once seduced by, and now leaders of, a world of consumerism dominated by lifestyle images of the affluent West. On the face of it, these two constructions – one of Oriental essentialism, the other of Western universalism – seem diametrically opposed.

This chapter attempts to explore and theorise these cultural constructions of the new rich in Asia. It draws on both the published literature as well as the other chapters that make up this volume. In the first section, I look critically at the concept of culture that underpins the commonly invoked binary divide between East and West. Yet I argue that a cultural understanding of Asia's new rich is vital, and a necessary corrective to the narrow political-economic approaches that have often been employed in this area. In advancing an approach that combines cultural and political-economic modes of analysis, I conclude the section by outlining a social relational perspective on culture, class and social differentiation. The second section examines the changing configurations of class and status in Asia, and is particularly concerned with tracing the status transformation of the capitalist from pariah to hero. The third section describes and analyses the Oriental, ethnic and ethno-nationalist representations of wealth production and the new rich in contemporary Asia. Its explanatory focus centres on the identity politics of international status relations, and their consequences for domestic class relations. The fourth and fifth sections examine the representation of Asia's new rich as high-status consumers, also with reference to international and domestic class relations. The sixth section deals with the cultural labelling of the new rich in Asia. This is followed by a conclusion which draws together the main arguments.

CULTURE, POLITICAL ECONOMY AND CLASS

The binary cultural divide between East and West that is expressed in the opening quotation from Tai has a long heritage and continues to inform the way in which large sections of humanity imagine each other. What is most interesting about this perspective is its persistence, despite ample evidence and numerous studies, that demonstrate: first, the wide cultural variance in both Asia and the

West; secondly, the interconnected processes of cultural change and globalisation in which all societies are to differing degrees caught up; and thirdly, the significant tensions centred on class and status differences that are present throughout Asia as well as the West. These points are demonstrated throughout this book.

The East/West cultural distinction rests on a dualism that, for a long time, has informed the literature on social change and industrialisation in Asia, Africa and Latin America. This concerns the relationship between Europe and its Other, the former colonies that make up most of the so-called Third World (Said 1978; Barker *et al.* 1985; Bhabha 1994). One influential paradigm, associated with 1960s' modernisation theory, is that which distinguished between the 'modern' cultures of the West and 'traditional' cultures of the 'Third World'. More recently, discussions have been concerned with differences between the European industrial revolution and the industrial transformation that has been taking place in Asia over the last few decades. Much of this discussion bears a strong resemblance to modernisation theory, the difference now being that Asia's traditions are seen to be propelling it forward rather than backward, as was asserted in the earlier model.

Where the earlier model looked for embryonic Western social and cultural elements as a sign of development, today these elements are often looked upon as superficial, or, in Tai's words, as a 'facade'. Thus proponents of this culturalist paradigm now tend to look sceptically upon the use, in Asian contexts, of a social theory developed in the context of industrialising Europe (Pye 1985: 7–10). Some are especially concerned about the use of class theory, and the adoption of such concepts as 'bourgeoisie' and 'proletariat', which are thought to carry with them too much Eurocentric cultural baggage. This problem is evident in a large body of literature which argues that Asian capitalists and, indeed, Asian capitalism are somehow spurious because they do not conform to an idealised model based on the European experience.[3]

Undoubtedly there are significant dangers in superimposing on contemporary Asian societies concepts and ideal types that were developed in nineteenth-century Europe. Even apart from variant socio-cultural milieux, the passing of the colonial era and marked differences in technology, communications, corporate organisation and global political relations, all make the contemporary industrialisation of Asia different to that of eighteenth- and nineteenth-century Europe. Yet there are also significant commonalities. First, capitalist transformation in both periods and regions has entailed the generalised production of commodities and the rise of owners of capital to positions of social prominence. Secondly, even if there may be significant historical differences between the two periods, there are important shared contemporary experiences founded in a global political economy that is no longer so constrained by spatial considerations (Harvey 1989; Sassen 1991). Thirdly, concepts like class that have arisen in the West continue to be debated and qualified. It may be less the case that analytical concepts developed in nineteenth-century Europe are limited or inadequate in dealing with contemporary Asia, than that they have also been limited or inadequate in dealing with the West. Indeed, some writers in the West have recently disputed the general empirical and conceptual validity of class (Pakulski and Waters 1996; Lee and Turner 1996). Yet, as will be argued in this and other chapters of this book, class differences and relations, however problematic they may be conceptually and analytically, are fundamental to an understanding of the cultural construction of Asia's new rich.

In assessing the East/West cultural divide, which has been so important in the identity construction of the new rich in Asia, it is also necessary to look critically at the particular concept of culture upon which it is based: like the sociological concept of class, it too has its origins in Western academic discourse. There have been two principal conceptions of the term 'culture' (Williams 1981: 10–14; Jenks 1993), both of them used in commentaries on Asia. The earlier concept uses culture as a synonym for civilisation, or what is sometimes called high culture; its opposite being that which is seen to be uncivilised, vulgar and backward. This understanding rests both on a sociological distinction, which posits the coexistence of a people who are civilised and a people who are not, and a historical trajectory of progress from a state of barbarity to one of civilisation. It is this latter idea that is embedded in early modernisation theory which posits a historical shift from tradition to modernity.

The second principal conception of culture, elaborated most fully in the discipline of anthropology, refers not to culture in the singular, as a state of civility or refinement, but to cultures in the plural, as the ways of life or symbolic universes that characterise different societies or peoples. With the 'Asian economic miracle', there seems to have been a paradigm shift from culture to cultures.[4] Thus, traditions in Asia are no longer seen as inferior or historically frozen antecedents of European modernity; rather they are now cultural traditions that rank alongside the cultural traditions of Europe, coexistent but separate and essentially different.

The relativism and multiplicity evident in this understanding of culture clearly reverberate with present popular representations of Asia in the West, and with the general growth of ethnic and cultural self-consciousness (Smith 1981; Kahn 1995), but by no means is there consensus. Anthropologists have long debated the concept of culture. Indeed, with the emergence of cultural studies and postmodern theory, the debate over culture has become more far-reaching, and is arguably the most central to contemporary social thought (see Rosaldo 1989; Keesing 1990; Hannerz 1992; Nelson *et al.* 1992; Featherstone 1990, 1995; Jenks 1993; Chaney 1994; Dirks *et al.* 1994; Kahn 1995).

Four criticisms of the concept of multiple cultures are of particular significance to our concern with the new rich of Asia. First, many versions of this model of culture, particularly those which emphasise socialisation or culture as learned behaviour. have difficulty acknowledging or theorising human agency. Secondly, culture as a bounded way of life, or system of symbols and meanings, fails to deal adequately with social change and historical process. Thirdly, humans do not live in clearly bounded groups with clearly bounded ways of life, or clearly bounded values and predispositions. If they ever did, this is no longer the case, and one is particularly hard-pressed maintaining this model of culture in a context of increasing globalisation of economic and political forces. Fourthly, this model of culture has a limited capacity to deal with social differentiation or social structure, where this entails contention or dissent (Hall 1980; Marcus and Fischer 1986; Sider 1986; Austin-Broos 1987; O'Hanlon 1989; Keesing 1990, 1991; Hannerz 1992; Dirks *et al.* 1994).

Because of conceptual difficulties with overly inclusive 'way of life' definitions, the culture concept is now most fruitfully limited to the sphere of symbols and meanings (Keesing 1974). However, the danger with this usage, is that it becomes reified or disembodied from the material world of lived social experience, as is evident in the Geertzian tradition (Keesing 1990; Roseberry 1991), and in some streams of postmodern thought which conceive of a world of cultural constructions virtually independent of agency or political-economic structure (Ulin 1991; Jenks 1993: 136–50). One attempt to deal with this problem of symbols and meanings, and the parallel danger of materialist reductionism, is to transcend both spheres with concepts such as 'practice' (Bourdieu 1977). Another attempt, adopted in this chapter, is to conceive of the relationship between the two spheres as a broadly dialectical one, whose path is historical and largely indeterminant (Murphy 1972; Keesing 1974: 94).

While there is still no consensus on the meaning of culture, the above criticisms have been widely acknowledged in anthropology, sociology and cultural studies, and are variably built into the contemporary use of the culture concept in these disciplinary areas.[5] Moreover, in these disciplines, the culture concept is now often deliberately linked with other analytical concepts. Through the development of cultural studies, in particular, power relations and social differentiation have been made integral to much contemporary cultural analysis (Turner 1990; During 1993; Dirks *et al.* 1994; Kurtz 1996; Grossberg 1996).[6] Indeed, arguably the best cultural analysis is that which contributes to our understanding of power and social differentiation.

Today, it is in political science, management theory and among a few born-again economists that culture has taken on its most ossified and simplistic form. Particularly prominent in these disciplines is an equation of culture with behaviourism, normative determinism and changeless monolithic custom. Unfortunately, these disciplines have dominated public and academic debate on the place of culture in industrialisation and development in Asia. For example, in a recent political science text on political and economic change in the Asian Pacific region, Simone and Feraru (1995) describe culture as 'a taken for granted...constant' made up of 'habits (customs), values, beliefs, and attitudes we inherit'. They then counterpose this to ideologies which are 'self-conscious patterns of ideas and images that redefine human beings' relationships', and proceed to explore the relationship between Asia and the West in terms of Asia having cultures and the West having ideologies (Simone and Feraru 1995: 213–14).

Of course there are other traditions of analysis in these disciplines, and in the study of transformation in Asia, most notably political economy, the analytical perspective adopted in the first two volumes of this series. It is hardly surprising, in light of the above-mentioned criticisms of the culture concept and the simplistic way in which writers like Simone and Feraru continue to use it, that many political economists, like Robison and Goodman (1996a) and Rodan (1996), either ignore cultural analysis or else cast their own modes of analysis in opposition to it. The arguments presented in this volume suggest that they throw the baby out with the bathwater: first, in sidestepping the questions of identity construction and related issues that have been crucial to the making of Asia's new rich; second, in not exploring far enough the hegemonic shifts that have accompanied the emergence of the new rich in Asia; and third, in not dealing reflexively with their own class constructions of the new rich.[7]

The perspective adopted in this volume does not assume the primacy of cultural explanation, and rejects any attempt to encapsulate the region as a whole, or individual countries within it, by reference to a particular culture. Nor does it adopt the view that cultural constructions are mere epiphenomena of base economic or political processes. Indeed, a central argument in the volume is that a cultural understanding of the new rich is integral to an analysis of these processes. Though individual contributions vary, the overall perspective is a dialectical one, which locates the construction or maintenance of belief, value and meaning, in reference to questions of power and inequality, in a context of shifting social, political and economic relations. According to this view, the cultural realm is a realm of variance, tension, contestation, ambiguity and fluidity, into which social actors are thrust, through which they may pursue advantage, and in which they may be subjugated. At each of these points the realm of meanings and symbols is crucial, not just in dialectical relation to political-economic structures, but also in dialectical relation to human agency. Thus, on the one hand we need to consider how people create and convey meaning through symbols, yet on the other, how these meanings and symbols may become embedded in habitual practice, orientations and institutions which appear to assume a life of their own, conditioning the way in which people think and behave. What has to be established here are the power structures and social relations through which meanings and symbols are generated, circulated and consumed. In addressing this last point, Hannerz (1992) thus describes culture as 'the social organisation of meaning'.

The first place to begin then is to ask what positions do the new rich occupy in the class structures of Asian societies? The answer to this question in the first volume of the series (Robison and Goodman 1996a) focuses on the emergence of a heterogeneous layer of capitalists, and salaried professionals, managers, administrators and technicians who have risen into these positions, and thus into new wealth, through the growth of capitalist enterprise and related state agencies in their particular countries. In that volume, and in the second, the political character of the new rich is also explored with reference to their attachments to the state, their involvement in opposition politics and their variable placement in the changing configuration of classes.

The contributors to this volume find Asia's new rich to be located in the same structural positions, as is the case in the country studies of the first volume, and we too share a concern with exploring the relationship between the new rich and the changing configuration of classes. For us, though, this concern necessitates a more open understanding of class and, in particular, one that is sensitive to questions of social and cultural identity. This means looking not only at productive or economic relations, or overt political behaviour, but also at how each of these is connected to status relations, differences in lifestyle, consumption codes and practices, interpersonal conduct, ethnic affiliations, moral dispositions and social imagery. How, and to what extent, are the various elements of the new rich constituted, by themselves and by others, as socially, culturally and economically distinctive? What moral influence do they wield and how? How are they related to, or distinguished from, the 'old rich' or the 'old' and 'new poor'? Do they constitute new classes? To what extent are they absorbed by existing classes, and how have they influenced the character of these classes? These questions cannot be answered within a narrow political-economic framework.

Any study concerned with the relationship between culture and the new rich of Asia must begin by problematising what Tai denies, and what many others ignore, namely that the new rich are emerging in contexts of substantial material inequality and social tension, and that these characteristics are changing rather than disappearing. In the absence of a distinctive theoretical literature that takes such a position in reference to Asia, it is useful to consider briefly the way in which the relation between culture and class in capitalist societies has been theorised in the West, most notably within the Marxist and Weberian traditions.[8] In doing so, I reject the argument that such a literature is inappropriate because it is Eurocentric. There are a number of difficulties with this argument: one is that the literature and the realities to which it refers are themselves highly variable over space and time; another is that much of this literature has been fruitfully adapted by intellectuals in Asia to the study of their own societies.[9]

There appear to be three broad theoretical positions on the connection between culture and class, which I call the economistic, inclusive and social relational. The economistic position recognises cultural distinctions between classes or strata within a wider social totality, explaining them on the basis of differences in economic position, interest or experience. Thus, in popular representations of class, differences in lifestyle are commonly presented as a direct consequence of income differentials. Veblen's (1979) classic account of the American leisure class, for example, explains conspicuous consumption, and the hierarchy of prestige that accompanies this practice, as more or less the simple outcome of wealth differences. In an often more abstract vein, Marxist accounts of class consciousness commonly give direct explanatory weight to the positions people occupy in the relations of production, or the material interests associated with these positions. These sorts of argument are now widely criticised for their inclination to reductionism (Williams 1977; Larrain 1986; Grossberg and Nelson 1988).

In the inclusive position, class differences may be acknowledged, but are seen to be lost in the deadening embrace of mass society or consumer capitalism, or are largely subsumed under pervasive national cultures or great cultural epochs, like modernity, or postmodernity (see Marcuse 1968; Jay 1984; Featherstone

1991; MacCannell and MacCannell 1993; Slater 1997). I return to aspects of this literature below.

The social relational position, which I wish to develop here, contains elements of both of the above. In the Marxist tradition, this position sees class as having an elementary economic component. But here class cultures are not so much directly traced to economic conditions as to the social relations through which people, differentially located by these conditions, constitute each other socially and culturally through the practices of daily life. For social historians, like Thompson (1968) and Genovese (1976), the key element to these relations is struggle. Relational approaches to class and culture owe much to Gramsci (Hall *et al.* 1978; Mouffe 1979), as is evident in the number of recent studies that work within the rubric of hegemony and resistance (O'Hanlon 1989; Rebel 1989; Kurtz 1996).[10] It is at this point, as Bocock (1986: 83–102) argues, that there is significant convergence with Weber.

Arguably the Weberian concept that is missing, but implicit, in the accounts of developing class communities, class consciousness and class struggle in the work of writers like Thompson and Genovese, is that of status honour. This concept, combined with structural understandings of class, in both the Marxist and Weberian traditions, is invaluable in exploring the cultural constructions of Asia's new rich. For Weber, status honour denotes a 'specific style of life' (Gerth and Mills 1970: 187), associated with the exclusive possession of particular material, political and symbolic resources, according to which groups and individuals are stratified or differentially located in relation to each other (Gerth and Mills 1970: 186–8, 190–1; Turner 1988: 4–7).[11] Thus classes, defined either in terms of production relations, after Marx, or in terms of market capacity, after Weber, may or may not become status groups.

Contrary to the way in which status honour has been used by many writers – as an alternative to class analysis – there are two important ways in which the concept compliments, and indeed enriches, the tradition founded in Marx.[12] It does this, first, by addressing the symbolic, moral and stylistic ways in which shared structural class positions may translate into social groups and practices. And it should be remembered that Weber specifically identifies the possession of property and the performance of 'common physical labour' as two qualities which 'in the long run' or 'quite generally' are recognised for 'status qualification' or 'disqualification' (Gerth and Mills 1970: 187, 191). Moreover, in reference to the middle classes, which, among Marxists, continue to evade unambiguous structural definition (Abercrombie and Urry 1983; Robison and Goodman 1996b), an understanding of the processes of status formation through the shared symbols of lifestyle and consumption would seem to be crucial. This is of particular significance here, where, as various contributors to this and other volumes in the series indicate, the new rich of Asia are commonly identified with the middle class, or are noted for their structural heterogeneity. The importance of the conceptual distinction between class and status is brought out further, in relation to this volume, in Weber's reference to the parvenu who has property, but is not fully accepted by established high-status groups (Gerth and Mills 1970: 192). This is precisely the lot of many new rich in Asia, and lies behind the usually deprecatory label, *nouveaux riches*.

The second way in which the concept of status honour may contribute to an understanding of class and culture, and, more particularly, to our understanding of the new rich, is by providing a conceptual means for recognising groups and identities that do not correspond to classes, but which have consequences for them, and may be partly understood in relation to them. Of most importance here are the cultural identities of ethnicity, nation and gender, according to which Asia's new rich are often variously understood. As argued below, it is the cultural construction of the new rich in terms of ethnic or ethno-nationalist identities that has commonly been so important to the hegemonic positions they are coming to assume.

The most important conceptual development in the literature on these various forms of status honour has involved a shift in focus away from groups or communities as such, to the symbolic construction and maintenance of the social boundaries that separate, and hence define, them (Barth 1969; Cohen 1985; Lamont and Fournier 1992; Anthias and Yuval-Davis 1992; Vermeulen and Govers 1994).[13] While these conceptual developments may have occurred in reference to ethnicity, race, nation and gender, they also provide a useful way of dealing directly with the social and cultural relations of class. Inasmuch as the class experience entails the differential evaluation of people, and the creation of varied identities, lifestyles and groups, all in a relational or dialogical context, the concept of symbolic boundary is particularly useful. Most ethnographic and historical accounts dealing with culture and class have not only been limited to the West, but have also tended to concern themselves with describing distinctive ways of life variously circumscribed by work relations, income, occupational prestige, educational status or place of residence.[14] For the most part, they have not focused on the social relations or symbolic boundaries through which these groups or classes acquire their distinctiveness. One important exception is Frykman and Lofgren's (1987) account of the ways in which members of the Swedish bourgeoisie cultivated a lifestyle and moral code through which they were able to distinguish themselves from, and elevate themselves above, the old elite and peasantry. Bourdieu's (1989) work on class and taste in France is another exception which is dealt with later in the chapter, as is Lamont's (1992) study of the upper middle class in France and the United States.[15]

The positions occupied by Asia's new rich are not simply to be understood in reference to the internal class relations and social organisation of the nation-states to which they belong. Their existence is premised on the structures and growth of capitalism, which are global as well as local. Thus, the new rich are also uniquely positioned in a global and international context, in which their societies have long been subjugated and disadvantaged. Indeed, the emergence of Asia's new rich represents a major change in this state of affairs, both structurally and in terms of international status relations. Thus, it is with reference to these two structural axes, the local and global, that we explore the cultural construction of the new rich in Asia.[16] On the face of it, these axes appear to correspond respectively with each of the two dominant representations of Asia's new rich, noted earlier: as Oriental producer and global consumer; one rooted in local traditions of social and economic order, the other in the free-flowing global commodity market. Yet, as is evident in the remainder of this chapter, and in those that follow, each of these representations of the new rich in Asia needs to be understood in reference to both the global and the local, and, most significantly, the interplay between them.

Indeed, it is this interplay, mediated through the unprecedented movement across state borders of people, capital, consumer goods, fashion and lifestyle images, and contending politico-religious ideologies, that underpins the heightening of both cosmopolitanism, and ethnic or nationalist differentiation in Asia.[17] Advertisers, media programmers, intellectuals and political ideologues – many of them, themselves new rich – thus often play a pivotal role in the shaping of new rich identities, as shown in most chapters in this book. Yet these identities also vary in relation to the particular organisational or institutional settings in which the newly rich make their wealth (see Smith and Buckley, this volume).[18] Those who are most dependent on the state tend to assume identities heavily tied to the nation or locality (Antlöv, Shamsul, Smith), while those whose wealth and livelihoods are based on private global capital seem more likely to develop transnational identities, to some degree dislodged from the nation (Young, Chua and Tan). Yet this pattern is not at all clear-cut: new rich identities may be strongly conditioned by ongoing local ties, independent of the state (Smith), or may arise in the playing out of broader ethno-national or religious tensions, even among diasporic new rich communities (Lakha). Furthermore, as Young argues in his chapter, it is commonly in the more amorphous experiences and practices of everyday life – in such places as shopping malls and housing estates – that new rich identities are fabricated.

In the remainder of the chapter I explore the principal cultural constructions of Asia's new rich with reference to the relational framework outlined above. In particular, I want to draw attention to the differential status honour awarded to people on the basis of the structural positions they occupy, and to examine how these come to constitute cultural boundaries through which social relations are negotiated and constituted.

CHANGING CLASS AND STATUS CONFIGURATIONS IN ASIA

The phenomenon of new wealth in many parts of contemporary Asia evidences not only a rise in economic growth, but also fundamental shifts in class structure and the cultural organisation of social relations. Not only are the new rich the possessors of new wealth; their emergence represents a substantial regional shift in the ways of making wealth, of being wealthy and of attributing prestige.

Though the new rich capitalists and salaried professionals have their antecedents earlier in twentieth-century Asia (see, for example, Bergère 1986;

Lakha 1988), their present numbers and, more significantly, their social, political and cultural influence, far exceeds the power they assumed in the past.[19] This is perhaps most evident in the prestige the new rich of Asia are now accorded in the upper reaches of society, both at home and abroad. Indeed, they are commonly represented within their countries, as well as outside, as the heroes of the 'Asian Miracle'.[20] Over the past three decades, the positions assumed by Asia's new rich have become increasingly hegemonic, though not uncontested, as a number of chapters in this volume indicate (especially Antlöv's). Historically, the present era represents a watershed, not only in the economic and industrial transformation of many societies in Asia, but also in their systems of social and cultural order.

In most of contemporary Asia, the eminence attributed to successful capital-ists among the privileged classes and in the mass media contrasts dramatically with the lowly placement of merchants and artisans – their closest counterparts – in the status hierarchies that dominated most of Asia well into the twentieth century. In the agrarian societies of China and India, under the great traditions of Confucianism and Hinduism, the roles of merchant and artisan were identi-fied as demeaning or servile and formally codified towards the bottom of the ideal status hierarchy of occupation and social position (Fairbank 1994: 55, 100, 108; Dumont 1972: 106; Evans 1993).[21] While the Confucianist order of East Asia and Vietnam formally provided for the social mobility of men into the ruling state bureaucracy, it was through scholarship, land acquisition and inter-marriage rather than money-making entrepreneurial skills (Fairbank 1994: 180; Osborne 1985: 39). Elsewhere, in what are present-day India, Thailand, Malaysia and Indonesia, highest social honour was formally attributed through the birthright of kingship, caste and nobility. In all of these systems, highest social rank was variously acted out, celebrated and confirmed through sump-tuary laws, refined courtly etiquette and elaborate ceremonial display (Palmier 1960; Dumont 1972; Steinberg *et al.* 1975: 59–86; Geertz 1976: 227–60; Osborne 1985: 38–53). Direct engagement in economic pursuits or mundane material production, while underpinning this exclusive world of power and privi-lege, was also its cultural antithesis. The economic power of those who assumed positions of cultural eminence was made possible through their political or spiri-tual authority, embedded in the institutions of the tributary state, from the sultanates of the Indo-Malay world, to the dynastic states of imperial China (Fairbank 1968; Steinberg *et al.* 1975: 30–6; Osborne 1985: 16–35).

While these socio-cultural arrangements generally held sway, they were also, to varying degrees, threatened and compromised by the independent economic power of merchants, despite their formally low status. Indeed, in practice, the tributary or patrimonial systems that prevailed through most of the region relied heavily upon trading relations, both within and beyond their domains of influ-ence (Skinner 1957: 97; Riggs 1966: 251; Wickberg 1965: 3–41; Brenner 1991; Fairbank 1994: 179–82). In some cases independent merchants were controlled through state repression; in others they were incorporated through the bestowal or sale of noble titles (Skinner 1957: 149; Shamsul). Nobles or gentry commonly had to enter into alliances with powerful merchants, and in some cases, they themselves operated as merchants. In imperial China, tributary relations, linking the emperor with other peoples and states, served as a principal vehicle for commercial exchange (Fairbank 1968; Mancell 1968). There were also ideological challenges, notably from the great tradition of Islam, introduced through South and Southeast Asia by Arab traders and missionaries, which attributed relatively high status to the activity of commerce. Notwithstanding these tensions, and the increasing importance of commerce, the state, class and status structures found within the region continued to be organised around ruling nobilities, whose chief claim to legitimacy lay in hierarchical principles based on aristocratic birthright, spiritual authority or scholarly achievement, not in economic entrepreneurship.

The impact of European expansion and colonisation on indigenous status hierarchies and class configurations was contradictory. On the one hand, economic life in colonised societies was increasingly commercialised and made more dependent on international as well as internal trade, thereby elevating the power of local trading communities. On the other, colonial rule subordinated, yet also reinforced, the local political authority and social rank of indigenous elites through their incorporation into the colonial state, and through the consolidation of agrarian social and economic structures, linked through merchant capital to the industrialising West. The exclusive courtly privileges of old royal families, and the principles of noble birthright, continued to be honoured, and social prestige continued to be organised largely in reference to aristocratic ideals, even if somewhat modified, as in the case of the Javanese *priyayi* tradition (Legge 1964: 107–8). In the case of the Philippines, which for the most part lacked a pre-colonial state tradition, Spanish and American colonial rule produced a quasi-aristocratic indigenous elite whose power lay in landownership and political office. The status markers and way of life of this elite were modelled largely on those of the Spanish nobility, though they developed their own unique form of patrimonialism (Lopez-Gonzaga 1991; Anderson 1988).

While the colonial bureaucracy provided a vehicle through which indigenous nobilities continued to exercise administrative power and high social rank, it also generated opportunities for a new class of officials, not recruited on the basis of ascription or noble patronage. In India, Indonesia, Malaya, the Philippines and elsewhere, colonial rule thus generated a substantially new bureaucratic middle class whose prestige rested principally on occupation rather than birthright (Misra 1961; Legge 1964: 107–8; Doeppers 1984; Shamsul). Of particular significance was the expansion of formal education as an associated meritocratic means of upward social mobility, and, more generally, of Western education as a new pathway to, and indicator of, social power and prestige (Legge 1964: 109; Lakha). In Thailand, which avoided colonisation, the state was the domain of a bureaucratic nobility recruited not principally through birthright but through the formal conferment of noble title (Skinner 1957: 149). With the rapid expansion of the Thai state bureaucracy in the early part of the twentieth century, it too served as the major vehicle for status mobility and middle-class formation during the era of colonialism (Riggs 1966). Likewise 'modern education' became an increasingly important credential in gaining a position in the state bureaucracy (Pasuk and Baker 1995: 236).

In all of these developments, as in the pre-colonial era, independent merchants, artisans and, by now, the growing number of entrepreneurial capitalists continued to be excluded from the realm of high social status and respectability. While some were rewarded, it was not through their money-making, as such, but through marital alliance, formal education or conferment of noble title, as in the case of Thailand and Malaya (Fairbank 1994: 180; Shamsul), a pattern similar to that of industrialising Europe (Neale 1985: 73; Pilbeam 1990: 14). That these economic operators often sought prestige within a status order dominated by ideas of noble birth, cultural refinement or scholarship probably indicated not only their opportunism, but also something of their acceptance of and deference towards this order. That increasing numbers of high-state officials or powerful landlords, with noble or quasi-noble status, were entering the world of commerce directly, or through personal alliances, suggested something of the economic transformation that was taking place around them, and anticipated later developments in which the state became a major vehicle for private investment and capital accumulation (Deyo 1987; Hewison *et al.* 1993).

Many of the cultural tensions and differences surrounding the organisation of privilege, power and economic activity in many Asian societies were also played out through ethnic conflict and the politics of nationalism. In most Southeast Asian countries, status relations between nobilities-cum-bureaucratic elites and merchants also found expression as an ethnic relationship between indigenous populations and Chinese migrant communities. That these relations have oscillated between open hostility, strategic alliance and acculturation reflects something of the structural tensions between merchants and nobles. The widespread perception among indigenous populations in Indonesia, Malaya and the Philippines that the ethnic Chinese were foreign economic opportunists enriching themselves at the expense of local people, was also fostered by the presence of colonial powers, whose commercial interests or needs seemed to favour the Chinese (Wickberg 1965: 6, 63; Osborne 1985: 109). The British presence in peninsular Malaya, initially built around the mainly Chinese populated straits settlements and the importation of Chinese and Indian workers and managers for colonial business ventures, was particularly influential in establishing ethnicity as a basis of identification and conflict (Shamsul, Smith).

In such situations, rising nationalist sentiment, generated through the experience of colonial rule, took on the form of ethno-nationalism (Shamsul, Heryanto). As such, it was directed not only at the institutions of colonialism, but at what were perceived as the races or ethnic groups responsible for and associated with it. The attainment of political independence in the years following the end of the Second World War consolidated ethno-nationalism in the institutions of the state, and as a principal ideology through which dominant classes maintained hegemony. Again this tended to confirm the largely pariah status of independent merchants or capitalists belonging to minority ethnic groups, notwithstanding the instrumental alliances made between politicians, senior civil servants and members of these groups.

Formal political independence proved to be a limited and passing phase in the pursuit of nationhood. Left unresolved were the experience of economic disadvantage and the associated national or racial stigmatisation that had come with colonialism and continued through subsequent decades of political independence. In the context of a more closely integrated global community of nations, dominated by the West, this problem became increasingly severe. Hence, throughout the region, national elites, politicians and intellectuals have been propelled towards the pursuit of 'national development', drawing variously on ideologies of free-market capitalism, communism and ethno-nationalist essentialism. For the past half-century, the pursuit of national development has been the most powerful discourse guiding political and economic life in the region. Though its content has varied widely, reflecting the particular histories of individual peoples and nations, its direction has had to be charted in the context of an increasingly integrated global political economy, dominated by large transnational corporations with their origins in the West and Japan (on the latter, see Smith).

Small numbers of moderately successful capitalists, mainly from backgrounds in commerce, had emerged in many countries in the region, commonly through state protection under import substitution policies. But the spectacular economic growth of the so-called 'Asian Miracle' is a phenomenon of the 1970s–1990s, and has seen the emergence of many highly successful capitalists, some of whom have founded enterprises that have become large international conglomerates (McVey 1992a; Robison and Goodman 1996a).[22] Of crucial significance has been the fact that, over this time, the various political quests for national development in Asia have intensified in a context of global economic restructuring. This has involved a substantial relocation of industrial manufacture from the West into East and Southeast Asia, through the agency of transnational corporations seeking out cheaper and more controllable sources of labour, increasingly via subcontracting or other post-Fordist arrangements (Harvey 1989; Deyo 1997; Hutchison and Brown, forthcoming).[23] Related growth in services and the domestic consumer market has combined to make Asia the world's most economically dynamic region for most of the 1980s and 1990s. However, this growth has also been uneven, as some countries with earlier- or faster-growing economies have shifted away from cheap labour areas of production into more highly skilled areas, while others have taken over their former mantle. Through these processes, and the increasing movement of capital and labour between different countries, the region's national economies have become increasingly entwined and unequal.

Because of its largely state-based and corporate character, economic growth in most of Asia is not easily attributable to the ideal personage of neo-classical economics: the free-wheeling, individual capitalist entrepreneur. Though the ideology surrounding this character prevails in some quarters, it has generally been subordinated to culturalist or ethno-nationalist ideologies, usually associated with the state. For much of the 1970s–1990s, a major stumbling block to sustaining the idea of the transacting individual capitalist has been the corporate monopoly character of world capitalism, in which even the most highly placed and powerful individuals are commonly salaried managers. It is largely the predominance of monopoly capital that has made it impossible for many entrepreneurs in Asia to succeed independently. Here the role of the state in promoting local business has been decisive, whether through the formation of state corporations or monopolies, favoured access to loans, contracts and licences, or other such practices (Deyo 1987; Hewison *et al.* 1993).

While there have been significant differences between the more legal-bureaucratic manner in which the Singaporean state has promoted local capital, and the particularistic and nepotistic practices that often link state and capital in other countries, the common legitimising umbrella of 'national development', founded in the experience of Western colonialism and imperialism, has been crucial throughout the region. Aside from the special case of Singapore, an island of largely second- and third-generation migrants, there also appear to be significant historical continuities. In many cases, the state is seen not only as the locale of administrative authority, but as a vehicle of privilege for high-status families, or ethnic groups, through which they may establish their own businesses, or else form profitable alliances with wealthy, but less honourable business people. These ideas and practices retain a certain continuity because of their efficacy under changed circumstances of state-led development.[24]

However, the economic and political forces at work here are complex and changing. Post-Fordist restructuring, along with the growth in service industries and the retail trade, which have followed the initial surge in manufacturing, have opened up new opportunities for capitalist entrepreneurs, independent of particularistic state assistance. There has also developed, in many countries, a powerful negative discourse on 'corruption' and 'cronyism'. In countries like the Philippines, this discourse has gained ground among the growing numbers of capitalists and new middle class who are not particularly dependent on, or beholden to, the state, as well as among the broader populace (Pinches). Whether or not this discourse becomes stronger in the context of the economic crisis that has been experienced in several countries in the region from 1997, remains to be seen. Should this happen, we might expect greater celebration of the idea of the independent individual capitalist entrepreneur, as has occurred in the Philippines, post-Marcos (Pinches). Alternatively, in Indonesia, where the crisis has been most severe, discourses which attribute it to Western capital or to domestic Chinese business also have a strong hold, and are clearly less damaging to the incumbent regime. Should they prevail and the economy recover, the ideal image of the new rich capitalist will most likely continue to be cloaked in collective ethno-nationalist symbolism.

The idea of accumulating wealth through private investment, independent of the state and quasi-noble or ethnic privilege, enjoys significant prestige and moral standing among many capitalists, technocrats and professionals in the region, a lot of them educated in the West, or influenced by similar education in their own countries. Moreover, as most chapters in this volume attest, there has been a widespread shift in occupational prestige, among the middle layers of society from civil service employment to private enterprise. Today, the most coveted job appears to be that of the business executive. However, by no means has the idea of the free-wheeling, individual capitalist been naturalised in the way it has in the West. Though the figure of the capitalist is now widely celebrated among the privileged classes across the region, it is most often as meritorious Asian, nationalist or ethnic cohort.

WEALTH PRODUCTION: CONFUCIANISM, ETHNICITY AND THE NEW RICH

Capitalist enrichment in many parts of Asia is commonly represented neither as the product of individual entrepreneurial endeavour and acumen, nor as a consequence of political-economic structures and processes – the explanations of wealth accumulation that have hitherto predominated in Western academic texts. The most striking representation of the new rich in Asia – in the mass media and, to a lesser extent, in academic discourse – attributes their wealth, in whole or part, to the traditions of Confucianism, 'Asian Values' or some other culturalist variant, supposing the unique normative, social or spiritual qualities of Asians, Japanese, Chinese, Malays or other ethnic groups in the region. In the West, the first wave of thinking along these lines centred on Japan. More recently, it has been other parts of East and Southeast Asia, and, for some, the whole Asian region.

At its most general level, the ideological arena in which new-rich identities are being constructed is defined in terms of the East/West dualism. At another level, the divide is played out in terms of Western liberal democracy versus the great traditions of Confucianism, Islam and Hinduism. Below this are various contending ethnicities and nationalisms.[25] These different layers of meaning and rhetoric clearly do not neatly collapse into each other but, as will become evident, new-rich identities are commonly constructed as if they did. In this section, I first consider how particular 'traditions', ethnicities and nationalisms in the region are being redefined around the figure of the new rich, and in contradistinction to the West. Secondly, I outline some of the tensions that are played out between different ethnicities and nationalities in reference to the rise of the new rich. Thirdly, I look at the significance of these ethnicities and nationalities for contemporary class relations in the region.

The most prominent of the contemporary culturalist explanations of new wealth in Asia have centred on Confucianism and the ethnic Chinese (for instance, Berger and Hsiao 1988; Tai 1989a; Clegg and Redding 1990; Redding 1990). In their most simplistic form, Confucianist representations of new wealth in Asia simply extrapolate a causal relation from the coincidence of rapid industrial growth, and Confucianist tradition in the countries of East Asia, and among the Chinese ethnic minorities of Southeast Asia. In their more nuanced forms, they are presented as a partial explanation alongside 'economic', 'institutional' or 'structural' factors (Clegg and Redding 1990; Redding 1990). A central proposition is that Confucianism and Chinese ethnicity constitute the new 'spirit of capitalism' in Asia, the counterpart of Weber's Protestantism in industrialising Europe (Redding 1990). According to Berger (1988), the countries of East and Southeast Asia are so culturally distinctive as to represent a 'second case of capitalist modernity' built around the traditional principles of family and community solidarity, and deference to authority, as against the individualism that is said to have characterised capitalism in the West. The other most-often mentioned principles, of industriousness, discipline and frugality, seem little different from those of Weber's Protestant ethic (Weber 1970; Chua 1995: 151). According to the proponents of this model, Confucianism constitutes an ethos that continues to shape consciousness and behaviour among the peoples of East Asia, and the ethnic Chinese of Southeast Asia, and is largely responsible for economic growth in the region. Naisbit (1996) even suggests that it is possible to speak of an overseas Chinese economy that transcends national boundaries.

There are several major difficulties with the explanatory claims of the Confucianist or Chinese ethnicity models of new wealth in Asia (Mackie 1989; Lim 1992; McVey 1992b: 18–21; Young, Chua and Tan), particularly in their more simplistic forms, though they have generated useful data on business networks and associated normative codes (Redding 1990, 1995). However, of most significance to us is the importance of Confucianist and Chinese ethnicity models to the cultural construction of the new rich in Asia. Just as Weber's Protestant Ethic, and Adam Smith's model of economic man, played an important part in distilling and promulgating the ideal capitalist and societal ethos in industrialising Europe, so too does this appear to be the case with those who advocate Confucianism or Chinese ethnicity as the hallmarks of capitalist growth in contemporary Asia.

Whereas the bourgeois ideals of Europe were constructed against the Other of feudalism or barbarity, from within as well as without, Confucianist and Chinese ethnic representations of Asia's new rich are formulated with the West as their primary Other. It is largely in this light that we can understand the appeal to tradition, continuity and antiquity built into these models, in contradistinction to the radical historical break that is supposed in Western bourgeois ideology. Similarly, we can understand the emphasis on family and 'moral community', the supposed Other of Western individualism. In the cultural construction of Asia's new rich, these simple oppositions cultivate an identity that is unambiguously distinctive and morally superior. As one writer on business practices says: '[the Chinese] pay more attention to human relations than to "things"…In the West "things" are more important than human relations' (Shui-shen Liu quoted in Tai 1989c: 19). That the intellectuals who proffer this sort of divide are to be found both in Asia and the West testifies not only to the growing cultural confidence in many parts of Asia, but also to what some see as the growing cultural malaise in the West (Chua 1995: 150).[26]

In some contexts, Confucianism has come to stand for Asia *vis-à-vis* the West and, in this sense, merges with the larger, looser concept of 'Asian Values', which likewise declares the cultural pre-eminence of family and community over individualism. However, the ideology of Confucianism has also focused more specifically on the reconstitution and elevation of Chinese identity across East and Southeast Asia, both in reference to the majority populations in Singapore, Taiwan and Hong Kong, and the minority ethnic Chinese in the industrialising societies of Indonesia, Malaysia, the Philippines and Thailand. In this sense, it is not only the West that constitutes the Other of Confucianism, but also the non-Chinese ethnic groups or nations of Asia, which to varying degrees have articulated their own identities through discriminatory treatment and characterisations of the Chinese, centred both on the latter's prominent roles in commerce, and on their purported lack of cultural refinement (Gosling 1983; Heryanto, Pinches). The reconstitution of the ethnicity of the 'overseas' Chinese around the newly elevated status of Confucianism and China challenges these negative stereotypes.

In their loosest and most general form, Confucianist representations construct the new rich of Asia as simply the peoples and nations of East Asia; in their narrower sense, they construct them as the 'overseas' Chinese, either as ethnic majorities or minorities in particular nation states. In both senses there is indeed a broad empirical correspondence: a high proportion of Asia's newly wealthy have Confucian or Chinese ancestries, and a high proportion of those who are not from such backgrounds do not possess new wealth. Thus, the efficacy of this cultural construction variously rests on its apparent explanatory value, its broad empirical correspondence with those who have new wealth, and its double-edged moral identity claims *vis-à-vis* the West, in a region long dominated by European and American interests, and *vis-à-vis* non-Chinese Asians, who have often been hostile to the Chinese. However, the Confucianist ideology that has been used to characterise Asia's new rich is distinctively modern. A fundamental deviation from classic Confucianism, which appears not to have been problematised in the literature, involves the elevation of the successful capitalist to the top of the status hierarchy, in some cases alongside the high-state official, as the hero of industrialisation and economic prosperity. As noted earlier, in classic Confucianism, the capitalist's former counterparts – the merchant and artisan – were virtual outcasts. And contrary to the ideal gender relations of classic Confucianism, growing numbers of the region's celebrated ethnic Chinese capitalists are women (Licuanan 1992).[27]

Confucianist and Chinese ethnic representations of Asia's new rich have mainly been the work of politicians, academics and journalists, both within the region and outside. A major thrust of their cultural production has been to 'orientalise' and nationalise values like diligence, work discipline and merit, with the new rich as their principal exemplars. While the Confucianist model of new wealth in Asia has been promulgated by intellectuals in each of the island Chinese states of Taiwan, Singapore and Hong Kong, it has been most assiduously developed as authoritarian state ideology in Singapore. On top of its other claims and functions, Confucianism in Singapore has been promoted as a source of national identity (Chua 1995; Lingle 1996). Within this rubric, the ruling People's Action Party (PAP) has attempted to capture the country's experience of economic growth, and its people's associated sense of ethno-national pride, both in reference to a past of shared poverty and in counter-distinction to the West and the non-Chinese of Asia, particularly in the neighbouring countries of Malaysia and Indonesia.

According to Chua (1995: 36), PAP leaders see themselves, in the Confucian tradition, as 'a group of honourable men'. What remains unclear is whether, or to what extent, others among Singapore's new rich and, indeed, among ethnic Chinese new-rich capitalists and professionals elsewhere in Asia constitute themselves in this way.

Undoubtedly the politicians and intellectuals responsible for the Confucianist and ethnic Chinese argument have exerted a significant influence on the self-perception of many newly rich in Asia: both through the mass media and formal education, most notably through business colleges, such as Manila's Asian Institute of Management, and a number of similar institutions in the West. Many of the region's technocrats, managers and professionals enrolled in such places have been exposed to a growing volume of literature linking business management and entrepreneurial skills to particular cultures and ethnicities, much of this literature expressly celebrating Confucianism or some other variant of Asian Values.[28] Nevertheless, the presence and affects of such ideologies are clearly uneven. Chua (1995: 36), for example, argues that Confucianism has not taken hold among the wider population of Singapore, notwithstanding the self-images of the PAP leadership. Indeed, the irony, according to Chua (1995: 27, 33), is that as state ideology Confucianism was inspired by conservative Western academics, and came after a period in which Singaporeans were lauded for their successes through an ethos of individualism.

It may be revealing in some ways to highlight the broad correlation between the ethnic Chinese and the new rich of East and Southeast Asia. Moreover, Chinese ethnic self-consciousness is clearly important among many new rich. However, Chinese business people are often selective in invoking ethnic attachments (Lim 1983), and as Young argues in Chapter 2, there are multiple Chinese ethnicities in the region, which have been variously shaped by different national settings and social relations with other ethnic groups. The social identities assumed by new-rich ethnic Chinese are often more national than they are 'Chinese'.[29] Indeed, Chua and Tan argue in Chapter 5 that national and class identities are far more important to Singaporeans than ethnic identities. In the case of new-rich ethnic Chinese minorities elsewhere in Southeast Asia, ethnic identity may be best viewed as a series of hybridities drawn from various ethnic and national attachments (Hall 1992: 310; Ang 1994) and constructed in relation to particular ethnic Others. Thus in Thailand, Chan and Tong (1995) reject the commonly held view in the literature that Thais with Chinese ancestry have simply been assimilated into Thai society, but argue, nevertheless, that the Chineseness of the Sino-Thai has been constructed within a broader national identity. While most Sino-Thais have grown up speaking the national language, for example, Chinese culture and ancestry have been celebrated in Thailand in recent years, largely in association with the rags-to-riches success stories of many Chinese entrepreneurs and the role they have played in the country's economic boom (Pasuk and Baker 1996: 133–6).

It is possible that increased economic integration within the region, involving, in part, growing co-operation between successful ethnic Chinese from different countries, combined with the promulgation of Confucianist ideology, has produced some diasporic re-Sinification. Yet the significance of even this possibility should not be exaggerated, and it appears fanciful that Confucianism, or Chinese identity, could develop as a triumphant, self-conscious ideology of economic success and new-rich solidarity across Asia.

The cases of Singapore and Thailand underline the fact that Confucianism and Chinese ethnicity are not the only peculiarly 'Asian' identities constructed around, and by, the new rich. Thus, the expanding new rich Indian middle class has, in part, come to express itself through the rise of Hindu nationalism, not only within India, but also among Indian diasporic communities (Lakha). Similarly, the Malay and *pribumi* (indigenous) Indonesian new-rich, in part, come to express themselves through the rise of Islam in their countries. These attachments are not only defined in relation to the West, but also to other rival attachments, and, as in the case of Hindu nationalism, they draw boundaries within nation states, as well as between them. Of particular importance has been the remaking of the region's various nationalisms. Several countries in Asia have not only become richer, but have shifted from an officially sanctioned ethos of national austerity to one in which, to quote Deng Xiaoping, 'to get rich is glorious' or, according to Heryanto on Indonesia (Chapter 6), 'it is cool to be rich'. Leading the drive to national prosperity are the new rich, often possessed with feelings of national pride, sometimes sanctified by a sense of religious mission.

While Singapore's Lee Kuan Yew and Malaysia's Dr Mahathir may join hands in their advocacy of Asian Values, they cannot conceal the changing and often conflictual identities that surround them. Within nationalist discourses through much of Southeast Asia, the idea of a causal link between Chinese ethnicity and enrichment arouses much ambivalence. It may be a matter for celebration; but it is also central to much of the anti-Chinese sentiment that has characterised a number of countries. In the Philippines, it is a commonplace view that the new rich are the local Chinese, and, furthermore, that accumulating wealth through frugality and enterprise is intrinsic to their ethnic makeup. While some non-Chinese Filipino politicians and business people have applauded and sought to emulate these qualities, others hold to a tradition that sees the Chinese as aliens, and their money making attributes as exploitative and disadvantageous to indigenous Filipinos (Pinches). Some, in positions of political or bureaucratic power, have seen Chinese new wealth as presenting them with a rightful opportunity to enrich themselves further, through the quasi-noble or ethno-national privileges associated with state office.

This latter stance has been more evident in Malaysia and Indonesia, where, historically, anti-Chinese sentiments have been stronger than in the Philippines. In both countries, many indigenous politicians, bureaucrats and rising wealthy entrepreneurs have used state privileges to establish advantageous business links with wealthy Chinese capitalists (Shamsul, Heryanto). Notwithstanding the accusations of corruption that are sometimes levelled at them, these indigenous operators have also been highly influential in promoting ethno-nationalist ideologies in which they are located at the forefront of national development. These ideologies invoke not only the nationalist cause of Malays and *pribumi* Indonesians in the era of independence, but also an ethos of pre-colonial and colonial times, when the state was the major vehicle for economic enrichment. A major proponent of 'Asian Values' as the measure of the region's new wealth and non-Western cultural identity is Malaysia's prime minister, Dr Mahathir, whose government's New Economic Policy (NEP) has been explicitly directed against what many Malays see as the dominance of the ethnic Chinese in the nation's economy. From the popular Malay vantage point, the economic success that has come with the NEP era represents a nationalist victory over circumstances which previously assigned the country, and its indigenous people, to the position of economic backwater, the direct result of European and Chinese exploitation (Shamsul).

While many new-rich Malays have acquired their wealth through 'money politics', the most numerous of them, and the main carriers of Malay ethnonationalism, are the first generation of educated salaried managers and professionals. As is the case elsewhere in the region, they represent a significant departure from the old indigenous middle class, who were based in the state bureaucracy. Their emergence in the corporate sector reflects not only the structural reorganisation of Malaysia's and the region's economy, but also a cultural shift from a civil service ethos to one that is business-oriented (Smith). Just as modern Confucianist ideology represents a significant departure from the earlier form, with the elevation of the capitalist to a position of high honour, so has there been a shift in the meaning of Malayness. While the new rich may be appropriating an idealised version of Malay peasant life (Kahn 1992), many are also living lives of increased privatisation and class exclusivity, largely removed from the patronage bonds that not long ago would have tied them to their home villages (Smith). New-rich Malays are also playing a leading role in linking Malay identity more strongly with Islam, through heightened religious piety and participation in the Dakwa movement (Shamsul, Smith). As with Confucianism and Chinese ethnicity, capitalist development in Malaysia has brought with it a transformation in the meanings of privileged social identity, but in ways that have strengthened 'tradition', rather than undermined it.

Malaysia and Indonesia testify to different and apparently contradictory ways in which new-rich identities are being constructed. First, there is the impetus to draw those with Chinese ancestry into a pan-Asian community of new rich, centred on Confucianism and Chinese ethnicity. Second, state development strategies and ethno-nationalist ideologies have generated substantial layers of new rich – largely new middle class – whose identities are stridently indigenous and increasingly Islamic. The relationship between these two new-rich identities has varied from accommodating to volatile. Thus in Indonesia, prior to the crisis of 1997, rapid economic growth was accompanied by an increasing acceptance of cultural practices identified as ethnic Chinese (Heryanto), but since then Chinese merchants, in areas outside the major cities, have borne the brunt of increasing, apparently racist, hostility. As in Malaysia, the experience of new wealth in Indonesia has been matched by growing Islamisation among *pribumi* Indonesians (Heryanto), and it is Islam which some rioters have invoked in their confrontations with the mainly Christian, ethnic Chinese.

While national development and the new rich have primarily been constructed *vis-à-vis* the West and, in some cases, ethnic Chinese minorities, international status contention within the region itself may also feature in these processes. In Southeast Asia, at least some of the cultural impetus for achieving newly industrialised status in Malaysia, Indonesia and Thailand came from the earlier success of the ethnic Chinese-dominated nations. The Philippines is a particularly instructive case, because its recent drive to new wealth arose in the context of being widely branded the regional exception to economic growth, and of becoming nationally identified with its lowly paid, poorly treated, overseas contract workers. Thus, one powerful domestic rendering of the Philippines' recent economic growth, and of the newly rich associated with it, draws a morally loaded contrast between its own open, democratic order and the rigid authoritarian character of other countries in the region. As is the case elsewhere, this distinction is attributed in part to the uniqueness of the Philippine ethnonational cultural heritage (Pinches).

None of the above cultural constructions, centred on the making of new wealth in Asia, is overtly class-oriented. For the most part, they are nationally or ethnically inclusive, but within these discourses, it is the new rich who are elevated to positions of pre-eminence and legitimised as exemplars of national or ethnic prowess. Within these constructions, which privilege collective relations with the Western, ethnic, or national Other, the importance of domestic class, status and gender inequalities is ideologically obscured.

Like the Confucianist past to which it defers, modern Confucianist ideology also divides as it embraces. Besides its simple East/West moral inversion, and its Chinese/other Asian ethnic divide, its principal function is as a ruling ideology of states, bureaucratic elites and newly powerful capitalist classes *vis-à-vis* the broader populace of middle classes, workers and peasants. This double edge of unity and division is evident in the kind of rhetorical anomaly one finds in Tai's account, in which he notes, on the one hand, that East Asia has achieved its new wealth 'while maintaining equality of income distribution' (1989c: 27), and, on the other, that 'oriental workers are willing to work hard, to labor for long hours and to receive a relatively low pay' (1989c: 20). What Tai's account, like that of many others working within this paradigm, fails to address adequately is that the new rich of Asia cannot be accurately described as whole nations or particular ethnic groups. Just as anti-Chinese racists in Malaysia, Indonesia or the

Philippines have often seen the ethnic Chinese as synonymous with wealthy traders and business people, thus ignoring the large numbers of exploited Chinese workers, so too do many of the proponents of modern Confucianism. While it may be possible, as Chua and Tan observe (Chapter 5), to describe Singapore as a society of new rich, relative to the West and a past of shared poverty, Singapore is also, they argue, a society differentiated by pervasive class inequalities.

In attempting to contain the disruptive potential of these inequalities, the Singaporean leadership not only invokes Confucianism as a basis for collective national identity, but also the Confucianist principles of paternalism and merit. How ideologically effective these principles are among working and middle classes remains a moot point. Chua and Tan's chapter suggests that they do enjoy considerable legitimacy, even if Singaporeans do not directly associate them with Confucianism (see also Chua 1995). Yet among Singapore's youth, they also appear to arouse a degree of dissent (Chua and Tan).

The relationship between Confucianist ideology, the new rich and class relations in capitalist enterprise is also contentious. One of the few detailed ethnographic works to examine the operation of modern Confucianist ideas within corporate Asia is Janelli's (1993) account of a large company in South Korea. On the face of it, he observes, the ideology of company managers conforms to the popular culturalist image of Asian corporations, invoking both the great tradition of Confucianism, as well as the little tradition of village social life. According to Janelli, managers quite consciously and, even cynically, use these ideologies as a rhetoric for imposing discipline and establishing authority. Yet they are not always successful, and indeed, much of Janelli's account explores the ways in which professional and white-collar workers (many of them new rich) reject and resist this managerial ideology.

The idea of merit as a source of legitimation of class and status inequalities is clearly not peculiar to Confucianism and the ethnic Chinese. Throughout Asia ascriptive principles are invoked in relation to ethnic or national Others, but the emergence of the new rich represents an open challenge to the ascriptive privileges of old agrarian elites within ethnic or national groups (Shamsul, Lakha, Pinches). The expanding labour markets and public education that have been integral to rapid economic growth have engendered the development of meritocracy as the normative code through which internal social differentiation is often explained and legitimated. Thus, on the one hand, for example, the newly rich Malay capitalists and middle class stand ascriptively for the dignity of Malayness and of all Malays. Yet, through their wealth, occupational prestige and educational credentials, the new rich are constituted, on the other hand, as the nation's most meritorious Malays, the majority of them being seen to have risen from commonly humble village origins, through the agency of state scholarships, talent and dedication, to positions of high individual achievement (Shamsul, Smith). Moreover, because many Malay new rich can afford to make the pilgrimage to Mecca, and are in a position to assume a leading role in the Dakwa movement, they are more able than others to distinguish themselves as pious Muslims (Shamsul, Smith). Like Confucianism in Singapore, Malay ethno-nationalism, in combination with the principle of merit, thus tends to legitimise a social order which privileges the new rich over the majority of indigenous and non-indigenous people, who are not newly rich or, at least, not as rich as others. However, this order is often challenged from below, in some cases through alternative ideologies. Thus, while ethnicity and merit might provide some Malays with an adequate framework for identifying the new rich, others see the new rich as having prospered through black magic (Smith).[30] Even the ideologies or theologies associated with power and privilege may provide a vehicle for denouncing the new rich, as in the case of Sariendah villagers who accuse the local new rich of behaviour that does not accord with Islam (Antlöv).

Finally, while the traditions, ethnicities and nationalisms discussed in this section may have been shaped by and around the new rich, some sections of the new rich – notably those within the middle class who are beholden to the state – appear to be more enamoured by these attachments and identities than are others. As in the case of Janelli's Korean study, many new rich invoke these attachments and identities selectively and opportunistically, and some, it seems, not at all. This is true even in those nations best known for their ethnic tensions or ethno-nationalist zeal. At the top of Malaysia's social order, for example, is a layer of capitalists and senior corporate managers – both Malay and Chinese – whose mutual success and interlocking economic interests are matched by the development of a shared sociability, class lifestyle and disposition that are relatively devoid of ethnic attachments and religious fervour (Smith). They appear to be the counterparts of Singapore's leading capitalists, whom Chua and Tan describe in Chapter 5 as 'transnationalised individuals' who are largely removed from both state and ethnic ideologies.

As with these groups in particular, and the new rich in general, the cultural constructions in which class finds clearest public expression are to be found in the display of private wealth through various lifestyles and consumption patterns.

FROM FRUGAL CAPITALIST TO HIGH-STATUS CONSUMER

The classic European capitalist, celebrated in liberal economic thought, and in Weber's 'Protestant Ethic', is an individualist of ascetic tastes and lifestyle, devoted to entrepreneurial endeavour and the rational pursuit of profits, a man alone and at odds with the leisured extravagance of the aristocracy. His legendary feats are not only celebrated in the West; they also constitute a powerful reference point for politicians, business associations and intellectuals campaigning for, or seeking to explain, rapid economic growth in parts of Asia. Today his frugality, independence and industriousness have been transposed into the Confucianism or Asian Values of the collective Oriental capitalist. Despite

the powerful image, it is doubtful whether such a historical personage ever characterised the capitalist classes of Europe, or of contemporary Asia.

In Europe, not only were many of those who invested in capitalist industry
from prosperous landed aristocratic families, but others who entered from the
middle layers of society commonly tried to use industrial success to follow in the
footsteps of the nobility. Not only did many seek the security of rents over
profits, but they also sought out aristocratic titles, or at least an aristocratic
lifestyle of conspicuous wealth (Neale 1985: 73; Pilbeam 1990: 8–11, 14).
Wallerstein (1988: 101) argues simply, that on both economic and status grounds:
'the primary objective of every bourgeois is to become an aristocrat'. He
suggests that the distortion embedded in the popular image of the European
capitalist arose because theorists derived the personal character of the capitalist
from the systemic character of capitalism, rather than from the human beings
who constituted what was then referred to variously as the bourgeoisie and
middle class (cf. Pilbeam 1990: 1–4). Something similar seems to be taking place
today in relation to the Newly Industrialising Countries of Asia, except that here
the capitalist is given an Oriental profile, reflecting the shifting spatial centre of
capitalist production, and a global discourse preoccupied with cultural difference.[31]

While the systemic forces of capitalism may have inhibited the shift from
profits to rents – the preference that Wallerstein (1988: 101–3) attributes to the
successful capitalist – the pursuit of status rewards has always been given freer
rein. With the decline in the availability and value of formal aristocratic titles,
other vehicles for status recognition have been pursued by the bourgeoisie in the
West, among them the acquisition of former aristocratic properties and prestigious family names. But increasingly, capitalism has produced its own rewards,
most immediately in the way of a growing supply of luxury consumer goods and
associated lifestyles.

Two important shifts in the productive and organisational character of capitalism have affected the status relations of class. Because these shifts have been
global in character, they have been as much a part of the contemporary experience of capitalist development in Asia as in the West. The first is the substantial
growth of a new middle class, comprising highly educated salaried professionals,
technical specialists, managers and administrators who assume powerful positions in the running and servicing of large corporations and state agencies
(Burris 1986). The growth of this new middle class, possessing high levels of
formal education but not, for the most part, capital, has elevated the importance
of educational credentials as a status marker, and deepened the apparent
veracity of meritocracy as a system for ranking people (see Sennett and Cobb
1972).

The second is the massive growth in the production of consumer goods, and
the associated development of what is commonly referred to as consumer culture
(Tomlinson 1990; Featherstone 1991; Slater 1997). The connection between
these two shifts is not only to be found in the economic or structural logic of
capitalism, and the cultural intermediary role of many within the new middle

class in the design and dissemination of consumer images (Featherstone 1991: 43–6), but it is also evident in the unfolding politics of identity and status attribution. The massive growth in luxury consumer goods and the associated development of fashion and marketing of lifestyle have focused heavily on members of the new middle class and their capacity to spend, generating at the same time a plethora of consumer images for the wider population (Featherstone 1991: 108–9; Betz 1992). They have also focused heavily on women: both as reproducers responsible for home-making, where most private consumption takes place, and as the prime subjects and objects of desire (Bocock 1993: 95–6; Slater 1997: 55–8). The enormous growth of the fashion industry in clothing, cosmetics and accessories, along with the industries in domestic appliances and home decoration, has particularly targeted women as consumers.[32]

On the one hand, the widening commitment to a life fabricated through commodities evidences the deepening hold that capitalist production has over people everywhere. On the other, an increasing body of literature argues that consumerism, rather than production, has become the principal arena in which social relations and identities are constructed. For some, the sheer variety and massive replication of consumer items and lifestyle images currently on offer have created new possibilities for identity construction that remove old social boundaries, generating in their absence an atomised sea of postmodern individual consumers, shifting more or less at will within a plurality of arbitrarily defined fashion communities (Fiske 1989; Finkelstein 1996). While the intensity of contemporary consumerism and the way in which it tends to colonise desire (see Heryanto) are undeniable, much of this literature errs in denying or neglecting the fundamental links between consumption and class or status inequalities (Featherstone 1991: 16–20; MacCannell and MacCannell 1993; Crompton 1996). For all its complexity and fluidity, contemporary consumption patterns continue to evidence the playing out of class and status relations through differences in spending power and cultural capital. Notwithstanding the increased possibility of misreading status markers, or of individuals successfully assuming symbolic identities associated with different classes or status groups, gross differences in wealth and cultured identity – evident, for example, in speech, demeanour, gait and confidence – continue to assume a powerful significance in the construction of social boundaries (Bourdieu 1989: 21, see below).

The following discussion, along with the other chapters that make up this volume, attest to the crucial role played by consumption in the cultural constructions of Asia's new rich. As will be shown, the collective identities and symbolic distinctions that arise through the practices of consumption are crucial to the making of class, ethnic and international status relations.

WEALTH CONSUMPTION AND STATUS CONTESTATION

An upturn has definitely hit South and Southeast Asia, and the newest recruits to the middle class are shopping for culture.

(*Asiaweek*, 16 October 1992)

It's a Malaysia where [men's lifestyle magazine] readers drive BMWs and Mercedes, ride Harleys, punch data into laptop computers, drink tequila sunrises in Hard Rock cafés (in a predominantly Muslim country), visit Paris and pay for it all on platinum Visa cards and large salaries.

(*Financial Review*, 2 October 1995)

Since early this year, developers [in China's Guangdong province] have filled pages of Hong Kong dailies with full-spread colour advertisements touting mock-European architecture, fountains and landscaped gardens.

(*Far Eastern Economic Review*, 14 July 1994)

Today, keeping up with the Joshis is the accepted middle-class norm.

(*Far Eastern Economic Review*, 14 January 1993)

Spurred by the growth of the international media and the subsequent emergence of a pan-Asian consumer class, advertisers are increasingly trying to consolidate brands and strategies to carry across national borders. More important they want to mould Asia's massive, growing markets into a single mass entity.

(*Far Eastern Economic Review*, 25 February 1993)

The Maruti-Suzuki Esteems and Tata Sierras roll up towards midnight at the Fireball (Disco), and out get the young set of Delhi's affluent classes: blue Levis made in Bangalore, black tops, vamp lipstick, unisex short haircuts, muscles sculptured at the gym. Outside the door, kept back by security guards, are groups of Jat boys, sons of the dominant peasant caste in the surrounding Haryana countryside, who gape in censorious envy at the independent rich girls in skimpy clothes.

(*Financial Review*, 4 October 1995)

As Mercedes-Benzes and mansions begin to proliferate in countries where millions still toil in destitution, new affluence stirs old resentment…People admire the rich for their success, but resent how they enjoy the fruits and prestige of their achievement.

(*Asiaweek*, 8 September 1995)

We must emphasise the common ground between the well-off and the less well-off…If affluent Singaporeans flaunt their success and deliberately distinquish themselves from others less well-off by the way they dress, the lifestyles they lead, the overseas holidays they take, this will lead to unhappiness and resentment.

(Lee Kuan Yew, *Financial Review*, 3 October 1995)

[T]here is also an ugly face of the new rich, one that is becoming increasingly common in boardrooms, in airport lounges and on golf courses in most countries of the region. They are extravagantly dressed, conspicuous consumers and frenetic users of mobile telephones. Some appear to have modelled their manners on unpleasant characters in American TV soapies. A senior Australian diplomat in South-East Asia describes them as 'venal'.

(*The West Australian*, 11 February 1994)

The representation of Asia's new rich as the West's Oriental Other is one of two opposed stereotypes. The second represents the new rich of Asia as Westernised or globalised yuppies preoccupied with the same consumer items that are associated with their counterparts in places like Australia, the United States and Britain: expensive late-model cars, mobile phones, fashionable nightclubs, designer clothes, gourmet food, tasteful art objects, membership of exclusive golf or health clubs, overseas holidays and shopping excursions, and palatial houses or condominiums. On the face of it, the glossy fashion and lifestyle magazines, which have proliferated in most countries in the region, are indistinguishable from such magazines in the West, except perhaps for the language in which they are written and the predominant ethnic appearance of their models.

There is an interesting contrast here. As producers of wealth, Asia's new rich are most often represented as the West's Oriental Other; as consumers of wealth it is as if there was virtually no distinction, and that what there is, is rapidly diminishing. Undoubtedly part of the reason for this opposition centres on the political and industrial relations implications of Asian Values explanations of productive growth, and the commercial implications of supposing a universal consumer market.[33] The consumer stereotype of Asia's new rich reflects a more general commentary on the nature of globalisation, concerned with the international movement of consumer goods, and the projection of advertising and lifestyle images through a mass media that has become more and more free-ranging (Featherstone 1991; Barnet and Cavanagh 1995; Young, Lakha). Several chapters in this volume evidence the enormous growth in the consumption of these goods and images in Asia, and highlight the extent to which they have been integral to the making of the region's new rich.

In this section, I first consider the meanings of new-rich consumption within the context of global and international status relations, in particular between East and West. Secondly, I examine the meanings of new-rich consumption in reference to domestic class relations, in the light of the arguments of Veblen and Bourdieu.

Despite the complexity and fluidity of the global commodity market, prestigious consumer goods and images identified with the West generally remain the yardstick of luxury. Indeed, participating in and appropriating Western affluence are often quite explicit goals among the new rich in Asia. This is perhaps most obvious in consumer labelling practices, in Bangkok for instance, where middle-class housing estates are given names like California Ville and Le Château (Pasuk and Baker 1996: 121), or in Manila where fashionable boutiques owned and/or frequented by the new rich often go under names like The Best of New York and Italina (on similar practices in Indonesia and India, see Young and Lakha).

To some degree, the images of Japanese affluence rival those of the West, and their influence can be seen, for example, in the expansion of karaoke and the Japanese car market into other parts of Asia, as well as in the Look East policies of the Malaysian government (Shiro 1994; Smith 1994). It can also be seen in the increasing recreational travel into Japan by newly wealthy people from elsewhere in the region. Yet, the pursuit of high living in Japan itself continues to be framed largely in reference to images of European luxury (Wakao 1989).[34] Thus, while new rich Asians may travel increasingly to Japan for holidays, some of their most popular destinations are Tokyo Disneyland and theme parks like Puroland, in which they will be treated to a pastiche of medieval Europe (Tanikawa 1997).

Notwithstanding this widening global fascination with Western luxury, the meanings of particular consumer items and repertoires, and the manner in which they are used, are not as self-evident as one might suppose from popular representations of consumer culture and new wealth in Asia. The mistake lies in assuming that the meanings of consumer goods and consumption patterns are transparent and universal (Appadurai 1988; Friedman 1994; Miller 1995). At a narrow economic level, it is undeniable that the consumption of particular cars, television programmes or fashion accessories indicates something of a development of Westernisation and global commonality. And there is no doubt that luxury continues to be associated, in large part, with images of the West. But increasingly, as the case of Japan's Puroland indicates, these images have been dislodged, in both space and time, from their original source, and shaped according to principles that are new and local. Even where the commodities consumed are materially identical, the particular meaning they have for consumers, and audiences, may vary immensely.

What most interests us here is the way in which the meanings of consumption and consumer items gravitate towards, or are mobilised around, particular social and political relations to become a basis of distinction and collective identity construction.[35] The first and broadest of these relations has come to be expressed as that between Asia and the West. Asia's identity as a major part of the 'Third World' has long been expressed in terms of consumption, evidenced in numerous statistical reports and dossiers comparing frequencies of 'modern' dwellings, 'modern' amenities, automobile ownership, hospital beds, schools, radios and television sets. These statistics have come to stand not just as a quantitative empirical record, but, more fundamentally, as a statement of asymmetrical social and cultural distinction, in which the West is cast as developed, and Asia as backward.

Decades of five- and ten-year plans, of nationalist developmental rhetoric and of regimes legitimising their authoritarianism with the promise of modernity testify to the enormous symbolic, as well as material, power embedded in the desire to dissolve this distinction. The increasing levels of industrialisation and material affluence, and the emergence of a substantial layer of people who can be described as newly rich, have meant that many nations in Asia have achieved, or are achieving, this dissolution. The conspicuous consumption often associated with Asia's new rich is thus, in large part, oriented to a Western audience, as well as to a collective subjective experience of past disadvantage. In a sense then, the cultural construction of Asia's new rich, most obviously expressed in their heightened consumption, is as national and regional ambassadors before a Western audience, both real and imagined. However, the dissolution of the old distinction has not involved a simple process of Westernisation, cultural convergence or capitalist absorption, even though there may be aspects of all of these. Rather, the relationship between East and West is being redefined in ways advantageous to the East. The leading personages in this redefinition are Asia's new rich. In Chapter 6, for example, Heryanto argues that in Indonesia Western cultural forms are becoming less authoritative, and more the subject of creative, often playful, indigenisation.

Not only are differential meanings attributed to identical consumer items, in reference to changing East/West power relations, but there has also been a deliberate promotion of ethno-national symbols as a selling point in many forms of consumption in Asia. Bangkok may be home to California Ville, but it also has new housing estates with names like Nichada, Thani, Laddawan and Chaiyapreuk, which are said to have been drawn from a tradition of Thai fantasy (Pasuk and Baker 1996: 121). And Manila, like all other major cities in the region, may have its McDonald's and KFC, but some of the most popular restaurants among the new rich have names that invoke local village traditions (Pinches). Moreover, the meaning and even the substance of food from international chains like McDonald's are, in large part, determined locally (Heryanto, Lakha). Similarly, while American films and variety programmes on international cable television are patronised by the new rich, so too, and often more frequently, are local films and programmes (Pasuk and Baker 1996: 123–5; Lakha). In some cases, particular imported consumer goods may be rejected because they fail to comply with local moral or linguistic codes, as in the poor sales in Singapore of the Nissan Bluebird, which some attribute to the fact that the name sounds like the Hokkien expression for the male sex organ.[36] There are numerous examples of consumer practices among the wealthy of Asia that constitute an assertion of local cultural preferences, in some cases explicitly concerned with the theme of national identity. This is evident in the recent upsurge in the construction of national theme parks (Kahn 1992; Acciaioli 1996) and the restoration of buildings deemed to be a part of the national heritage (Lim 1991; Askew and Logan 1994).

An interpretation of the above points is implicit in the opening quotation from Tai. Instead of reading this statement for its literal veracity, it might be better understood for its identity politics, set against a historical background of Western domination and belittlement. According to this reading, Tai's statement might best translate as: 'the new rich of Asia have achieved all that Western modernity has to offer, but more than that, they have done so by maintaining their own cultural distinctiveness'. While this kind of identity politics might be implicit in aspects of consumer practice throughout the region, it has also been variously promoted in state ideologies, most aggressively in Malaysia, Singapore and Indonesia, as a means of legitimising the authority of incumbent regimes, as I noted earlier in relation to 'Asian Values'. While these regimes benefit from heightened levels of consumption, they also selectively invoke anti-Western or anti-materialist sentiment in trying to prevent forms or degrees of consumption that might arouse excessive resentment, or be conceived as posing a challenge to the dominant political morality (Heryanto, Chua and Tan).[37] The response in the West to heightened levels of consumption in Asia has been favourable among business people and politicians seeking new markets. But there is also evidence of continued claims to status superiority. Thus, while commentators in the West may marvel at the diligence, Oriental business acumen and paternalistic authority of Asian capitalists, some – such as the *West Australian* journalist featured in the last quotation at the beginning of this section – simultaneously look upon them as lacking the civility and cultivation that might be expected of the Western bourgeoisie.

Another set of relations, played out through changing lifestyles and consumption practices, are those between different nations within Asia. Even if the West remains the principal Other of Asian economic success, the countries of Asia are also divided as competitors for regional economic, political and cultural advantage. With the end of the Cold War, the relative decline of the American presence in Asia and the heightened global status of the Asian region, one might expect this status competition within the region to become increasingly important. Having been caught up in a common quest for modernity and development, officials, national elites and rising middle classes have used heightened levels and overtly nationalist forms of consumption as national status claims *vis-à-vis* other countries and peoples in the region. This is played out, for instance, among the tens of thousands of new rich in Hong Kong, Singapore and Malaysia whose lifestyles include being served by maids from the Philippines and Indonesia. Not only is the fact of having Filipino or Indonesian servants a private source of consumer status for the new rich; it also stands as a symbol of collective ethno-nationalist achievement *vis-à-vis* the Philippines and Indonesia. In the case of the Philippines, this, in turn, has contributed to a nationalist counter-quest for prosperity and renewed regional honour (Pinches). Through their consumption, the new rich of Asia appear as exemplars of national development and prosperity, in relation to both the West and other, less wealthy, countries in the region.

The most immediate way in which the new rich of Asia are constituted through consumption is in relation to other layers of people within their own societies: the 'old rich', workers, peasants and less prosperous elements among the middle classes. The members of old-established elites throughout the region are well known for their titles, family reputations, political dynasties, landholdings and businesses. They are also known for their often lavish lifestyles, their consumption of prestigious goods and services, and, sometimes, their philanthropy and patronage of the arts. Over recent decades their standing has been challenged by many apparently anonymous figures, whose consumer spending power rivals and even surpasses their own. Previously, these established elites could deal with small numbers of new rich by granting them titles or incorporating them through marriage, but old modes of asserting privilege have been undermined, if not swept aside.[38] As large numbers of newly rich people have emerged, as ideologies of meritocracy displace those of ascription, within, and to a limited extent across, ethnic boundaries, and as social prestige is increasingly mediated through the market, so has commodity consumption become more central to the construction of social identity. More and more, consumer items operate as the principal signifiers of standing and achievement. While these characteristics mark the arrival of the new rich at the upper reaches of society, they also mark their departure from those groups located in the lower and middle layers, as well as the status disparities that are opening up among the new rich themselves.

Elsewhere, in periods and places of rapid capitalist expansion, where significant numbers of people from the middle or lower ranks have risen to become newly prosperous industrialists or professionals, there has often been an explosion in status claims made on the basis of conspicuous consumption. Such a period and place was late nineteenth-century North America, the subject of Veblen's (1979) classic study, which documents the elaborate status strategies of 'conspicuous consumption', 'conspicuous leisure' and 'pecuniary emulation' on the part of America's newly risen 'leisure class'. According to Veblen, the very act of possessing wealth had come to be seen as meritorious and conferring of honour (1979: 29). Thus, the newly rich of North America displayed their wealth in order to win public recognition and prestige, and, in so doing, to elevate themselves above others. In order to maintain a position of social exclusivity, they had to demonstrate their continued ability to spend, and so they generated new fashions in order to keep at bay others of lesser means, who may have been able to emulate their earlier forms of display.

Similar processes seem to be at work in Asia today. Thus, as Young's chapter suggests, a key way in which the new rich in some parts of Asia distinguish themselves from the majority of the population comes by way of their possessing a 'discretionary income' and the consumer goods which they purchase with it. As some of the quotations at the beginning of this section indicate, the positional goods that separate the new rich from the less advantaged seem to be almost universal: late model cars, expensive dwellings, designer-label clothes, mobile phones and so on. Thus, one of the key ways in which the new Thai middle class is popularly represented, and identified with street democracy, is through their public display of the mobile phone (Ockey). Similarly in Malaysia, Smith (Chapter 4) observes that the middle class distinguish themselves from the working class through new car ownership as against the ownership of older, reconditioned cars. For Malay Muslims, the making of the pilgrimage to Mecca also serves as an income marker separating the new rich from the less privileged, both as an item of great expense in itself, but also as a religious duty whose fulfilment legitimises a subsequent lifestyle of high secular consumerism (Smith).

A particularly interesting case is that of Singapore in which state-supplied items of collective consumption make for an apparent homogeneity of lifestyle. Yet, according to Chua and Tan (Chapter 5), this situation throws into sharper relief the consumer items – in particular, the private car and apartment, or house on the ground – with which the new rich distinguish themselves from the working class and poor (see also Yao 1996). Many among the middle class in Singapore make all sorts of sacrifices in devoting themselves to the acquisition of these 'icons of success' (Chua and Tan).

In some settings, the positional consumer goods of the new rich may be acknowledged unambiguously as the measure of high social status. Yet often status claims are subject to disputes that have to do with the manner and style of consumption, and not simply with the monetary value of accumulated consumer goods. While Veblen's account centres on the acquisition of prestige through the simple display of material wealth, his own disapproving, satirical voice highlights the presence of another scale of evaluation. In part it is that of the liberal economic theorist in search of the rational capitalist entrepreneur, who is more intent on profitable investment than unprofitable gratification, a position echoed by some contemporary Indian politicians who have coined the phrase 'microchips not potato chips' in reference to what they see as the wasteful consumerism of the Indian middle class.[39] But Veblen's (1979) disapproval is also that of the cultural sophisticate. Indeed, his account of consumption and prestige not only documents the practices of a leisured class, it also contributes to the creation of powerful derogatory stereotypes known in the English-speaking world as the *nouveaux riches*, a people with wealth but no taste.[40] This is precisely the characterisation that is often levelled at Asia's new rich. While the new rich may use consumption to win high status, successfully distinguishing themselves from those with less wealth, including former peers, others with established positions of high status commonly try to defend themselves against newcomers by practising forms of exclusionary behaviour based on criteria other than the mere possession of material wealth.

Here it is instructive to consider the work of Bourdieu (1989), who uses the concept 'cultural capital' to explore similar practices in France. First, Bourdieu draws attention to the symbolic power embedded in the operation of Culture ('high culture') as an aesthetic code through which people are attributed differential social value (1989: 11–32). Thus, he refers to the differential possession of cultural capital, cultivated through family and formal education, and by which individuals demonstrate variable levels of ease or awkwardness in the realm of 'legitimate' taste or 'high culture' (1989: 252). The 'ease' which Bourdieu says characterises the manner and lifestyle of the bourgeoisie is pervasive in its influence 'because it represents the visible assertion of freedom from the constraints which dominate ordinary people' (1989: 255). Cultural capital thus has a parallel existence to 'economic capital'; in general, the two reinforce each other, and one can be used to acquire the other. Though it is economic capital that ultimately proves the more powerful asset, and is more likely to guarantee the reproduction of privilege across generations, the two capitals need to be seen as separate, as they constitute different means by which people acquire power and prestige – one pyramid headed by the cultivated intellectual or artist, the other by the wealthy capitalist. For the most part, the bourgeoisie is comprised of people who are privileged in both, but social tensions arise over differences in the primary attachments of particular segments. We might expect these to become particularly acute in the case of the new rich.

Secondly, while the variable possession or lack of cultural capital has social consequences for all, Bourdieu does not simply posit a hierarchical continuum of differential prestige; he also distinguishes three different forms of taste dynamics identified with the bourgeoisie, the petite bourgeoisie and the working class. Thus, whereas the working class might seek cleanliness, the petite bourgeoisie look for comfort and fashion, while the bourgeois, who simply assume both, pursue harmony or refinement (1989: 247). The major qualitative divide is to be found between the 'legitimate' aesthetics of the bourgeoisie and the 'popular' aesthetics of the working class. A crucial aspect of Bourdieu's argument here is its materialist line of explanation. For Bourdieu, the detached, abstract and formalist Kantian aesthetics of the French bourgeoisie is founded in its 'distance from necessity' (1989: 53–4, 254–5). Conversely, proletarian taste is said to be rooted in the practical concerns of everyday life (1989: 41–4, 254, 372–96), yet Bourdieu also claims that this often combines with the domination of bourgeois-taste goods, as is evident in the popularity of what he calls 'cheap substitutes' (1989: 386).[41]

For Bourdieu, the taste dynamics of the petite bourgeoisie or middle class, whose position would approximate most closely the majority of the new rich in Asia, is to be understood in terms of their intermediate position. On the one hand they struggle to distinguish themselves from the working class, with reference to such qualities as sobriety, rigour and neatness; on the other, they go out of their way to emulate the bourgeois, but in doing so are distinguished by the bourgeoisie as 'pretentious' and 'flashy' (1989: 246–7). Hence the middle-class man:

> is bound to be seen – both by the working classes, who do not have this concern with their being-for-others, and by the privileged classes, who, being sure of what they are, do not care what they seem – as the man of appearances, haunted by the look of others and endlessly occupied with being seen in a good light.
>
> (1989: 254)

In making these points, Bourdieu seeks to combine two kinds of explanation, one rooted in the economic, the other in social relations. The second is the basis of 'the symbolic struggles between the classes' (1989: 250) and concerns the way in which each class defines itself *vis-à-vis* another in terms of various binary oppositional qualities (1989: 246–7). Bourdieu also draws attention to the internal complexities of the bourgeoisie and, in particular, the struggle over what constitutes distinction or legitimate taste (1989: 254).[42]

A third point in Bourdieu's account, which has immediate relevance to our understanding of the new rich in Asia, is his reference to the class trajectories of the 'new bourgeoisie' and the 'new petite bourgeoisie'. We already have a sense of the way in which the cultural identity of the growing middle classes might be built around an uneasy striving for the lifestyle and assured personal qualities associated with the established bourgeoisie. The further point about cultural capital is that it cannot be acquired quickly, as may be possible with monetary wealth; rather, it is cultivated over generations to become something ingrained, and more or less unconscious, embedded in one's habitus (socialised predisposition), hence the qualities of ease, assurance and nonchalant detachment that are said to characterise those with high cultural capital. Thus, we might expect the new bourgeoisies of Asia to be striving for, but lacking, these qualities. But Bourdieu also says something else about the new bourgeoisie, suggestive both of a greater level of self-assertion and of a shifting set of economic conditions that generate new styles and modes of consumption. Here his account comes closest to that of Veblen:

> The new bourgeoisie is the initiator of the ethical retooling required by the new economy from which it draws its power and profits…The new logic of the economy rejects the ascetic ethic of production and accumulation based on abstinence, sobriety, saving and calculation, in favour of a hedonistic morality of consumption, based on credit spending and enjoyment. This economy demands a social world which judges people by their capacity for consumption, their 'standard of living', their lifestyle, as much as their capacity for production.
>
> (1989: 310)

There is a significant difference between Veblen's and Bourdieu's accounts which helps to throw some light on the nature of class, consumption and status in contemporary Asia. While Bourdieu deals with a society in which there is an old rich elite who use cultural capital to distinguish themselves both from the new rich and the petite bourgeoisie, Veblen's account deals with a society in which there is arguably no old rich in possession of an established store of cultural capital by which to denounce, exclude or cultivate the upwardly mobile.[43] Where Bourdieu's reference to the pretensions of the petit bourgeois seems to reflect the prejudices of the French bourgeoisie, Veblen's satire is levelled at the American bourgeoisie itself and comes from without. Moreover, in contrast to Bourdieu's French bourgeoisie, Veblen's account of America's leisure class in the 1890s, and Lamont's (1992) of the American upper middle class a century later, suggest the continued predominance in the United States of an ethos concerned less with the cultivated manner of consumption than with the volume of wealth and the capacity to accumulate it. While the French case suggests something of a capitalist society founded slowly, and within a formerly aristocratic cultural milieu, the case of the United States starts with economic capital and seems to celebrate, more than anything else, the speed with which individuals accumulate it. Yet

Bourdieu's reference to a new era of 'hedonistic consumption' in France concurs with a picture of contemporary consumerism that may have had its origins in the United States, but which has become increasingly global.

In industrialising Asia today we see a number of the above elements. As noted already, the social standing of the new rich, and of those they have left behind, is measured largely by their different levels of material wealth. In addition, there is a strong impetus to reward the new rich with high standing as the leaders and heroes of national development, in part because of their divergence from the old rich, who are often associated with national poverty and backwardness (Lakha, Pinches). Thus the old rich in Asia do not stand as the unambiguous guardians of high honour in the way they appear to in Bourdieu's France.

However, taste and style clearly matter to the new rich. Not only are the new rich commonly demeaned for their alleged vulgarity and ostentation, but many also go to great pains to acquire sophistication and refinement, if not for themselves, then at least for their children. They work at this in a number of ways, one of which is through formal education. Not only have the majority of new rich acquired higher levels of formal education than their parents' generation, but many are also more inclined than their parents to provide their children with something beyond technical or vocational training. In the Philippines, for example, many new-rich Filipino-Chinese families are now sending their children to prestigious universities to study arts and humanities (Pinches). Many new rich also work on their taste and presentation of self by using the services of cultural specialists, like interior decorators, architects, beauticians, grooming consultants and gallery operators. Many more, notably those of lesser means, attempt to cultivate themselves more informally, through selective reading, television viewing and window shopping. As Young argues in Chapter 2, the cultivation of a new aesthetic language commonly takes place in the informal contexts of everyday life, perhaps most notably in shopping malls, where it is not only possible to study the taste codes embedded in the goods on display, and to consult the salespeople who are knowledgeable in these codes, but also to use the mall as a venue in which to practise one's newly cultured identity. The cultivation of a fashionable or sophisticated self may even be an explicit requirement of employment. Companies in Singapore, for example, spend millions of dollars annually on training courses in grooming and etiquette for their young professional employees.[44]

What are the aesthetic codes by which the new rich are evaluated and to which many of them aspire, and where do they come from? The answers to these questions are a good deal more complex and variable than seems to be the case in Bourdieu's France, and in the absence of detailed studies of such matters in the region, it is impossible here to do any more than make some preliminary points. If the high-status authority of the established elites is compromised by their association with past economic backwardness, the bourgeoisies of the West are similarly compromised by the very fact that they are Western. Nevertheless, it would appear that the principal arbiters of aesthetic prowess come from the artistic and intellectual communities found within and between these local and foreign classes. However, these communities are clearly changing, and vary in inclination and influence across the region. And because of their compromised authority and the growing social power of the new rich, they are also subject to influences from without. Indeed, following Bourdieu, the constitution of high taste represents an important area of symbolic struggle between these various social forces.

Clearly there are important differences here which reflect the varied breaks and continuities in the political and social structures of particular nations, as well as the differential engagement of particular societies and classes with the world beyond. In some settings, old elites and intelligentsias retain significant influence, while in others their influence has been eliminated or marginalised. For example, while members of the contemporary Indonesian elite normally preside over national ceremonial events wearing *batik tulis* (written batik cloth), in deference to the attire of the former *priyayi* nobility, on similar occasions ruling officials in China either wear what are variously known as Sun Yat-Sen or Mao suits, or else 'Western' business suits, as deliberate alternatives to the scholarly robes associated with the Confucian tradition.[45] In Chapter 5, Chua and Tan suggest that there are significant cultural differences between the national elites of Singapore, Hong Kong and the Philippines, in the extent to which they see it as becoming to display private wealth publicly. Within particular countries, there may also be rival high-taste regimes defined in terms of different ethnic traditions. It is highly doubtful that these sorts of variations can be accommodated in reference to the Kantian aesthetics identified by Bourdieu as the hallmark of legitimate taste in France.

These variations and complexities are compounded by the fact that contentions over taste evaluation between the new rich and the old rich may be played out in reference to national identity constructions and the symbolic contentions between East and West. In some countries, the traditions of local landed or bureaucratic elites have been selectively recast or renewed by nationalist intellectuals, and professionals or business people from old elite families. This is evident, for example, in the widespread renovation and renewed display of historic public buildings and old stately homes, and in the production of scholarly literature on these architectural forms. Though such activities often serve commercial ends, they are also inscribed with ideas of national identity, which not only address foreign audiences, but also the local population, most notably the upwardly mobile who are seeking out both old and new forms of respectability. Yet there are also cases, often in the same societies, where other nationalist taste arbiters, and sections of the new rich, have distanced themselves from the high-culture practices of old elites, by appropriating and redefining elements of indigenous 'tribal' or 'peasant' culture. These sections of the new rich and nationalist intelligentsia may seek to represent themselves not only as exemplars of national economic success, but also as the cultural re-embodiment of the nation. This is evident in Kahn's (1992) study of the Malay middle class who have been the major force behind such projects as Malaysia's new national theme parks. According to Kahn (1992), the unifying symbols of the traditional peasant community have been idealised and transformed by the Malay middle class into their own class symbols. Similar processes are demonstrated by Heryanto in Chapter 6, which describes the efforts of newly wealthy Indonesian tycoons to legitimise their social positions by participating in the popular tradition of public poetry recitals. Similarly, in the Philippines, it has become increasingly fashionable among wealthy business people and professionals to have among their household art collections a display of 'tribal Filipino' artefacts (Pinches).

Consumer fashions and aesthetic standards have become increasingly fluid in the Asian region and, to varying degrees, new, looser, status structures are being negotiated by and around the new rich. Some of the symbolic struggles entailed in this cultural restructuring have been over national identity and the appropriation of Western luxury, but they have also been over the status of particular classes and groups. While Bourdieu's characterisation of France suggests a relatively stable configuration of status relations with the petite bourgeoisie perennially caught in a position of cultural subordination to the taste standards and practices of the bourgeoisie, the case in much of contemporary Asia seems more contentious and uncertain. Although some elements among the old elites may assert their cultural capital in such ways as to exclude newcomers, others have found their economic and cultural foundations moving from under them. That many from the old elites remain wealthy and influential is some measure of their preparedness to move with the new rich (Pinches), as well as with global fashion trends. Prior to the 1997 economic crisis, this seems to have been evident in Thailand and Indonesia, in the increased acceptability of cultural practices identified with the newly rich ethnic Chinese (Pasuk and Baker 1996: 133–6; Heryanto).

Indeed, in a number of countries in the region, one popular representation of societal change is to speak of the emergence of a new generation comprising sections of the new rich, as well as the still prosperous offspring of the old rich, who, in some ways, may have distanced themselves from their parents' generation (Ockey, Pinches). While the new rich are often accused of vulgarity and ostentation among local artistic and intellectual circles, at least some high-culture specialists are happy to play a role in cultivating the more privileged and socially ambitious new rich, and in acknowledging the gains they have made (Pinches). Ultimately, the livelihoods and cultural authority of these specialists depend on their doing this; so too does the social standing of those new rich in a position to rise above the status levels of the mainstream middle classes.

Notwithstanding these contentions, uncertainties and newly forged alliances, there is also ample evidence of hierarchy in the restructuring of consumer-status relations within the societies of Asia. Poor-worker neighbourhoods in many cities throughout the region continue to be bulldozed, not only on legal or bureaucratic grounds, but because the privileged classes consider them unsightly and offensive to their sensibilities.[46] While there is significant social mobility at the middle and upper levels of society, the new rich themselves are widely variegated. Despite their attempts at cultivating sophistication and refinement, a great many will continue to be looked upon by those in more privileged positions as lacking these qualities.

Clearly not all new rich are able or inclined to study, or have their children study, at elite institutions at home or abroad. Nor are they equally able to avail themselves of sought-after professional culture specialists. Many new rich have to cultivate their tastes by relying instead on some of the more informal methods noted earlier. And in doing so, they have to negotiate a plethora of shops, lifestyle magazines and television programmes that are not only various, but also commonly stratified by market researchers, advertisers and business operators, in such a way as to attract some consumers and repel others (Young). Even items of 'tribal' or 'peasant' material culture that have become popular symbols of national identity among elites and middle classes in the region are commonly ordered by similar taste codes as are other commodities: the most 'tasteful', rare and expensive items coming from specialist dealers; the more common, cheaper and less 'tasteful' items coming from popular craft and department stores. Some measure of the symbolic codes and status distinctions at stake here is given in Kahn's remark on the Mini Malaysia theme park in Malacca: 'Expecting a taste-less Malaysian Disneyland, we were surprised to find an elegant layout of traditional Malay houses' (1992: 169), the implication being that other sectors of the Malay middle class may not have been so fortunate in their quest for respectability.

One of the attractions of Bourdieu's work on cultural capital and distinction is that he extends these concepts to practices that might not ordinarily be seen as being about taste or aesthetics. For example, a principle which seems to be an important part of cultural capital and social distinction in Singapore concerns not so much the question of taste for particular consumer items, as a question of restraint and timing. Promoted by the government, and set against a backdrop of shared poverty and insecurity, this principle, described by Yao (1996), centres on the virtue of being able to time the acquisition of prestigious consumer items with particular moments in the trajectory of upward social mobility, when they are 'deserved'. Just as the accusation of ostentation may be used to exclude many new rich from entry into the cultural world of those with established privilege, so too may the virtue of timing and restraint be used by some new rich as a prin-ciple for excluding others – perhaps the 'anxiety-laden' described by Chua and Tan – from entry into their world of consumer propriety.

The consumer markers used to identify different layers of new rich as distinc-tive social categories are also important in the cultural construction of social groups and interpersonal networks among the new rich, whose lifestyles are commonly developed collectively in particular places: at worksites, housing estates, golf clubs, bars, shopping centres so on. Although the new rich often live unusually private lives (Smith), these places may also engender relations of inter-dependence and class sociability. Indeed, within a social world that is circumscribed by differences in lifestyle and consumer status, there may be little choice but to use these markers as instrumental devices in building social rela-tions. Playing golf, for instance, may simply be a lifestyle statement, but it may also be a useful career strategy (Smith, Pinches). This point is brought out clearly in Buckley's study (Chapter 8) of the Chinese new rich in Beijing who use 'calculated extravagance' and expensive gift-exchange rituals in order to establish interpersonal business networks and a reputation for honour and trustworthiness. In this case ostentation is integral to staying rich and becoming richer, but it also circumscribes a moral world of collective solidarity.

While the lifestyles and business interests of the new rich may be engendering new norms and moralities of intraclass conduct, they also seem to be associated with the development of sharper, more impersonal inter-class cleavages. In spite of persistent characterisations of Asia as a place of ubiquitous patronage, paternalism and personalistic social ties (for example, Pye 1985), a number of studies of capitalist and class transformation in the region suggest a changing and more complex picture.[47] For example, while the corporation examined in Smith's study (Chapter 4) may have cultivated an ethos of paternalism, personalised bonds of patronage centred on the old Malay junior managers appear to have been giving way with the emergence of a new layer of Malay managers, distanced from their villages and from factory workers. Their lifestyles – centred on religious piety and privatised consumption – seem to separate them altogether from dealings with the working class, and it is apparent that they prefer it that way. The new rich in Antlöv's study (Chapter 7) continue to reside in their home village – their livelihood and status are dependent on it – but other villagers complain that they have socially withdrawn and no longer fulfil their communal obligations. Encouraged by the Indonesian government, a key function these new rich see themselves performing is not that of generous patron, but of local role model, whose wealth accumulation and private consumption should inspire other villages along the path to modernity and affluence. Similarly, though conspicuous consumption may be a vehicle for gift exchange among new-rich peers in China, its effect and apparent intention, in relation to less privileged classes, is to communicate superiority and exclusion.

The symbolic struggles over national identity and cultural capital that have been dealt with in this section have concerned privileged classes in the Asian region, and have focused, in particular, on the relationships between the new rich and old rich, and between different layers of new rich. A more complete account of the cultural construction of the new rich would look more closely at the ways in which they are seen and represented among the working classes and peasantries. As Shamsul argues in Chapter 3, this question has been largely overlooked in academic discourse. Some people from these classes may look upon the new rich as embodiments of national pride, or as meritorious individuals. However, as consumers, the new rich appear to arouse a good deal of resentment and antagonism from those they have left behind. Certainly, these sorts of concerns are evident in some of the quotations that open this section.

However, the sentiments of resentment against the new rich appear to invoke varied perspectives on the status of high consumption. In Smith's chapter on Malaysia (Chapter 4), workers struggle for respectability in much the same way as the middle-class new rich, except that workers can afford only reconditioned cars and small houses, rather than the new cars and larger houses of the middle class. A similar picture on Singapore is presented by Chua and Tan in Chapter

5. While this may suggest the incorporation of the working class under the legitimate aesthetic culture of the bourgeoisie, to return to Bourdieu's model, it is also consistent with the potentially disruptive sentiment of envy, referred to in one of the opening quotations. Antlöv's chapter on Indonesia (Chapter 7) documents a different perspective on the consumer practices of the new rich. In this case, villagers resent the new rich, not so much out of envy, but rather because the conspicuous private consumption of the new rich flies in the face of the 'traditional' morality of community reciprocity. This morality lies outside the dominant aesthetic described by Bourdieu. Indeed, arguably it lies outside the aesthetic realm altogether, though it is used in judgement of it. It may be that in many cases worker and peasant constructions of the new rich incorporate both envy and moral condemnation.[48] What is perhaps most interesting is that either way, they may ultimately threaten the security of the new rich and of the wider social, political order. This, at least, seems to be the concern in the second last quotation from Lee Kuan Yew.

LABELS, CATEGORIES AND CLASSES: EAST AND WEST

Although this chapter variously uses terms like new rich, middle class and bourgeoisie to describe and analyse, it must also be acknowledged that these terms are themselves cultural constructions and hence form part of the world we need to explore and problematise. The term 'new rich' was chosen by the editors of the series for its apparent descriptive simplicity, but also because of the fact that it is an expression that is commonly used in some parts of Asia to describe the emergence of a new social phenomenon. Indeed, perhaps the clearest evidence that a 'new rich' has acquired significance in Asia is to be found in the emergence and popular usage of new class vocabularies centred on those meanings that have been discussed throughout this and other chapters in the volume.

The most widely used label identifying newly rich people across the region seems to be the English term 'middle class', as is evident from a number of chapters in this volume. As with its use in the West, the term has taken on various meanings exemplified in Ockey's chapter on Thailand (Chapter 9). Two points in Ockey's account are of particular interest in this context. The first is that after a long absence, the term 'middle class' reappeared in academic writing on Thailand only after the upturn of industrial growth and increasing affluence. While there had long been occupational data that would have supported retention of the term in accordance with its past usage, the apparent significance of its reappearance seems to be that it reflected more the perception of a newly powerful social force than a mere statistical increase in particular occupations. The second point is that the term 'middle class' has been at the centre of increasing discursive elaboration in Thailand, such that it variously denotes prestigious occupations, high educational attainment, high income levels, affluent consumer lifestyles and democratic political practices, all of them represented as transformative of Thai culture and society, but none of them neatly coincident with the others.

In Chapter 6 on Indonesia, Heryanto refers to the increasingly used term *kelas menengah*, an apparent literal translation from the English 'middle class', noting its centrality to local discourse on the new rich. Though much less common, bourgeoisie is a term that is also increasingly used in Asia, in some cases adapted into popular language, as in the expression *burgis*, commonly used in the Philippines (Pinches). There are also terms of indigenous origin that come closer to the English expression 'new rich', and that have become increasingly important to everyday conversation. The most obvious case seems to be the abbreviation OKB, widely used in Indonesia and Malaysia, which stands for *Orang Kaya Baru*, or 'new rich person' (Shamsul, Antlöv). Shamsul traces its first emergence as an everyday Malay expression to the 1950s, and its original reference to those indigenous Malays who rose to positions of wealth independently of high ascriptive office. While the term has positive high-status connotations in some quarters, it is also used pejoratively by many peasants and workers in Indonesia and Malaysia, both in denoting envy and moral condemnation (Antlöv, Shamsul). The officially sanctioned term *Melayu Baru*, which in Malaysia has, to some extent, replaced the popular expression OKB, translates as 'new Malay'. Like OKB, it denotes new wealth, but now this quality is subsumed under an identity that is ethno-nationalist. With the *Melayu Baru* we witness a cultural construction of the new rich that is present in other ways throughout Asia, namely one that distinguishes both locally and globally.

Both the value and limitation of words like those that are used to identify the new rich are that they classify within a world of continuity. On the one hand they signify that which is remarkable and important, on the other they do so through the artificiality of boundaries. When the terms 'middle class' and 'bourgeoisie' were popularised in industrialising Europe, they represented an attempt to apprehend and label the emergence of powerful new social forces which challenged the feudal order of estates and aristocratic authority. The two terms were commonly used interchangeably, and were invested with a shifting range of meanings, both moral and descriptive, reflecting something of the elusiveness and complexity of the phenomenon at hand, as well as the different social vantage points from which it was experienced. Morally, the terms 'bourgeoisie' and 'middle class' conveyed feelings of respect and contempt, of honour and scorn, suggesting 'solid citizen', as well as mediocrity (Williams 1976: 38; Wallerstein 1988: 92). Descriptively, they referred to people who were 'neither lord nor peasant', who were 'well-off', living comfortable lifestyles of 'order, social convention, sobriety and dullness' (Wallerstein 1988: 92). According to Pilbeam (1990: 3), the bourgeois of this era 'would not be king or labourer, but he might be a state official, a man of letters, a professional, merchant, banker, industrialist or academic'.

While the meanings of these two terms continue to be debated, their usage in particular schools of academic writing has become more refined and narrow, in part reflecting a certain crystallisation of the social forces to which they refer, but often, more tellingly, the desire to produce concepts of analytical rigour rather than descriptive accuracy. Thus, in contemporary political economy, the terms 'bourgeoisie' and 'middle class' are defined structurally, positioning actors differentially through their varied relations to the means of production. In this tradition, the two terms are now distinguished, the bourgeoisie referring to those who own capital, the middle class to salaried managers, the self-employed or others similarly defined.[49]

The danger is that it is often forgotten in this kind of writing that the terms 'bourgeoisie' and 'middle class' are cultural constructs as well as analytical concepts. While their refinement in the academic literature may produce sharper analytical tools, this same process also eliminates the range and ambiguity of meaning that are produced both through academic reflection and popular discourse. In looking at the terms 'bourgeoisie' and 'middle class' as cultural constructions, it is their varied, ambiguous and sometimes contradictory, everyday meanings that assume greatest significance, and communicate most directly the experience of class. What is striking about the early popular representations of bourgeoisie and middle class in western Europe is their similarity to the labels and cultural constructions of the new rich that have emerged in industrialising Asia. As is evident from the above, there are important differences, concerning, in particular, the changed global circumstances in which these labels and constructions have arisen, but in both cases it has been in a context of capitalist transformation.

CONCLUSION

The task of this volume, and others in the series, is to develop an understanding of Asia's new rich and the role they are playing in shaping particular societies in Asia, as well as the region as a whole. Part of this understanding comes with the recognition that the new rich comprise mainly capitalists and salaried managers or professionals, whose very positions and success evidence the capitalist transformation that is taking place through most of the region. That the success of a great many of the new rich has been heavily dependent upon the state and foreign capital is also indicative of the key role the latter two forces have played in this transformation. Thus, many of the characteristics of the new rich are to be understood in reference to the structures of change and political-economic organisation entailed in contemporary capitalist development, and to the various ways in which they have unfolded in particular countries and localities.

However, I have argued that this kind of understanding of the new rich in Asia, while necessary, is limited. What is also needed is a cultural analysis of the making of the new rich, in reference to class and international relations. Such an analysis focuses on the way in which power is exercised and contested through symbols and meanings. While the new rich are positioned in the structural sense mentioned above, they have also been positioned discursively through the construction of symbolic boundaries which place and identify them in relation to a range of counter identities: global, ethnic, moral, national, stylistic, religious and so on. In this chapter I have highlighted, and attempted to analyse, the two major ways in which the new rich have been thus identified: as Oriental producers and as global consumers. In so doing, I have sought to problematise and explain, rather than take at face value, those essentialist accounts which simply represent the new rich either as a manifestation of some particular Asian tradition or as the blind followers of some universal cultural logic of capitalist modernity.

Through the structural and symbolic transformations taking place in Asia, the new rich have emerged not only as people with considerable wealth and corporate or state power, but also as a powerful hegemonic force, variously identified as the heroes of national or regional development, meritorious achievers and high-flying consumers. As both producers and consumers of wealth, Asia's new rich are presented as embodying the region's achievement of having overturned the condition of backwardness and stigma *vis-à-vis* the West. Within the region, they are also seen to have done this as the representatives of particular nations or ethnic groups *vis-à-vis* other nations or ethnic groups. The symbolic power of their construction as wealth producers rests heavily on the idea that their success is a direct outcome of their cultural traditions, which variously distinguish them from the West, and from other groups in Asia. Yet this construct also contains a certain tension: on the one hand, the new rich are seen as the embodiments of particular regional, national or ethnic identities; on the other, the honour they are seen to have brought to these identities comes through the representation of the new rich as successful players in the global arena of capitalist accumulation. Through the new rich, 'traditional' regional, ethnic, national and religious identities are uneasily reconstructed in terms of global capitalism. A similar tension is evident in the construction of Asia's new rich as global consumers. While in this case the initial emphasis is on the globalised or Westernised nature of new-rich consumer lifestyles, it also becomes clear that these are given distinctive meanings which largely have to do with elevating national and local identities. This is given clearest expression in the promotion of particular consumer goods and practices as explicit symbols of national, ethnic or religious tradition.

The class efficacy of these constructions of the new rich lies in the very fact that they are most overtly concerned with the redefinition and transformation of regional, national and ethnic identities in terms of capitalist growth. Each of these identities implicitly transcends class, but in such a way as to equate collective sentiments and interests with the sentiments and interests of the new rich. The hegemonic power vested in the new rich through these constructions substantially undermines the ascriptive and high-culture claims of the old aristocratic landowning and bureaucratic elites. In some cases, it similarly undermines the legitimacy of those older sections of the bourgeoisie associated with economic backwardness and state protection. At the same time, within particular national and ethnic boundaries, it also elevates the ideas of merit and spending power as the bases upon which social inequalities are explained and legitimised. Accordingly, those who have been left behind by the new rich – the peasantry,

working class and sections of the middle class – are encouraged to judge themselves individually as lacking the necessary talent to enjoy the same level of
success and social standing.

Although the new rich constitute a powerful hegemonic force in the industrialising countries of Asia, they have also been characterised in ways that dispute
their claims to legitimacy and high social standing. In some cases these characterisations come from old elite and intellectual circles, and centre on the
purported cultural vulgarity of the new rich. Such practices of exclusion and
denigration are likely to continue, particularly in reference to the expanding
middle classes. However, it also appears that there is significant impetus for
accommodation and the pursuit of mutual advantage, including the selective
suspension of ethnic distinctions, among the most powerful sections of the new
rich and old elites.

What seems more problematic and potentially unstable is the relationship
between the new rich and those they have left behind. Considerable work still
needs to be done to demonstrate the extent to which the dominant constructions
of the new rich penetrate the social consciousness of subordinate classes.
Certainly the emulation of new rich consumer practices that have been observed
among some less privileged groups suggest deference and normative consensus.
Yet in other instances the new rich are represented as people who have acquired
their wealth illegitimately, or who have withdrawn from their collective social
and moral obligations to those less fortunate than themselves. In these cases, the
national and ethnic identities that appear to unite all classes around the new rich
may themselves be disputed or subject to moral redefinition. Indeed, it may be
that the hegemonic constructions built around Asia's new rich are serving
primarily to generate consensus among the elites and middle classes rather than
across whole nations or ethnic categories.[50]

NOTES

I wish to thank Loretta Baldassar, John Gordon and the two anonymous
reviewers for their comments on an earlier draft of this chapter.

1 This kind of characterisation is evident in much of the political science literature on
  patronage and paternalism in Asia, for example Pye (1985, 1988); as well as in some
  anthropological tracts on societal integration such as those by Dumont (1972) on
  India, and Nakane on Japan (Hata and Smith 1983).
2 In Asia itself, this expression is most closely associated with political leaders Lee Kuan
  Yew (Singapore) and Mohamed Mahathir (Malaysia), but it is also an expression
  popular among Western journalists, for example Sheridan (1998). For critical discussion see Rodan *et al.* (1996).
3 One instance of this is Yoshihara (1988). For a critical account of this literature see
  Rutten (1994). See also McVey's (1992b) discussion and Pinches (1996).
4 Though it may be argued, in reference to the idea of 'great traditions', that the shift
  here is to an acknowledgement of multiple Cultures, rather than cultures, the opposition of civilisation to barbarity is relatively absent in the recent literature on Asia.

5 Kahn's (1991, 1992) response to some of the foregoing problems is to limit his concerns to the self-conscious construction of cultures by middle classes and intellectuals. This perspective is used to revealing effect in his work on the Malay middle classes, and parallels the 'culture builders' orientation found in Frykman and Lofgren (1987). The drawback in Kahn's effective abandonment of the culture concepts as an analytical device is that it tends to privilege the practices of the privileged.

6 Anthropological analysis has been particularly weak in dealing with culturally variegated class societies. However, it might be observed that as Cultural Studies has shifted from its Marxist origins under the influence of postmodernist thought, the question of social structure has receded in favour of an identity politics that is largely removed from the idea of the material.

7 The same could be said of my own contribution to the first volume in this series (Pinches 1996).

8 There are almost no socio-cultural accounts of privileged classes or status groups in industrialising Asia, but see Kahn (1991, 1992).

9 See for example Chakrabarty (1989).

10 But most of these have focused on subaltern or subordinate groups, providing only limited treatment of the cultural life of the bourgeoisie and middle classes. But see Abercrombie *et al.* 1980, 1990; Wilentz 1985.

11 In this general sense the term embraces distinctions of a formally 'ascribed' nature, as in the codified rankings of feudal Europe or pre-colonial Java (Geertz 1976: 227–60), and of the formally more open, 'achieved' kind, usually associated with capitalist societies, involving, for example, prestige rankings based on occupation, education, income and consumption patterns.

12 See also Austin (1981) on the value of the status concept for class analysis.

13 In many respects these developments build on what Weber described as the strategy of social closure (see Parkin 1974).

14 Recent examples on the middle classes and bourgeoisie in Europe and the United States include Blumin (1989), Crossick and Haupt (1995), and Marcus and Hall (1992). One of the few detailed ethnographic accounts based in Asia is Vogel (1963).

15 This latter account explicitly focuses on the theoretical question of cultural boundaries (see also Lamont and Fournier 1992), and is directly comparable to Bourdieu's study. Its main ethnographic weakness is that there is very little about those classes in relation to which the upper middle class defines itself.

16 As is evident in the first volume in the New Rich in Asia series (Robison and Goodman 1996a), along with other literature on the region (for example, Deyo 1987; Hewison *et al.* 1993), the political-economic structures and processes, through which the new rich in Asia have emerged, have been complex and variegated. While it is useful for the purposes of this volume to make a broad distinction between the global and local, this is clearly a major simplification.

17 These issues have been the subject of a growing volume of literature: see for example Smith 1981; Friedman 1990; Featherstone 1990, 1995; Appadurai 1991, 1996; Foster 1991; Hall 1992; Gupta 1992; Robertson 1992, 1995; Hannerz 1992, 1996; Basch *et al.* 1994; Kearney 1995; Tønnesson and Antlöv 1996; Grossberg 1997.

18 Further reference to other chapters in this book will be made simply by listing the authors' names.

19 Because of its earlier industrialisation and prosperity, this chapter deals only minimally with Japan.

20 Note, for instance, the increasing interest in listing and profiling Asia's growing number of tycoons in the pages of journals such as the *Far Eastern Economic Review* and *Asiaweek*, and books such as Yoshihara (1988), Ch'ng (1993) and Hiscock (1997).

21 This was more clear-cut in the Chinese status order than in Indian caste, and nor were these ideologies uncontested (on caste, see Appadurai 1986). In China attitudes to commerce varied between classes and regions, as Skinner points out in relation to

the early Sino-Thais, whose ethos was more that of the merchant, than was the case with the Thai elite who looked upon commerce with disdain (1957: 93–5, 306). On a similar stance of the Japanese samurai towards commerce, see Sheldon (1958: 31–2).

22 See also note 20.

23 Post-Fordism, also called 'flexible accumulation', refers to a system of economic organisation in which labour processes, labour markets, product designs and consumption patterns are not rigidly structured and centrally controlled in the ways that were associated with Fordism, but rather are flexibly configured in ways which allow capital to be more immediately responsive to rapidly changing conditions and opportunities (Harvey 1989: 147–88).

24 Much of the discussion here centres on the so-called practice of rent seeking. See note 3.

25 What I have in mind here are a series of layered ideologies, rhetorics and modes of identification which are variously called into play in the context of identity politics. This framework thus differs, for example, from the more definitive world civilisations model found in Huntington (1996).

26 It should be noted that critics of these propositions also come from within the region as well as from outside (see Young).

27 The growth of the fashion and retail industries in the region appears to have provided many women with the opportunities to become successful capitalists. For more on gender and the new rich, see Sen and Stivins (1998).

28 See for example Berger and Hsiao (1988), Tai (1989a), Clegg and Redding (1990), Redding (1990), Berger (1991) and Weinshall (1993). Clearly students at such colleges are also exposed to managerial perspectives based on neo-classical economic principles. The pedagogical weight given to these different perspectives, and the influence they have on students from the region, would make for interesting research.

29 See also Gosling (1983) and Lim (1992).

30 Attempts to gain new wealth through such practices seem to be quite widespread. In Korea, for example, Kendell (1996) notes that most shamanistic rituals, once held primarily in response to life-threatening illnesses, are now held for the purposes of becoming rich. In Thailand, several new Buddhist movements, oriented towards business people and the new middle class, have come into being in Bangkok. Organised around the lifestyle constraints, dispositions and insecurities of the city's entrepreneurs and professionals, these movements have gained large followings. One cult to become popular in the 1990s centred on the mother goddess Kuan Yin, whom business people identify as the 'goddess of trade' (Pasuk and Baker 1996: 127–33).

31 On this last point see Kahn (1995).

32 Some of these matters are taken up in the Asian context in Sen and Stivens (1998).

33 Thus the work discipline, corporate harmony and low-wage regimes that are said to characterise Asian workers are commonly invoked by politicians and capitalists in the West as a means of controlling or dismembering their own working classes. Conversely, the impetus to expand markets is well suited by the proposition that the world is made up of keen, predictable consumers.

34 According to Wakao: 'It is often remarked that although Japan has become an economic superpower, the Japanese people do not feel affluent…in comparison with the lives of comparatively affluent people in the West….What we lack in our daily lives is the fragrance of a culture mellowed and refined over the years. This is what I mean by class' (1989: 30).

35 As recent work in this area indicates, commodity consumption might best be understood as an elaborate means through which the individual and collective self is constructed, and, to that extent, its meanings are quite idiosyncratic and context-specific (Friedman 1994). Ironically though, some of this literature (for example, Fiske 1989: 32–7) seems to move from rejecting the idea that consumer goods have

universal meaning, to positing the idea of the autonomous universal consumer subject.

36   My thanks to Joanna Tan for pointing out to me this and a number of other examples.

37   At one stage Malaysia's prime minister, Dr Mahathir, considered setting up a system of morality summer camps for the nation's youth on the grounds that economic growth had been associated with their moral corruption through the growing emulation of Western consumer lifestyles (*The West Australian*, 8 February 1997).

38   In China and parts of Indochina, of course, this had occurred earlier, in a far more radical way.

39   Salim Lakha, personal communication.

40   For an excellent exploratory article on the cultural identities of the *nouveaux riches* in contemporary eastern Europe, see Sampson (1994).

41   Here there appears to be an unresolved tension in Bourdieu's account between one model which supposes separate class taste communities, and another which assumes the hegemony of legitimate (bourgeois) taste. Indeed, Bourdieu's propositions on proletarian taste are the least convincing aspects of his argument

42   In his discussion of the symbolic struggles between and within classes, Bourdieu's account draws heavily on Weber's concepts of status and social closure. See also Lamont and Lareau (1988) and Jenkins (1992: 128–51).

43   Though it may be argued that the old rich who set the tone for the American bourgeoisie were based in western Europe.

44   'Money Mind' Television Corporation of Singapore, 6 April 1997; my thanks to the series' producer, Douglas Carr, for making this programme available to me.

45   My thanks to Greg Acciaioli and Bev Hooper, respectively, for their assistance with these two examples.

46   See for example Pinches (1994).

47   See for example Scott and Kerkvliet (1973).

48   This is something I try to deal with in Pinches (1992).

49   Much of the political-economic literature is of course a good deal more sophisticated and varied in its definitions than this statement suggests. Definitions of the middle class, in this and other theoretical traditions, have been especially varied (Burris 1986; Robison and Goodman 1996(b)).

50   Though this is suggestive of one of Abercrombie *et al.* (1980, 1990) major arguments, I do not wish to endorse their narrow rendering of the hegemony concept, nor their failure to explore the complex ways in which hegemony and resistance are interconnected in the practices of subordinate groups (see Pinches 1992).

BIBLIOGRAPHY

Abercrombie, N. , Hill, S. and Turner, B. (1980) *The Dominant Ideology Thesis*, London: Allen & Unwin.

——, —— and —— (eds) (1990) *Dominant Ideologies*, London: Unwin Hyman.

Abercrombie, N. and Urry, J. (1983) *Capital, Labour and the Middle Classes*, London: George Allen & Unwin.

Acciaioli, G. (1996) 'Pavilions and Posters: Showcasing Diversity and Development in Contemporary Indonesia', *Eikon*, 1: 27–42.

Anderson, B. (1988) 'Cacique Democracy in the Philippines', *New Left Review*, 169: 3–29.

Ang, I. (1994) 'On not Speaking Chinese: Postmodern Ethnicity and the Politics of Diaspora', *New Foundations*, 24: 1–18.

Anthias, F. and Yuval-Davis, N. (1992) *Racialized Boundaries*, London: Routledge.

Appadurai, A. (1986) 'Is Homo Hierarchicus?', *American Ethnologist*, 13: 745–61.
—— (1988) 'Introduction: Commodities and the Politics of Value', in A. Appadurai (ed.), *The Social Life of Things*, Cambridge: Cambridge University Press.
—— (1991) 'Global Ethnoscapes: Notes and Queries for a Transnational Anthropology', in R. Fox (ed.), *Recapturing Anthropology: Working in the Present*, Santa Fe: School of American Research Press.
—— (1996) *Modernity at Large: Cultural Dimensions of Globalization*, Minneapolis: University of Minnesota Press.
Askew, M. and Logan, W. (eds) (1994) *Cultural Identity and Cultural Change in Southeast Asia*, Geelong: Deakin University Press.
Austin, D. (1981) 'Ideology in Class Society', in P. Hiller (ed.), *Class and Inequality in Australia*, Sydney: Harcourt Brace Jovanovich.
Austin-Broos, D. (1987) 'Introduction', in D. Austin-Broos (ed.), *Creating Culture*, Sydney: Allen & Unwin.
Barker, F., Hulme, P., Iverson, M. and Loxley, D. (eds) (1985) *Europe and its Others*, Colchester: University of Essex.
Barnet, R. and Cavanagh, J. (1995) *Global Dreams: Imperial Corporations and the New World Order*, New York: Touchstone.
Barth, F. (1969) 'Introduction', in F. Barth (ed.), *Ethnic Groups and Boundaries: The Social Organisation of Culture Difference*, London: George Allen & Unwin.
Basch, L., Schiller, N. and Blanc, C. (1994) *Nations Unbound: Transnational Projects, Postcolonial Predicaments, and Deterritorialized Nation-States*, Amsterdam: Gordon & Breach Publishers.
Berger, B. (1991) *The Culture of Entrepreneurship*, San Francisco: ICS Press.
Berger, P. (1988) 'An East Asian Development Model', in P. Berger and H. Hsiao (eds), *In Search of an East Asian Development Model*, New Brunswick: Transaction Books.
Berger, P. and Hsiao, H. (eds) (1988) *In Search of an East Asian Development Model*, New Brunswick: Transaction Books.
Bergère, M. (1986) *The Golden Age of the Chinese Bourgeoisie 1911–1937*, Cambridge: Cambridge University Press.
Betz, H. (1992) 'Postmodernism and the New Middle Class', *Theory, Culture and Society*, 9 (2): 93–114.
Bhabha, H. (1994) *The Location of Culture*, London: Routledge.
Blumin, S. (1989) *The Emergence of the Middle Class: Social Experience in the American City, 1760–1900*, Cambridge: Cambridge University Press.
Bocock, R. (1993) *Consumption*, London: Routledge.
—— (1986) *Hegemony*, London: Tavistock.
Bourdieu, P. (1977) *Outline of a Theory of Practice*, Cambridge: Cambridge University Press.
—— (1989) *Distinction: A Social Critique of the Judgement of Taste*, London: Routledge.
Brenner, S. (1991) 'Competing Hierarchies: Javanese Merchants and the Priyayi Elite in Solo, Central Java', *Indonesia*, 52: 55–83.
Burris, V. (1986) 'The Discovery of the New Middle Class', *Theory and Society*, 15: 317–49.
Chakrabarty, D. (1989) *Rethinking Working-Class History: Bengal 1890–1940*, Princeton: Princeton University Press.
Chan, K. and Tong, C. (1995) 'Modelling Culture Contact and Chinese Ethnicity in Thailand', *Southeast Asian Journal of Social Science*, 23 (1): 1–12.
Chaney, D. (1994) *The Cultural Turn: Scene-Setting Essays on Cultural History*, London: Routledge.

Ch'ng, D. (1993) *The Overseas Chinese Entrepreneurs in East Asia*, Melbourne: Committee for Economic Development of Australia.

Chua Beng Huat (1995) *Communitarian Ideology and Democracy in Singapore*, London: Routledge.

Clegg, S. and Redding, R. (eds) (1990) *Capitalism in Contrasting Cultures*, Berlin: Walter de Gruyter.

Cohen, A. (1985) *The Symbolic Construction of Community*, London: Tavistock.

Crompton, R. (1996) 'Consumption and class analysis', in S. Edgell, K. Hetherington and A. Warde (eds), *Consumption Matters*, Oxford: Blackwell.

Crossick, G. and Haupt, H. (1995) *The Petite Bourgeoisie in Europe 1780–1914*, London: Routledge.

Deyo, F. (ed.) (1987) *The Political Economy of New Asian Industrialisation*, Ithaca: Cornell University Press.

—— (1997) 'Labour and Industrial Restructuring in South-East Asia', in G. Rodan, K. Hewison and R. Robison (eds), *The Political Economy of South-East Asia: An Introduction*, Melbourne: Oxford University Press.

Dirks, B., Eley, G. and Ortner, S. (1994) 'Introduction', in B. Dirks, G. Eley and S. Ortner (eds), *Culture/Power/History: A Reader in Contemporary Social Theory*, Princeton: Princeton University Press.

Doeppers, D. (1984) *Manila 1900–1941*, Quezon City: Ateneo de Manila University Press.

Dumont, L. (1972) *Homo Hierarchicus: the Caste System and its Implications*, London: Paladin.

During, S. (1993) 'Introduction', in S. During (ed.), *The Cultural Studies Reader*, London: Routledge.

Evans, G. (1993) 'Hierarchy and Dominance: Class, Status and Caste', in G. Evans (ed.), *Asia's Cultural Mosaic*, New York: Prentice-Hall.

Fairbank, J. (1968) 'A Preliminary Framework', in J. Fairbank (ed.), *The Chinese World Order*, Cambridge, MA: Harvard University Press.

—— (1994) *China: A New History*, Cambridge, MA: Belknap Press.

Featherstone, M. (ed.) (1990) *Global Culture: Nationalism, Globalization and Modernity*, London: Sage.

—— (1991) *Consumer Culture and Postmodernism*, London: Sage.

—— (1995) *Undoing Culture: Globalization, Postmodernism and Identity*, London: Sage.

Finkelstein, J. (1996) *After a Fashion*, Carlton South: Melbourne University Press.

Fiske, J. (1989) *Understanding Popular Culture*, London: Routledge.

Foster, R. (1991) 'Making National Cultures in the Global Ecumene', *Annual Review of Anthropology*, 20: 235–60.

Friedman, J. (1990) 'Being in the World: Globalization and Localization', in M. Featherstone (ed.), *Global Culture*, London: Sage.

—— (ed.) (1994) *Consumption and Identity*, Chur: Harwood.

Frykman, J. and Lofgren, O. (1987) *Culture Builders: A Historical Anthropology of Middle-Class Life*, New Brunswick: Rutgers University Press.

Geertz, C. (1976) *The Religion of Java*, Chicago: University of Chicago Press.

Genovese, E. (1976) *Roll Jordan Roll: The World the Slaves Made*, New York: Vintage.

Gerth, H. and Mills, C. (eds) (1970) *From Max Weber*, London: Routledge & Kegan Paul.

Gosling, L. (1983) 'Changing Chinese Identities in Southeast Asia: An Introductory Review', in L. Gosling and L. Lim (eds), *The Chinese in Southeast Asia: Identity, Culture and Politics*, Singapore: Maruzen Asia.

Grossberg, L. (1996) 'Identity and Cultural Studies: Is That All There Is?', in S. Hall and P. du Gay (eds), *Questions of Cultural Identity*, London: Sage.

—— (1997) 'Cultural Studies, Modern Logics and Theories of Globalisation', in A. McRobbie (ed.), *Back to Reality? Social Experience and Cultural Studies*, Manchester: Manchester University Press.

—— and Nelson, C. (1988) 'Introduction: The Territory of Marxism', in C. Nelson and L. Grossberg (eds), *Marxism and the Interpretation of Culture*, Urbana: University of Illinois Press.

Gupta, A. (1992) 'The Song of the Nonaligned World: Transnational Identities and the Reinscription of Space in Late Capitalism', *Cultural Anthropology*, 7 (1): 63–79.

Hall, S. (1980) 'Encoding/Decoding', in S. Hall, D. Hobson and P. Willis (eds), *Culture Media Language*, London: Hutchinson.

—— (1992) 'The Question of Cultural Identity', in S. Hall, D. Held and T. McGrew (eds), *Modernity and its Futures*, Cambridge: Polity.

Hall, S., Lumley, B. and McLennan, G. (1978) 'Politics and Ideology: Gramsci', in Centre for Contemporary Cultural Studies (ed.), *On Ideology*, London: Hutchinson.

Hannerz, U. (1992) *Cultural Complexity: Studies in the Social Organization of Meaning*, New York: Columbia University Press.

—— (1996) *Transnational Connections: Culture, People, Places*, London: Routledge

Harvey, D. (1989) *The Condition of Postmodernity*, Oxford: Blackwell.

Hata, J. and Smith, W. (1983) 'Nakane's Japanese Society as Utopian Thought', *Journal of Contemporary Asia*, 13 (3): 361–88.

Hewison, K., Robison, R. and Rodan, G. (eds) (1993) *Southeast Asia in the 1990s*, St Leonards: Allen & Unwin.

Hiscock, G. (1997) *Asia's Wealth Club*, St Leonards: Allen & Unwin.

Huntington, S. (1996) *The Clash of Civilisations and the Remaking of World Order*, New York: Simon & Schuster.

Hutchison, J. and Brown, A. (eds) (forthcoming) *Organising Labour/Globalising Asia*, London: Routledge.

Janelli, R. (1993) *Making Capitalism: The Social and Cultural Construction of a South Korean Conglomerate*, Stanford: Stanford University Press.

Jay, M. (1984) *Adorno*, Cambridge, MA: Harvard University Press.

Jenkins, R. (1992) *Pierre Bourdieu*, London: Routledge.

Jenks, C. (1993) *Culture*, London: Routledge.

Kahn, J. (1991) 'Constructing Culture: Towards an Anthropology of the Middle Classes in Southeast Asia', *Asian Studies Review*, 15 (2): 50–6.

—— (1992) 'Class, Ethnicity and Diversity: Some Remarks on Malay Culture in Malaysia', in J. Kahn and F. Loh (eds), *Fragmented Vision: Culture and Politics in Contemporary Malaysia*, North Sydney: Allen & Unwin.

—— (1995) *Culture, Multiculture, Postculture*, London: Sage.

Kearney, M. (1995) 'The Local and the Global: The Anthropology of Globalization and Transnationalism', *Annual Review of Anthropology*, 24: 547–65.

Keesing, R. (1974) 'Theories of Culture', *Annual Review of Anthropology*, no. 3: 73–97.

—— (1990) 'Theories of Culture Revisited', *Canberra Anthropology*, 13 (2): 46–60.

—— (1991) 'Asian Cultures?', *Asian Studies Review*, 15 (2): 43–9.

Kendell, L. (1996) 'Korean Shamans and the Spirits of Capitalism', *American Anthropologist*, 98 (3): 512–27.

Kurtz, D. (1996) 'Hegemony and Anthropology', *Critique of Anthropology*, 16 (2): 103–35.

Lakha, S. (1988) *Capitalism and Class in Colonial India: The Case of Ahmedabad*, New Delhi: Sterling.

Lamont, M. (1992) *Money, Morals and Manners: The Culture of the French and American Upper-Middle Class*, Chicago: University of Chicago Press.

—— and Fournier, M. (eds) (1992) *Cultivating Differences: Symbolic Boundaries and the Making of Inequality*, Chicago: University of Chicago Press.

—— and Lareau, A. (1988) 'Cultural Capital: Allusions, Gaps and Glissandos in Recent Theoretical Developments', *Sociological Theory*, 6 (2): 153–68.

Larrain, J. (1986) *A Reconstruction of Historical Materialism*, London: Allen & Unwin.

Lee, D. and Turner, B. (eds) (1996) *Conflicts about Class*, London: Longman.

Legge, J. (1964) *Indonesia*, Englewood Cliffs: Prentice-Hall.

Licuanan, V. (ed.) (1992) *Women Entrepreneurs in Southeast Asia*, Makati: Asian Institute of Management.

Lim, L. (1983) 'Chinese Economic Activity in Southeast Asia: An Introductory Review', in L. Lim and P. Gosleng (eds), *The Chinese in Southeast Asia: Ethnicity and Economic Activity*, Sinpapore: Maruzen Asia.

—— (1992) 'The Emergence of a Chinese Economic Zone in Asia', *Journal of Southeast Asia Business*, 8 (1): 41–6.

Lim, W. (ed.) (1991) *Architecture and Development in Southeast Asia*, Special Issue of *Solidarity*, nos. 131–2.

Lingle, C. (1996) *Singapore's Authoritarian Capitalism*, Barcelona: Edicions Sirocco.

Lopez-Gonzaga, V. (1991) *The Negrense: A Social History of an Elite Class*, Bacolod: Institute for Research and Development, University of St John La Salle.

MacCannell, D. and MacCannell, J. (1993) 'Social Class in Postmodernity: Simulacrum or Return of the Real?', in C. Rojek and B. Turner (eds), *Forget Baudrillard?*, London: Routledge.

Mackie, J. (1989) 'Chinese Businessmen and the Rise of Southeast Asian Capitalism', *Solidarity* 123: 96–107.

McVey, R. (ed.) (1992a) *Southeast Asian Capitalists*, Ithaca: Southeast Asia Program, Cornell University.

—— (1992b) 'The Materialisation of the Southeast Asian Entrepreneur', in R. McVey (ed.), *Southeast Asian Capitalists*, Ithaca: Southeast Asia Program, Cornell University.

Mancell, M. (1968) 'The Ch'ing Tribute System: An Interpretive Essay', in J. Fairbank (ed.), *The Chinese World Order*, Cambridge, MA: Harvard University Press.

Marcus, G. and Fischer, M. (1986) *Anthropology as Cultural Critique*, Chicago: University of Chicago Press.

—— and Hall, P. (1992) *Lives in Trust: The Fortunes of Dynastic Families in Late Twentieth-Century America*, Boulder, CO: Westview.

Marcuse, H. (1968) *One-Dimensional Man*, London: Sphere.

Miller, D. (1995) 'Consumption and Commodities', *Annual Review of Anthropology*, no. 24: 141–61.

Misra, B. (1961) *The Indian Middle Classes*, London: Oxford University Press.

Mouffe, C. (1979) *Gramsci and Marxist Theory*, London: RKP.

Murphy, R. (1972) *The Dialectics of Social Life: Alarms and Excursions in Anthropological Theory*, London: George Allen & Unwin.

Naisbit, J. (1996) *Megatrends Asia*, London: Nicholas Brealey.

Neale, R. (1985) *Writing Marxist History: British Society, Economy and Culture since 1700*, Oxford: Blackwell.

Nelson, C., Treicher, P. and Grossberg, L. (1992) 'Cultural Studies: An Introduction', in L. Grossberg, C. Nelson and P. Treicher (eds), *Cultural Studies*, New York: Routledge.

O'Hanlon, R. (1989) 'Cultures of Rule, Communities of Resistance', *Social Analysis*, 25: 94–114.

Osborne, M. (1985) *Southeast Asia*, London: George Allen & Unwin.

Pakulski, J. and Waters, M. (1996) *The Death of Class*, London: Sage.

Palmier, L. (1960) *Social Status and Power in Java*, London: Athlone Press.

Parkin, F. (1974) 'Strategies of Social Closure in Class Formation', in F. Parkin (ed.), *The Social Analysis of Class Structure*, London: Tavistock.

Pasuk, P. and Baker, C. (1995) *Thailand: Economy and Politics*, Kuala Lumpur: Oxford University Press.

—— and —— (1996) *Thailand's Boom*, St Leonards: Allen & Unwin.

Pilbeam, P. (1990) *The Middle Classes in Europe 1789–1914: France, Germany, Italy and Russia*, London: Macmillan.

Pinches, M. (1992) 'Proletarian Ritual: Class Degradation and the Dialectics of Resistance in Manila', *Pilipinas*, 19 (Fall): 67–92.

—— (1994) 'Modernisation and the Quest for Modernity: Architectural Form, Squatter Settlements and the New Society in Manila', in M. Askew and W. Logan (eds), *Cultural Identity and Urban Change in Southeast Asia*, Geelong: Deakin University Press.

—— (1996) 'The Philippines' New Rich: Capitalist Transformation Amidst Economic Gloom', in R. Robison and D. Goodman (eds), *The New Rich in Asia*, London: Routledge.

Pye, L. (1985) *Asian Power and Politics: The Cultural Dimensions of Authority*, Cambridge, MA: Belknap Press.

—— (1988) 'The New Asian Capitalism: A Political Portrait', in P. Berger and H. Hsiao (eds), *In Search of an East Asian Development Model*, New Brunswick: Transaction Books.

Rebel, H. (1989) 'Cultural Hegemony and Class Experience: A Critical Reading of Recent Ethnological-Historical Approaches', *American Ethnologist*, 16 (1 and 2): 117–36 and 350–65.

Redding, S. G. (1990) *The Spirit of Chinese Capitalism*, New York: Walter de Gruyter.

—— (1995) 'Overseas Chinese Networks: Understanding the Enigma', *Long Range Planning*, 28 (1): 61–9.

Riggs, F. (1966) *The Modernization of a Bureaucratic Polity*, Honolulu: East-West Center Press.

Robertson, R. (1992) *Globalization: Social Theory and Global Culture*, London: Sage.

—— (1995) 'Globalization: Time–Space and Homogeneity–Heterogeneity', in M. Featherstone, S. Lash and R. Robertson (eds), *Global Modernities*, London: Sage.

Robison, R. and Goodman, D. (eds) (1996a) *The New Rich in Asia*, London: Routledge.

—— (1996b) 'The New Rich in Asia: Economic Development, Social Status and Political Consciousness', in R. Robison and D. Goodman (eds), *The New Rich in Asia*, London: Routledge.

Rodan, G. (ed.) (1996) *Political Oppositions in Industrialising Asia*, London: Routledge.

——, Muzaffar, C. and Jayasuriya, K. (1996) 'Debate: Asian Values', *The Asia-Pacific Magazine*, 3: 50–2.

Rosaldo, R. (1989) *Culture and Truth: The Remaking of Social Analysis*, Boston: Beacon.

Roseberry, W. (1991) *Anthropologies and Histories: Essays in Culture, History, and Political Economy*, New Brunswick: Rutgers University Press.

Rutten, M. (1994) *Asian Capitalists in the European Mirror*, Amsterdam: VU University Press.

Said, E. (1978) *Orientalism*, Harmondsworth: Penguin.

Sampson, S. (1994) 'Money without Culture, Culture without Money: Eastern Europe's Nouveaux Riches', *Anthropological Journal on European Cultures*, 3 (1): 7–30.

Sassen, S. (1991) *The Global City*, New York: Princeton University Press.

Scott, J. and Kerkvliet, B. (1973) 'The Politics of Survival: Peasant Response to "Progress" in Southeast Asia', *Journal of Southeast Asian Studies*, IV (2): 241–68.

Sen, K. and Stivens, M. (eds) (1998) *Gender and Power in Affluent Asia*, London: Routledge.

Sennett, R. and Cobb, R. (1972) *The Hidden Injuries of Class*, Cambridge: Cambridge University Press.

Sheldon, C. (1958) *The Rise of the Merchant Class in Tokugawa Japan 1600–1868*, New York: J. J. Augustin.

Sheridan, G. (1998) 'Fortunes Crumble but Asian Values Hold', *The Australian*, 8 February.

Shiro, H. (1994) 'East Asia's Middle Class Tunes in to Today's Japan', *Japan Echo*, XXI (4): 75–9.

Sider, G. (1986) *Culture and Class in Anthropology and History: A Newfoundland Illustration*, Cambridge: Cambridge University Press.

Simone, V. and Feraru, A. (1995) *The Asian Pacific: Political and Economic Development in a Global Context*, New York: Longman.

Skinner, G. (1957) *Chinese Society in Thailand: An Analytical History*, Ithaca: Cornell University Press.

Slater, D. (1997) *Consumer Culture and Modernity*, Cambridge: Polity.

Smith, A. (1981) *The Ethnic Revival*, Cambridge: Cambridge University Press.

Smith, W. (1994) 'Japanese Cultural Images in Malaysia: Implications of the Look East Policy', in K. Jomo (ed.), *Japan and Malaysian Development*, London: Routledge.

Steinberg, D., Wyatt, D., Smail, J., Woodside, A., Roff, W. and Chandler, D. (1975) *In Search of Southeast Asia*, Kuala Lumpur: Oxford University Press.

Tai Hung-chao (ed.) (1989a) *Confucianism and Economic Development*, Washington DC: Washington Institute Press.

—— (1989b) 'Introduction: The Oriental Alternative?', in Tai Hung-chao (ed.), *Confucianism and Economic Development*, Washington DC: Washington Institute Press.

—— (1989c) 'The Oriental Alternative: An Hypothesis on Culture and Economy', in Tai Hung-chao (ed.), *Confucianism and Economic Development*, Washington DC: Washington Institute Press.

Tanikawa, M. (1997) 'Fun in the Sun: Newly Rich Asians Help Sustain Japan's Theme Parks', *Far Eastern Economic Review*, 29 May: 56–7.

Thompson, E. (1968) *The Making of the English Working Class*, Harmondsworth: Penguin.

Tomlinson, A. (ed) (1990) *Consumption, Identity and Style: Marketing, Meanings and the Packaging of Pleasure*, London: Routledge.

Tønnesson, S. and Antlöv, H. (1996) 'Asia in Theories of Nationalism and National Identity', in S. Tønnesson and H. Antlöv (eds), *Asian Forms of the Nation*, London: Curzon Press.

Turner, B. (1988) *Status*, Minneapolis: University of Minnesota Press.

Turner, G. (1990) *British Cultural Studies: An Introduction*, Boston: Unwin Hyman.

Ulin, R. (1991) 'Critical Anthropology Twenty Years Later', *Critique of Anthropology*, 11 (1): 63–89.

Veblen, T. (1979) (orig. 1899) *The Theory of the Leisure Class*, New York: Penguin.

Vermeulen, H. and Govers, C. (eds) (1994) *The Anthropology of Ethnicity*, Amsterdam: Het Spinhuis.

Vogel, E. (1963) *Japan's New Middle Class*, Berkeley: University of California Press.

Wakao, F. (1989) 'Learning to Live the Good Life', *Japan Echo*, XVI (2): 30–4.

Wallerstein, I. (1988) 'The Bourgeois(ie) as Concept and Reality', *New Left Review*, 167: 91–106.

Weber, M. (1970) *The Protestant Ethic and the Spirit of Capitalism*, London: Unwin University Books.

Weinshall, T. (ed.) (1993) *Societal Culture and Management*, Berlin: Walter de Gruyter.

Wickberg, E. (1965) *The Chinese in Philippine Life 1850–1898*, New Haven: Yale University Press.

Wilentz, S. (1985) *Rites of Power: Symbolism, Ritual and Politics since the Middle Ages*, Philadelphia: University of Pennsylvania Press.

Williams, R. (1976) *Keywords*, Glasgow: Fontana.

—— (1977) *Marxism and Literature*, London: Oxford University Press.

—— (1981) *Culture*, Glasgow: Fontana.

Yao, S. (1996) 'Consumption and Social Aspirations of the Middle Class in Singapore', *Southeast Asian Affairs*, pp. 337–54.

Yoshihara, K. (1988) *The Rise of Ersatz Capitalism in Southeast Asia*, Quezon City: Ateneo de Manila University Press.

2 Consumption, social differentiation and self-definition of the new rich in industrialising Southeast Asia

Ken Young

INTRODUCTION

Rapid industrialisation and urbanisation are changing the face of Southeast Asia. Established scholarly paradigms of economy, society and culture are becoming less reliable because these societies are changing so rapidly. The very substantial growth of new bourgeois and middle-class groups is one of the most significant of these changes.

In seeking answers to questions about the political and cultural influence of these new groups, it is natural to look to the current writings of indigenous intellectuals, or the prescriptions of influential political and religious leaders. However much such intellectual discourses might formalise, or seek to influence, the outlooks of the new rich, a more secure basis of these people's sense of their place in society is built around their day-to-day social experience. This experience fosters the growth of lasting predispositions grounded in mundane behaviour, in the practices of everyday life. Behaviour of this kind can be observed in familiar institutions such as the home, workplace, school, mosque or cinema – and in numerous urban shopping malls. In such locales, the new rich display their fluent employment of the behavioural codes of a middle-class 'lifestyle', but at the same time, unobtrusively, they also show that they possess the values, social orientations and distinctions that mark their group out from other parts of society.

In this chapter I argue that consumption behaviour, learned and perfected in the ubiquitous shopping malls in the major cities of the region, contributes significantly to identity construction and social differentiation. The mundane, apolitical character of consumption practices disguises the key contribution they make to a broader integrated pattern of behaviour that not only fulfils the practical ends of everyday life for the new rich, but also gives material form to their 'particular narratives of self-identity' (Giddens 1991: 81). Together, these habitual behavioural patterns constitute a 'lifestyle' (Giddens 1991; Castells 1997).[1] I do not attempt here to characterise the entirety of that lifestyle. However, to illustrate the connections between consumption, lifestyle and social differentiation, I look briefly at the development of housing estates in Jakarta.

My main interest, then, is in the apparently apolitical processes of identity formation through consumption. One cannot fail to note, however, that what is being built up here are patterns of association and representations of collective identity of surprising durability, and this has clear political significance. As Castells (1997: 7) observes: 'the social construction of identity always takes place in a context marked by power relationships'. These are matters that states in the region, seeking to secure their own legitimacy, to build national consciousness and exercise social control, attempt to direct through their command of an array of major institutions (education, media and so on). Thus consumption practices may be overwhelmingly apolitical in intent, but still have significant political consequences.

The new sites and practices of consumption are rendered even more effective in shaping new lifestyles and identities because the emerging wealthy elites are themselves so new. As the leading Thai social scientist Anek Laothamatas observes, 'historically speaking, most [of the Thai] middle classes are from uneducated parents, either merchants or farmers' (*The Nation* 1994: 78). This quality of newness of the new rich is found in most of the other industrialising countries discussed here. The people who form these elites are mostly new, and their social environment – a globalised urban-industrial milieu – is also new. The upwardly mobile seek models of behaviour appropriate to their new elevated status. Many of those at the margin – excluded for many reasons, but most immediately because they do not have any money – nevertheless show a fascination with the cultural codes associated with the wealth and power of the new elites.

On the one hand, my arguments will show that consumption and lifestyle contribute to the formation of new elite identities. Global influences and the complexities of the urban milieu serve to some extent to uncouple the new rich from established national and communal identities. They are more internationally oriented, constructing novel narratives of themselves and their place in the world from creative blends of their own cultural inheritance and global influences (see Heryanto, this volume). Ethnicity frequently has low significance for the higher reaches of these elites (see Smith, Shamsul, Heryanto, this volume), concurring with McVey's observation of Southeast Asia's capitalists that 'both business interests and cultural forces bring together Chinese and indigenous elites into a common cosmopolitan *nouveau riche* consumer style which offers itself as the high-culture model for modern capitalist Southeast Asia' (McVey 1992: 22; see also Lim 1983; Hewison 1993: 168; Rodan 1993a). These considerations tend to reduce the association of wealth with ethnicity in the region.

On the other hand, there is another tendency that has attracted a lot of speculation – the high proportion of ethnic Chinese among the new rich throughout the region. This alternative perspective gives greater emphasis to the 'Chineseness' of the new rich, linking the adaptability and cultural distinctiveness of the new rich less to sociological factors and more to a shared cross-national Chinese heritage (the more invidious version of this line of 'explanation' casts doubt on their commitment to local societies on the grounds that their forebears were mere 'sojourners' (Wang 1996, 1991) with shallow roots in their local society). I argue that conclusions of this kind are specious. I indicate the difficulty of establishing a coherent, authoritative understanding of what it is to be Chinese in the late twentieth century, even in a place like Singapore, let alone in other parts of the diaspora (see Lee 1996: 263f.).

To discuss industrialising Southeast Asia within a single chapter, one must be selective. I compare four important Southeast Asian countries: Indonesia, Thailand, Singapore and Malaysia. Singapore is at an advanced stage of socio-economic development. Thailand and Malaysia are moving into more skill- and knowledge-intensive sectors of the global economy, while Indonesia, in spite of sustained rapid industrial growth in the decades prior to the 1997 crisis, still depends heavily on the comparative advantage of cheap labour for most of its industrial growth. Associated with the varying nature of the spread of industrial transformation are differing configurations of the new rich in each country. Other historical, political and cultural influences contribute to the variations between each country, yet there is sufficient similarity between them all to make comparison fruitful. The comparisons that follow consider selective examples from these countries. A systematic comparison of each is possible, but not within the confines of a single chapter. So, too, does the evidence here deal only with part of industrialising Southeast Asia. There are many strong and interesting parallels with the Philippines, for example, but a wider range than the ones chosen would be unwieldy.[2]

The new rich are, within and between the countries under consideration, heterogeneous and varied on most of the criteria I will use.[3] I will not pursue here issues of definition beyond a brief indication of the main internal groupings a conventional class analysis would discern within the new rich. Such an analysis would invoke categories such as the bourgeoisie; the affluent middle classes (managers, professionals and others in clearly contradictory class locations); the lower middle classes (structurally closer to the working class); and, cutting across the boundaries of these middle-class strata, intellectuals. In structural terms, the middle classes are diverse. That diversity cannot be fully overcome by formulations – useful as they are – that classify them together as occupants of contradictory class locations. Rather, if they have unity at all, it does not derive clearly from structural location within society and economy, but more from subjective self-definition buttressed by a minimal material capacity to maintain realistically certain petit bourgeois aspirations, such as those related to social advancement through education, and a subjective belief (misplaced or otherwise) in their economic security and life-chances. Working-class people harbour fewer illusions about such matters.

There are three common threads that are striking in the comparative study of Southeast Asia's new rich. One is the variable but consistent importance from nation to nation of good connections between capitalists and the state, and, less uniformly, between the middle classes and the state. The second is the disproportionate and seemingly problematic 'Chineseness' of the bourgeoisies in most countries, and the high proportion of people of Chinese descent among the middle classes more broadly. The third is the striking newness of the new rich.

The extent and social consequences of industrialisation vary considerably among the countries under consideration, with Singapore lying at one end of the spectrum, and Indonesia at the other. Nevertheless, the experience of wealth, rapid social mobility and urbanisation (not Singapore) barely spans two generations for large numbers of these people. The more recent waves of middle-class expansion have been in the private sector and have opened up careers for skilled workers, well-educated professionals, managers, knowledge workers in more advanced, higher value-added sectors, and growing numbers of groups that command high wages internationally (the people Robert Reich (1992) calls 'symbolic analysts'), with Indonesia still lagging in the earlier stages of labour-intensive industrialisation.

Historically, the state and large corporations have played major roles in the modernisation of society and economy in these countries. This has had obvious and important effects on the growth of domestic bourgeoisies, and on their values. It produced, at first, broader middle classes whose composition and social orientations correspond to this pattern of economic development. They have been, for example, far less independent of state patronage than 'typical' Western middle classes (Young 1990). In every case the intervention of the state has been crucial.

However, the influence of the state, and the importance of careers as state functionaries, gave way to accelerated integration into the global economy, backed by vast flows of foreign investment, and the pre-eminence of the private sector in export-led growth. For Malaysia, Thailand and Indonesia, this started in about the 1980s; for Singapore, much earlier. The size and composition of today's new rich is directly linked to the shifts in economic policy and the nature of the mix of government and private sector development. The history of these economic changes is dealt with elsewhere (Robison and Goodman 1996; Higgott and Robison 1985; Hewison *et al.* 1993; Kahn and Loh 1992). It is sufficient to note that the national experiences were different, and led to differently composed elites of wealth in each country, as well as to considerable heterogeneity within each of them.

Many of these new elites are people who have achieved far higher levels of education than their parents and grandparents. They have had to adapt to the many-faceted pressures of modernisation in little more than a generation. But alongside the very recent development of these middle-class groups, it is important to stress the marked shift towards wealth and influence generated in the private sector, and the shifts in outlook and identity that go with that change. The new rich are bearers of 'new forms of wealth generated through new systems of accumulation', so that:

> the explosion of an elite culture of materialism, individualism and conspicuous consumption based on growth of private disposable wealth is in sharp contrast to the culture of the state and the official. A growing middle class based on educational qualification and expertise confronts old networks of patronage and loyalty.
>
> (Robison and Goodman 1996: 8–9)

In important ways these people are still discovering their place in a transformed Southeast Asia. Among the locales where they find appropriate ways of declaring their success are urban shopping malls and housing estates. Not only are Javanese, Malay and Thai business people now active in the economy; values have shifted so that material possessions and wealth are now seen as legitimate sources of power, and are valued at least as much as the prestige of office (McVey 1992: 18–20).

To the extent that this is true, then, the new patterns of consumption and public display we will examine here are an important unifying force among the elites in the region and within the individual countries under discussion. However, we have yet to address the second of the common traits found among the wealthy of Southeast Asia mentioned above. That is the equally widespread association of this new wealth with 'Chineseness'. The widespread resentments that this can create (especially in Indonesia) oblige us to address this question first of all. Are the principal unifying characteristics of these new elites to be found in their ethnicity, rendering issues of consumption of secondary importance?

ETHNIC IDENTIFICATION OF THE NEW RICH?

These confident new capitalists and middle-class professionals, particularly Thais, Malays and *pribumi* Indonesians, may be the type of new rich individual that political leaders in the region would like to encourage as part of their vision for modern, industrialised, Asian nations. But are their fellow citizens comfortable with this ideal type? Are the middle classes in general dedicated to this and related ideas, especially middle-class intellectuals? And what of the ethnic Chinese, be they citizens of Southeast Asian nations, born and raised there, or more recent immigrants? What is their place in these vibrant emerging industrial societies? If we are talking of Southeast Asia's new rich, are not the Chinese, more than any other group, the constant between these otherwise rather different societies? Do they not in some senses transcend local political and cultural boundaries to constitute a common thread in this success story?

On the other hand, apart from the case of Singapore, the ethnic Chinese do not control the governments of Southeast Asian countries. Indeed, part of the record of the success of ethnic Chinese bourgeoisies in amassing wealth in Southeast Asia has been their skill at achieving an accommodation with governments. This has yielded them significant opportunities to make profits, but they cannot command those governments. Indeed, much of the resentment directed at the Chinese as a group in Indonesia, and elsewhere, has been because of the blatant rent-seeking deals done between key politico-bureaucrats and a handful of favoured ethnic Chinese entrepreneurs. Given the significant part the state has had in encouraging development, it is necessary, at the very least, also to understand the relationship between so-called 'pariah entrepreneurs' and the indigenous groups who control the government and military apparatus.

Is there a case to answer that simplifies the issue of the new rich in Southeast Asia by asserting that this group is distinguished throughout the region primarily by its 'Chineseness'? Naisbit (1996: 4), for example, suggests that: 'the economy of the borderless Overseas Chinese is the third largest in the world...outranked only by the US and Japan'. According to him, most of these people are politically loyal to their country of residence, but retain an apolitical loyalty to China, moderated among the younger generation by a 'global mindset' (Naisbit 1996: 14–17). Like much else in Naisbit's book this is simplistic and superficial, but it nevertheless articulates a widespread perception which must be answered, since it suggests that this ethnic-cultural identification may be the single most significant characteristic of Southeast Asia's new rich.

These issues are too complex to settle conclusively here, but I will indicate the speciousness of this perspective by giving most attention to the case of Singapore. Singapore would appear to be, on the surface, the one country where the issue of Chinese identity is least problematic. I will restrict the discussion mainly to issues of cultural identity and its significance for social action.[4] While 'explanations' that link Chineseness and wealth have the attraction of providing a key factor which tidily explains several complex issues at once, the simple association of 'Chineseness' and wealth, and the assumption that we can think of the diasporic collectivity as a coherent whole, independent of non-Chinese national loyalties, is almost entirely illusory. The empirical fact that wealth in these countries is disproportionately concentrated in the hands of ethnic Chinese is striking and undeniable. Yet it cannot be explained by reference to a common schematic account divorced from the great differences of time, place and historical experience. Rather, as Mackie, Kwok and others have argued, any attempt to understand how this situation developed must deal with particular cases in their full historical, socio-economic and political contexts (see Mackie 1992a, 1992b; Kwok 1994).

The fact is that the meaning of what it is to be Chinese has varied historically within and between the emerging nations of Southeast Asia. It has been contested among the leading Chinese intellectuals who have sought to define their situation (people such as Lim Boon Keng, Song Ong Siang and Lee Kuan Yew in Singapore – see Kwok 1994: 27f.). The pragmatic orientations of different waves of emigrants over the nineteenth and twentieth centuries have frequently meant that individuals faced with the practical claims of everyday life have tended to put aside sentimental claims of an ill-defined shared identity (Kwok 1994). Long before the word 'postmodern' was fashioned, the existential situation of overseas Chinese gave rise to multiple identities (Wang 1991: 199; Kwok 1994: 300). They found themselves subject to the fragmentary pull of different loyalties so that there is now 'the simultaneous presence of many *kinds* of identity, e. g. ethnic, national (local), cultural and class identities' (Wang 1991: 217; Kwok 1994: 30). Even in the case of Singapore, which might on the surface seem to be a place where there would be relatively few challenges to questions of what it means to be Chinese, there have been major shifts and real tensions among intellectual protagonists, influenced by both local historical developments as well as those emanating from China itself. Lee Kuan Yew articulated one clear point of view of the contemporary reality in a recent address to Chinese entrepreneurs in Hong Kong:

> We are ethnic Chinese, but we must be honest and recognise that at the end of the day our fundamental loyalties are to our home country, not to China…After two or three generations away from China, we have become rooted in the country of our birth. Our stakes are in our home countries, not China where our ancestors came from. The Chinese Thai is a Thai, and in the end he wants Thailand to prosper…So too, Chinese-Singaporeans, Chinese-Indonesians, Chinese-Malaysians and Chinese-Filipinos.
>
> (Hicks and Mackie 1994: 47)

The issue here is not whether Southeast Asians of Chinese descent take pride in their ethnic and cultural origins. Plainly they do, and with great passion on some occasions (for example, Gilley 1996). The overseas Chinese, many of whom identify first with the nation to which they belong, nevertheless find themselves deemed to be Chinese,[5] and to be part of the Chinese diaspora. Most of these diasporic groups are in a situation where their 'Chinese cultures are both Chinese and Other to China, just as they are Other' to the mainstream culture of their Southeast Asian homeland (Lee 1996: ix). The cultural inheritance of Southeast Asians whose ancestors came from provinces in southern China (Guangdong, Fujian and so on) were culturally plural in the Chinese context, and are plural in the diaspora (Lee 1996: 264–71). The 'folk models' of contemporary Guangdongese (Cantonese) leave little doubt that their culture is different to that of northerners and other southern regional groups (Hakka, Chauzhou Lo, Hoklo and others) and certainly to the overseas Chinese (Guldin 1998). That is not to say that the Guangdongese do not think of themselves as Chinese – they do, and consider themselves to be the best Chinese (Guldin 1998). Thus notions of Chineseness embrace a plurality of cultures (Lee 1996), and the question that then arises is whether the shared sense of Chineseness is sufficient to sustain the kinds of coordinated action that can overcome the cultural and other differences that exist between regional cultures within China and the cultures of the diaspora. I do not intend to solve that issue here, even though I do note that the real complexity of the issue of Chinese identity does not sit comfortably with the tidy schemas found in works like Naisbit's (1996).

The situation is further complicated by the fact that there are pressures on Southeast Asian communities to reinterpret their narratives of identity in terms of the unity of Chinese culture. From Beijing's perspective, much depends on maintaining unity in 'greater China' (The People's Republic, Hong Kong and Taiwan), and these pressures, though not directed at Southeast Asian populations, have important effects. So, too, do the efforts of wealthy overseas philanthropists who have donated vast sums to museums, educational institutions and foundations dedicated to the preservation of (often pre-revolutionary) Chinese culture. The Singapore government has intervened in encouraging the

Chinese community there to assimilate to the former's reading of Chinese culture (including the acquisition of Mandarin rather than the southern Chinese languages of their forebears). The natural sentiments of pride in the inheritance of Chinese civilisation are therefore joined by official pressures that foster an authorised (and unitary) reading of 'Chineseness'.

Such pressures in a highly controlled city-state like Singapore might seem to be overwhelming. What reasons might there be for supporting Kwok Kian Woon's scepticism about whether the state, or any other social agency, can create coherence in the realm of culture and values in a modern, instrumentally rationalised and 'logically' functioning society (Kwok 1994: 26)?[6] A partial response is offered below in my explanation of the construction of components of lifestyles through consumption and other practices in a globalised marketplace. As Singapore advances to the conditions of 'late modernity', might not the 'puzzling diversity of options and possibilities' of our contemporary 'risk culture' (Giddens 1991: 3) stand against the continued success of the government's directives? Giddens argues that identities in late modernity originate much less from dominant institutions, and are drawn from multiple sources as individuals organise their social world via biographical narratives of the self.[7]

There is an abundance of examples of the lasting identification of the overseas Chinese with China. The problem, at the level of sustained social action, is in part with clarifying just what 'China' is. The shutdown of Penang, Singapore or Hong Kong for Chinese New Year; the pride in Chinese art, food, fashion, sporting, intellectual and business achievements; the continuing celebration of the family; the maintenance of temples and temple associations;[8] the popularity of tours to China; investment in China; the wish to be buried in one's (ancestral) home district on the mainland – these and many other examples show the strong value that is placed on Chinese origins in the Southeast Asian diaspora. There are qualifications to these examples, but none that deny their broad significance (though they might put a brake on the overenthusiasm of some). Tours to China remain popular in Singapore, but many Singaporeans report sobering bouts of 'culture shock' after encountering the difference of China as it is.[9]

The Singapore government's eagerness to build a dynamic industrial city of 600,000 people in the 70 km² Suzhou Industrial Park, west of Shanghai, has run into difficulties. These were sufficiently serious to provoke stern public criticism from Mr Lee Kuan Yew. There are other problems with major projects in China that suggest that broad cultural affinity only goes so far in cooperative ventures (*The Economist* 1998c: 25). The spontaneous popular anger in Taiwan, Hong Kong and Southeast Asia against the Japanese government's willingness to tolerate landings by right-wing Japanese extremists on the disputed Diaoyu islands (north of Taiwan) in 1996 also speak of a widely shared identification with China. Government responses, however, from Hong Kong, Singapore and Taiwan were variable (Gilley *et al.* 1996). Beijing itself tried to subdue the issue to the disappointment of overseas nationalists (Gilley 1996; Forney *et al.*1996). Examples and qualifications can be multiplied endlessly. The enthusiasm for China at the level of rhetoric and sentiment is not troubled by the lack of clarity about what 'China' is, and what 'Chineseness' means. But sustained social action is another matter.

Beyond the very real loyalties that ethnic Chinese feel to their countries, and the pragmatic recognition that their fates, and those of their children, depend on the fortunes of the nations to which they now belong, there is the far more serious difficulty of the maintenance of a unitary 'Chinese' cultural identity. In dynastic China, Chinese identity was much more a cultural or civilisational consciousness than it was a national identity. It was sustained by the meanings, rituals and symbols of the Middle Kingdom. The institutions of Imperial China gave coherence to Chinese culture since they articulated standards according to which people identified themselves as Chinese (Cohen 1991: 114). These have long disappeared under successive waves of indigenous social movements bearing various discourses of modernisation, the penultimate, most far-reaching and catastrophic of which was Mao's Cultural Revolution. At each stage of reform since the nineteenth century, governments in China have tried to give definition to the post-dynastic unity of the people they claimed to rule, defining the Chinese successively in terms of civilisation, then as citizens (liberal Republicans), then as members of the Chinese race (the Kuomintang), and then, under the Communist Party, as citizens qualified by social class. None of these attempts succeeded (Fitzgerald 1995: 76–85). Today, according to Fitzgerald (1995: 103), 'the relationship between nation and state is under negotiation in China to an extent that defies all precedent'. The fear of movements that break from the centre is intense, not only because of incipient nationalism in Taiwan, but because of the dangers of fragmentation within China itself (Fitzgerald 1995). Since cultural distinctiveness may foster separatist claims, the desire to uphold the cultural integrity of China is very strong. Yet the issue remains unresolved, a thorny problem for China itself. If this is so in China, what is the basis of the purported solidarity of the overseas Chinese?

The old unitary symbolic universe has gone, and cannot plausibly be resurrected, notwithstanding the efforts of wealthy patrons in the Chinese diaspora. Even in Singapore where Chinese identity is encouraged by the state as part of its policy of multiracialism (alongside Malay and Indian identities), this state-sponsored Chineseness is not one rooted in community experience or based on

> deep historical memory. It is rather a Mandarinization of Chinese culture, [that emphasises] the high culture or great tradition that all Chinese Singaporeans putatively shared with their ancestors and their counterparts in the Chinese diaspora – bypassing its internal contradictions in modern Chinese life and the processes of the localisation of the community in Singapore life.
>
> (Kwok 1994: 31)

State and privately sponsored interpretations of the Chinese tradition (such as the museum of the Chinese diaspora in Singapore) will be unavoidably particularised in the absence of central institutions of cultural reproduction in China itself (McLaren 1994). As Kwok (1994: 30) sums up:

> the landscape of modernity in the world and in Singapore has fundamentally changed. In the case of Chinese modernity, there was a massive transformation in the meaning of Chineseness. Chinese identity was traditionally rooted in a symbolic cosmos, a ritual life that was standardised by the imperial state and localised everywhere that the Chinese found themselves – even, I would argue, in Singapore. But the early twentieth century saw the forces of modern rationalism and scientism penetrating throughout the non-Western world; in time the traditional symbolic universe became more and more implausible. At the same time, there developed a new definition of Chineseness grounded in nationalism, severing its rootedness in the traditional cultural or religious system.

Kwok's fine essay (1994) offers a historical account of the vicissitudes of Chinese identity in Singapore during the nineteenth and twentieth centuries. He points to the loss of the old symbolic universe in China itself where, to quote Cohen (1991: 133), being Chinese 'no longer involves commonly accepted cultural standards; existentially, however, being Chinese is far more problematic, for now it is as much a quest as it is a condition'.

In Singapore, the fact that the ethnic majority is Chinese (around 76 per cent of the population)[10] could lead to the misleading impression that the values of this apparently unitary ethnic group would assume a certain 'naturalness' in society as a whole. That is even more so given the recent entrenchment of the role of communitarianism (Chua 1995: ch. 9) in this multiracial society. That impression disguises the reality that many important lines of social cleavage cut across these community boundaries. At the time of independence, the Chinese population was stratified internally between a political and economic elite of English-speaking (and disproportionately Christian) ethnic Chinese and a larger Chinese working class whose household languages were various southern Chinese tongues (Hokkien, Hakka, Teochew, Cantonese, Hainanese and others). To some extent this cleavage persists today. However, beginning in the period of the union with Malaysia, steps were taken by the government, primarily through the public housing system (Chua 1995: ch. 6) and the education system (Tham 1989; Tremewan 1994: chs 4, 5), to break the strength of the older (mainly working-class) language-based communities. The bilingual education policy favoured English as the shared language. Community second languages of Malay and Tamil matched the language of the Malay and Indian communities, but the ethnic Chinese (including the *peranakan* Chinese who spoke Malay) are now taught in Mandarin (Shotam 1989). While the English-speaking Chinese group predominate in the middle class, the sustained emphasis on Mandarin for the Chinese puts pressure on them too to conform to the government's social engineering of racially based communities.

After breaking down the older communities of culture and language, and eschewing cultural chauvinism, the People's Action Party (PAP) forged a more individualised meritocratic society. However, from the late 1970s and early 1980s it became concerned about the trend towards Westernisation and loss of the cultural ties of community. The stages of these various initiatives in favour of Asian Values, Confucianism and the 'promotion of Mandarin as the symbolic language of all Chinese, whether or not they spoke it, set up a communal equation of ethnicity and language which had not previously existed' (Tremewan 1994: 140). The entire story is too involved to trace here, but the Chinese population of Singapore has been moulded by a sustained process of social engineering in which their language, values and identity have been minutely prescribed through the major institutions of society. Taught first to separate from their communities of origin, they are now exhorted to celebrate a Chinese identity drawn from the high culture of the mainland (Clammer 1993). Cultural identity here is manifestly linked to the state's strategies of governance, development and social control. It fosters 'Chineseness' but not a sense of Chinese identity that is 'rooted in community experience or based on deep historical memory' (Kwok 1994: 31). How much this state-sponsored Chinese identity has in common with the diverse Chinese populations of the Southeast Asian diaspora is unclear. However, the need within Singapore itself for such a sustained effort to forge ethnic cultural unity in a compact city-state ought to inspire caution about the existence of region-wide cultural homogeneity among the Chinese.

It is noteworthy too that the PAP turned back to communitarianism in the face of concerns about values, excessive Westernisation, individualism and mindless materialism. With due caution about the adequacy of these labels, they are attributes that Singaporeans tend to acquire in the arenas of globalised consumption – open recognition that the 'mindless' activities of consumption and the lifestyle associated with these practices do have potent effects on values and identity. That is arguably the case in Hong Kong as well, where neither the old colonial power nor the People's Republic of China favoured the growth of a strong local identity – yet, perversely, and pointlessly, that is what grew there (Lee 1996: 264–71; Chow 1992; Turner 1996).[11]

The issues engaged here are too complex to settle conclusively, though I hope enough has been said to support my disinclination to regard the connection between Chineseness and wealth as the key cultural characteristic of the new rich in the region. While ethnicity, religion, language and other cultural differences remain important, the most obvious means by which the new rich distinguish themselves in society is found in the way they live. They assert their material advantages, and their claims to superior competence in the new internationalised urban-industrial environment, over members of their own cultural group no less than against others. The most public demonstrations of their superiority – and these are primarily differences of class and status – are in their patterns of consumption.

CONSUMPTION, CLASS AND IDENTITY

The diverse occupations of the new rich share at least one common quality: they leave individuals and households with a margin of income beyond what they need to secure the necessities of life. This discretionary income allows them to exercise consumer choices in ways that lower-ranking social groups cannot readily manage. Secure discretionary incomes can be saved or mortgaged. The demonstration of the newly elevated social rank of the new middle classes is displayed in patterns of savings, investment, residential patterns, private trans-portation and other lifestyle choices that give definition to who they are. So, too, does the greater individuation of their life choices – the middle class are far less dependent on the solidarity of communal support mechanisms for their own needs, and tend to withdraw from direct participation in residential groups commonly found in poor urban neighbourhoods (Sullivan 1995). Their deep concern with their own and their children's education is a quintessential element of middle-class values.

For the sake of brevity I will concentrate on consumption. I am not referring here to the unsatisfactory attempts often made to classify social groups as 'middle-class' by assembling statistical data on household consumption patterns. My concern is rather one that goes well beyond the usual empirical interest in identifying the middle classes by the amount and nature of their possessions, or amusement at the public manners (or lack of manners) of phone-toting *nouveaux riches*(*The Nation* 1994: 76f., 30; Tanter and Young 1990). The serious business of marking oneself off from the rest, of boundary maintenance between status and class groups, is first of all integral to the organisation of middle-class households. Most significantly – and that is one reason why the *nouveaux riches* are almost universally mocked[12] – it is a matter not just of knowing *what* to consume and having the means to do so, but of knowing *how* to consume (Bourdieu 1989). The 'connoisseur' is literally that – one who 'knows' how to consume not just in a physical sense, but who can do so in a manner that celebrates the special quali-ties of the consumed object (food, music, wine, literature, education, travel). These goods and services have their greatest potency when they can be appreci-ated and consumed in the appropriate manner, only by the initiated (Mintz 1985; Douglas 1987; Mennell 1985; Finkelstein 1989, 1991). A very important part of the construction of the personal and social identity of the new rich is developed through their consumption patterns, from major decisions about where to live, and how to educate their children, to far less vital but still highly significant matters of personal adornment.[13]

Consumption patterns are important therefore, not only because they have some utility in measuring 'class' differences (see, for example, the fairly typical survey in *The Nation*1994: 9–10), but because they constitute a significant propor-tion of the symbolic codes through which the middle classes, and the new rich more broadly, differentiate themselves. However, as in many other modern soci-eties, intellectuals in Southeast Asia worry about materialistic rootlessness (Elegant 1996a, 1996b; *The Nation* 1994: 76) and the incursion of international (mainly American) cultural influences. Thus, the conspicuous consumption of the new rich has given further stimulus to localised intellectual yearnings for normative expressions of identity and social cohesion that nostalgic reconstructions of the past attribute to the pre-industrial world (Chua 1994a). Secular and religious intellectuals (almost entirely of middle-class origin) are articulating perspectives (Elegant 1996b) that attempt to give coherence and meaning to the new world I have been describing – a situation in which old ethnic and cultural codes have been radically redefined (often by the state), and in which nationalist and other Utopias (but not nostalgia, see Chua 1994a) have lost part of their unifying force. Yet, aside from these attempts to influence values, the practices of everyday living, notably consumption practices, contribute no less significantly to the construction of new identities.

Many, if not most, of the new rich have had to adapt to their enhanced social status in a remarkably short time, within one or two generations, or even less. This applies to the extremely wealthy controllers of the vast conglomerates that are at the heart of these rapidly growing economies, as much as to the much more numerous upwardly mobile middle classes. The psychological and cultural adjustments that the major capitalists presumably had to make are huge if one contemplates their relatively obscure and economically marginal beginnings in the 1950s and 1960s.[14] As all the different social elements of the new rich have advanced themselves, they have had to learn, or to define for themselves, identities and roles appropriate to their new status. Moreover, the patterns of growth in Malaysia, Thailand and Indonesia, from the mid-1980s to the mid-1990s, have brought large numbers of people, who now work in a much wider variety of mainly private firms, into new occupational groups and into the ranks of the middle classes. Again, one of the striking characteristics of these groups is their newness, the very recent entry of many people with relatively little previous direct experience of affluence.

When large numbers of people are adjusting to new ways of life in a new or transformed urban environment they draw upon their established cultural repertoire to some extent. They do so in given institutional settings in which particular models of behaviour are deemed to be prestigious. Some draw upon older cultural models, as, for example, have senior Indonesian civil servants who have maintained to a significant extent the traditions and cultural orientation of the Javanese *priyayi*.[15] The adjustment may therefore partly involve the creation of new forms of behaviour, and it may also in part require the newcomer to learn from, and conform to, available models of correct behaviour. The new malls and residential estates of Southeast Asia's major cities are sites where middle-class styles can be absorbed with a greater degree of creativity – though, certainly, the pressures to conform to given codes of behaviour are also present. There are many other sites of more formal acculturation, such as schools, universities, professional workplaces, training institutes for civil servants and the military, and so on. To a significant degree, these are relatively closed institutions which inculcate established models of behaviour and identity. When the middle classes were more closely tied to the state for employment and training, they acquired many of their normative models in institutions of this kind, so that these formal institutions had a more significant influence on the broader character of middle-class mores. However, we have seen that in Malaysia, Thailand and, to a lesser degree, Indonesia, the latest patterns of growth are bringing a much more diverse range of people into the ranks of the well-off.

At the further extreme from formal training institutions are the mass media. Here the upwardly mobile are presented with many models, both national and international, of modern urban sophistication. Shopping malls lie somewhere in between relatively diverse sources of socialisation like the media,[16] and prescriptive institutions such as civil service training institutes. They are open to a very wide part of society,[17] yet full participation comes at a price which only the middle class can pay with ease. There is prescriptiveness here, yet there is also some scope for individual flair and originality. These are places where broad elements of the new rich display their mastery of the new codes of behaviour, and can observe and comment on others. They are also venues where more marginal groups can learn and assimilate the same codes at little cost, as they seek ways to participate in a seductive but imperfectly understood prosperity, so brilliantly displayed, so accessible, yet frustratingly out of reach.

OPEN ACCESS ACADEMIES OF SOCIAL DIFFERENTIATION

We should not underestimate the cultural role of shopping centres, malls, redeveloped 'heritage' precincts, theme parks, and redeveloped downtown commercial areas with interior pedestrian zones (Harvey 1989). Kevin Hewison observes pithily that the new shopping malls are the public parks of Bangkok (Hewison 1995).[18]They provide all manner of indoor, air-conditioned amusements for the public. Families wander through their halls and corridors, absorbing instruction in consumption behaviour and developing status associations with brand names. Many come simply to window-shop, often a reasonably serious activity and a costless form of consumption. In Singapore 'shopping' is a major pastime, and much of this activity is 'simply' window-shopping. In Bangkok, some capitalists were so confident in the early 1990s about both national economic growth and the efficacy with which their malls created felt needs among consumers that they said that they were untroubled by the high numbers of visitors who simply came to look and bought nothing. As incomes rise in the decade ahead, the investors claimed, today's window-shoppers will have been psychologically prepared to come and spend their disposable incomes in the developers' stores. Thus, there is a lot happening in these places besides buying and selling. The cool vastness of the malls also offers relief from a hot and polluted environment. Most importantly, as John Clammer (1992: 195) claims: 'shopping is not merely the acquisition of things; it is the buying of identity'. Significantly, one does not have to buy to engage in practices of identity formation in these spaces. And while they are public places, they are sufficiently diverse internally to provide for, and even to constitute, social differentiation among the public (Shields 1992: 14, 108). Shields (1992: 14) observes: 'The desegregated market of "life styles" and "consumption classes" (Saunders 1978) reflects both the cross-hatching of socio-economic stratification with cultural groupings and the absence of any truly "mass" culture.' Religious leaders in Bangkok raise the lament that the malls are the new temples of modern Bangkok. Nobel Prize nominee Sulak Sivaraksa muses (*The Nation* 1994: 95):

> At present Buddhism is manipulated by the state and when the state becomes weak, consumerism fills the vacuum and manipulates religion…Monks who used to splash holy water on marine frigates nowadays perform the ritual in front of an automatic telling machine. They perform for American Express, for Coca Cola. Do they realise what a sinful mistake they are committing?

So, malls are variously described as public parks, as the new temples of the great new cities of Asia. I would submit a further metaphor to characterise their multiple social functions – they are open-access academies of middle-class consumerism. In the most opulent malls of central Jakarta (such as Plaza Indonesia, Plaza Menteng, Sarinah Store), or in prestige locations like Pondok Indah, Pasaraya Blok M or Citraland Mall, one can spend hours walking past a seemingly endless array of specialist boutique shops, large national and international department stores, supermarkets, banks, franchised food outlets and the like. In these prestige locations, buyers are relatively few compared with window-shoppers, although in many cases these stores create environments that discreetly discourage casual browsers (Chua 1992: 119). International tenants outnumber local retailers, partly because of the exorbitant rents that are charged (Seek 1996), and the mix of people is towards the more affluent in society, with a good leavening of foreigners. Yet, even here, there is an admixture of teenagers in school uniform, sightseers, couples on dates in the restaurants and fast-food outlets. The merchandise is carefully viewed, though few are buying at the luxury end. What is being studied most assiduously are the elements of middle-class style.

In stores and markets close to the main complexes, in the malls adjacent to the residential estates, or in suburban and less uniformly opulent settings away from the city centre, the shoppers are far more varied and interesting. More are buying, and the stores are more likely to be leased by local firms selling goods that middle-class people can afford. It is much more bustling, noisy and vibrant. Yet the display of style is still important. It is still a long way in social distance from the crowded urban *pasars* (markets) where household servants and working-class people shop for provisions and inexpensive mass-produced goods. In these less intimidating malls one still dresses, performs and displays one's virtuosity with middle-class behaviour for the benefit of peers and aspirant class members alike.

The socialisation acquired in shopping malls is qualitatively different, though often complementary to, the passive absorption of cultural messages from advertising and other sources in the mass media. In shopping malls, people make conscious choices or deliberately conform to accepted practices as they consume, disport themselves, and display their virtuosity in these assertively modern environments. These practices, mundane, self-indulgent and sometimes frivolous, nevertheless are repetitive and concrete manifestations of people's visions of modernity and of their own place in the social order. They have 'symbolic, spatial, economic, class and gender aspects' (Clammer 1992: 197); they provide 'an aesthetics of self', which establishes one's 'social being' (Shields 1992: 15; see also Clammer 1992). In Japan, Clammer argues, 'this is true even of the consumption of "necessities" in any situation where choice reflects decisions about self, taste, images of body and social distinctions' (Shields 1992: 15).

In the case of many of the emerging mega-cities of Asia, such as Bangkok and Jakarta, these practices of self-definition are more exigent than in, say, Singapore, precisely because of the newness not only of the new rich, but of the vast urban population as a whole. Large numbers are from rural villages, or belong to families who migrated from the country only a generation ago. The wealthy in these cities are gravitating to the large new estates and condominium developments found everywhere in the region. The scale of both these great cities and of residential/retail developments like Muang Thong Thani on the fringes of Bangkok defy nineteenth- and early twentieth-century models of new industrial cities (Sudjic 1993: 9). Muang Thong Thani is much larger than even the Jakarta estates discussed below. By 2010 its population could be as large as one million. Sudjic (1993: 11) observes:

> Just four years ago the site was nothing more than an expanse of rice fields close to Bangkok airport, crisscrossed by drainage canals. Now there are enough high rise apartments marching across the site in a strip two kilometres long to house 250,000 people, and close to 750,000 sq. metres of offices, shops and factories have been completed. A city bigger than Ghent, Salzburg or Cork has come into being since 1989.

In Jakarta, the transformation has been vast and very rapid,[19] no doubt contributing to particular kinds of social and cultural dislocations to be discussed below.

There are therefore processes of learning and of self-definition at work in malls and other prestige sites which influence even the long-established middle classes. For the newly socially and geographically mobile, the degree of novelty is much greater. For all concerned, I would argue, the mastery of new codes of behaviour can best be understood in terms of a model of language acquisition. The grammar and vocabulary are acquired gradually, assimilated through mimicry and repetition in the context of social interaction. Fluency and understanding tend to follow the earlier stages of mastering patterns and learning the contexts in which it is appropriate to use them. Like language, the codes of behaviour for consumption are generative structures, so that, once mastered, they can be used to create original but appropriate responses in novel situations. But these codes, especially the globalised codes of middle-class consumption, are invariably acquired in particular cultural and historical contexts, so that consumption practices found in major cities around the world acquire quite specific meanings in different local situations (Friedman 1994: ch. 8). Thus the paradoxical counterpart of the apparently homogenising influences of global commercialisation is the generation of local particularisations of the same set of symbolic codes. The processes of enculturation are less simple than they appear at first glance.

The malls of Jakarta are clearly designed for the new rich. Yet they are open to all. In principle, anyone who is prepared to pay the cost of shopping there is welcome. While the specialised fashion and jewellery shops are beyond the finan-cial reach of most Indonesians, there are department stores and food outlets that are accessible to large numbers of people who are not especially rich. It might then be thought that there are levelling and democratising forces at work here alongside those that demonstrate social differentiation. This is only partly true at best. Certainly there is the tendency long recognised by sociologists for marginal and lower groups to participate by buying mass-produced elite goods, or close copies of them, while the elite move on to create new and exclusive definitions of what is fashionable (Simmel 1904; Chua 1992). Further, just as sugar, tea, coffee, tobacco and other consumption goods were once luxuries affordable only by the wealthy, so too is there a frequent movement of elite goods into goods of mass consumption (Mintz 1985). The mobility of the market should not disguise the fact that shopping precincts are as differentiated as housing estates. The price of goods is only one of the mechanisms of exclusion. Chua Beng Huat, in a study of women's fashion shops in Singapore, documents the methods by which exclu-sive shops operate in public places, yet maintain themselves as preserves for consumers from higher elite groups (Chua 1992: 119). He notes how the windows and doors intimidate browsers. He further observes (1992: 119):

> The setting is intimidating in its emptiness; the emptiness being itself a measure of exclusivity. As soon as one passes the glass doors, one is immedi-ately the centre of attention of the salespeople, for there are generally more staff than clients in the shop and anyone not used to such attention can only respond with nervousness. Occasionally, an inadvertent browser may break the seal and wander into the shop, only to be shocked by the price tags on the display items and beat a hasty retreat out of the shop without uttering a word.

The mechanisms Chua Beng Huat describes for Singapore are to be found in Jakarta and elsewhere too. The malls themselves cater for different blends of people. In Jakarta, for example, one could contrast the exclusivity of Plaza Indonesia with the more diverse middle-class multi-storey mall at Mangga Dua, or the inner suburban mall at Plaza Arion, Rawamangun. Yet, having allowed for the variation in social range from one mall to another, it is also true that the spectrum of visitors within them is wide – more extensive, certainly, than the list of tenants would lead one to expect. That is part of the sociological interest in these places. They serve to educate many more categories of people than those who can afford to shop there regularly. Having observed that, there clearly are significant numbers of city dwellers who don't go to malls, unless it is to deliver goods, clean and otherwise service the operation of the complexes.

Those city dwellers who do regularly visit malls, however, are a diverse and interesting range of people. A practised sociological eye can soon identify who is who among the apparently casual and variegated visitors.[20] The staff, and indeed the regulars themselves, become no less adept at classifying people and their activities. The small numbers of regular customers who compensate for the frequent emptiness of fashion boutiques by the frequency of their visits (almost daily according to Chua (1992) !) have no need of display except to their peers. They are the bearers of international taste and manners since they shop with equal ease in America, Europe and other parts of Asia. Aside from this group, however, there are many who come to be seen, as well as to shop and consume. They not only seek recognition and acceptance by their peers but also like to set themselves off from the rest. The potential taxonomy of the evanescent, but constantly renewed, groups that congregate in malls is in fact very complex.

It is doubtful whether the regulars in Pondok Indah or Sarinah display the kind of behavioural cohesiveness suggested by the term 'tribe' which is used by Shields (1992: 108, 14) to characterise spontaneous group formation in malls.[21] Nevertheless, a wide range of recognisable middle-class groups are there to be seen. It is at this level of analysis that broader social constants manifest themselves as well. There are, for example, observable differences in the predominance of ethnic Chinese customers at certain malls, while civil servants, expatriate residents and other groups tend to favour certain malls over others. The presence of some groups is sometimes little more than accidental where a mall happens to be adjacent to civil service offices or schools, near military headquarters, major religious centres and so on. There is a fair representation of those who serve the middle classes too – minding children, buying goods in the supermarket and so on. The malls are places for young people to meet and be seen. They even serve as places where attractive young singles might meet eligible partners from a good family. High-school children come to buy books, eat in the stalls or franchised food outlets, or just to be seen, and to learn. At the margins are all sorts of interesting people, some with less than honourable intentions, but most eager to participate in learning the ways of the successful in the modern world, to show that they are part of it too.

As social rank decreases, there is a lack of congruence between the experience and practices of the mall and the rest of daily experience in the home, neighbourhood and workplace. It is not a well-integrated aspect of a class lifestyle. The cultural behaviours appropriate to the mall may be executed with precision and even with ease, but the meanings attached to them can be somewhat dislocated. The language has been learnt with degrees of fluency, but it is still rather too much a foreign language; foreign, not primarily in the sense of being from outside the country, but from a world of class experience that is unfamiliar. Still, the constant impression I have from people in Jakarta and elsewhere is that this doesn't matter too much. The important thing for most is to have a part in the modern world.

To this point, much of what can be observed in Jakarta will hold for other cities in other parts of Asia, after allowing for some variations in historical and cultural experience. These are familiar variations on what takes place in many societies where consumption plays a key part in establishing cultural differentiation and thereby marking out, claiming and defining social position. Consumption is linked to other key regions of social life such as work, education, neighbourhood, and forms of association in constituting one's social identity. It is not merely a utilitarian part of material reproduction of one's self. It is a symbolically charged part of the activities that reproduce one's selfhood, one's identity, since it belongs among the most significant distinctions that contribute to the differential definition of both individuals and social groups (Friedman 1994).

FROM CONSUMPTION TO LIFESTYLES: HOUSING ESTATES

In 1995, I studied a number of residential estates in Jakarta; estates with names such as Lippo City, Taman Kebun Jeruk, Permata Hijau, Sunrise Gardens, Green Garden. The naming of estates seeks to associate the area with the good life, or the serenity of a lost rural past (nostalgia again), or with the proprietor (Lippo), or prestige and prosperity, or international sophistication (the use of English names), or combinations of these. The naming strategies bear interesting resemblances to those used in Penang (see Goh 1996) or comparable developments I have observed in Johore Baru, Malaysia. In Penang, developers have chosen names like Bella Vista, Belle Vue, Arcadia, Sri Emas, Desa Mas, Fortune Heights and so on (Goh 1996). By contrast with malls, which attract a wide selection of people, the new residential estates achieve much greater internal homogeneity. There are grades of wealth and status within the residential estates, but these are slight compared to those that separate the people who can afford to live in them and the people who cannot. These estates deserve mention, however, for a number of reasons. The first of these is that, for a significant proportion of the social groups we are calling 'the new rich', the consolidation of a distinct consciousness is not built around one institution or arena of social behaviour such as the mall, but around a fairly comprehensive way of life.

Schooling, transportation, recreation and many other domestic routines are integrated through the facilities provided in neighbourhoods of this kind. Consumption and other behaviours are melded – they become habitual and even normatively sanctioned among one's peers – into a lifestyle. A lifestyle 'can be defined as a more or less integrated set of practices which an individual embraces, not only because such practices fulfil utilitarian needs, but because they give material form to a particular narrative of self-identity' (Giddens 1991:

81). On the one hand consumption choices and other elements of lifestyle achieve a definite coherence between groups and even classes (Bourdieu 1989), and thus become basic aspects of social differentiation. Consumption and lifestyle choices 'are decisions not only about how to act but who to be' (Giddens 1991: 81).

The estates allow the wealthier members of society to move in a much more socially homogeneous environment. Many have their own shopping precincts, or even an adjacent mall, to complement their facilities (for example, the Mega Mall at Lippo City in Jakarta). The two belong quite naturally together. A report in the Singapore *Business Times* (2 December 1995) notes that middle-class consumers pick up many of their ideas on 'interior design in the shopping malls they visit, in the hotel dining rooms they frequent and, often, in the workplace'. Home, mosque, temple, school, market, office, transportation systems, clubs, sporting venues, health services, entertainment and many other aspects of life can be knit together in a relatively socially homogeneous continuum of experience, with only the dense pollution and gargantuan traffic jams to remind the middle-class commuters of the difficult urban environment beyond the boundaries of their controlled and comfortable estates, malls and offices. What developers are selling in Jakarta – and in Malaysia (Goh 1996) – is entry into a comprehensive modern lifestyle. This is conspicuous consumption, certainly. Even more surely, it is the conscious but often unreflective creation of identity. By living in this way, and internalising many of the lifestyles' implicit values, the residents are giving material form to particular narratives of self-identity.

There are grades of development too, beyond the large and opulent estates that I have mentioned. Some are built in Indonesia by government housing agencies in peri-urban areas. Mohamad Sobary (1991, 1995) has written an interesting study of one such place, Suralaya in Tangerang, West Java. In it he traces the gradual bifurcation of status in the settlement between the original villagers and the urban middle-class commuters who moved into the new housing complex built next to the existing village in Suralaya. The forms of self-classification he found there contrast *orang kampung* (villagers) with *orang komplek* (newcomers living in the complex); *orang tidak berpendidikan* (uneducated) with *orang pendidikan* (educated); *orang miskin* (poor person) with *orang kaya* (rich person) (Sobary 1991: 33– 34). Other expressions of these same binary oppositions were *orang kampung* (villagers): *orang kota* (townspeople): *tani* (farmers) : *pegawai kantor* (office workers): *orang kecil* (commoners): *priyayi* (elite) (Sobary 1991: 54). I visited Suralaya in 1995 with Pak Sobary, and was able to observe the changes since his original research. In spite of the social distance between the villagers and the middle-class residents of the housing complex, relations between the communities were mostly harmonious (Sobary 1991, 1995). However, Sobary's earlier study also referred to a very large upmarket development of a new residential town built by large capitalists nearby on the site of a former rubber plantation. The new town, Bumi Serpong Damai,[22] is only accessible to the more affluent elements of the middle classes. The residents do not readily mix with either the office-workers or the farmers from Suralaya. I was told in Suralaya that locals were concerned not just about the exclusivity of Bumi Serpong Damai; they were also worried about the new town being flooded by wealthy emigrant Chinese. 'One does not hear Bahasa Indonesia spoken among them', I was told.

Again, considerations of ethnic differences rise along with strong inter-class differences. It is worth noting, in this respect, that there are people of Chinese descent living in Suralaya itself, families of traders who had settled there several generations ago. They regard themselves as not different from other villagers (apart from being Christian in a large Muslim community), and the common feeling is that they (the Chinese) are: '*sama-sama orang sini juga* (they are also Suralayanese)' (Sobary 1991: 50–1). Thus, although one can observe expressions of ethnic resentment directed at the exclusive expensive estate with its high proportion of Chinese residents, the simplistic association of wealth and Chineseness is not borne out. The tensions and accommodations between the residential groups are too complex to be represented in this way.

This case draws our attention to a number of things. Like shopping malls, middle-class estate developments vary considerably, and it is only the most opulent that achieve the kind of closure of affluent lifestyles referred to above. The range of malls and estates in fact service different though overlapping publics. They are sites of practices in everyday living that express, construct and consolidate the reality and consciousness of social differentiation in the new cities of Southeast Asia. And in that process, broader social currents of ethnicity, religious and linguistic difference find expression too. They are among the strategic sites for the construction of individual and social identity.

Giddens (1991) stresses the centrality of lifestyle choices of this kind for the construction of narratives of identity. Consumption and lifestyle are central because of certain postulates that Giddens advances about 'late modernity'. He observes that: 'in conditions of high modernity, we all not only follow lifestyles, but in an important sense are forced to do so – we have no choice but to choose' (Giddens 1991: 81). He characterises these conditions as 'post-tradi-tional', meaning, amongst other things, that in a globalised late capitalist environment, there has been an inevitable breakdown of the capacity of the major institutions of society to sustain unitary normative models of identity for its members. This has real implications for the nation-building projects of states like those in Indonesia, Singapore and Malaysia, which in part animates the efforts of governments to influence identity formation.[23] Yet to the extent that authors like Giddens (1991) and Castells (1996, 1997) are correct about the redundant role of state institutions,[24] how far do their analyses extend in Southeast Asia?

CONCLUSION

The (not so) Veblenesque model of *La Distinction* [Bourdieu 1989] may tell us a great deal about the role of cultural differentiation in the definition of social position, a process whereby a particular 'class'-determined *habitus* distinguishes itself in the cultural marketplace by identifying itself with a clearly defined set of products and activities, a lifestyle.

(Friedman 1994: 103)

There are current public debates of considerable significance among Muslim intellectuals in Indonesia (Hefner 1993; Ramage 1995) and Malaysia (Anwar Ibrahim 1996; Kahn and Loh 1992; Elegant 1996a, 1996b) about values, self-identity, modernity and the relations between civil society and the state. These debates are of great interest, especially as they contribute to the constitution of distinctive Asian modernities, and the paradoxical quest for a traditionalism that is cosmopolitan and a cosmopolitanism that is traditionally or religiously grounded (Kwok 1994: 29).

Nevertheless, all these efforts at persuasion, the attempts to reach the hearts and minds of the new urban classes, are perhaps excessively focused on the cognitive level and take insufficient account of how large numbers of people are already predisposed to certain manifestations of modern identity by the practices of everyday life. The arguments put forward in this chapter have tried, through reference to several Southeast Asian countries, to show how the normative and political consequences of consumption and lifestyle are too often underestimated.

One should not exaggerate the degree to which the consumption patterns and lifestyles of the Asian new rich have transported urban residents into the existential condition of global societies characterised by choice and a 'puzzling diversity of options and possibilities' (Giddens 1991: 3). Yet, nor do such trends have negligible impact. It varies, according to the degree of industrial (and post-industrial) transformation, the nature of the city in question, and the historical and cultural circumstances of each case. Furthermore, one could suggest that the perceived cultural separateness of more affluent ethnic Chinese in these different cities may have more to do with the fact that their wealth and hybrid lifestyles set them apart, than with some improbable notion that they constitute some form of transnational cultural, economic (and potentially political) entity. I have shown the implausibility of viewing the Chinese diaspora as being culturally unified to any effective extent.

Social analysts like Giddens and Castells posit their analyses on 'post-traditional' situations.[25] I would not want to characterise the cultures of the urban complexes of any of these countries as 'traditional'. Yet, beyond the concerns of governments with shaping national values and identities – for lofty reasons sometimes, but always to buttress social control – there are social groups and social movements that have similar concerns. They do want to sustain their collective identity even though they find it necessary to redefine themselves in an environment of greater wealth and urban cosmopolitanism. The response of some Muslim groups in Indonesia provides instances of this (Heryanto, this volume; Mahasin 1990).

The experience of industrial transformation is very new, the new rich are themselves recently arrived, and global integration is very uneven. These are also societies with a strong sense of their own cultural heritages, and memories of the humiliations of the colonial era. Like their governments, most are apprehensive about the consequences of social fragmentation. The context is markedly different to the societies that best fit Giddens's account of high modernity. Nevertheless, the concern of the argument in this chapter has not been about the influence of major social institutions in shaping identity, but about the seemingly ideologically neutral world of consumption and lifestyle. The practices that become habitualised in this arena also shape identity to a remarkable degree, and their influence is greatest where major institutions are losing their power to do so. As I suggest, there are strong institutions in civil society that may continue to be very influential in some of these countries. The institutions that are most strongly challenged in the present globalised era are those of the state. The current brutal spectacle of the IMF (and financial markets) imposing reforms that no domestic force could contemplate (for example, stripping financial privileges from the Suharto family, the attempts to 'veto' Dr B. J. Habbie's nomination for vice-president) bears out the reality of loss of sovereignty and loss of policy discretion for contemporary states everywhere (Castells 1997: ch. 5; Strange 1996; Horsman and Marshall 1994; Ohmae 1995). Whether globalisation can erode the normative influence of major social institutions to the same degree in Southeast Asia remains to be seen. To varying degrees, most governments have had a paternalistic orientation towards their citizens. The lifestyles of the new rich shake them loose from these controls, even if in an apparently apolitical fashion. One should not be surprised if this creates a certain anxiety among their rulers.

NOTES

1 Giddens (1991: 81) understands 'lifestyles' as: 'sets of actions chosen by individuals to give material form to their particular narrative of self-identity'.

2 The more practical reason for this choice is, of course, that I have conducted field studies in Indonesia, Malaysia and Singapore and have investigated Thailand closely from secondary sources. They are a useful guide to more general Southeast Asian trends.

3 Provided we recognise that 'the new rich' is a term that marks out a range of social groups for investigation, rather than precisely identifying in advance a tightly specified group, the term has definite heuristic utility. It is useful for a number of reasons identified by the editor, including the fact that it is: 'conceptually open...thus [raising] questions of political, economic and cultural identity in a way which, for instance, a single class designation would not' (Pinches 1995: 1).

4 I do so since these are the issues that concern this chapter. Simply to contain the chapter within the limits of the themes of the chapter, I will not engage the closely related arguments about the connections between economic success and Confucian culture (Berger and Hsiao 1988). However, when considering the links between entrepreneurship and Confucianism, I again draw readers' attention to the gap between the simplistic enthusiasms of Naisbit (1996) and the nuanced and scholarly article by Mackie (1992a).

5 Even after intermarriage and abandonment of the use of a Chinese language.
6 Dr Kwok's theoretical stance is heavily influenced on this point by Weber and Gellner. See Kwok 1994.
7 'The reflexive project of the self, which consists in the sustaining of coherent, yet continuously revised, biographical narratives, takes place in the context of multiple choice as filtered through abstract systems' (Giddens 1991: 5).
8 Even though, in Singapore, their social role is much diminished.
9 A rather more familiar experience to many Hong Kong people, whose stereotypes of mainlanders are found in popular culture, TV soap operas and so on (Lilley 1993).
10 The other main ethnic groups are Malays (15 per cent) and Indians (7 per cent).
11 'So it was that the gathering identity of Hong Kong people during the last years of the sixties was not the civic loyalty of the citizen, not an identity of community interest, which in any case was denied by the philosophy of laissez-faire. It was rather an identity of life-style, a shared recognition of similar self-images, real or desired, of existential choices, from food to education, that had to be made now that Hong Kong people could no longer be guided either by Chinese tradition, or (since the demise of Shanghai) Chinese modernity – Tradition, as well as modernity, would now have to be re-made in Hong Kong, if not by scholars, then by the Shaw Brothers' (Turner 1996: 23).
12 Of course, large numbers of the wealthy urban citizens of these countries have experienced rapid – in some cases dazzling – advances in prosperity. Many have learnt very rapidly, others not. Sulak Sivaraksa in Thailand, for example, laments the vulgar ostentation and rootlessness of such people (*The Nation* 1994: 76): 'The very moment I see one, I can spot them a mile off. Middle classes are people who if they are rich, flaunt their wealth. If they are educated, flaunt their knowledge. They want bigness, but not in the sense of excellence.'
13 The political scientist Graham Little wrote a persuasive account of how, even given the minimal clothing used on an Australian beach, a middle-class woman could effortlessly declare her status by the way she wore a ribbon in her hair (personal communication, 1972).
14 I would like to thank Professor Jamie Mackie for this observation, and for pointing to the great potential there is for biographical studies of these major entrepreneurs.
15 *priyayi*: Javanese aristocrat or senior Javanese official.
16 How relative the media's diversity is varies of course from country to country. The media in Indonesia, for example, is reasonably diverse, though hardly free from state intervention (or the public outrage of, for example, Muslims on certain issues).
17 Not to everyone certainly. Mike Davis (1990) examines the phenomena in Los Angeles, and shows how the malls are actually designed to make the poorest ranks of society feel ill at ease and out of place. If they don't take the liberally provided hints, they attract direct attention from security staff to dissuade them from spoiling the relative social homogeneity of the mall. Chua Beng Huat (1992: 119) reports how the upmarket boutiques in Singapore are deliberately designed to dissuade casual shoppers from entering, and once in, from staying.
18 I extend my thanks to Professor Hewison for his advice and for material supplied in researching this chapter.
19 Since the currency crisis, the amount of overdevelopment has become obvious. Surprisingly, given the number of malls, high-rise condominiums and opulent housing estates in Jakarta in 1996, business sources at that time (Seek 1996: 52) suggested that the market was nowhere near saturation:

> Indonesia…has only 200,000 square meters of retail space for its 195 million population according to a survey by the Indonesian retailing business association…Currently there are 55 million Indonesians residing in major cities, 6

million of which are of the so-called a and b class who have monthly disposable income between Rp. 1 and 4 million (500–2000 US dollars). Shopping malls in Jakarta and other big cities play a significant role in developing retail business…In Indonesia, companies wishing to rent a room in a shopping mall have to pay five years of rent in advance. Under such terms plus the current high interest rate of about 20 per cent, it's very hard for small and medium retailers to enter the shopping malls.

20 I was fortunate in Jakarta to have the assistance of Mr Hanneman Samuel from Universitas Indonesia and Swinburne University to draw my attention to many sociological aspects of both malls and estates.
21 Shields (1992: 108) notes: 'Tribe-like but temporary groups and circles condense out of the homogeneity of the mass…The impulse of sociality founds class coalitions at the local, neighbourhood scale, effectual cliques and clubs: a chain reaction of neighbourhoods, counterspaces, heteronomies, local "tribes".'
22 'Bumi Serpong Damai' means 'the peaceful land of Serpong'.
23 Aside from their oft-stated aversion to the corrupting influences of 'Western values'.
24 Castells argues that in the 'network societies' that are emerging beyond Giddens's 'high modernity', dominant social institutions lose completely their capacity to define the identity of citizens.
25 'The more tradition loses its hold, and the more daily life is reconstituted in terms of the dialectal interplay of the local and the global, the more individuals are forced to negotiate lifestyle choices among a diversity of options – Reflexively organized lifeplanning – becomes a central feature of the structuring of self-identity' (Giddens 1991: 5).

BIBLIOGRAPHY

Anderson, B. R. O'G. (1990) 'Murder and Progress in Modern Siam', *New Left Review*, no. 181: 39–40.
Anek Laothamatas (1988) 'Business and Politics in Thailand: New Patterns of Influence', *Asian Survey*, 28 (4): 451–70.
——— (1992) *Business Associations and the New Political Economy of Thailand*, Boulder, CO: Westview Press.
Anwar Ibrahim (1996) 'The Ardent Moderates: A Top Malaysian Leader Describes how His Region's Muslims Came to Choose "The Path of Magnanimity"', *Time*, 23 September: 24–5.
Berger, P. and Hsiao, M. (eds) (1988) *In Search of an East Asian Development Model*, New Brunswick, NJ: Transaction Books.
Bourdieu, P. (1977) *An Outline of a Theory of Practice*, Cambridge: Cambridge University Press.
——— (1989) *Distinction: A Critique of a Theory of Taste*, Cambridge: Cambridge University Press.
Castells, M. (1991) *Four Asian Tigers with a Dragon Head: A Comparative Analysis of the State, Economy and Society in the Asia Pacific Rim*, Universidad Autonoma de Madrid, Instituto Universitario de Sociologia de Nuevas Technologias, working paper no. 14.
——— (1996) *The Information Age: Economy, Society and Culture*, Vol. I: *The Rise of the Network Society*, Oxford: Blackwell.

—— (1997) *The Information Age: Economy, Society and Culture*, Vol. II: *The Power of Identity*, Oxford: Blackwell.

Chow, R. (1992) 'Between Colonizers: Hong Kong's Postcolonial Self-Writing in the 1990s', *Diaspora*, 2 (2): 151–62.

Chua Beng Huat (1992) 'Shopping for Women's Fashion in Singapore', in R. Shields (ed.), *Lifestyle Shopping: The Subject of Consumption*, London: Routledge.

—— (1994a) *That Imagined Space: Nostalgia for the Kampung in Singapore*, Singapore: National University of Singapore, Department of Sociology working paper no. 122.

—— (1994b) 'Arrested Development: Democratisation in Singapore', *Third World Quarterly*, 15 (4): 655–68.

—— (1995) *Communitarian Ideology and Democracy in Singapore*, London: Routledge.

—— and Kuo, Eddie C. Y. (1991) *The Making of a Nation: Cultural Construction and National Identity in Singapore*, Singapore: National University of Singapore, Department of Sociology working paper no. 104.

Clammer, J. (1985) *Singapore: Ideology, Society, Culture*, Singapore: Chopmen Publishers.

—— (1992) 'Aesthetics of the Self: Shopping and Social Being in Contemporary Urban Japan', in R. Shields (ed.), *Lifestyle Shopping: The Subject of Consumption*, London: Routledge.

—— (1993) 'Deconstructing Values: The Establishment of a National Ideology and its Implications for Singapore's Political Future', in Garry Rodan (ed.), *Singapore Changes Guard*, Melbourne: Longman Cheshire.

Cohen, M. L. (1991) 'Being Chinese: The Peripheralisation of Traditional Identity', *Daedalus*, 120 (2): 113–34.

Davis, Mike (1990) *City of Quartz: Excavating the Future in Los Angeles*, London: Verso.

Deyo, F. C. (ed.) (1987) *The Political Economy of the New Asian Industrialism*, Ithaca, NY: Cornell University Press.

Douglas, M. D. (1987) *Constructive Drinking: Perspectives on Drink from Anthropology*, Cambridge: Cambridge University Press.

The Economist (1998a) 'Why Did Asia Crash?', *The Economist*, 10 January: 70.

—— (1998b) 'Which Way to Safety?', *The Economist*, 10 January: 66–7.

—— (1998c) 'The Trouble with Singapore's Clone', *The Economist*, 3 January: 25.

Elegant, S. (1996a) 'Between God and Mammon', *Far Eastern Economic Review*, 9 May: 58–60.

—— (1996b) 'All the Right Reasons', *Far Eastern Economic Review*, 9 May: 59.

Featherstone, M. (ed.) (1990) *Global Culture*, London: Sage.

Finkelstein, J. (1989) *Dining Out: A Sociology of Modern Manners*, Cambridge: Polity.

—— (1991) *The Fashioned Self*, Oxford: Polity.

Fitzgerald, J. (1995) 'The Nationless State: The Search for a Nation in Modern Chinese Nationalism', *The Australian Journal of Chinese Affairs*, no. 33: 75–105.

Forney, M., Moffett, S. and Silverman, G. (1996) 'Ghosts of the Past: China Tries to Keep the Lid on Diaoyu Protests', *Far Eastern Economic Review*, 10 October.

Friedman, J. (1990) 'Being in the World: Localisation and Globalisation', in Mike Featherstone (ed.), *Global Culture*, London: Sage.

—— (1994) *Cultural Identity and Global Process*, London: Sage.

Giddens, A. (1991) *Modernity and Self-Identity: Self and Society in the Late Modern Age*, Stanford, CA: Stanford University Press.

Gilley, B. (1996) 'Controlling Interest: Beijing Plays Diaoyu Dispute in a Low Key', *Far Eastern Economic Review*, 26 September.

——, Moffett, S., Baum, J. and Forney, M. (1996) 'Rocks of Contention', *Far Eastern Economic Review*, 19 September.

Goh Beng Lan (1998) 'Modern Dreams: An Enquiry into Power and Cultural Difference in Contemporary Urban Malaysia', in Joel S. Kahn (ed.), *Southeast Asian Identities; Culture and the Politics of Representation in Indonesia, Malaysia, Singapore, and Thailand*, Singapore: Institute of Southeast Asian Studies.

Gold, T. B. (1993) 'Go with Your Feelings: Hong Kong and Taiwan Popular Culture in Greater China', *China Quarterly*, no. 136: 907–25.

Guldin, G. (1980) 'Whose Neighborhood is This? Ethnicity and Community in Hong Kong', *Urban Anthropology*, 9 (2): 243–63.

—— (1998) 'Hong Kong Ethnicity: Of Folk Models and Change', in G. Evans and M. Tam (eds), *The Anthropology of Hong Kong*, (forthcoming).

Harvey, D. (1989) *The Condition of Postmodernity*, Oxford: Basil Blackwell.

Hefner, R. (1993) 'Islam, the State, and Civil Society: ICMI and the Struggle for the Indonesian Middle Class', *Indonesia*, no. 56: 1–35.

Hewison, K. (1989) *Bankers and Bureaucrats: Capital and the Role of the State in Thailand*, New Haven: Yale University Southeast Asia Series.

—— (1993) 'Of Regimes, States and Pluralities: Thai Politics Enters the 1990s', in Kevin Hewison, Richard Robison and Garry Rodan, *Southeast Asia in the 1990s: Authoritarianism, Democracy and Capitalism*, Sydney: Allen & Unwin.

—— (1995) 'Emerging Social Forces in Thailand: New Political and Economic Roles', in Richard Robison and David Goodman (eds), *The New Rich in Asia: Economic Development, Social Status and Political Consciousness*, London: Routledge.

—— and Maniemai Thongyou (1993) *The New Generation of Provincial Business People in Northeastern Thailand*, Perth: Murdoch University, Asia Research Centre, working paper no. 16.

——, Robison, R. and Rodan, G. (1993) *Southeast Asia in the 1990s: Authoritarianism, Democracy and Capitalism*, Sydney: Allen & Unwin.

Hicks, G. and Mackie, J. A. C. (1994) 'Overseas Chinese: A Question of Identity', *Far Eastern Economic Review*, 14 July: 46–8.

Higgott, R. and Robison, R. (eds) (1985) *Southeast Asia: Essays in the Political Economy of Structural Change*, London: Routledge & Kegan Paul.

Horsman, M. and Marshall, A. (1994) *After the Nation-State: Citizens, Tribalism and the New World Disorder*, London: HarperCollins.

Ien Ang (1993) 'To Be or not to Be Chinese: Diaspora, Culture and Postmodern Ethnicity', *Southeast Asian Journal of Social Science*, 21(1): 1–17.

Jesudason, J. W. (1989) *Ethnicity and the Economy: The State, Chinese Business and Multinationals in Malaysia*, Singapore: Oxford University Press.

Kahn, J. S. (1992) 'Class, Ethnicity, and Diversity: Some Remarks on Malay Culture in Malaysia', in Joel S. Kahn and Francis Kok Wah Loh (eds), *Fragmented Vision: Culture and Politics in Contemporary Malaysia*, Sydney: Allen & Unwin.

—— (1993) 'Culture Wars: Observations on Identity and Globalisation in Southeast Asia', paper presented at the panel on 'The Dynamics of Identity in the Global System' at the International Studies Association Conference in Acapulco, 23–7 March.

—— (1994) 'New Class Contradictions between the Urban and Rural Contexts in Southeast Asia', paper given to conference on 'Emerging Classes and Growing Inequalities in Southeast Asia', held by the Nordic Association of Southeast Asian Studies, 23–5 September, at Gl. Vraa Slot, Tylstrup, Denmark.

—— and Loh, Francis Kok Wah (eds) (1992) *Fragmented Vision: Culture and Politics in Contemporary Malaysia*, Sydney: Allen & Unwin.

Keyes, C. F. (1987) *Thailand: Buddhist Kingdom as Modern Nation-State*, Boulder, CO: Westview.

Kuo, Eddie C. Y. (1992) *Confucianism as Political Discourse in Singapore: The Case of an Incomplete Revitalization Movement*, Singapore: National University of Singapore, Department of Sociology working paper no. 113.

Kwok Kian Woon (1993) 'The Moral Condition of Democratic Society', *Commentary*, 11 (1): 20–9.

—— (1994) *Social Transformation and the Problem of Social Coherence: Chinese Singaporeans at Century's End*, Singapore: National University of Singapore, Department of Sociology working paper no. 124.

Lee, G. B. (1996) *Troubadours, Trumpeters, Troubled Makers: Lyricism, Nationalism and Hybridity in China and its Others*, Durham, N.C.: Duke University Press.

Lilley, R. (1993) 'Claiming Identity: Film and Television in Hongkong', *History and Anthropology*, 6 (2–3): 261–92.

Lim, L. Y.-C. (1983) 'Singapore's Success: The Myth of the Free Market Economy', *Asian Survey*, 23 (6): 752–64.

Mackie, J. A. C. (1992a) 'Overseas Chinese Entrepreneurship', *Asian-Pacific Economic Literature*, 6 (1): 41–64.

—— (1992b) 'Changing Patterns of Chinese Big Business in Southeast Asia', in Ruth McVey (ed.), *Southeast Asian Capitalists*, Ithaca, NY: Cornell University, Southeast Asia Program.

McLaren, A. (1994) 'Reconquering the Cultural Heritage: Regionalism in Popular Culture Studies in China', *Asian Studies Review*, 18 (1): 77–88.

McVey, R. (1992) 'The Materialization of the Southeast Asian Entrepreneur', in Ruth McVey (ed.), *Southeast Asian Capitalists*, Ithaca, NY: Cornell University, Southeast Asia Program.

Mafesoli, M. (1988) *Les Temps des Tribus*, Paris: Meridians Klincksieck.

Mahasin, Aswab (1990) 'The *Santri* Middle Class: An Insider's View', in R. Tanter and K. Young (eds), *The Politics of Middle Class Indonesia*, Melbourne: Centre of Southeast Asian Studies, Monash University.

Mahathir bin Mohamad (1970) *The Malay Dilemma*, Singapore: Donald Moore.

Mennell, S. (1985) *All Manner of Food*, Oxford: Blackwell.

Mintz, S. (1985) *Sweetness and Power: The Place of Sugar in Modern History*, New York: Viking.

Naisbit, J. (1996) *Megatrends Asia: The Eight Asian Megatrends that are Changing the World*, London: Nicholas Bradley.

The Nation (Bangkok) (1994) Yearend Book 1994: *The Rise of the Thai Middle Classes*.

Ohmae, K. (1995) *The End of the Nation State: The Rise of Regional Economies*, London: HarperCollins.

Pinches, M. (1994) 'Modernisation and the Quest for Modernity: Architectural Form, Squatter Settlements, and the New Society in Manila', in Marc Askew and William S. Logan (eds), *Cultural Identity and Urban Change in Southeast Asia: Interpretative Essays*, Melbourne: Deacon University Press.

—— (1995) 'The New Rich and Changing Cultural Constructions of Social Inequality in East and Southeast Asia', unpublished paper dated 8 February 1995.

Ramage, D. (1995) *Politics in Indonesia: Democracy, Islam and the Ideology of Tolerance*, London: Routledge.

Reich, Robert (1992) *The Work of Nations: Preparing Ourselves for 21st Century Capitalism*, New York: Alfred Knopf.

Robison, R. (1985) 'Class, Capital and the State in New Order Indonesia', in Richard Higgott and Richard. Robison (eds), *Southeast Asia: Essays in the Political Economy of Structural Change*, London: Routledge & Kegan Paul.

—— (1986) *Indonesia: The Rise of Capital*, Sydney: Allen & Unwin.

—— (1993) 'Indonesia: Tensions between State and Regime', in Kevin Hewison, Richard Robison and Garry Rodan (eds), *Southeast Asia in the 1990s: Authoritarianism, Democracy and Capitalism*, Sydney: Allen & Unwin.

—— and Goodman, D. S. G. (1996) 'The New Rich in Asia: Economic Development, Social Status and Political Consciousness', in Richard Robison and David Goodman (eds), *The New Rich in Asia: Economic Development, Social Status and Political Consciousness*, London: Routledge.

——, Higgott, R. and Hewison, K. (eds) (1987) *Southeast Asia in the 1980s*, Sydney: Allen & Unwin.

Rodan, G. (1993a) 'The Growth of Singapore's Middle Class and its Political Significance', in Garry Rodan (ed.), *Singapore Changes Guard*, Melbourne: Longman Cheshire.

—— (1993b) 'Introduction: Challenges for the New Guard and Directions in the 1990s', in Garry Rodan (ed.), *Singapore Changes Guard*, Melbourne: Longman Cheshire.

Saunders, P. (1978) 'Domestic Property and Social Class', *International Journal of Urban and Regional Research*, no. 2: 233–51.

Seek, N. H. (1996) 'Institutional Participation in the Asia Pacific Real Estate Markets: Are the Benefits Worth the Risk?', *Real Estate Finance*, 12 (4): 51–8.

Shields, R. (ed.) (1992) *Lifestyle Shopping: The Subject of Consumption*, London: Routledge.

Shotam, Nirmala Puru (1989) 'Language and Linguistic Policies', in K. S. Sandhu and P. Wheatley (eds), *Management of Success: The Moulding of Modern Singapore*, Singapore: Institute of Southeast Asian Studies.

Simmel, G. (1904) 'Fashion', in G. Willis and D. Midgley (eds), *Fashion Marketing*, London: Allen & Unwin.

Sobary, Mohamad (1991) 'Piety and Economic Behaviour: A Study of the Informal Sector in Suralaya, West Java', MA thesis, Monash University.

Sobary, Mohamad (1995) *Kesalehan dan Tingkah Laku Economi*, Yogyakarta: Yaysan Bentang Budaya.

Strange, Susan (1996) *The Retreat of the State: The Diffusion of Power in the World Economy*, Cambridge: Cambridge University Press.

Suchit Bunbongkarn (1993) 'Thailand in 1992: In Search of a Democratic Order', *Asian Survey*, XXXIII (2): 218–25.

Sudjic, Deyan (1993) 'The Metropolis, Present and Future', *Polis*, 1: 8–15.

Sullivan, J. (1995) *Local Government and Community in Java: An Urban Case-Study*, Singapore: Oxford University Press.

Tanter, R. and K. Young (1990) *The Politics of Middle Class Indonesia*, Melbourne: Monash University, Centre of Southeast Asian Studies.

Tham, Seong Chee (1989) 'The Perception and Practice of Education', in K. S. Sandhu and P. Wheatley (eds), *Management of Success: The Moulding of Modern Singapore*, Singapore: Institute of Southeast Asian Studies.

Tremewan, C. (1994) *The Political Economy of Social Control in Singapore*, London: Macmillan.

Turner, M. (1996) 'Hong Kong 60s/90s: Dissolving the People', in M. Turner and I. Ngan, *Hong Kong Sixties: Designing Identity*, Hong Kong: Hong Kong Arts Centre.

Wang Gungwu (1991) *China and the Chinese Overseas*, Singapore: Times Academic Press.

—— (1996) 'Sojourning: The Chinese Experience in Southeast Asia', in A. Reid (ed.), *Sojourners and Settlers: Histories of Southeast Asia and the Chinese*, Sydney: Allen & Unwin.

Walsh, J. (1996) 'The New Face of Islam', *Time*, 23 September: 18–23.

Wee, Vivienne (1988) *What Does 'Chinese' Mean? An Exploratory Essay*, Singapore: National University of Singapore, Department of Sociology working paper no. 90.

Yao Souchou (1995) 'Heavenly Book, Earthly Script: Literary Pleasure, Chinese Cultural Text, and the "Struggle against Forgetting"', unpublished paper presented at the Torque Symposium, 24–6 March 1995, Perth Institute for Contemporary Art, Perth, WA.

Young, K. R. (1990) 'Middle Peasants, Middle Bureaucrats: Middle Class?', in Richard Tanter and Kenneth Young, *The Politics of Middle Class Indonesia*, Melbourne: Monash University, Centre of Southeast Asian Studies.

—— (1994) 'The Urbanisation of the Rural: A New Political Context?', in D. Bourchier and J. D. Legge (eds), *Democracy in Indonesia: The 1950s and 1990s*, Melbourne: Monash University, Centre of Southeast Asian Studies.

—— and R. Kunanayagam (1998) 'Mining, Environmental Impact and Dependent Communities: The View from Below in East Kalimantan', in C. Warren and P. Hirsch (eds), *The Politics of Environment in Southeast Asia*, London: Routledge.

3 From *Orang Kaya Baru* to *Melayu Baru*

Cultural construction of the Malay 'new rich'

A. B. Shamsul

> Does any culture seek inferiority?…We studied how non-Western cultures alter their societies in an effort to attain equality or superiority, but we used criteria and a framework that relegated them to an interpretive position as the perpetual inferior.
>
> (Tanaka 1993: ix)

In the introduction to the first volume in the series on the 'new rich' in Asia, editors Robison and Goodman (1996) note that the 'imprecise' nature of the new rich, both in analytical and empirical terms, concerns the 'imprecise' nature of the new rich as an analytical tool (Robison and Goodman 1996: 5). Indeed, this conclusion is evident throughout the volume. Moreover, the major component concepts under the rubric of the new rich, namely 'the middle class' and 'the bourgeoisie', suffer the same problem of imprecision. In fact, some of the contributors go as far as to demonstrate not only the imprecise nature of these concepts but also their elusiveness. After some twenty pages of interpretation on the 'growth, economic transformation, culture and the middle classes in Malaysia', one author declares, in a Kafkaesque ending, that: 'I have here avoided the question of what I mean by "middle classes"' (Kahn 1996: 48–75).

However, Robison and Goodman do provide a general statement, regarding those they consider the new rich in Asia as: 'the new wealthy social groups that have emerged from industrial change in Asia, particularly during the past two decades' (1996: 5). They also emphasise from the outset that the main task of the research is to provide an analysis of the new rich in contemporary Asia, defined within the criteria and framework of academic interpretation and the 'political economy' approach (Robison and Goodman 1996: xi–xii, 5–10). This could also be understood to mean that the research, conducted by middle-class academics, is interested only in the social group called the 'new rich': who they are, what they do, how they live, how they think and what their future is in Asia. How the rest of the society, especially those from the lower class and the peasantry, think about or perceive the new rich would appear to be of no real consequence to this study. Inevitably, this has resulted in the unintended exclusion of two significant factors pertinent to the 'cultural construction' of the new rich in Asia: first, the changing idiom, texts and contexts of popular discourse that shape the social meaning of the new rich in the public sphere, past and present; second, the role of 'cultural politics' in the formation of the new rich. These factors go beyond a narrow focus on consumer culture, epitomised by such status symbols as mobile phones and McDonald's, referred to in the subtitle of the first volume. Within the 'political economy' approach, each of these two factors is frequently dismissed.

What is significant here is the failure on the part of most of the contributors to the inaugural volume to take into account the fact that a conceptualisation of the new rich is inscribed and embedded in the private and public histories of ordinary people: in vernacular rhetorics and local idioms, in the stories of actual lives scripted by dreadful unpredictability, untidiness, ordinariness and splendour. In other words, we should expect that the 'ordinary people' in Asia, consciously and unconsciously, have been constructing their own 'everyday paradigms' of the 'new rich'. Through shared experience they have developed their own vernacular vocabulary and language to describe, accept or criticise the new rich, both as a social phenomenon, and as people belonging to their local community or wider society. In the Malay-speaking world, the people's 'everyday paradigm' of the new rich is embedded in the popular terms *Orang Kaya Baru* (lit. the new rich person), and *usahawan* (entrepreneur) (Van Der Kroef 1956). These concepts came into being before the 1960s. Whether similar popular concepts or discourses exist among the Cantonese-, Tagalog-, Korean-, Thai- and Japanese-speaking peoples of East and Southeast Asia is a matter that has not been explored.

Therefore, one of the tasks of this chapter is to consider the experience of the 250 million or so Malay-speakers who inhabit the contemporary geopolitical areas of Brunei, Indonesia, Malaysia, Singapore and Pattani of southern Thailand, and to consider the changing ways in which they have constructed an understanding of the new rich. For instance, among the Malay-speakers in Malaysia, the term *Orang Kaya Baru* has recently been replaced by *Melayu Baru* (lit. the New Malay), hence the popular recognition of the fact that there is an 'old' and 'new' Malay new rich. What this implies is that parallel to the process of academic knowledge construction on the new rich, there has been in existence all along a similar popular construction, ignored by academics. Thus, part one of this chapter examines the cultural construction of the Malay new rich, both among the new rich and the non-new rich.

The second part of the chapter explains the emergence and cultural construction of the 'new' Malay new rich, or *Melayu Baru*, in reference to key social, political and economic forces at work in Malaysian society. In particular it situates the origins of the *Melayu Baru* in the historical trajectory of 'Malay nationalism', from before the Second World War to independence and to the recent past. Finally I comment on the cultural predicament of the 'new' Malay new rich.

THE MALAY NEW RICH: POPULAR IDEAS AND
ANALYTICAL ELABORATIONS

There are at least two ways of looking at the new rich in the Malaysian context; first, from the academic viewpoint and, second, from the popular perspective. While they are not mutually exclusive, they have to be treated as equally important. What is obvious though is the fact that there seems to be a 'time-cum-intellectual lag' between the two perspectives. The new rich have long been popularly recognised as a significant social phenomenon and hence have been the subject of lively public discourse. Only recently has academia begun to generate its own focused discourse on the new rich, a subject which had been discussed previously under a variety of broader sociological themes.

Let us start by examining briefly what has happened in the academic sphere in Malaysia. In the first volume of *The New Rich in Asia*, Kahn (1996: 49–75) presents a concise and sophisticated interpretive overview of the kind of empirical and conceptual challenges confronting any attempt to analyse the emergence of Malaysia's middle class, but amazingly avoids, as he says at the end of his chapter, 'the question of what I mean by middle classes' (1996: 71). Yet earlier in the chapter he unwittingly provides one answer by drawing attention to the failure of social scientists studying Malaysia 'to clarify the use of the concept in Malaysian conditions, or to assess its impact on the taken-for-granted contours of Malaysian society' (1996: 49).

It could be argued that the 'elusiveness' of the 'new rich' concept has discouraged Malaysianists, both local and foreign, from tackling the concept head on. Like Kahn, many Malaysianists have taken an indirect approach, subsuming the discussion of topics such as the middle class under broader and more general themes or concepts like 'class, ethnicity, diversity' (for example, Chandra Muzaffar 1984; Kahn 1992a), 'modernity, subalternity and identity' (Idrus 1981; Kahn 1991, 1994; Kessler 1992), 'modernity and agrarian transformation' (Shamsul 1986; Stivens *et al.* 1994), 'matriliny and modernity' (Stivens 1996), 'gender and social change' (Stivens 1994, 1996; Wazir Karim 1990), 'religion and modernisation' (Ong 1995; Shamsul 1995b, 1997b) and the like. In the light of this, Kahn's (1996: 49) disappointment over the 'outpouring of studies of peasants, factory women, ethnicity and Islam...[with]...the growth of the middle class...largely ignored' is both misplaced and premature.

Based on his survey of the Malaysian situation, Kahn seems to suggest quite a different interpretation of what constitutes the new rich to that outlined by Robison and Goodman (1996: 1–16). The latter suggest that the 'new rich' has two main components, namely, the middle class and the bourgeoisie, not unlike the way the recently coined term *Melayu Baru* is meant and used in Malaysia. As understood in both the official and popular sense, the term *Melayu Baru* refers to Malays who are the *para tokoh korporat*, or the 'corporate figure-players' (read 'the bourgeoisie'), as well as the *golongan usahawan dan eksekutif*, or the 'entrepreneurs and executives group' (read 'the middle class'). But Kahn uses the term 'new Malays', or *Melayu Baru*, to refer only to Malays who are 'in the corporate sector and political elites' (Kahn 1996: 67), or 'the bourgeoisie' (Robison and Goodman 1996: 5), but not those in 'the middle class(es)', who, according to him, are the 'new rich'. In other words, Kahn seems to have half-understood the term *Melayu Baru* as it is used in Malaysia, both in the public and academic sphere.

In the Malaysian academic discourse, from the 1950s until the 1970s, components of the Asian 'new rich', as understood by Robison and Goodman (1996: 1–15), were each studied and analysed separately, often subsumed, under the broader sociological themes noted above. This reflects both the nature and development of social scientific studies on and in Malaysia as much as the prevailing social reality. For instance, in the 1950s and early 1960s, topics related to the components within the present-day concept 'new rich' were investigated under the broad topic 'economic development and cultural change' (Ungku Aziz 1951, 1975; Swift 1965). From the mid-1960s onwards they were discussed in the context of the study of social stratification, social mobility and occupation (Husin Ali 1964; Mokhzani 1965; Alatas 1967). Mokhzani (1965) suggested two reasons for this: first, the absence of an academic department of sociology and anthropology in the local university (until 1970, Malaysia had only one university: the University of Malaya) and, secondly, the 'cultural' (read 'orientalist') orientation of past writers on Malaysian subjects.

It was only in the 1970s, after the setting up of new universities in Malaysia, that academic departments of anthropology and sociology were established in three of the five universities. The academic teaching and research activities, as well as academic discourse generated by these departments, opened up new foci of research informed by a variety of theoretical orientations. Some of these concerned the significance of Malaysian stratified society for the conceptualisation of social status and rank (Abdul Kahar Bador 1967, 1970), social consciousness and entrepreneurship (Papenoe 1970; Tham Seong Chee 1973a, 1973b, 1977; Abdul Kahar Bador 1973), leadership (Husin Ali 1975), and the distribution of benefits from so-called planned development projects (Tham Seong Chee 1973b; Rudner 1994; Shamsul 1977). By the mid-1970s, the research topics had begun to narrow, focusing on 'new rich'-related themes, concerning middle-class bureaucrats (Nordin Selat 1976), elite formation (Lee 1980; Scott 1978; Khasnor 1984), and professional groups and entrepreneurs (Lee 1976; MacAndrews 1977; Mohd. Fauzi Yaacob 1981; Shamsul 1986). In the 1980s, the focus narrowed further, dealing with such topics as educated groups and the rise of Islamic revivalism (Zainah Anwar 1987; Chandra Muzaffar 1987), and emerging corporate groups (Jesudason 1989; Gomez 1990; Lim Mah Hui 1985). Debates over the applicability of different analytical concepts – like 'plural society', 'class', 'ethnicity/race', 'political economy' and 'gender' – to dissect Malaysian society also became commonplace (Brennan 1982; Lim Mah Hui 1980; Jomo 1986; Shang 1976; Kua Kia Soong 1981). These were followed by a series of studies on the 'politics and poetics of identity' (Nagata 1979; Hirschman 1986; Strauch 1981; Peletz 1993; Tan Leok Ee 1988).

It could be said that for the first four post-war decades, there was a steady nurturing and maturing of scholarly interest and analytical sophistication in dealing with various components of the new rich in Malaysia. From the mid-1980s onwards, social scientific knowledge and analysis of the new rich, as understood both by Robison and Goodman, and by Kahn, began to take shape in Malaysia, in response to changing social reality (Mohd. Nor Nawawi 1985, 1991; Gomez 1990, 1991, 1994; Lee Oon Hean 1994; Kahn 1988–9; Stivens 1995a, 1995b; Saravanamuttu 1989; Saravanamuttu and Maznah 1989). Indeed, commencing in early 1996, there have been a number of research projects on the Malaysian middle class conducted by groups of Malaysian social scientists, generously funded by the government under the IRPA (Intensive Research Priority Areas) Research and Development Program of the Ministry of Science and Environment, as well as by foreign funding bodies.

What is both exciting and revealing in my present examination of the new rich in Malaysia is the fact that it reminds me of the 'old' concept of the 'new rich' which has existed in the popular realm of social life in Malaysia. The term *Orang Kaya Baru*, which literally means 'the new rich person', was already in vogue when I was at primary school in the mid-1950s. This was later confirmed by my field research in the early 1980s when its usage was still commonplace, and by my recent conversations with those of my parents' generation. According to Hans Antlöv (this volume), the term *Orang Kaya Baru* has also been around for some time in his field research area of West Java, and is used in a popular manner, not unlike in Malaysia. It has also been popular in West and North Sumatra, according to four Indonesian researchers-cum-doctoral candidates at the National University of Malaysia, who have been conducting field research in their regions of origin in Sumatra on the theme of 'politics and culture'. They kindly alerted me to the fact that in the mid-1950s academic discourse on the Indonesian middle class was in place, but was usually linked to an examination of the concept and community of *usahawan* (entrepreneurs) (Van Der Kroef 1956).

Written or printed sources in Malaysia seem to suggest that the term *Orang Kaya Baru* has been used since the early 1950s in daily conversation, vernacular weeklies and dailies, movies, lyrics of songs, radio comedy shows, short stories, election campaign speeches and *pojok* columns of local Malay newspapers. The term is often alluded to in everyday conversation simply by its abbreviation, OKB. It is used in the singular or the plural, because the word *orang* could refer to an individual (for example, *orang itu* meaning 'that person') or a group of people (for example, *Orang Melayu* meaning 'the Malay people'; *orang putih* meaning 'the white people'), or else be used as a neutral descriptive term (for example, *jadi orang baik* meaning 'to become someone good'; *orang alim* meaning 'religious persons').

There are two major explanations as to how the expression OKB came about in the Malaysian context. The first 'theory' traces the origin of the concept to the Malay feudal system; and the second one to the more subaltern circumstances and contexts among the grassroots. In the former, it is argued that the formation of an 'achievement-based' non-feudal class of Malay elites during and after colonial rule – first as civil servants and later as Members of Parliament and State Legislative Councils – threatened the 'ascribed' traditional Malay feudal class. On the one hand, the latter do not really wish to absorb these 'new men' into their ranks, and thereby lose the symbolic standing of their position. On the other hand, they fully realise that for the Malay polity to function in the most harmonious fashion possible, as well as for sheer practical reasons, the persistence of rigid caste-like social distinctions could be detrimental to their position. Hence, a compromise has been worked out. A system of honours, after the traditional model, was instituted, through which the Sultans – as 'the Fount of Nobility' – create life-*Datos* and other 'Awards' granted to 'deserving' civil servants, politicians and other private individuals (Abdul Kahar Bador 1973: 148–9). Many of these individuals are very rich entrepreneurs, including non-Malays who willingly accept the Malay titles.

For each of the life-*Datos* awarded, there are specific, often very long, titles, some of which begin with *Orang Kaya* (lit. rich person) or *Orang Besar* (lit. big person). Some, such as *Orang Kaya Maharajalela Pahlawan* or *Orang Besar Mahligai Alam*, are not dissimilar – at least in naming style and grandeur – to those already used to designate ascribed traditional aristocrats. Such titles also appear in the numerous texts of Malay *hikayats* (classical literature texts), some of which have been used as textbooks for government secondary-school examinations. Numerous parts of these *hikayats* have been incorporated into folk and oral litera-ture or staged in the various traditional Malay performing arts, such as *bangsawan, Mak Yong, wayang kulit, randai* and the like (Sweeney 1987). Therefore, the term *Orang Kaya* is one of the most popular titles known to the Malay and non-Malay public at all levels of society. According to one 'theory', the adoption of this term in popular colloquial and written forms, along with that of *Orang Besar*, was basically to denote new wealthy social groups within the community. They largely consisted of the *rakyat biasa*, or commoners, rather than the aristo-crats, but were given a quasi-royal title, something not uncommon in the 1950s. The emphasis in this particular usage is on the phrase *Orang Kaya*, which has its roots in the existing feudal order, implying honour, status and dignity, thus providing a social levelling effect on those commoners referred to as OKB. By implication, the silent opposing term, *Orang Kaya Lama*, or 'old rich person', is generally understood as referring to those belonging to the aristocratic class.

A second 'theory' seems to suggest that the term *Orang Kaya* came into use in daily conversation, in both a positive and negative sense, as part of gossip or rumour-mongering. Here it is commonly used as an expression of envy or jeal-ousy directed at individuals who belong to the same class (usually peasants or workers), but who have recently become wealthy and who often unashamedly flaunt their new-found riches. What makes such behaviour 'irritating' to friends and foes in the same class is what they see as its sheer 'outlandishness' or 'ridicu-lousness'. Sometimes such behaviour is simply perceived as 'odd', for example when people buy electrically powered refrigerators in a village without electricity and use them instead as cupboards in which to keep clothes (Shamsul 1986: 64). Thus, according to the second 'theory', the term *Orang Kaya Baru* was coined and came into popular use to refer to people who had just recently become rich, or to *orang yang baru jadi kaya*, whose behaviour is rather odd and 'not really like the "real" rich people'. The way it is used in this context indicates that the emphasis is on the word *Baru*, not on *Orang Kaya*, because the term as a whole refers to those who have just become rich, but who adopt behaviour that is perceived as not in the repertoire of the 'really rich'. Similarly it is used for those who are not really rich, but who behave oddly in trying to make out that they are.

It could be suggested that the second 'theory' represents a strong subalternist tendency, because the way *Orang Kaya Baru* is understood and used – such as in the form of gossip, rumour-mongering or through the expression of envy or even uncouthness – conforms with the practices that Scott (1985) describes as 'weapons of the weak', or as an articulation of 'everyday forms of peasant resistance'. Antlöv (this volume) observes that in West Java the term 'OKB' has these subalternist or 'negative' connotations, because to call someone an OKB is considered derogatory and is sometimes meant to insult the person.

A closer examination of how the term 'OKB' has been used in the Malaysian public arena reveals that it is popular among the rich (*kaya*), the 'comfortable' (*senang*) and the poor (*miskin*). In fact, amongst the elite in Malaysia, both rural and non-rural, the term 'OKB' has frequently been used in election campaigns where it is meant to criticise or to accuse, in an indirect manner, people who become well off through corrupt means. In movies, songs and comedies it has been used to expose the ironies in the behaviour patterns of individuals or groups of OKB individuals, such as the instance I mentioned above involving refrigerators in a village without electricity.

Interestingly, amongst Malay-speakers in Malaysia, the term *Orang Kaya Baru* has recently been replaced in the popular parlance, and in scholarly analysis, by another term, *Melayu Baru*, referring mainly to Malays who have become *senang* (lit. comfortable) or *kaya-raya* (very wealthy) as a result of the implementation of the long-term pro-Malay affirmative action policy, called the New Economic Policy (NEP), between 1971 and 1990 (Rustam A. Sani 1993). Viewed from the top down, the *Melayu Baru* consist of corporate players, political elites and the professional middle class, a perspective on the 'new rich' not dissimilar to the one suggested by Robison and Goodman (1996: 5). But, it is significant to note that the term also has an 'everyday' meaning at the grassroots level – in daily conversation by Malaysians from all ethnic groups and walks of life, be they Chinese workers, Malay peasants or Indian schoolchildren. In this context the term is used as a phrase or cliché to 'make fun of' others, both negatively (*perli, giat, kutuk* – an expression of ridicule) and positively (*puji, sokong, ampu bodek* – an expression of praise).

This cultural construction of the social meaning of the new rich in Malaysia is in itself an interesting phenomenon to observe. It enriches our knowledge regarding how the new rich are being perceived and inscribed into popular minds and memories. In analytical terms, 'the people' themselves – in this case Malay-speakers – are social actors who contribute and witness actual lives, acting as their own historians. They are aware of the phenomenon of the new rich as they experience it. In their own individual and collective ways they invent, through their vernacular understanding and language, particular terms, related phrases or poetic clichés to describe and label the new rich and, simultaneously, construct and inscribe cultural meanings into the term. When things around them change, they are also quick to introduce new terms to capture and internalise, as well as to come to grips with, the new circumstances: hence a redefined cultural scenario. This is evident in the way the term *Orang Kaya Baru* became *Melayu Baru* in Malaysia, capturing the stories of actual lives with all their internal contradictions.

IDENTITY POLITICS AND CULTURAL PREDICAMENT OF THE NEW MALAY NEW RICH

It is not unusual for us, as students of society, to be caught in the 'historian's predicament', torn between what we would like the story to be and what the evidence shows it really is. This could be resolved if we accept the principle that fictional story writers enjoy a licence, while we in the human sciences have a responsibility. It is imperative for us to explain the emergence of the new classes in Asia, particularly their materialist (read 'political economy') underpinnings, as demonstrated in the inaugural volume edited by Robison and Goodman (1996). However, it is also the responsibility of researchers to trace the historical origins and trajectories of these classes within the realm of 'cultural politics' or 'nationalist discourse'. It is also necessary to take cognisance of the central role of the 'social engineering' strategy adopted by the state. This part of the chapter intends to do just that.

Making *Orang Kaya Baru*: the economic dimension of a nationalist project

The making of a Malay nationalist ideal and movement revolves around the politico-ideological problem of resolving the elemental character of the Malay as a 'race' or *bangsa*: what constitutes 'Malayness' and, subsequently, what is the vision and nature of the 'Malay nation'. Such a preoccupation is a direct response to the European colonial presence and the influx of the Chinese migrant population into Malaya from the mid-nineteenth century. Initially, it resulted in the formulation of a popular expression of group identity by the long-established peasant Malays. However, later, with the introduction of census and 'race-based' laws during the colonial era, informed by the principles of 'scientific racism' (Hirschman 1986), the popular expression of 'Malay' group identity was transformed into a definite and legal category, namely, 'a race', with all its Darwinian underpinnings (Milner 1994; Shamsul 1995a).

Therefore, the concept 'Malay', as a race and as a source of identity, became popular and was readily accepted, developed, debated and elaborated by Malay journalists, creative writers, literary figures and intellectuals. They included such people as Abdullah Munshi in the late nineteenth century, Mohd. Eunos

Abdullah in the first decade of the twentieth century, Syed Sheikh Alhadi in the 1920s, Za'aba and Kajai in the 1930s, Ishak Hj. Muhammad in the early 1940s, and the 'young' Mahathir Mohamed, under the pen-name of C. H. E. Det, in the late 1940s (Shaharuddin Maaruf 1988; Ariffin Omar 1993; Khoo Boo Teik 1995).

The protracted discussion on what should constitute 'Malayness' eventually shaped the two central agendas of the Malay nationalist movement in colonial Malaya, namely, the political and the economic. The political agenda was rather complex and so became a source of continuous contestation. Though clear and simple in their objectives, the programmes of the economic agenda were unclear, and their future uncertain (Roff 1967; Milner 1994).

In political terms, there was a general consensus among the three major factions within the Malay nationalist movement – the administrator-aristocrat or 'administocrats' faction, the Malay left faction and the Islamic faction – as to what should constitute 'Malayness', namely *'bahasa, agama dan raja'* (language/Malay, religion/Islam, and royalty/sultan-chiefs). All agreed that the Malay language should be the sole medium of official communication and education in their proposed 'Malay nation' or 'nation-of-intent' (Shamsul 1996a). But they differed as to the order of importance of religion and royalty in each of their preferred options for national identity. The 'administocrat faction' emphasised the symbolic importance of royalty as the custodian of Malay culture and religion; the 'Malay left' recognised the importance of religion but not royalty; and the 'Islamic group' felt that the ultimate form of a Malay nation was an Islamic one (Roff 1967; Ariffin 1993; Milner 1994).

The British, after having to abort their own nation-of-intent programme, namely, a 'unitary nation' in the form of the Malayan Union in 1946, opted for a 'federation-based nation' favoured by the Malay administocrat faction, to whom the British eventually entrusted the running of the independent Federation of Malaya in 1957. This occurred after elites from the said faction underwent various stages of political internship in the management of a multi-ethnic government. The administocrats formed UMNO (United Malays National Organisation) in 1946 and, together with MCA (Malaysian Chinese Association) and MIC (Malaysian Indian Congress) – both set up in the early 1950s – formed the Alliance. This coalition political party was blessed by the British, won its first national election in 1955, and continues to enjoy success. It now operates under a much expanded coalition called the National Front (Ariffin 1993).

The adoption by the British of the administocrat-endorsed federation concept meant that the primacy of each of the Malay states (*negeri*), and its sultan and chiefs as rulers to whom all Malay should be loyal, came to be recognised and institutionalised, first, in the Federation of Malaya Agreement in 1948 and, later, in the constitution of the independent Federation of Malaya in 1957. It could be argued that the administrocrats (read UMNO) had no clear concept of 'nation', or *bangsa*, but strongly upheld the province, or *negeri*-based concept of *kerajaan*, or indigenous governance (Milner 1982), thus institutionalising the internal plurality of the Malay as a *kaum*, or race. It is not surprising, therefore, that they too accepted, without meaningful debate, the British-endorsed 'plural society model' as the model of their 'Malay nation'.

Significantly, the Malayan Constitution was considered by many as a 'social contract' between the different ethnic groups in the country. The British always acted as the 'mediator' in negotiations between different ethnic groups. For instance, under the constitution, the immigrant population (mainly Chinese and Indian) were made Malayan citizens overnight, but, under the same constitution, they had to accept the special position, rights and privileges of the Malays. In other words, 'Malay dominance', or *ketuanan Melayu*, was written into the constitution. However, the constitution also guaranteed the right of freedom of speech of all citizens. Hence the Chinese and Indians, as rightful citizens, could question the special position, rights and privileges of Malays. From then on, the issue of special rights and privileges became one of the central contentious issues in inter-ethnic relations in Malaysia (Shamsul 1995a).

In sum, the federation concept, practised since 1948 in Malaya (later Malaysia), recognised Malay dominance as central to its existence because it was put together and introduced to the British by the administocrat faction of the Malay nationalist movement in the wake of Malay opposition towards the British proposition of a Malayan Union. The protection of Malay dominance by the constitution means the protection of the three pillars of Malayness, namely, *bahasa, raja dan agama* (lit. language, royalty and religion). In a way it also signaled the successful struggle for the Malay nationalist ideal, at least in the political sphere.

In spite of the clear success of the political agenda of the Malay nationalist movement, its economic agenda remained unfulfilled, even a decade after independence. Not only was this because its details were unclear, but also because it was overwhelmed, for a long time, by activities motivated by the perceived need to control the 'political sphere' first. This was understandable in view of the fact that the British were in total control of the economy while conducting negotiations for a peaceful transfer of power to the locals. The British were concerned that the bitter experience of the Dutch in Indonesia would not be repeated in Malaya.

The British were also aware that the economic agenda of the Malay nationalist movement was closely linked to the political one. The link was provided by the perceived experience of 'being dispossessed at one's own home' (*dirampas segalanya di rumah sendiri*), with the colonialist and the immigrant population perceived as the 'dispossessors'. Hence the idiom of the Malay nationalist struggle was always put in terms of 'repossessing' (*merampas kembali*) or reclaiming political and economic dominance from the British and the immigrant population (Roff 1967; Husin Ali 1984; Milner 1994; Shamsul 1995a).

In reference to the economy, the Malay nationalists argued that before the coming of the European colonialists and immigrant population, the Malays enjoyed a period of economic independence and were involved in sophisticated commercial dealings with the Chinese, Indians, Arabs and others. They further argued that native commerce was arrested, and that indigenous economic development was marginalised by colonial subjugation and immigrant encroachment. However, Malay nationalists, such as Sheikh Al-Hadi and Zaaba, argued that there were other 'Malay cultural traits', such as lack of awareness of time, lack of rationality, fatalism and a '*tak apa*thy' attitude towards work, that had contributed to 'Malay economic backwardness'. In this context Al-Hadi and Zaaba were referring to the Malay peasants' inability to break the 'vicious circle of poverty' that imprisoned them. In another context, having the Malay entrepreneurs in mind, Al-Hadi and Zaaba suggested that Islamic ideas and values are compatible with capitalistic values, and that it is not a sin to become rich and have a lot of money (Ungku Aziz 1975; Shaharuddin 1988).

In a series of articles written for the *Sunday Times* (September 1948–April 1950), the young Mahathir also lamented the problems: first, of rural Malays who were unable to understand the difference between 'property', 'land' and 'money', and who were continuously subjected to exploitation by Chinese middlemen: and secondly, of the incipient rural and urban Malay entrepreneurial class, who were denied a fair share of colonial capital accumulation (Mahathir 1995). Although education was important in changing these conditions, it was capital and skill which the Malays needed most to transform their disadvantaged economic condition (Khoo Boo Teik 1995).

In short, the nationalists were clear that the struggle in the economic sphere was to regain control both in the rural agricultural sector (dominated by British- and Chinese-owned plantation and mining) and in the urban commercial sector (dominated by British agency houses and Chinese family businesses). A successful implementation of this agenda, they contended, should help to solve both the poverty problem among the poor rural Malays and the problem of creating a niche for Malay entrepreneurs (old and new) in the ever-expanding urban business sphere. Unlike the political agenda, the economic one remained for a long time on the drawing board; it was never seriously followed up, detailed or discussed with the enthusiasm that surrounded talks about the issue of Malayness or the Malay nation (Shamsul 1997a).

It was not until 1950, when the colonial Draft Development Plan 1950–1955 (DDP) was launched, that the Malay nationalist economic agenda was mentioned again. By this time the political context was quite different. It was perceived by Malay administocrats as being a 'victorious' one, because they had now become part of the ruling power. They had had their federation concept – protecting Malay special rights and privileges – endorsed by the British, they had successfully formed a political alliance with the elite-led Chinese and Indian political parties, and there was even talk about independence in the air (Shamsul 1977, 1986).

The British were quick to react and they institutionalised the concept of affirmative action in the said five-year DDP plan, which was pro-Malay in that it was clearly worked out within the special rights and privileges framework. A number of special economic programmes emerged from this effort, but others were built into the overall development planning strategy and implementation. For instance, the British established a semi-government body called RIDA (Rural Industrial Development Authority) in 1953 under the DDP, to assist rural Malay entrepreneurs to obtain capital and skill either to start or expand their own small and medium businesses. In 1956, under the First Five-Year Malaya Plan 1956–60 (FFYMP), another semi-government body called FELDA (Federal Land Development Authority) was set up, specifically to help the very poor and landless Malays.

When Malaya gained independence in 1957, the political agenda of the Malay nationalist was well in place, but not the economic one. The colonial government did what it could, but obviously without endangering the well-entrenched Chinese and British commercial and economic interests. Besides, in a country devastated by a major war, no amount of money and planning could change anything very much within a decade. The big push to fulfil the nationalist economic agenda came after independence. It was targeted at both Malay peasants as well as old and new Malay entrepreneurs.

It began in 1959 with the setting up of a Ministry of Rural and National Development by Razak, the then deputy prime minister, who later became the architect of the NEP. A massive rural development programme was launched countrywide to provide infrastructural facilities to rural Malays. Not long after that the Green Revolution came to Malaysia. Politically, these programmes were meant to buy rural votes for UMNO, which was facing fierce opposition from Parti Islam and the Socialist Front Party. For the urban-based Malay businessmen, the Ministry of Commerce and Industry set up a National Investment Company in 1961 to allow Malay civil servants and professionals to buy shares allocated for Malays in the mostly foreign-owned pioneer manufacturing companies. Then, in 1963, the same ministry set up an organisation for the National Timber Industry, mainly for Malays who were involved in logging and timber-based enterprises. Other forms of support were also made available for those conducting business in mining, transportation and construction (Faarland *et al.* 1990).

Seen from another angle, the 1960s rural development programmes, awash with funds, were really the NEP before the NEP, especially for those who were already in UMNO. As a result, UMNO politicians became not only more keen on the 'business of politics', but also increasingly knowledgeable in 'the art' and 'the politics of business', particularly in the 'business of rural development' – generating income, wealth and influence from projects related to the rural development programmes. Because most of these 'development projects' were infrastructural in nature, they largely involved construction works where business was dominated by the Chinese. Tenders and contracts for these projects were won by the UMNO politicians, but eventually subcontracted to the Chinese contractors. The former received a certain percentage from the latter, literally for doing nothing. Therefore, it is not difficult to understand the script and plot of the larger picture which, in the 1970s, featured the rise of a class of Malay OKBs who were predominantly 'rentier capitalists'.

It was then that many young Malays and aspiring Malay entrepreneurs hit upon the idea that there seemed to be a short cut, or a method, to make the 'materialist leap', to become rich rather quickly, to climb the social ladder, to enjoy a better social status and, at the same time, to have power: 'the political way'. This reflected strongly the pre-war Malay nationalist priority of getting access to 'the economic' through politics. For the grassroots Malays of the 1960s, it established the idea of *jadi ahli politik untuk buat duit* (lit. be a politician to make money). This became a popular folk political philosophy at the grassroots. In fact, it was adopted as an unwritten 'guiding ethos' for many young Malays who were keen to become entrepreneurs or who simply wanted to be rich. Thus, the link between 'politics' and 'money' was firmly established in Malay politics in the 1960s (Shamsul 1988).

In this way the 1960s saw the rise of a nascent Malay entrepreneurial class from rural Malays who were predominantly peasants, petty traders and owners of cottage industries. Many of them benefited greatly from the endless 'development projects' made available to them by Razak's massive rural development programmes. The traditional Malay capitalists, mainly from the aristocrat families, were generally urban-based, though many owned large acreages of rural agricultural land, urban real-estate properties and large timber concessions. Other urban-based Malay entrepreneurs were involved mainly in transportation, mining and contracting. Many began to make their way into the 'business of development'. However, the real explosion and expansion of Malay interests in business and commerce was in the rural sphere, especially with the rise of the new Malay entrepreneurs through the business of rural development. The rural and urban Malay entrepreneurs were able to put their act together for the first time in the mid-1960s, by giving a 'political voice' to their economic interests and pitching it to a level loud enough to attract the government's attention.

This resulted in the first *Kongres Ekonomi Bumiputera* in June 1965, a meeting which, for the first time since the advent of Malay nationalism, successfully planned detailed strategies and programmes to implement the nationalist's economic agenda. Before this, there were numerous *kongres bahasa Melayu* (Malay language congresses), *perhimpunan parti politik* (political party conferences), *muktamar ulamak* (conferences of religious leaders), not to mention regular *persidangan raja-raja* (conferences of rulers), but never a *kongres ekonomi* (economic congress). This finally happened about half a century after the Malay nationalist movement came to the scene and scored many political successes. In a matter of three years, in September 1968, another *Kongres Ekonomi Bumiputera* was held to evaluate the success rate of programmes outlined and implemented since 1965, as well as to make additional future plans. Both the congresses were significant, in various ways, in carving the 'socio-economicscape' which eventually contributed to the rise of Malay OKBs of the 1970s, 1980s and eventually the *Melayu Baru* in the 1990s.

The 1968 *Kongres* successfully outlined, in some detail, the perceived trajectory of and strategy for the general 'upliftment of the Malay economic position' in Malaysia. Secondly, it established the much needed institutional structures for the advancement of Malay capitalist enterprise, such as banks and other financial institutions, commercial organisations (as distributors, wholesalers and agency houses for imported and local consumer goods), educational and vocational training institutes, and economic and urban development bodies, all of which were government-funded. Thirdly, it was the first time Malay bureaucrats, technocrats, professionals, petty traders, academics and others met one another, exchanged ideas and tabled their visions of the future for the Malay economy, setting the target to be achieved, and planning how this could be realised (Mohd. Fauzi Yaacob 1981; Jesudason 1989).

Ironically, the 1969 ethnic riot was a blessing in disguise for Malay entrepreneurs and politicians. It provided them with a reason, if not an occasion, to push further the implementation of the nationalist 'economic agenda'. Previously it was done under the political umbrella of 'Malay dominance' but, after 1969, it was carried out within a redefined and constrictive political ideology of 'Malay hegemony'. This was made possible by the tightening up of various legislations or the introduction of new ones, such as the Sedition Act 1970, which prohibited any discussion on matters relating to what constituted 'Malayness' and 'Malay special rights', concerning the Malay language, Islam and royalty. With the new 'political rules' clearly spelt out, the Malay economic march towards the full realisation of the Malay nationalist ideal in the economic sphere began in earnest (Shamsul 1977, 1986).

The NEP, launched in 1971, can be seen as the product of the efforts of Razak, the then prime minister, and his 'backroom boys', comprising Malay bureaucrats, academics and technocrats, most of whom were also responsible for the successful organisation of the *Kongres Ekonomi Bumiputera* in 1965 and 1968. In fact, a group of them produced a book called *Revolusi Mental* (1970), edited by Senu A. Rahman, in an attempt to provide a kind of conceptual framework for a plan of action for the future of the Malay cause. Many Malaysians were also encouraged to reflect on and explain the causes of the 1969 ethnic riot, and many books were published with that intention.

The most famous and the most widely read of the lot, entitled *The Malay Dilemma* (1970), was written by Dr Mahathir Mohamed, the present prime minister. It was banned as soon as it appeared for its supposedly 'ultra-Malay' views. In the book, Mahathir tried to explain a number of things: his ideas on the problematic nature of inter-ethnic relations, especially between the Malays and the Chinese before 1969; why the need to recognise the 'primordiality and indigenousness' of the Malays in Malaysia; the socio-biological factors in the making of the Malay race; the relationship between Malay cultural traits and economic backwardness; the need for state intervention to protect the Malays in their development; and some methods on how Malays could improve themselves.

If seen from the Malay nationalist perspective, the two central objectives of the NEP – first, to 'eradicate poverty'; and second, 'to restructure society' – are essentially parts of the overall nationalist economic agenda, the former for the Malay rural poor, and the latter for the Malay entrepreneurs. It is not uncommon, therefore, for the NEP to be referred to by some analysts as a form of 'Malay capitalistic/economic nationalism' (Shaharuddin 1988: 154–6), which is not entirely incorrect, at least from the social actors' perspective.

From *Orang Kaya Baru* to *Melayu Baru*: old and new Malay new rich

In the NEP's second objective, it was specifically stated that within two decades (1971–90) the successful implementation of the policy should be able to create a 'community of Malay entrepreneurs'. This was to be done not only through direct government intervention and economic support, but also through an aggressive training and educational strategy that would create the much needed professionally trained Malay manpower to participate in various fields into which Malays had not ventured before. These were mainly in the economic-cum-commercial sphere, involving non-manual 'mental production' processes that called for bureaucrats, company executives, technocrats, academics, accountants, computer-chip engineers, information technology specialists and a host of other professions demanding high or specialist education and training. Thus, the implementation of the NEP's second objective has successfully created and expanded the Malay middle class. In fact, many of its members have become extremely rich and are now active corporate players in the country and globally.

However, my own study (Shamsul 1986) indicates that through the implementation of its first objective of 'poverty eradication', the NEP has ironically also created many new Malay entrepreneurs, mostly rural-based, who, in the eyes of the 'ordinary people', are the *Orang Kaya Baru*. Most of them, unlike their educated urban counterparts, are not involved in the non-manual 'mental production' process. Rather, they are usually involved in traditional, manually oriented, small- and medium-size businesses, such as construction and food or handicraft manufacture, or are self-employed in the wholesaling of primary products or direct selling activities. Most of these emerging grassroots Malay new rich have been politically active in, or connected to, the local UMNO branch, some of them as top district-level UMNO politicians. By establishing their own companies and then awarding them lucrative government contracts, they have managed to turn rural development projects, initially aimed at eradicating poverty, into rich financial resources for themselves. However, without the support, both in capital and skill, of local Chinese tycoons, the grassroots Malay new rich would not have risen so quickly. Of course, the Chinese *towkays*, or tycoons, like their Malay partners, benefited tremendously in financial terms from this 'fulfilling and harmonious' relationship (Gomez 1994, 1991, 1990).

From the above, it is noteworthy that the contemporary Malay new rich, along with both its bourgeoisie and middle-class components, are not internally homogeneous. The latter are divided into at least two broad analytical categories, namely the 'old', manually oriented middle class (for example, small-business people, the self-employed), popularly known as *Orang Kaya Baru*, and the 'new', non-manual and mentally oriented middle class (for example, professionals and bureaucrats), recently labeled, together with Malay corporate players, as *Melayu Baru*. The 'new' middle class is based mainly in big cities, such as Kuala Lumpur, Penang, Johare Baru, Kuching and Kita Kinabalu. But the 'old' middle class is based both in the big cities and in the small rural towns and villages.

There is a noticeable difference between these two categories of middle class, at least in the Malay case in Malaysia. Those in the old, manually-oriented middle-class, most of whom are rural-based, seem to be dominated by the 'rentier' kind, comprising individuals who have little or no previous background in the world of business. In fact, most of them are children of Malay peasants. They, or their family members, are not seriously involved in business either, except as 'sleeping partners' to Chinese *towkays*, or tycoons, earning large sums of money in commissions for getting government contracts using their political positions or contacts. They are between 45 and 50 years of age, with secondary-school qualifications, but their main asset is that, over the years, they have built an enormous political power base at the grassroots by virtue of working and living mostly in the rural areas. They became rich and joined the middle class through the 'business of development projects' for the rural poor (Papenoe 1970; Mohd. Fauzi Yaacob 1981).

I call these new rich Malay 'rentier' middle-class politicians whose position is akin to *telor dihujung tandok* (lit. an egg perched precariously on a sharp horn), and whose success or survival is largely dependent on personal resources and initiative as political entrepreneurs and middlemen. Their rise and continued existence as 'middlemen middle-class' Malays, who are not really highly educated but who are extremely influential and powerful at the grassroots, rest heavily on 'patronage politics', which now takes the form of 'money politics' within UMNO (Gomez 1990). They seemed to be UMNO's main source of support and strength and, at the same time, its weakness, because they can literally be bought and sold. This is evident in the period since the advent of the NEP, when UMNO has struggled and staggered from one leadership crisis to another and, indeed, was 'brought back from the dead' after being deregistered in 1988 (Shamsul 1988).

Although the majority in the new middle class were once *kampung*, or village, kids, now they are based in urban areas where most of them are employed. That they are what they are and where they are now is directly related to the implementation of the NEP's second objective of 'restructuring society', particularly in the field of education. Since the advent of the NEP, the government has created a number of special education-related programmes, which I call 'express lane programmess' – fully funded by the government – to increase the number of qualified Malays rapidly, not only in the field of science and technology but also in non-science fields (Siti Zaharah Sulaiman 1975). Within a period of ten years (1976–85), thousands of graduates from these special programmes flooded the Malaysian job market, some having graduated from local tertiary institutions, and others from institutions in the USA, Australia and the UK. Since 1988, after overcoming early unemployment woes, the government has managed to create employment for these 'NEP graduates'.

Most of them have been employed as 'managers of material resources' – primarily a private sector concern – such as in banks, insurance companies, other financial institutions, real-estate and business management organisations. Many of these institutions and organisations were set up, and partly funded, by the government to cater for Malay economic and corporate interests through privatisation programmes and the like. Other 'NEP graduates' ended up as 'managers of human resources', both in the private and public sector, mainly in management activities relating to education, material and non-material assistance, 'internal security' and legal sanctions, propaganda programmes and 'care programmes' (health, welfare, corrections and the like), most of which are government- initiated and -funded.

It is interesting to note that it is among this new middle class that the influence of Islamic resurgence, or *dakwah*, is felt most (Shamsul 1995b, 1997b, 1998). In fact, the *dakwah* movement in Malaysia was initiated in 1969 by members of this new middle class, some of whom are running the country at present (for example, cabinet ministers, senior bureaucrats, corporate figures, and academic bureaucrats). It began at the campus of the University of Malaya (then Malaysia's only university) soon after the ethnic riot of 1969. It then spread to the newer Malaysian universities established in the early 1970s. By the 1980s, many Malaysian students, who have been sponsored by the government in the special educational 'express lane programmes' have gone to study abroad. There they have joined many different types of overseas-based *dakwah* groups (for example, Iranian or Pakistani), and later returned to Malaysia to join the 'management team', both in the private and public sector.

There are at least two major *dakwah* factions – the 'moderate' (modernist) and 'radical' (fundamentalist) – and one non-*dakwah* faction – the 'ordinary Muslim' – represented within the new middle class in Malaysia. Most of the moderates found employment in the private and public sector. They are also firmly placed within the ruling party, UMNO, and have succeeded in 'mainstreaming' Islam into the everyday activities of Malaysia's multi-ethnic-oriented economy and society. For example, Muslims and non-Muslims now participate in Islamic banks and insurance. This contrasts with the past when Islam was dominant only among the Malays, especially in the symbolic political sphere which only indirectly affected non-Muslims. The radicals are fragmented and generally peripheralised. Some have joined groups which are openly disfavoured by the government.

The members of the non-*dakwah* faction within the Malay new middle class, who are neither homogeneous nor united, are simply called 'secular Malays' by the *dakwah* members, a label which has either been ignored by or carries no meaning for those who have been branded so. In fact, many of them prefer to be referred to as simply 'ordinary Muslims'. They view the *dakwah* Muslims, especially the moderates, whom they perceive as their main competitors, as a self-righteous lot peddling religiosity and spiritualism for political and materialist gain. Nonetheless, numerically, the so-called 'secular' Malays, though fragmented and disorganised, still form a big and influential group within the new middle class whose political clout is most felt during UMNO party elections.

The '*dakwah-isation*' of the Malay new middle class has highlighted the 'neo-liberalist' tendencies within it, particularly its internal contradictions. On the one hand, it is highly in favour of the continued expansion of the market and promotion of aggressive individualism, thus making it hostile to tradition. On the other hand, its political survival depends upon the manipulation and persistence of tradition for its legitimacy, hence its attachment to conservatism, notably in areas concerning the nation, religion, gender and the family. Having no proper theoretical rationale, its defence of tradition in these areas normally takes the form of fundamentalism of sorts. Therefore, it is not difficult to understand why many observers quickly label the *Melayu Baru*, who belong to the middle class, a confused or schizophrenic lot.

Since the mid-1970s the rise of the new Malay middle class has also created a series of leadership crises within UMNO, the main partner in the ruling party coalition in Malaysia (Shamsul 1988). Initially, this was the result of conflict between the 'old' leadership, surviving on support from rural Malay peasants and petty local officials, and the 'new' leadership, consisting of bureaucrats and technocrats who were the architects of the NEP, and who had plenty of development projects to buy political support. In the early 1980s, the conflict was between the rentier entrepreneurs and the corporate entrepreneurs within the new Malay middle class. In the late 1980s and early 1990s it was dominated by the contest between the rich corporate Malay entrepreneurs, namely, the 'royalty', and the 'non-royalty' (Khoo Boo Teik 1995).

CONCLUSION: THE *MELAYU BARU* CULTURAL PREDICAMENT IN MALAYSIA'S POST-TRADITIONAL SOCIAL ORDER

In conclusion, one could advance the argument that the NEP, as an economic agenda of the Malay nationalist movement of the 1920s, has not only gone a long way to achieving its ultimate aim of repossessing the country's wealth from foreigners through the creation of a community of *Orang Kaya Baru* and, subsequently, *Melayu Baru* decades later, but has also established a community which has complex internal divisions fractured by a host of economic, political and cultural factors. In turn, this has unleashed a variety of consequences, both short-term and long-term, which created what I call the 'new' Malay dilemma and the dilemma for the 'new Malay', that is the 'new' Malay new rich.

The major predicament facing the contemporary Malay community, to my mind, is the result of the reconstitution of the concept of Malayness itself, so that its meaning is now quite different to that which informed the Malay nationalist political agenda, in particular its notion of a Malay nation. In fact, the reconstitution of Malayness in the next century may be more suited to the creation of a 'united Malaysian nation'. I now briefly examine this 'new Malay' cultural predicament.

When the Malay nationalist movement first initiated its political and economic agendas, it was during the Great Depression and in the colonial era. The priority was quite clear then: politics first and economics second. This was eventually translated into action in the form of the creation of a 'Malay nation' first, and then the creation of an economy with Malays playing an active role along with other ethnic groups, particularly the Chinese. The political agenda became a reality when Malaysia became independent in 1957; but not the economic agenda, not until thirty-five years later, and even then it did not result in the control of the economy by the Malays. Nonetheless, the Malay economic presence had become strongly felt and widely recognised, especially after the NEP was implemented. The expansion of the Malay middle class was definitely rapid, but the expansion of the Malay new rich was even faster and more extensive, if not phenomenal. However, it did not arise without a 'cultural cost'.

The recent success of the Malay nationalist economic agenda has rendered the original political agenda, especially the 'three pillars of Malayness', open to public discussion and interrogation, especially by the OKBs. This has been interpreted by some observers as a sign of the growth of Malay 'social reflexivity' among the highly educated Malay middle class. This has resulted in a dislocation between knowledge (about nationalist discourse, ideals and history) and control (via implementation, governance, state intervention, planning and social engineering). Both knowledge and control, when combined previously, formed the 'authoritatively defined social reality' for Malays. This could be observed and interpreted only as Malayness or as the Malay nation. Now that the authoritatively defined social reality is being questioned and doubts are raised about it by the Malay new middle class and other groups within the Malay new rich, particularly at the individual level, what was once accepted as 'constructed certainty' (for example, Malayness) has now transformed into a kind of 'manufactured uncertainty' (whither the three pillars of Malayness). This is exactly what the cultural predicament of the Malay new rich is all about – Who is the new Malay? Are we Malay first or *bumiputera* second, or the other way around? When do we become Malaysian?

This tension characterises a post-traditional social order in Malaysia, in which the collaboration between modernity and tradition, crucial to the earlier phases of post-war and post-colonial social development, has been redefined and moved into another phase. As a result, tradition, as a medium for the reality of the past, does not disappear but only changes its status into a form that is open to discourse and interrogation rather than accepted blindly as it once tended to be. Thus, 'Malayness' and 'Malay tradition', as authoritatively defined social realities, are now being questioned, debated and refuted by some extremely influential, wealthy Malay corporate figures, and by others from within the equally well-off Malay new middle class. This critical stance reflects the way in which these 'new rich' experience everyday social reality, in particular the process of globalisation, and the transformation of the individual actor's personal contexts of social experience. The latter often stands in opposition to the former because it encourages 'false autonomy'. It accentuates, for instance, local ethnic identities (*Malayism, Ibanism* or *Kadazanism* within *bumiputeraism*) while the former promotes the creation of unified large-scale systems, such as satellite communications.

The introduction of the term *Melayu Baru* by the Malaysian prime minister, Dr Mahathir Mohamed, in 1991 (Mahathir 1991), and its populist use since then have demonstrated that globalisation is not a single process but a complex mixture of processes, which often act in contradictory ways, producing conflicts, conjectures and new forms of stratification, involving for instance the emergence of the new rich. The 'new Malay', declared Dr Mahathir, is a community of completely rehabilitated Malays who have gone through a mental revolution and cultural transformation, thus leaving behind feudalistic and fatalistic values. They are a people, he declared, who now possess a culture suited to the modern period, who are capable of meeting all challenges, able to compete without assistance, learned and knowledgeable, sophisticated, honest, disciplined, trustworthy and competent. Mahathir further argued that although the 'new Malay' originated from families of peasants and fishermen, they have now become heads of departments, scientists, actuaries, nuclear physicists, surgeons, experts in the fields of medicine and aviation, bankers and corporate leaders. According to him, some of these Malays have become managers of major conglomerates with world-wide assets worth billions of *ringgit*. They are equipped to participate in mergers and acquisitions which are complex and sophisticated, not only in Malaysia and Southeast Asia, but also globally.

These are the Malay entrepreneurs and the non-government Malay professionals who broadly make up the 'Malay commercial and industrial community', or the Malay new rich. They were invented through the 'social engineering' of the state, informed by the so-called logic of securing inter-ethnic parity. This is the group that Mahathir feels will carry the 'Malay flag', as it were, into the next century, competent, skilled and able to compete with the best in Malaysia and the world. This is the 'new Malay' proclaimed by Mahathir (Cheong Mei Sui and Adibah Amin 1995).

The cultural predicament of the Malay new rich has been materially motivated, as is evident when they questioned the 'excesses of the Malay royalty', an accusation that was initiated by Mahathir himself in the so-called constitutional crises of 1983 and 1993. Mahathir was essentially voicing the interests of the 'new Malay', in interrogating one of the pillars of Malayness which informed the Malay nationalist vision of the Malay nation. When Mahathir suggested that English should be reintroduced as a medium of instruction at the tertiary level, he was also articulating the so-called global interest of the Malay new rich and new middle class, who are vigorously expanding their interests outside Malaysia, and who perceive that this could be done only through the use of English. Such a suggestion, as some Malay nationalists saw it, puts in doubt the future of the Malay language as the sole medium of instruction in national and government-funded institutions. This suggestion directly questions, yet again, one of the pillars of Malayness. Similarly, when Mahathir and his cabinet endorsed the amendment of the Education Act in 1996, allowing foreign tertiary institutions to set up their branches in Malaysia and conduct their courses in English, it was perceived by some Malays as compromising the position of the Malay language as a central pillar of Malayness.

Finally, one could argue that the challenge that the Malay new rich have to confront, both at present and in the future, is not simply 'materialist' or 'political-economic' in nature. If observed from Granovetter's perspective (1985), the Malay political economy is deeply embedded in, and symbiotically linked with, Malay 'cultural politics', both at the popular and non-popular levels. The significance of the latter is often understated because studies of Malay politics have always been too institutionally oriented and insufficiently concerned with the practices of conflict, co-operation and negotiation involved in the use, production and distribution of resources among Malays and between Malays and other social groups. If we do not take into serious consideration the cultural construction aspect of the Malay new rich, we are indeed, at best, offering only half of a story.

Note

My thanks, first, to Universiti Kebangsaan Malaysia for its invaluable support in allowing me to complete my research on 'Identity formation in Malaysia'; secondly, to Michael Pinches who has been responsible for making my contribution readable; finally, to Wendy Smith for her generous moral support.

Bibliography

Abdul Kahar Bador (1967) 'Traditional and Modern Leadership in Malay Society', PhD thesis, London School of Economics.
—— (1970) *Political Authority and Leadership in Malay Society in Perak, Malaysia*, VRF Series no. 5, Tokyo: Institute of Developing Economies.
—— (1973) 'Social Rank, Status-Honour and Social Class Consciousness amongst the Malays', in Hans-Dieter Evers (ed.), *Modernization in Southeast Asia*, Singapore and Kuala Lumpur: Oxford University Press.
Alatas, S. H. (1967) 'The Grading of Occupational Prestige amongst the Malays in Malaysia', a paper for the International Conference on Comparative Social Research, New Delhi, India, 21–3 April 1967.
Ariffin Omar (1993) *Bangsa Melayu: Malay Concept of Democracy and Community 1945–1950*, Kuala Lumpur: Oxford University Press.
Brennan, Martin (1982) 'Class, Race and Politics in Modern Malaya', *Journal of Contemporary Asia*, 12 (2); 188–215.
Chandra Muzaffar (1984) 'Has the Communal Situation Worsened over the Last Decade? Some Preliminary Thoughts', in S. Husin Ali (ed.), *Ethnicity, Class and Development in Malaysia*, Kuala Lumpur: Malaysian Social Science Association.
—— (1987) *Islamic Resurgence in Malaysia*, Petaling Jaya: Fajar Bakti.

Cheong Mei Sui and Adibah Amin (1995) *Daim: The Man Behind the Enigma*, Petaling Jaya: Pelanduk.

Faarland, Just, Parkinson, J. R. and Saniman, Rais (1990) *Growth and Ethnic Inequality: Malaysia's New Economic Policy*, Kuala Lumpur: Dewan Bahasa & Pustaka.

Gomez, Edmund Terence (1990) *Politics in Business: UMNO's Corporate Investments*, Kuala Lumpur: Forum.

—— (1991) *Money Politics in the Barisan Nasional*, Kuala Lumpur: Forum.

—— (1994) *Political Business: Corporate Involvement of Malaysian Political Parties*, Townsville, Australia: Centre for South-East Asian Studies, James Cook University.

Granovetter, Mark (1985) 'Economic Action and Social Structure: The Problem of Embeddedness', *American Journal of Sociology*, no. 9: 481–510.

Hirschman, Charles (1986) 'The Making of Race in Colonial Malaya: Political Economy and Racial Ideology', *Sociological Forum*, Spring: 330–61.

Husin Ali, S. (1964) *Social Stratification in Kampung Bagan: A Study of Class, Status, Conflict and Mobility in a Rural Malay Community*, Singapore: The Malaysian Branch of the Royal Asiatic Society.

—— (1975) *Malay Peasant Society and Leadership*, Kuala Lumpur: Oxford University Press.

—— (1984) 'Social Relations: The Ethnic and Class Factors', in S. Husin Ali (ed.), *Ethnicity, Class and Development in Malaysia*, Kuala Lumpur: Malaysian Social Science Association.

Idrus, F. K. (1981) 'Leisure Interests of Young People in Malaysia: A Cross-cultural Study', PhD thesis, University of Aberdeen, UK.

Jesudason, James (1989) *Ethnicity and the Economy: The State, Chinese Business and Multinationals in Malaysia*, Kuala Lumpur: Oxford University Press.

Jomo, K. S. (1986) *A Question of Class: Capital, the State and Uneven Development in Malaysia*, Kuala Lumpur: Oxford University Press.

Kahn, Joel (1988–9) 'Constructing Malaysian Ethnicity: A View From Australia', *Ilmu Masyarakat*, no. 14, January 1988–June 1989: 6–8.

—— (1991) 'Constructing Culture: Towards an Anthropology of the Middle Classes in Southeast Asia', *Asian Studies Review*, 15 (2): 50–6.

—— (1992a) 'Class, Ethnicity and Diversity: Some Remarks on Malay Culture in Malaysia', in Joel Kahn and Francis Loh (eds), *Fragmented Vision: Culture and Politics in Contemporary Malaysia*, Sydney: Allen & Unwin.

—— (1992b) 'Constructing Ethnicity in Contemporary Malaysia', in Joel Kahn and Francis Loh (eds), *Fragmented Vision: Culture and Politics in Contemporary Malaysia*, Sydney: Allen & Unwin.

—— (1994) 'Subalternity and the Construction of Malay Identity', in Alberto Gomes (ed.), *Modernity and Identity: Asian Illustrations*, Bundoora, Victoria, Australia: La Trobe University Press.

—— (1995) *Culture, Multiculture, Postculture*, London: Sage.

—— (1996) 'Growth, Economic Transformation, Culture and the Middle Classes in Malaysia', in Richard Robison and David S. G. Goodman (eds), *The New Rich in Asia*, London and New York: Routledge.

Kessler, Clive (1992) 'Archaism and Modernity: Contemporary Malay Political Culture', in Joel Kahn and Francis Loh (eds), *Fragmented Vision*, Sydney: Allen & Unwin.

Khasnor, Johan (1984) *The Emergence of the Modern Malay Elite*, Kuala Lumpur: Oxford University Press.

Khoo Boo Teik (1995) *Paradoxes of Mahathirism: An Intellectual Biography of Mahathir Mohamed*, Kuala Lumpur: Oxford University Press.

Kua Kia Soong (1981) 'Class Formation and Communalism in Malaysia', PhD thesis, University of Manchester, UK.

Lee, Edwin (1976) *The Towkays of Sabah*, Singapore: Singapore University Press.

Lee, K. H. (1980) 'Education, Earnings and Occupational Status in Malaysia', PhD thesis, London School of Economics.

Lee, Oon Hean (1994) 'Fenomena Kelas Menengah: Suatu Analisis Teoretikal dan Sosiologikal di Malaysia serta Implikasinya', Academic Exercise, Department of Anthropology and Sociology, Universiti Kebangsaan Malaysia.

Lim Mah Hui (1980) 'Ethnic and Class Relations in Malaysia', *Journal of Contemporary Asia*, 10 (1–2): 130–54.

—— (1985) 'Contradictions in the Development of Malay Capital: State, Accumulation and Legitimation', *Journal of Contemporary Asia*, 15 (1): 37–61.

MacAndrews, Colin (1977) *Mobility and Modernisation: The Federal Land Development Authority and its Role in Modernising the Rural Malays*, Jogjakarta: Gadjah Mada University Press.

Mahathir, Mohamed (1970) *The Malay Dilemma*, Singapore: Donald Moore.

—— (1991) 'Malaysia: The Way Forward', paper for the inaugural meeting of the Malaysian Business Council, 28 January.

—— (1995) *The Early Years 1947–1972: Compilation of Writing by Mahathir Mohamed*, Kuala Lumpur: Berita Publishing.

Milner, Anthony (1982) *Kerajaan: Malay Political Culture at the Eve of Colonial Rule*, Tucson, Arizona: University of Arizona Press.

—— (1994) *The Invention of Politics in Colonial Malaya*, Melbourne: Cambridge University Press.

Mohd. Fauzi Hj. Yaacob (1981) *Peniaga dan Perniagaan Melayu: Satu Kajian di Kota Baharu Kelantan*, Kuala Lumpur: Dewan Bahasa dan Pustaka.

Mohd. Nor Nawawi (1985) 'The New Economic Policy and the Malay Middle Class in Malaysia', PhD thesis, University of Bristol, UK.

—— (1991) 'Dasar Ekonomi Baru, Perpaduan Nasional dan Kelas Menengah', in Khadijah Muhamed and Halimah Awang (eds), *Dasar Ekonomi Baru dan Masa Depannya*, Kuala Lumpur: Persatuan Sains Sosial Malaysia.

Mokhzani, B. A. R. (1965) 'The Study of Social Stratification and Social Mobility in Malaya', *East Asian Cultural Studies*, no. 4: 138–62.

Nagata, Judith (1979) *Malaysian Mosaic*, Vancouver: University of British Columbia Press.

Nordin Selat (1976) *Kelas Menengah Pentadbir Melayu*, Kuala Lumpur: Utusan Publications.

Ong, Aihwa (1995) 'State versus Islam: Malay Families, Women's Bodies, and the Body Politic in Malaysia', in Aihwa Ong and Michael Peletz (eds), *Bewitching Women, Pious Men: Gender and Body Politics in Southeast Asia*, Berkeley: University of California Press.

Papenoe, O. (1970) 'Malay Entreprenuers: An Analysis of the Social Background, Careers and Attitudes of the Leading Malay Businessmen in Western Malaysia', PhD thesis, London School of Economics.

Peletz, Michael (1993) 'Sacred Texts and Dangerous Words: The Politics of Law and Cultural Rationalisation in Malaysia', *Comparative Studies in Societies and Histories*, 35 (1): 66–109.

Robison, Richard and Goodman, David (1996) 'The New Rich in Asia: Economic Development, Social Status and Political Consciousness', in R. Robison and D. Goodman (eds), *The New Rich in Asia: Mobile-Phones, McDonald's and Middle-Class Revolution*, London: Routledge.

Roff, William (1967) *The Origins of Malay Nationalism*, Kuala Lumpur: University of Malaya Press.

Rudner, Martin (1994) *Malaysian Development: A Retrospective*, Ottawa: Carlton University Press.

Rustam A. Sani (1993) *Melayu Baru dan Bangsa Malaysia: Tradisi Cendekia dan Krisis Budaya*, Kuala Lumpur: Utusan Publications.

Saravanamuttu, Johan (1989) 'Kelas Menengah dalam Politik Malaysia: Tonjolan Perkauman atau Kepentingan Kelas', *Kajian Malaysia*, 7 (1–2): 106–26.

—— and Maznah Mohamad (1989) 'Correspondence: Deconstructing a Construction of Malay Ethnicity from Australia: A View from Malaysia', *Ilmu Masyarakat*, 15, July–September: 92–3.

Scott, James (1978) *Political Ideology in Malaysia*, New Haven: Yale University Press.

—— (1985) *Weapons of the Weak: Everyday Forms of Peasant Resistance*, New Haven: Yale University Press.

Shaharuddin Maaruf (1988) *Malay Ideas on Development: From Feudal Lord to Capitalist*, Singapore: Times Books International.

Shamsul, A. B. (1977) *Rancangan Malaysia Kedua, Tujuan dan Pelaksanaannya*, Kuala Lumpur: Dewan Bahasa dan Pustaka.

—— (1986) *From British to Bumiputera Rule: Local Politics and Rural Development in Peninsular Malaysia*, Singapore: Institute of Southeast Asian Studies.

—— (1988) 'The Battle Royal: The UMNO Elections of 1987', in Mohammed Ayoob and Ng Chee Yuen (eds), *Southeast Asian Affairs 1988*, Singapore: Institute of Southeast Asian Studies.

—— (1995a) 'From Melayu to Bumiputera: Bureaucratic Management of Identity in Malaysia', unpublished paper presented at the Joint Seminar, National Museum of Ethnology, Osaka, Japan, 19 July.

—— (1995b) 'Invented Certainties: The Dakwah Persona in Malaysia', in Wendy James (ed.), *Pursuit of Certainty*, ASA Monograph, London: Routledge.

—— (1996) 'Malaysia's Nation-of-Intent', in Stein Tønnesson and Hans Antlöv (eds), *Asian Forms of the Nation*, London: Curzon.

—— (1997a) 'Economic Dimension of Malay Nationalism: The Socio-Historical Roots of the New Economic Policy and its Contemporary Implications', *Developing Economies*, 35 (3): 240–61.

—— (1997b) 'Identity Construction, Nation Formation, and Islamic Revivalism in Malaysia', in Robert Hefner and Patricia Horvatich (eds), *Islam in the Era of Nation-States: Politics and Religious Renewal in Muslim Southeast Asia*, Honolulu: University of Hawaii Press.

—— (1998) 'A Question of Identity: A Case Study of Malaysian Islamic Revivalism and the Non-Muslim Response', in Tsuneo Ayabe (ed.), *Nation-State, Identity and Religion in Southeast Asia*, Singapore: Singapore Society of Asian Studies.

Shang, A. E. L. (1976) 'Political Development and Class Formation in an Ethnically Divided Country: A Case Study of Peninsular Malaysia', MA thesis, University of Sussex, UK.

Siti Zahara Sulaiman (1975) 'Mara Junior Science College: Student Selection and its Implication for Educational Development in Malaya', PhD dissertation, Cornell University, USA.

Stivens, Maila (1994) 'Gender and Modernity in Malaysia', in Alberto Gomes (ed.), *Modernity and Identity: Asian Illustrations*, Bundoora, Victoria, Australia: La Trobe University Press.

—— (1995a) 'The Gendering of the New Malay Middle Class', a working paper presented at the conference on 'Sex and Power in Affluent Asia', 13 February 1995, Murdoch University, Australia.

—— (1995b) 'The New Malay? Who is She? Gender, Class and Nation in Middle-Class Malaysia', a paper for the Inaugural Conference of European Association of Southeast Asian Studies, 1–3 July, Amsterdam.

—— (1996) *Modernity and Matriliny: Sexual Politics and Social Change in Rural Malaysia*, Sydney: Allen & Unwin.

——, Ng, C. and Jomo, K. S. (1994) *Malay Peasant Women and Land*, London: Zed.

Strauch, Judith (1981) *Chinese Village Politics in the Malaysian State*, Cambridge, MA: Harvard University Press.

Sweeney, Amin (1987) *A Full Hearing: Orality and Literacy in the Malay World*, Berkeley: University of California Press.

Swift, Michael (1965) *Malay Peasant Society in Jelebu*, London: Athlone.

Tan Leok Ee (1988) *The Rhetoric of Bangsa and Minzu: Community and Nation in Tension on the Malayan Peninsula, 1945–1957*, working paper no. 52, Melbourne: Centre of Southeast Asian Studies, Monash University.

Tanaka, Stefan (1993) *Japan's Orient: Rendering Pasts into History*, Berkeley: University of California Press.

Tham Seong Chee (1973a) 'Child Rearing in the Malay Business Family', *Journal of Southern Seas Society*, 28 (1–2): 12–23.

—— (1973b) 'Ideology, Politics and Economic Modernization: The Case of the Malays in Malaysia', *Southeast Asian Journal of Social Science*, 1 (1): 41–59.

—— (1977) *Malays and Modernization*, Singapore: Singapore University Press.

Ting Chew Peh (1987) *Hubungan Ras dan Etnik: Suatu Pengantar*, Kuala Lumpur: Pustaka Dimensi.

Ungku A. Aziz (1951) *Some Aspects of the Malayan Rural Economy Related to Measures for Mobilising Rural Savings*, Bangkok: ECAFE, paper E/CN. II/I.

—— (1975) 'Footprints on the Sands of Time: The Malay Poverty Concept over 50 years, from Za'ba to Aziz and the Second Malaysia Plan', in Stephen Chee and Khoo Siew Mun (eds), *Malaysian Economic Development and Policies*, Kuala Lumpur: Malaysian Economic Association.

Van der Kroef, J. (1956) 'Entreprenuer and the Middle Class', in J. Van der Kroef, *Indonesia in the Modern World*, Bandung: Masa Baru.

Wazir Karim (1990) *Women and Culture: Between Malay Adat and Islam*, Boulder, CO: Westview.

Zainah Anwar (1987) *Islamic Revivalism in Malaysia: Dakwah among the Students*, Petaling Jaya: Pelanduk.

Zawawi Ibrahim (1978) 'A Malay Proletariat: The Emergence of Class Relations on a Malay Plantation', PhD thesis, Monash University, Australia.

4 The contribution of a Japanese firm to the cultural construction of the new rich in Malaysia

Wendy A. Smith

INTRODUCTION

Over the two decades before the currency crisis of late 1997, Malaysia experienced rapid industrialisation and increased prosperity. This was achieved through the implementation of the New Economic Policy (NEP) of 1971–90, and particularly through Prime Minister Mahathir's successful repositioning of the economy from an agricultural to a manufacturing orientation, relying on high levels of foreign investment, especially from Japan. These factors were effectively combined under Mahathir's Look East Policy (LEP) of 1981, which gave even more emphasis to the importance of Japan in Malaysia's economic development, and enhanced the NEP in its decisive role in shaping the social and cultural character of Malaysia's new rich. Principally through its 'social engineering' strategy favouring the Malays *(bumiputera)*, the NEP fostered the creation of a large new middle class and waged working class, both of whom constitute Malaysia's 'new rich'.[1] In part, this process centred on high levels of Japanese investment which created many positions for professional managers, technicians and process workers in the new factories. The transplant of Japanese work ethics and systems of management, with associated training and exchange programmes, also influenced people's mentalities and life strategies. Finally, the predominance of Japanese consumer goods had great impact in the sphere of consumption and lifestyles (Smith 1994b).

In this chapter I will focus on the cultural construction of new rich Malays. In Malaysia's multi-ethnic society – comprising the indigenous Malay majority and ethnic Chinese and Indians of immigrant ancestry – industrialisation has had its greatest effect on the Malay population, particularly on those of peasant origin. They have experienced substantial increases in income; especially those who entered the growing urban middle class or the urban proletariat through opportunities generated by the NEP. While the Malay new rich share an increasing preoccupation with the status attributes and lifestyles of global consumerism, other important factors particular to the Malays, such as fundamentalist Islam, also contribute to their social identity and consciousness.

The expansion of the Malay new middle class was aided by the active support and participation of existing members of the Chinese and Indian middle class.[2]

In Malaysia, the way in which people construct their individual identities varies depending on their social class. For instance, working-class Malaysians emphasise their ethnic identity over class solidarity, because there is more to be gained as individuals in activating the networks of patronage based on vertical ties between members of the same ethnic group (Smith 1994a: 179). On the other hand, the middle class and the really wealthy of all ethnic groups come together in residential areas, hotels, clubs and resorts. Their lifestyles demonstrate a preference for class over ethnic values.[3] The weakening of ethnicity as the dominant factor in the self-identity of middle-class individuals is exemplified by the fact that it became a fashion in the 1980s for urban new-rich Malay families to decorate their homes with Chinese rosewood/pearl-inlay furniture and wall panels. In other contexts there may be a degree of antipathy between the Malays and the Chinese, but here the furniture is installed because it looks 'expensive' and this is more important than the fact that it looks 'Chinese'.

Spending power clearly differentiates the middle class from the proletariat, and this is reflected in the fact that the former usually purchase new cars while the latter, at best, can afford only old reconditioned cars, shipped from Japan.[4] Housing size and quality are other key areas of difference.[5] However, because of their urban lifestyles and ability to purchase consumer goods, the proletariat may also be classified as 'new rich' *vis-à-vis* unwaged villagers. Villagers who are without regular cash incomes rely on remittances from relatives who are factory workers to buy consumer items. Conversely, factory workers rely on these villagers for childcare and the organisation of weddings and funerals 'at home' in the village (*kampung*), outside a commercial context.

The major argument underlining the analysis of this chapter is that the cultural constructions of a large proportion of Malaysia's new middle class and proletariat must be understood not only at the macro level, by focusing on historical relations between state and capital, and the politics of ethnicity, but also on the micro level of management systems and work relationships in modern organisations such as large foreign firms. It is this environment which structures the careers, income levels and hence consumption patterns of the new middle class and those below who aspire to their standards of living.

The company chosen for the analytical purpose of this chapter is a Japanese joint venture in the food manufacturing industry, established in Kuala Lumpur in the early 1960s. It is called Iroha (M).[6] I conducted a longitudinal study of this company using the firm's records from 1964 until 1997, as well as data gathered by the anthropological method of participant observation (1976–97). Being a longitudinal study, it encompasses the NEP era and, more significantly, the LEP era, during which the government used Japanese work ethics and management styles as the primary model for Malaysian industrial development. Because these have been used as key elements of a state philosophy in the second half of the NEP era, Japanese investment in Malaysia takes place in a highly politicised context.

The chapter is divided into three sections. It begins with a brief survey of Malaysia's industrialisation process and, in particular, Japan's contribution through direct investment and the LEP. Section two presents an ethnography of the cultural construction of the new rich in the context of the Japanese firm Iroha (M). Here, I begin with a brief description of the firm, and then examine how the internal dynamics within the firm's management system, combined with external factors, influence the recruitment process of local managers and shape their subsequent career development as executive officers resulting in their entry into the middle class. Several brief biographical case studies of these managers are presented to illustrate their class origin and the cultural construction of their social life as new-rich members of post-NEP Malaysian society. Section three reflects on the need to understand the intricate linkages between the economy and cultural practice from macro to micro levels of focus.

MALAYSIA'S INDUSTRIALISATION

State, culture and class

Compared with other plural societies, Malaysia shows an unusually balanced ethnic structure made up of two dominant groups: the indigenous groups, or *bumiputera* (Malays and others), who make up about 62 per cent of the population, and the immigrant groups (Chinese and Indians) who make up the rest. Malaysian society as a whole is characterised by highly diversified cultural practices in terms of language and religious beliefs which provide the sanctions for diet, dress and other behavioural codes, creating a challenging situation for social interaction between Malaysians, both in the workplace and in the community at large. For example, while eating together is a fundamental way of developing social cohesion, there are many contexts where religious taboos prevent Malaysians of different ethnic origins from eating and drinking together.[7]

The correlation between ethnic identity, on the one hand, and economic function, educational performance, political dominance and cultural practices, on the other, has become a matter of concern for both the state and the people: it continuously dominates everyday discourse, as well as grassroots and formal political processes. Indeed, it shapes social interaction at all levels of the society. The situation can be characterised as one of stable tension (Shamsul 1994), although the ethnic riots that occurred in May 1969 demonstrated the fact that the ethnicisation of the economy and popular political discourse can result in open bloody conflict.

The state justified the launch of the NEP of 1971–90 as the solution to some of the problems related to this incident. The policy clearly favoured Malays and other indigenous groups, and aimed to redress their grievances by promoting economic growth to eradicate poverty and to restructure society away from the perceived correlation of economic function with ethnic identity. In substance, the pro-Malay affirmative action approach of the NEP aimed to create entrepreneurial opportunities which would place 30 per cent of national equity in Malay hands by 1990.[8] This was to be achieved by economic growth rather than the redistribution of existing shares, although there was redistribution at the expense of foreign, mainly Western, investors. This policy further increased Malaysia's reliance on foreign investment, largely from Japan, to provide partners, capital and technical know-how, for fledgeling Malay capitalists. It is in this context that industrialisation has special significance in Malaysia, particularly after the NEP, because of its stimulus towards social as well as economic change. In the economic sense it promised economic growth and more waged occupations for the population. In the social sense it promised raised living standards and symbols of modernity, but these are only to be achieved within the social matrix of highly politicised ethnic diversity.

Despite the fact that a large Malay working class has been generated by the NEP, the union movement has been emasculated in the process (Smith 1996: 45). Moreover, a significant byproduct of the NEP era has been the transformation of the class consciousness of the workers into a preoccupation with ethnic rivalries and consumer ideals.

Although Malay participation in the national economy has increased significantly under the NEP which provided education opportunities, capital loans and other benefits, on a population quota or even discriminatory basis in favour of the Malays, poorer Malays benefited least. Indeed, the NEP hastened the development of the middle class of all ethnic groups, as Chinese businessmen acted as silent partners of new, inexperienced Malay entrepreneurs. More important for this chapter is the fact that NEP-led industrialisation generated a class of managers and other professionals in occupations involving the 'mental production' process.[9]

Despite rapid growth of the middle class and its more or less common lifestyle, foreign companies employing these new Malaysian professional managers cannot avoid the pervasive ideology of ethnic division. Under the Industrial Coordination Act (ICA) of 1974, ethnic percentages which mirror national population ratios must be represented at all levels of the organisation. Until the mid-1980s there were not enough Malays with the necessary tertiary qualifications to fill managerial positions in many new large corporations. To fulfil the conditions of the ICA, companies were forced to recruit large numbers of Malay graduates and promote them to positions of responsibility before they were sufficiently experienced. This led to accusations of ethnic favouritism in promotions, and also to a stereotype that the Malays were incompetent. Foreign managers also encountered ethnic tensions on the shop floor, though some learned to use these to the company's advantage (Smith 1994a: 170).

At all levels of Malaysian society, consumerism is a powerful force, sometimes mitigating the forces of ethnic traditionalism, sometimes strengthening them. The material gains of the new middle class – urban housing, ownership of Proton Saga motor cars, the ability to shop in large shopping malls, many of them designed around a Japanese department store – are clearly visible to factory workers. Although they do not have the income levels to replicate the lifestyles of the middle class, they aspire to them and, in their limited way, emulate them (Hing 1985: 152).[10] Consumerism also redefines the symbolism and representation of particular values. For instance, most Malay workers come from a peasant background where status in the community is primarily demonstrated by the possession of material things. This reinforces the strength of consumerism and the practice of demonstrating one's status in modern society with material symbols.

Despite the Islamic prohibition against young Muslim women leaving the house unaccompanied by male kin, Malay fathers now willingly allow their young unmarried daughters to work night shifts in factories, far from their villages. Village parents ignore such fundamental religious values because they desire the electric fans, TV sets and other consumer goods which make village life more comfortable, and which are purchased with the cash remittances from their daughters (see Stivens 1987: 102).

The growth of consumerism has generated new sources of competitive conflict among the new rich.[11] Often this has intensified the recourse to 'traditional strategies' of conflict management or resolution. These strategies accord with a powerful village-based ethos of interpersonal harmony: openly to express anger is to sever a relationship and the possibility of future cooperation for ever. Yet beneath the surface, bitter rivalries exist over competition for status and wealth. In village society, if you dislike someone, you might anonymously wound their water buffalo, an attack which hurts the individual by damaging his property, without affecting the outward cordiality of social relationships. In more serious cases, individuals attempt to harm or even kill other individuals by black magic.

Thus in factories we observe the expression of conflict in ways that will not be attributable to any one individual, and hence will not damage ongoing relationships or the employer–employee contract. Mass hysteria among young female industrial workers is an example of this (see Ong 1987). Employees in modern companies sometimes also resort to anonymous magical attacks against rivals for promotion or to take revenge against an enemy, in the same way they would in the village.[12] Convergence theory predicts that such behaviour would die out as individuals from traditional societies begin to participate in modern organisations and occupations such as industrial labour, where principles of efficiency and rationality predominate. But the evidence in Malaysia suggests that as the level of benefits increases, traditional practices like those above become even more common.[13]

Japanese management

In formulating the Look East Policy, the Malaysian government sought to transplant an ideal model of Japanese management and work ethics for both ideological and organisational reasons. Some of the values fundamental to this model were already well established in Iroha (M) through fifteen years of factory management by expatriate Japanese managers. An understanding of the nature of the Japanese management system and how it is transferred is necessary in order to understand the career strategies and aspirations of the Malaysian managerial class. Hence it is briefly explained below.

In its barest form the Japanese management paradigm consists of 'Three Pillars': lifetime employment (*shushinkoyo*); a seniority principle in wages and promotions (*nenko joretsu*); and enterprise unionism (*kigyobetsu kumiai*). Lifetime employment refers to the informal compact between the company and its employees that the latter have a job for the whole of their careers and will not be retrenched in the face of a recession until all other measures have been tried by the company. In return for this job security, employees are expected to give loyal and productive service. Companies recruit employees directly from secondary school or university. They recruit them for their general education rather than for any special skills or trade certificates they possess, because the company trains them in its own corporate values and work practices as well as in technical matters relating to the goods or services it produces.

According to the seniority principle in wages and promotions, a significant component of an employee's wage is determined by the length of his or her service in the company. A wage rise gives workers a periodic reassurance that they are being compensated for their loyalty to the company and that they are making progress in their careers. If an employee were to leave and be re-employed in another company, he or she would start again at the bottom of the wage scale. This would entail little sacrifice early in a person's career, but would involve a considerable financial loss if they were to leave later on.

Enterprise unionism is a system whereby membership in the union is purely on the basis of being an employee of that company. Such a union includes all blue- and white-collar regular employees of non-managerial status in the company in all factories or offices around Japan. It also includes employees posted to overseas subsidiaries or joint ventures, even though those employees may have managerial status while they are away from Japan. Workers are thus organised in the first instance into vertical lines of allegiance to their own company rather than on a cross-cutting horizontal class basis. Hence the interests of workers in the enterprise union are directly bound up with the fortunes of the company in the long term. Given workers' individual expectations of lifetime employment, this long-term perspective is reinforced. Since membership in the union is based on the fact of employment only, not in the context of a specific craft, there are no demarcation lines except those drawn by the company for its own functional convenience. There can be no disputes with the union on this score and this allows the company to deploy workers freely around the workplace to perform diverse jobs at management's convenience.[14]

Thus lifetime employment, the seniority system and enterprise unionism are mutually reinforcing aspects of an integrated system. The system was most evident in practice in the boom years of the Japanese economy in the 1970s and 1980s, when it applied only to a quarter of the total Japanese labour force (nearly all of them are males), who were regular employees in the large companies (*daikigyo*). The success of its application was made possible by the existence of a 'buffer zone' of less privileged women and men, who worked as part-time or temporary labourers on lower wages with no training or promotion opportunities and no union representation. Although the system is now collapsing in Japan in the face of a recession, it has been adopted as a model by developing countries eager to emulate the Japanese economic miracle.

MANAGERIAL CAREERS – THE CASE OF IROHA (M)

Iroha (Malaysia) was established in Malaysia in 1961 as the third overseas manufacturing investment of the parent company in the post-war era. One of the earliest Japanese companies to invest in Malaysia in the 1960s, when Japanese investment began, it was set up to produce a highly specialised food item formerly imported into the local market.

Production is highly technical in nature, involving a series of continuous chemical reactions. This requires only a small workforce of unskilled and semi-skilled male workers organised into three shifts to regulate and observe the process. Most workers started with the company at the age of seventeen. In many cases it was their first regular job and they stayed on because of the job security. Hence the workforce aged with Iroha (M), and by the 1990s there were many 'veteran' employees with close to thirty years' service. From 1978 to 1988, the workforce decreased by 20 per cent under a vigorous management rationalisation campaign. Again, according to typical Japanese management policies, workers were not retrenched, but those who resigned were not replaced.

Recruitment of local managers

Although Iroha (M)'s top posts were filled by expatriate Japanese,[15] local managers were present at all three management levels in the organisation. Managers and section chiefs (the equivalent of *Bucho* and *Kacho* in Japan) are considered to be senior management, and unit chiefs (*Kakaricho*) are junior management.

After Iroha (M) was established in 1961, the company advertised for local management staff, emphasising the need for applicants to have a university degree. They tried to recruit unmarried males in the first instance because they wanted to send them to Japan for an extended period of technical training. They also tried to recruit Malays, although before the NEP, Malays with science or engineering degrees were few in number and preferred to seek employment in the public service. Nevertheless, the original batch of managerial recruits, who received an initial six months' training in Japan, comprised four Chinese (all science graduates, one female) and three Malays (with incomplete science degrees, all male). Of these, three resigned from Iroha (M) and four remained for over three decades, until they reached retirement age. There were two other early recruits, a Chinese graduate and an Indian who did not complete his undergraduate engineering course. These six (four Chinese, one Malay, one Indian) constitute the present local senior management group, both in the sense of their long service and because they occupy senior positions, including those of production manager, engineering manager, personnel manager and sales manager. Their experiences demonstrate the transfer of the principle of seniority in management policies of Japanese ventures overseas and also the lack of emphasis placed on formal educational status.

In the 1970s, the managerial levels were top-heavy with Chinese. This can be attributed to a number of factors. There were few Malay science graduates, especially those willing to work in the private sector. If Malays could not attain the status and security of a job in the public service, then money was their priority.[16] Income levels are critical for urban Malays, not only for private status and personal consumption, but also because of obligations to support various kin, through gifts of money, or board, food and educational allowances to children from home villages also seeking a prosperous future in the city. When one member of the extended kin group attains middle-class status, he or she is used as a springboard to help other relatives do the same. Pressure is put on such individuals to maintain their high level of income in order to help the whole family advance economically and socially. Hence, job hopping for higher pay was common among Malays who did enter the private sector.

For Malays in the 1970s, the need for money was linked with the need for that money to come from a secure, high-status occupation. The status of one's job accrued to all the relatives in the village as well, and this was always a consideration for the individual Malay manager who may have become the first member of his or her family to gain a tertiary qualification. Having a sideline business to earn money like the Chinese would not satisfy job frustrations. Nor did the Malays have an established socio-cultural milieu in which to do this until the latter half of the NEP era when the preferential loans granted to Malays under the NEP, and the entrepreneurial ethos it promoted, created many new Malay entrepreneurs as well as first-generation professionals.

The growing number of large firms needing professional managers in the NEP era gave educated Malays new opportunities beyond the comparatively low-status, low-paid occupations formerly available to them in the immediate post-colonial era as clerks or members of the police or armed forces, and so on. Because of the need for large companies to employ a significant percentage of Malays at higher managerial levels, Malays also had more mobility than non-Malay professionals.

The Japanese were also able to appeal successfully to Chinese Confucian notions of loyalty to the company after the Chinese had been trained in Japan. Compared with Malays, the Chinese were more willing to take salaried jobs in the private sector, and to stay in one position rather than job hop, because of their ability to satisfy the frustrations of working in one particular company through sideline activities. Under NEP, Chinese professionals had fewer prospects of job mobility than their Malay counterparts.

The early Japanese managers in Iroha (M) felt an affinity with the more business-like, urbane approach of Malaysian Chinese managers, and despite the pro-Malay emphasis of the NEP, this did not change in the NEP era. Moreover,

Chinese and Japanese could drink alcohol together so there were more contexts for socialising outside of working hours. Until the Malay NEP graduates matured, the Chinese were perceived by the Japanese managers to have superior ability to the Malays, in terms of work ethics and technical skills. Because of these factors there were accusations of favouritism towards Chinese over Malays in management-level promotions.

However, after the NEP Iroha (M)'s policy to 'indigenise' top-management positions began in earnest, the Malay managers' confidence in their security of tenure and future promotion within the organisation strengthened. Between 1976 and 1981, the senior management level received six new members at the level of section chief: three young graduates (two Malays, one Chinese), two Malay 'mid-career' recruits in their thirties, and one Malay from the company's rank and file. By 1988, the company had recruited seven more Malay NEP graduates and two more Chinese graduates.

New-rich career paths

I will now present case histories of three Iroha (M) managers who attained the status of 'new rich' through different routes: Sanusi, one of the first managerial recruits, a non-graduate from the old middle class who attained senior managerial status through the seniority principle; Rahman, an NEP graduate, first-generation middle-class by virtue of his tertiary education; and Ridzuan, son of a working-class family who rose from the ranks to become a manager.

Sanusi – old middle class to manager

Sanusi, one of the 'old guard' recruited in 1963, was in the production side until 1972, after which he was moved to personnel and administrative roles. He became personnel manager in 1976, and by the early 1990s had become personnel and general affairs manager, and a director of the company. Sanusi was a former pupil of a famous English-medium colonial school. His father was an English-educated bureaucrat, giving the family a footing into the old middle class. As is the case with such families, Sanusi's wife stayed at home, a sign of their affluence. They lived in a single-storey bungalow in a middle-class area of Petaling Jaya adjacent to Kuala Lumpur. Sanusi sent one of his sons to the USA for tertiary education. After this Sanusi helped him to set up a business, which Sanusi plans to join upon his retirement from Iroha (M).

Unlike the new middle class, where it is common for both husband and wife to have professional jobs, and to be concerned with maximising only the interests of the nuclear family, Sanusi's concern extended more widely. When new employees were needed, the company advertised internally for friends or relatives of existing employees. Sanusi recruited many relatives and other residents of his native village. He was close to most of the veteran workers, in the older village-style patron–client sense, and went out of his way to assist them in various ways. For instance, a Malay worker asked the company – through Sanusi, in the latter's capacity as personnel manager – for a loan to purchase a motorcycle. Sanusi's Japanese superior refused the request, so rather than pass on a flat refusal, Sanusi lent the worker money out of his own pocket. This was both to save face personally, and to smooth over relations between workers and the Japanese management because Sanusi knew that the latter did not understand workers' real needs.

Indeed, the Japanese managers did not appreciate the fact that Sanusi always played this key role as cultural interpreter, and was the main channel for worker–management communication. He knew the Japanese way, but he did not accept it where he saw it as detrimental to the workers' interests. Sanusi appeared to be very lazy to the Japanese because he insisted on leaving the office at 4.30pm each day, the official office closing time. In the late 1970s the Japanese managers showed their lack of appreciation of his conduct by giving him a slightly lower bonus than that given to the Chinese managers, even though they had equal seniority. What they did not understand was that he left at this time in order to play golf at a prestigious golf club in Petaling Jaya, whose members included many high-ranking Malay bureaucrats. His after-hours networking was crucial for the company's welfare if problems arose with labour, consumer groups, environmental issues and so on. Unknown to the Japanese, Sanusi had used these connections on many occasions to smooth over potential problems for the company. He also used these networks to gain himself a position on the board of directors of the company.

The Japanese managers also did not appreciate his informal efforts in the Malay cultural context to promote the smooth running of labour relations in the factory. He was a personal friend of the Malay secretary of the company's works committee before the two became personnel manager and union leader respectively. Even though Sanusi's status was now much higher and, in class terms, opposed to that of his friend, he took pains to maintain the relationship. Sometimes Sanusi took his friend to prestigious golf clubs. If his friend came to him with a complaint from a union member, he would say, 'Please try to calm the issue. You don't want to embarrass me in front of the Japanese do you?' Through this informal bargaining or 'microdealing' (Boulanger 1992: 333), many labour disputes were defused. By maintaining a peaceful industrial relations climate in the factory, Sanusi was able to campaign for higher wages and benefits for workers when he was part of the (mainly Japanese) team representing management during collective bargaining negotiations. Over the years he made personal loans to many workers, which were quite unrecoverable, and in this way personally diffused dissatisfaction with the Japanese management's policies. But the Japanese did not observe these activities and gave him no credit. Rather, the Japanese were more impressed by the behaviour of Cheng, the Chinese production manager who always stayed back late at work and was seen to be busy on the job. But Cheng had no established personal links with workers outside of the factory context, and thus exercised limited influence. He conformed more to the Chinese community's mode of behaviour which preserves class and status differences.

Sanusi's successful attempt to be represented on the board of directors reflected a concern that the company's long-term interests were not adequately represented by the large proportion of Japanese from the parent company, who were resident in Japan, or by the transient expatriate Japanese managers in Malaysia, whose personal career interests were primarily with the parent company.

But Sanusi's quest for a director's position also concerned his personal ambition to receive a measure of recognition and status among the local managers within the company. As the only senior Malay manager, recruited before the *bumiputera* policy, he was always marginalised. Although it was the common practice to have Malays in the position of personnel manager, Malays who achieved positions of prominence in business or academia before the affirmative action advantages under the NEP did so in the face of considerable handicaps.

Approaching retirement age, Sanusi could expect to be rehired on a contract basis for several years and perhaps located in a subsidiary company. Afterwards his son's company would provide a source of income. Sanusi's successful career and entry into the new rich was founded on a combination of the NEP *bumiputera* policy and aspects of the Japanese management system promoting lifetime employment and the principle of seniority. Recruited from university, but with an incomplete science degree, his career in the Japanese company had generally served him well, while not making him extremely wealthy. It provided him and his family with security and a comfortable middle-class lifestyle. In the Japanese management system of the time, there was no likelihood that talented juniors would leapfrog over him. Though Sanusi displayed managerial skills based on village-style patron–client ties, he also showed a degree of 'Japanese-style' loyalty to the company; as a *bumiputera* manager, he could have moved to another foreign company quite easily, but did not.

Rahman: NEP graduate to manager

The first new top-management candidate to be recruited after the old guard was an NEP Malay science graduate, Rahman. He was appointed section chief in the technical department in 1976, several years after the position had been left vacant. Rahman was being groomed for a manager's post after the Japanese were to leave in 1980, before the Look East Policy reversed the 'nationalisation of top management' policy of the first decade of the NEP.

Rahman resigned to take up a university tutorship after one year with the company but, for a number of reasons, returned to Iroha (M). He was persuaded by his relatives not to leave a job with such good promotion prospects in the private sector. They were concerned about his ongoing ability to contribute to them financially. The Japanese took Rahman back because it would be costly for them to retrain a new recruit. And his momentary 'disloyalty' in resigning put him in a weak bargaining position within the organisation for the rest of his career. Japanese management had adopted a similar recruiting strategy in taking the failed graduates among the management recruits of 1963.

In the 1980s, as the NEP incentives for Malays to enter business brought concrete results, a business ethic emerged which overtook the old Malay world-view that jobs in the civil service had the most prestige. Making money for its own sake and acquiring status through the possession of certain material goods – like European cars,[17] renovated houses and elaborate furniture – became legitimate goals for Malays in the latter half of the NEP era. Not only did Prime Minister Mahathir introduce the LEP as a source of work ethics, but he also introduced the 'Look to Islam' campaigns which linked 'productivity and piety', and extolled success in business, as long as it did not involve cheating people or usury. The first wife of the Prophet Mohamed, Khadijah, a wealthy and successful businesswoman, was quoted as a role model.

However, the Japanese managers failed to convert the primary loyalty of Malay managers to the *kampung*, the family and Islam into loyalty to the firm, as had been more possible in the case of most Chinese. The firm was large, its market position was very secure and its remuneration of local executives was reasonable, so Malay managers did stay, and to a certain extent were influenced by the lifetime employment aspect of the corporate culture. But the case of Rahman illustrates a common pattern: it was his relatives' perception of the company as a good long-term economic prospect that caused him to stay, rather than an intrinsic loyalty to the firm. His loyalty as a member of the new Malay middle class lay elsewhere, particularly towards Islam. The following case demonstrates this.

In 1988, Rahman asked for two months' leave to perform the *haj*, or pilgrimage to Mecca, one of the five pillars of Islam and mandatory for all Muslims who are able to do so in terms of health and wealth. But the management refused to give Rahman the leave because the Japanese had made a policy not to give leave longer than fourteen days at a stretch, saying that if they could do without him for two months, the usual time taken for the trip to Mecca, then they could do without him for good. However, the Japanese were not able to refuse his request as it would have become a sensitive issue under the pro-Malay, pro-Islam mood of the NEP. Rahman performed the *haj* and was away for over two months, without being dismissed. A number of explanations could be offered as to why the parties acted the way they did during this episode.

For Rahman, performing the *haj* involved choosing between identity and productivity. He felt that he needed to make the pilgrimage to get respect from people in his community. As he came from a pious family and had always been pious in his outward presentation of self, there would have been pressure on him to perform the *haj* once his income made it possible for him to do so. Family and friends would have questioned his religious devotion had he, for instance, purchased an expensive car before making the pilgrimage. This could also explain why many other young Malay professionals were making the *haj* so early. Before the NEP era, people usually did not perform the *haj* until they were elderly, and when they had accumulated enough savings to make the trip. The *haj* can be quite dangerous – often accompanied by injury or death as a result of heatstroke, stampedes and unavoidable physical exertion – and pilgrims set off with the expectation that they may never return. With the rise of prosperous young middle-class Malays, it became financially possible for couples with young children to perform the pilgrimage. To do so became a simultaneous public demonstration of status and piety: *Hajis* (male pilgrims) wear a small white skull-cap and *hajas* (female pilgrims) a white headscarf in daily life as a symbol of their new ritual status.

The social expression of Malay identity had become crucial given the NEP *bumiputera* policies. As the NEP era progressed, Malay identity was articulated more and more through Islam. For the NEP-generated new middle-class Malays, prosperity and Islamic piety went hand in hand. Making the pilgrimage tied these two phenomena together, and it has become commonplace for professional Malay couples to leave even very young children with relatives or servants in order to perform the *haj*.

Upon his return to Iroha (M), Rahman wore his white *haji* skull-cap to work. Despite his absence, he was promoted to deputy production manager and became the first of the NEP new graduates to achieve this level of seniority. While maintaining a stronger loyalty to his religious beliefs than to Iroha (M), Rahman still reaped the benefits of the Japanese system in his career.

Ridzuan: worker to manager

The Japanese were not averse to promoting veteran workers to management roles. All the unit chiefs were from the rank-and-file worker levels except for four in engineering who were recruited at unit chief level by the Japanese factory manager in the 1980s. Three veteran workers were promoted to assistant section chief level and one to deputy manager level. This follows the Japanese management strategy of taking advantage of long-term relationships and loyalty by promoting capable veterans to areas such as security, sales and marketing. Ridzuan's case exemplifies this. It also exemplifies the Japanese practice of transferring employees between quite disparate areas in the organiation, as was also the case with Sanusi.

Ridzuan was born in 1947, as one of four children, thus in a small family by Malay standards of the time. His father worked for a European firm making air conditioners in Kuala Lumpur. This gave the family an entry into the urban lifestyle, quite unusual for Malay families from rural origins in the pre-NEP era. Ridzuan was able to attend an English-medium school and passed Form 5. He wanted to go on to teacher training, but at that time his father was on strike, and was left with no income to support the family. Thus Ridzuan had to get a job. A neighbour who was working at Iroha (M) saw the family's predicament and gave Ridzuan some application forms.

Ridzuan was employed as a process worker in 1966, thinking he could still study to become a teacher. However, with the 3-shift system and the prohibitive cost of fees and books, he found it impossible. He tried to find other employment that would enable him to study, but was not successful. After marrying in 1970, Ridzuan gave up his teaching plans and decided to stay at Iroha (M).

The Japanese preferred their male employees to be married as they saw it as a sign of stability and maturity. Ridzuan's wife, Suriani, became a 'housewife' in that she did not work for wages, but like many Malay wives she supplemented the family income by engaging in small business activities. Despite Ridzuan's disapproval, Suriani became a dealer in Pyrex plates which she sold on a hire purchase scheme to neighbourhood wives and friends.

Ridzuan received good evaluations, and a double pay increment in 1974. In that year he was promoted to assistant charge hand, the first supervisory role after process worker. Then in 1975 he was promoted to assistant unit chief, a management category. This sudden promotion, which bypassed three supervisory grades, caused people to be very suspicious, as Ridzuan was active in the national union at the time, and the promotion meant he would have to leave behind his union activities. Ridzuan had become deputy secretary of the works committee in the company when one of the other Malay leaders left the company for another job. This was halfway through the first collective agreement negotiations in 1974. At the time, Ridzuan said, he was respected by both his fellow workers and by management. Although he supported the union, he was worried about becoming a union official: 'If I come to the union, I may lose my good name. I just want to have a peaceful life, rest, enough food and money. But I didn't see anyone else who could do the job.' When he was offered the management position, Ridzuan realised he would have to resign from his union posts and was placed in a dilemma. The dramatic leap in status made his position even more suspect:

> People said, 'You are betraying the union and being bought out by management'...I am a simple man. I thought about it for six months. I considered it might be better to get out of the union and the company altogether, get a job in Monsanto or Magnolia [other large multinational companies, but not Japanese]. But my father-in-law advised me, 'If you are scared, you had better not live.'

Ridzuan accepted the promotion but had to survive his loss of face for several years. The substantial pay rise he received was most welcome at the time as his wife had just had their second child, and his father-in-law was helping him to buy a house (a small bungalow) in a new lower middle-class housing estate on the outskirts of Kuala Lumpur. Yet Ridzuan was to suffer from the responsibility of his position because he was now expected to be available at all hours to deal with any technical problems that arose in his production section. The Japanese managers were always prepared to do this and they expected Ridzuan to follow suit. Part of the problem for Ridzuan was that, like many Malays of his generation (see Chew 1993: 108), he did not have a science background and struggled with the basic on-the-job tuition he received in chemistry and maths from the Japanese technical manager.

Nevertheless, as Ridzuan's supervisory responsibilities increased, his relationship to the Japanese technical manager became closer. Sometimes the two of them went to dinner together, and in this way Ridzuan started to participate in middle-class activities. After his promotion to assistant unit chief, he was sent to Japan for three months' training in July 1976. In the main factory, he worked with operators on shift duty and was surprised to find that they owned cars, and that some of them had been on overseas trips to Hawaii or the Philippines, perhaps, he thought, for their honeymoon. Their living standards were obviously different to those that he was familiar with: 'Here we have our honeymoon in the *kampung*', he said.

Ridzuan went on to be a popular junior manager, and his career was nurtured by Sanusi (case one, above). When it became clear that he was not technically competent to be promoted to section chief level in production – these roles were being given to newly recruited Malay science graduates – Ridzuan was shifted to administration and given the role of section chief of security. Later he was moved to public relations, under another new manager, Othman, who for a time became Ridzuan's patron: the two used to play golf together at a budget nine-hole golf club. Ridzuan aspired to a comfortable, high-status middle-class lifestyle, but his income was not sufficient to participate in the truly middle-class activities of shopping at supermarkets for imported goods, and having membership of the more exclusive golf clubs. Like other senior workers and senior managers, he could afford to take his family to fast-food outlets, like Long John Silver or McDonald's. But Ridzuan complained that the food at Long John Silver was expensive and not at all nice. According to him, they 'were eating status rather than food' by patronising these establishments.

Ridzuan was caught between the generations, a phenomenon experienced by all educated Malays in the NEP era. He had respect for the opinions of his family regarding his career, and he had the simplicity of life values of the pious, but not fundamentalist, Malays of old *kampung* society. Yet he was touched by new middle-class consumerist values, and he had internalised the Japanese ethos of working hard for the company.

Ridzuan continued to live in the private housing estate on the fringe of Kuala Lumpur, where all the houses were free-standing single-storey residences. He renovated and expanded the house to accommodate his wife, three children and several relatives, all of whom could be supported on his salary from Iroha (M). He was also able to invest in real estate for his future security.

The Japanese system of lifetime job security and horizontal transferring away from an employee's original section guaranteed Ridzuan a stable career in the firm and the financial security to consolidate his membership of the middle class, despite his lack of tertiary education. Other companies, regarding his technical ability as limited, may have kept him in a lower supervisory role in the production side, limiting his career prospects and his income. It is said that only in a Japanese company in Malaysia could a worker become a manager, reflecting the situation in Japan itself. This possibility, coupled with the patronage of local managers such as Sanusi and Othman, projected Ridzuan into a middle-class life, not only in financial terms, but also in terms of lifestyle.

SOCIETY, CULTURE AND MALAYSIA'S NEW RICH

Lifestyle and social interaction

Employment in the Japanese company at managerial level, combined with key NEP outcomes such as tertiary education opportunities and ethnic quotas in organisations which guaranteed them promotions, was a sure path to 'new rich' status for the Malays. Even working-class Malays were able to participate in some aspects of new rich lifestyles, and a few attained middle-class status through their careers in the company. For the Chinese it was less easy, although the pre-NEP Chinese recruits became senior managers in the company under the seniority principle and there was one case of a Chinese employee who was promoted to manager status from the rank and file.

New-rich status was guaranteed by managerial levels of income, but in comparison with the village context, even factory workers could be classified as new rich because their working-class wage allowed them to participate to some extent in urban consumer lifestyles. So it is lifestyle rather than income which may be said to define the new rich.

Moreover, social interaction with the Japanese, both during social activities organised by the company and on a personal basis, gave new opportunities for local managers and workers to participate in middle-class lifestyles. For instance, there were cases of friendships based on affinity between individuals. Kunino, the production control manager, sold his car for a very reasonable price to Ridzuan when he left for Japan and even gave him back $500 in cash to pay for repairs. This was the first car that Ridzuan owned.

On the whole, social interaction between the Japanese and the local managers was based on formalised invitations in the context of company business or the ritual yearly events of the Malaysian cultural calendar, such as the festival days. In the 1970s there was an annual ten-pin-bowling night for all the local and Japanese managers, a very middle-class activity at that time. Afterwards they went for dinner at the halal Chinese restaurant area in Brickfields, where those non-Malay managers who wished to drink alcohol could order beer, but at least the Chinese food was prepared in a way that was acceptable to the Muslim dietary rules.

Individuals from both groups played golf, but the local managers complained that the Japanese did not play with them voluntarily in their free time but only on the annual golf day when the two groups played together as a company event. This event served to introduce many of the local managers to the game, and some, like Ridzuan, took it up as a career strategy thereafter.

Senior managers: patronage and ethnicity

Although patron–client relations exist in Japanese society too, it is on a more individual level in the context of a pervasive and long-established middle-class ethos in the society. In contemporary Japan, patron–client relations would serve the strategic interests of individuals involved, for instance, in politics or in business. It would thus be difficult for individual Japanese managers to understand the obligations that middle-class Malays feel to the less-well-off in their society, not just to their immediate kin, but to a wider circle of relatives and members of the same village or to 'Malays' in general. This custom of distributing wealth from rich to poor is reinforced by the notion of giving charity in Islam. For instance, cousins or nieces and nephews of an urban middle-class Malay would reasonably expect financial support with their education. Even more distant relatives would not necessarily be turned away, especially for more temporary help, such as assistance in receiving treatment in the urban Western-style hospital. And a Malay from one's *kampung* who came to the house asking for help would not be turned away without some form of assistance.

However, even among the Malays, there is slowly developing the inwardly closed focus typical of the Western middle-class nuclear family which looks after its own members' financial interests and social advancement to the exclusion of other kin or members of society, except in the form of tax payments or formal donations to charity. This is because the cash required for status consumption in one's own nuclear family is so much that Malay parents cannot afford to be too generous to numerous relatives and still maintain the prevailing status symbols of the middle class of other ethnic groups. This has been exacerbated by urban living where the ethnic groups live together in modern housing estates and their children attend the same schools.

The present generation of middle-class Malays, however, are still only one generation removed from a village existence with a peasant social ethos, where patron–client relations are a matter of honour and shame in a face-to-face small-scale community where the boundaries of kinship and friendship are blurred. Older Malays feel these ties more strongly. Thus Sanusi, the personnel manager, conducted his relationships within the factory as if it were a village and practised generalised patronage towards the Malay workers. In doing so he sometimes went beyond the boundaries of the contractual and contextually-specific relationship patterns typical of modern organisations.

The senior local managers who were mainly Chinese were from established middle-class origins and were much less likely to express their ethnicity overtly in terms of material symbols or behaviour. Because of the prohibitions on consuming pork and alcohol for Malays, the local senior managers only got together for eating and drinking on the occasion of a work-related event, a dinner in the general manager's house, or when entertaining a former Japanese expatriate manager who was passing through Kuala Lumpur, and so on. On such occasions halal Chinese restaurants in the large hotels – inreasingly patronised by the Malay middle class – or other restaurants associated with Japanese, French or other national cuisines would be chosen. The managers did visit each other's homes for the 'open house' gatherings (see Armstrong 1988) of their respective festival days, Chinese New Year, Deepavali, Hari Raya, Christmas and so on. To do so was not merely an expression of friendship, but a mandatory demonstration of respect for a work colleague. Not to visit without a very good excuse would tend to be regarded not as a passive act of omission but rather as a calculated act of hostility.

The senior managers therefore were 'friends', but they were quite middle-class in the structure of their families and suburban lifestyles. They would argue that their private time was for their hobbies and pastimes, their own nuclear families or friends of the same ethnic group.

New graduates: work ethics and Muslim identity

As opposed to the senior local managers described earlier, who had direct personal experience to varying degrees with Japanese culture and who did not have much bargaining power with the company owing to deficiencies in their basic qualifications and other aspects of their careers, the new graduates, who were mainly Malay and who had been recruited largely on the basis of their tertiary qualifications in the technical fields, had bargaining power as *bumiputera*, despite their lack of experience in production.

Within the social organisation of the factory, they stood on their status as graduates and rarely left their air-conditioned offices. Unlike the first generation of managers, who helped set up the factory and who knew 'every valve and pump', and every worker personally, they did not know the workers so well and it was said that they did not care about them. As first-generation middle-class Malays themselves, the new graduates' generation, even if from *kampung* origins, had received affirmative action *bumiputera* scholarships to special science-stream secondary boarding schools set up under the NEP to 'hothouse' Malays into tertiary science education. Their social origins were similar to veteran junior managers' yet their experience on the way to becoming middle class was quite different. In these schools the Malay students experienced a very hard daily existence, living in hostels and eating the unpalatable mass-produced hostel food. To poor village families, the chance for one of their children to get a scholarship to one of these schools was a great blessing as the child's food and lodging were paid for: they did not have to depend on the generosity of a wealthier relative in the urban area to support their child at a good urban school. Secondly, the science-stream education assured their child of getting a place in a science course in the university, and perhaps even a government scholarship to study overseas.

Any hardship was bearable in the face of this social mobility through education. Often the schools were located in rural towns, so there was little recreation for the students, only a life of school lessons, homework, religious observances and the pressure to succeed. It was a very artificial lifestyle and the young people were deprived of the stabilising influences of warm family relationships in their adolescent years. These schools became a fertile ground for Muslim fundamentalism (Shamsul 1995), and there were even outbreaks of mass hysteria of the type found among Malaysian female industrial workers in the non-unionised semiconductor factories. Here workers are highly regimented and there are no formal avenues of protest (Ong 1987).

Thus we find that Malay middle-class culture in the post NEP era is often a mixture of what would seem to be paradoxically juxtaposed elements: fundamentalist piety and extreme materialism – the need to demonstrate status with expensive consumer items. The importance of performing the pilgrimage to Mecca for middle-class Malay couples in their thirties can be understood in this context.

With this background of being *bumiputera* graduates and having themselves experienced hardship during their schooling and a degree of social dislocation from their parents' social world, the new graduates had lost the thread of the patron–client village-style relationships maintained by older-generation Malays like Sanusi. They had become more individualist in their status orientations, demonstrating status with material possessions alone rather than combining this with a show of patronage to those less fortunate than themselves. In other words, they were becoming middle-class in the isolationist sense typical of the middle-class nuclear family in mature middle-class Western societies. They would not have observed first-hand the hardship experienced by the workers as squatters in the illegal *kampungs* on the outskirts of Kuala Lumpur in the 1970s, before these workers began to have income levels sufficient to purchase low-cost terrace houses in the 1980s. Even if they knew about the hardships of the workers' lives, they would not have reason to care since their success was an individual achievement, created by scholarships provided by the state and their own hard work, not by parents or wealthy relatives. This gave them a one-dimensional confidence and, with it, a degree of arrogance, the arrogance of those who are not really sure of themselves. They were obligated to the state, not to an individual patron, for their position, so they had no role model of patronage. Furthermore, any large act of generosity would jeopardise their ability to fund their own children's future (so much more expensive in terms of paid tuition, other activities and mandatory brand-name gym shoes costing $200 a pair, than the *kampung* childhood they had experienced).

Because the new graduates did not seem to care about the workers, it was said that the Japanese were able to use them from the 1980s onwards in support of policies which disadvantaged the workers in the name of productivity. Examples of this were the removal of male general workers from the packing room, leaving the ageing women packers to carry the heavy boxes formerly carried by the young male workers; the reduction of overtime, on which many workers depended to pay their motorbike loans, their housing loans and other hire purchase arrangements and so on. As Sanusi explained, there was no way the new graduates could envisage the financial hardship caused by the cutting of overtime levels that workers had come to expect, and on the basis of which they had committed themselves to many credit arrangements.

With monthly salaries of $1,200 the new graduates could not afford too much luxury but they sought to distance themselves socially and in the workplace from the workers. They rejected the fictive egalitarian approach of performing jobs with the workers in order to motivate them, as Cheng the senior Chinese production manager had done,[18] on the basis of their educational status. They were not willing to walk around the factory and get a feel of production, a practice which is regarded as extremely important by Japanese managers in Japan.

The new graduates had three roles to fulfil in their lives: (i) their professional role in the company, that is their status as managers; (ii) their technical roles, as science graduates, which were nevertheless not being developed because they were there in a token role only as *bumiputera* numbers in the management levels; and (iii) their social roles as young prosperous *bumiputera* in both the urban community and the rural community of origin. In their lives it was this latter role which ultimately assumed the most importance, and it provided the most difficulty for them as their behaviour was required to be different in some aspects in the two different contexts. The main common point in both urban and rural social contexts for the young educated Malay middle class was their Muslim identity, expressed through overt symbols of piety in speech, dress and ritual prayer. Otherwise there were great paradoxes in the coexistence of the two spheres, such as being expected to attend the weddings and funerals of a large number of distant relatives in the village social context while, on the other hand, being expected to keep up with a professional daily schedule of important meetings and appointments in the urban context. The individual trying to cope with these two disparate and mutually conflicting worlds suffered a schizophrenia in values and it was understandable that Islam, which bound the two together as the key factor identifying the *bumiputera* under the NEP and as the basis of *kampung* social relationships, came to be embraced so fervently by the young middle class.

The Japanese management were not able to divert their loyalty towards the company and the job and away from their religious and other social representations in the critical community of their families and peers in the Malay middle class.

CONCLUSION

Employment in the Japanese joint venture gave the opportunity of social mobility to different individuals to varying degrees. For the senior local managers, Chinese and one Malay, the experience of employment consolidated the middle-class status from which they had come. The fact that their parents had had sufficient means to educate them to tertiary level at the end of the 1950s is proof of their families' middle-class status. The junior local managers came from two groups: the veterans and the new graduates who had risen from the ranks. The veterans, in becoming managers after being workers, owed their mobility to the Japanese, as it was remarked that it was only in Japanese companies that one could become a manager from the unionised ranks. In fact, Ridzuan had been a union leader and this was a major factor in his promotion as this pattern of career advancement is typical in large companies in Japan itself.

The Malay new graduates, who were largely from rural peasant origins, owed their social mobility to the NEP. As *bumiputera*, they could have been employed in any large company, and they were highly mobile. But they tended to stay on in the Japanese company, not so much from a loyalty created by the Japanese corporate culture, but because of pressures from family and from their financial commitments, especially housing loans and the hire purchase of cars and consumer items, in order to maintain a stable income.

The workers on the whole remained working class, but in a privileged position. Through steady wage increments and security of tenure under the Japanese system, they were able, after over twenty years' employment in the company, to buy reconditioned cars and the simplest form of single-storey terrace housing.

The steady income, prospects of security of tenure and promotion for the local managers affected their relationships both within the organisation and in the wider social context. However, these were expressed in different ways by the different groups. The senior local managers demonstrated their middle-class identity with less emphasis on their ethnic identity. They lived in the mixed ethnic middle-class housing estates in the suburbs of Kuala Lumpur and Petaling Jaya. They joined prestigious golf clubs where members did not congregate in ethnically exclusive groups and where alcohol was openly consumed. Their wives did not work for wages. The Malays among them maintained their traditional ties with the *kampung* folks, but overall their focus was much more on the nuclear family, especially on the financial expenditure for their children's overseas education. Nevertheless, 'old school' middle-class Malays such as Sanusi extended patronage in a general sense, not just to immediate relatives and friends, but to workers in the company in a general sense, albeit mainly to Malays.

The Malay majority of new graduates among the local junior managers were of a different generation from Sanusi. They came from peasant origins and they owed their position not to personal patrons or family help, but to the state. They, with less confidence in their new-found middle-class status, expressed it much more overtly in terms of symbols of their ethnicity and with conspicuous consumption in the form of cars and furniture, and with religious observances, such as making the *haj* at an early age. Their wives, usually as educated as themselves, needed to work in professional occupations to help fund these family expenditures.

The veterans from the ranks who became junior managers were different from the new graduates. Their wives were not highly educated and either did not work or engaged in small business activities based at home. Thus the lifestyles of these veteran junior managers were not so opulent as those of the graduates. Still, they lived on lower-cost modern housing estates and usually were able to purchase a house larger than a single-storey terrace. They tried to learn golf at the cheaper clubs, but could not afford to join the prestigious clubs to which the senior managers and Japanese belonged.

At the level of the middle class, we observe that all ethnic groups show an increasing turning inward to the prosperity and lifestyle comforts of the nuclear family, expressed in the use of income to upgrade housing, make of car and leisure activities conducted in the context of prestigious clubs, resorts and expensive hotels. Significant investments were made also in children's education in expensive private institutions, often overseas. Specific to the Malay group were the remnants of wider community patron-client relations of the peasant village type, and also demonstrations of piety as a status device, through the performance of the *haj* at an early age.

The workers aspired to middle-class lifestyles and bought cheaper versions of the middle-class status items – the lounge suites, curtain materials, which were ostentatious and flashy, but of cheap quality on closer examination. Their cars were Proton Sagas or reconditioned Toyotas or Nissans. They used the middle-class supermarkets and shopping malls as a place of recreation, taking their children there and thus educating them unconsciously in middle-class lifestyles. As a special treat, they would take the family to fast-food restaurants such as Kentucky, or Pizza Hut, even though nicer, cheaper indigenous food was available at roadside stalls.

How did the Japanese firm in Malaysia contribute specifically to this?

First at the macro level, by its role in providing substantial amounts of direct foreign investment in the NEP era, Japanese capital and Japanese firms contributed to the formation of a new managerial class in Malaysia. Again, owing to the dynamics of the *bumiputera* focus of the NEP, a substantial number of these new positions went to Malays. Hence this helped to create among the Malays a new middle-class phenomenon, whose values and motivations contrasted with the old middle-class Malays. A distinction between old and new middle class was not so striking in the Chinese and Indian groups because their young professional generation had largely urban origins anyway and were not a product of 'hothouse' education schemes for the children of rural peasants. The rural Chinese and Indian children largely missed out on the benefits of the NEP although the urban Chinese business group benefited greatly from it by acting as business partners for the new class of Malay entrepreneurs.

Secondly, at the micro level, within the firm itself, transplanted systems of Japanese management, emphasising lifetime employment, seniority wage structures and systems of job transfer which are a feature of the enterprise union system in Japan itself, gave security of tenure to managerial employees, even in the face of demonstrated incompetence. This loyalty of the firm to the individual employee translated back into a loyalty of the individual to the firm. Thus job hopping was much less observable among Malay executives in Iroha, compared to the situation in the professional job market outside. Employment in the firm also gave first-generation professionals an introduction to middle-class lifestyles, hotel dining, golf and other middle-class leisure activities, although these influences were not specific to the Japanese firm and would have been experienced in any large foreign firm. However, the experience of employment in the Japanese system did have specific consequences for the Malaysian managerial class as outlined above.

Workers too experienced benefits specific to the Japanese firm. They had the opportunity to be promoted from the level of worker to manager. They experienced security of tenure, allowing them to make commitments to large projects like the purchase of a home or a car. The Japanese were less strict with shift schedules, allowing them to run side businesses and earn a second income in the informal sector (Smith 1988: 455). Thus their loyalties were diverted away from the company and from class solidarity to the pursuit of self-interested economic gain in the short term. Their working-class consciousness was subverted by a preoccupation with consumption and they relied on vertical links of patronage within their ethnic groups to fulfil these desires through access to promotions in the organisation or licences for petty trading activities outside it. In that sense, the Japanese management system promoted their social mobility both through their participation in the company organisation with its stable career and promotion prospects and in the wider range of economic activities it allowed them to engage in.

In this way, employment in the Japanese firm gave Malaysians of all classes and ethnic groups a foothold into the consumption-dominated lifestyles of Malaysia's 'new rich'. Different individuals used the resources available in different ways to maximise their status: Sanusi chose to consolidate his status as a patron figure in his ethnic group; Rahman chose to express his status through piety, even in the modern organisational context. The Japanese organisational structures allowed for these variations. Ultimately, considerations of highly politicised ethnicity constituted the basic reference point, but state-validated 'Malayness' could still be expressed through patronage or piety within the Japanese firm.

Notes

All cost and income figures presented in this chapter are expressed in Malaysian ringgit and were current for 1990 when the exchange rate was MYR\$2 = A\$1.

1 The members of the new rich whom I focus on in this chapter are the professional managers in a Japanese joint venture in Malaysia and, to a lesser degree, the workers whose stable incomes allow them to aspire to middle-class lifestyles and replicate them to some extent.

2 All members of the plural society are Malaysians, and strictly, we should refer to them as such, or as 'Malaysians of Chinese ethnicity', 'Malaysians of Indian ethnicity', and so on. 'Malaysian Chinese', 'Malaysian Indians' and 'Malays' is another way of referring to the members of these distinct ethnic groups. In this chapter, I am using the local mode of expression: 'Malays', 'Chinese' and 'Indians', but this should not be taken to mean people with Chinese or Indian nationality.

3 Ingenious arrangements are made to accommodate ethnic factors in a class context. As the key expression of their Muslim identity, Malays will not eat pork under any circumstances, even in mixed ethnic gatherings, although some individuals may relax the other food prohibition, the consumption of alcohol, and drink it with their non-Malay friends in certain contexts. Dining in top-class hotels, especially with a Western-style menu, is a way of expressing one's upper-class status. Hence large hotels serve 'beef bacon' for breakfast, so that Malays may participate in the English breakfast lifestyle without contravening the pork taboo in Islam.

4 In the 1990s, the 850cc Kancil based on the Daihatsu Mira has been marketed as a second car for middle-class families or as a potentially purchasable first car for working-class families.

5 Much is made in Malaysia of the type of house one lives in: bungalow (free-standing), semi-detached or terrace. These may be single- or double-storey. Factory workers could at best aspire to purchase a single-storey terrrace. The middle-classes will be content with single-storey semi-detached or double-storey terrace. Single- or double-storey bungalows are most prestigious. In a government housing estate, the occupational status of the residents is reflected in the house type they live in, as the government housing loans have ceilings for the different civil servant rankings, thus preventing people from purchasing a house type above their status. All groups seek to gain status over neighbours with the same basic house type by carrying out expensive renovations, which often transform the house so as to be unrecognisable from its original shape.

6 A fictitious name.

7 It is prohibited for Muslim Malays to eat pork or drink alcohol. Hindu Indians do not eat beef and may be strictly vegetarian.

8 The official level of Malay equity in 1971 was 2.4 per cent. By 1990 this had risen to 19.4 per cent (Osman-Rani 1990).

9 Refer to the chapter by Shamsul in this volume.

10 People from rural origins had always done without toilet paper or shampoo, but when they came to live in the urban areas, with urban regular cash wages to spend, they began to buy these cash items to demonstrate their urban status. Going to the supermarkets in the urban shopping complexes and purchasing these luxury consumer items was part of the fun of the urban lifestyle. Even neighbourhood provision shops were stocked with a glittering array of consumer items in modern, international-style packaging and prices which were just accessible to workers. It was difficult not to be tempted to purchase tubes of face wash for $5 or paper tissues for $3, things which had never been necessary before.

11 While conflict and competition have been exacerbated within classes, it has been alleviated between classes as the workers seek personal patrons within ethnic groupings to further their family self-interest, rather than trying to raise income levels through mass class action (Smith 1994a).

12 A case was observed of a manual worker whose hand became swollen to the extent that he could not work. Western-trained doctors could find no explanation and could not cure the hand either. The man consulted a shamanic healer and was told that his rival for promotion to the position of foreman had used an *orang asli* (aboriginal) type of black magic called *busong* (denoting a swelling phenomenon) to affect his hand so that he would not be able to do his job properly and hence would not receive the promotion. If not treated for the condition, he would eventually die. The shamanic healer was able to heal him, where Western medical science had failed after many months of trying. Although such magical practices are found within Malay culture, non-Malays also consult Malay shamans for help with the same range of human needs and foibles: illness, love relationships, conflict, revenge, law suits, economic gain and personal success (see Skeat 1967: 568; Gimlette and Thomson 1983: 32).

13 Magical practices remain dominant in the world-view of the people themselves as responses to and explanations for the effects of rapid economic development. Thus we see how the re-creation of tradition is often used to powerful effect by ruling groups and others aspiring to wealth and power in rapidly industrialising societies (Hobsbawm and Ranger 1983; Kessler 1992).

14 Despite the fact that workers in Iroha (M) were organised under a national industrial union, not an enterprise union, this feature is important as it is a key element in the ethos of flexibility in staff deployment in Japanese management systems, and this flexibility did exist in the Malaysian venture at the managerial level.

15 Japanese managers always filled the posts of general manager/managing director, administrative manager, factory manager and technical manager. There were usually two other Japanese managers present as well, although from the mid-1970s their roles

went from 'line' to 'staff' positions: engineering development manager (shadowing the local engineering manager) and production control manager (shadowing the local production manager).

16 The prestige of a pensionable job in the civil service, apart from the economic security of a permanent job and a pension after retirement, can be attributed to the fact that the British gave such positions to members of the royal families as a way of controlling their loyalty to the colonial regime.

17 Mercedes, Volvo, BMW.

18 This is a key element in Japanese corporate cultures – the company president may perform lowly tasks such as picking up rubbish or mopping floors in order to set company standards and encourage workers to do the same. In Malaysia, when some Japanese managers and local managers tried this, they merely lost the respect of workers by performing tasks below their status.

Bibliography

Armstrong, M. (1988) 'Festival Open Houses: Settings for Inter-Ethnic Communication in Urban Malaysia', *Human Organization*, 47 (2): 127–37.

Boulanger, C. L. (1992) 'Ethnic Order and Working-Class Strategies in West Malaysia', *Journal of Contemporary Asia*, 22 (3): 322–39.

Chew, C., Keng, L. C., Sugiyama, K. and Leong, S. (1993) *Human Resource Development in Malaysia: Japan's Contribution since 1980*, Kuala Lumpur: Centre for Japan Studies, ISIS Malaysia.

Gimlette, J. D. and Thomson, H. W. (1983) *A Dictionary of Malayan Medicine*, Kuala Lumpur: Oxford University Press.

Hing, A. Y. (1985) 'The Development and Transformation of Wage Labour in West Malaysia', *Journal of Contemporary Asia*, 15 (2): 139–71.

Hobsbawm, E. (1983) 'Introduction', in E. Hobsbawm and T. Ranger (eds), *The Invention of Tradition*, Cambridge: University of Cambridge Press, pp. 1–14.

Hobsbawm, E. and Ranger T. (eds) (1983), *The Invention of Tradition*, Cambridge: University of Cambridge Press.

Kessler, C. (1992) 'Archaism and Modernity: Contemporary Malay Political Culture', in J. Kahn and K. W. Loh (eds), *Fragmented Vision: Culture and Politics in Contemporary Malaysia*, Sydney: Allen & Unwin, pp. 133–57.

Ong, A. H. (1987) *Spirits of Resistance and Capitalist Discipline: Factory Women in Malaysia*, Albany: State University of New York Press.

Osman-Rani, H. (1990) 'Malaysia's New Economic Policy after 1990', *Southeast Asian Affairs 1990*, Singapore: Institute of Southeast Asian Studies, pp. 204–26.

Shamsul, A. B. (1994) 'National Unity: Malaysia's Model for Self-Reliance', in A. B. Shamsul *et al.*, *Malaysian Development Experience: Changes and Challenges*, Kuala Lumpur: National Institute of Public Administration (INTAN), pp. 3–26.

—— (1995) 'Invented Certainties: The Dakwah Persona in Malaysia', in W. James (ed.), *Pursuit of Certainty*, ASA Monograph, London: Routledge, pp. 112–33.

Skeat, W. W. (1967) *Malay Magic*, New York: Dover.

Smith, W. A. (1988) 'Skill Formation in Comparative Perspective: Malaysia and Japan', *Labour and Industry*, 1 (3): 431–62.

—— (1994a) 'A Japanese Factory in Malaysia: Ethnicity as a Management Ideology', in K. S. Jomo (ed.), *Japan and Malaysian Development*, London: Routledge, pp. 154–81.

136 *Wendy A. Smith*

—— (1994b) 'Japanese Cultural Images in Malaysia: Implications of the Look East Policy', in K. S. Jomo (ed.), *Japan and Malaysian Development*, London: Routledge, pp. 335–63.
—— (1995) 'The Japanese Management System in Malaysia: A Case Study of a Japanese Company Overseas', unpublished PhD thesis, Monash University.
—— (1996) 'Japan's Contribution to the Impact of Globalization on Malaysian Industrial Workers', *Hiroshima Journal of International Studies*, 2: 39–56.
Stivens, M. (1987) 'Family, State and Industrialization: The Case of Rembau, Negri Sembilan, Malaysia', in H. Afshar (ed.), *Women, State and Ideology*, London: Macmillan, pp. 89–104.

5 Singapore

Where the new middle class sets the standard

Chua Beng Huat and Tan Joo Ean

In a brief thirty years, Singapore has been transformed from a society that was relatively, homogeneously poor – unemployed or underemployed, undernourished and inadequately housed – to one where social stratification by income is increasingly apparent even to untrained eyes. This successful economic transformation is by now a well-told tale, heavy with its interpretations and controversies (see Rodan 1989; Drysdale 1985; Tremewan 1994; Chua 1995). Success itself has become a metaphor for Singapore.

Domestically, this successful political economy is characterised by the use of monopolistic statutory boards to provide a high level of basic collective-consumption goods and services for the entire population. These provisions have the apparent effect of homogenising the lifestyle of the nation: an overwhelming 85 per cent of the people live in subsidised public-housing flats within estates that have the same level of provisions of ancillary facilities for daily needs, for example, shopping facilities are everywhere; an overwhelming majority of children go to neighbourhood schools, where education is effectively free up to secondary level; and these public-housing residents are well served by the mass rapid transit (MRT) system, with the government undertaking the total development cost.[1]

The even spread of these provisions has engendered a certain homogeneity in the Singaporean culture of everyday life among public housing residents. For example, the MRT system, with terminals in every public-housing new town, is now being used to implement the decentralisation of employment and shopping facilities into four 'regional' centres, thus increasing employment and consumption opportunities for the residents, yet reducing the need to travel. Another example is the place of markets and hawker centres in the configuration of residents' routines. The fresh-produce markets operate only in the morning, compelling all housewives to schedule into their mornings a trip to the market. On these trips, they may develop some measure of familiarity with each other, breaking down one layer of impersonality associated with the monotonous high-rise housing estate and its large, heterogeneous residential population. In addition to acting as a hang-out for the retired, the hawker centres also provide ready access to local fast foods, making eating out an increasingly routine activity, especially for dual-income families (see Table 5.1). The culturally homogenising effects of these provisions combined to gloss over differences within the 'overwhelming majority'.

Table 5.1 Average proportion of expenditure spent on cooked food, by household size

	Number of Persons in Household		
	Two	*Five*	*Seven*
1977–8	40%	34%	34%
1982–3	50%	40%	41%
1987–8	53%	45%	46%

Source: Dept of Statistics (1979: 31, table 25); Dept of Statistics (1984: 112, table 83); Dept of Statistics (1989: 23, table 11).

Ironically, the apparent homogenisation in the routines of everyday life of the overwhelming majority also brings into high relief existing inequalities that demand attention and comparisons. For example, private apartments, houses-on-the ground and cars are coveted objects and are displayed as icons of success against the sea of dependants on public housing and public transportation. As we shall show later, every Singaporean has either to resign himself or herself to the position of never-to-possess such goods or to compete aggressively for them, often at the expense of other aspects of social and material life.

The significance and consequence of differences within a society that is apparently homogeneous are also observable in primary- and secondary-school education. In contrast to the ubiquitous neighbourhood schools, there emerged a number of 'independent' or 'autonomous' schools which, although aided by government grants similarly to the others, have greater freedom to raise school fees, determine curriculums, develop facilities and select students. There is a scramble for enrolling children in the kindergartens which are feeders to these schools at both primary and secondary levels.[2]

The competitions for positional goods, such as private housing and school placement for children, constitute the lines that broadly divide social classes, and in particular subdivide the middle class, in an increasingly stratified Singapore. This chapter is concerned with this emerging stratification structure and the cultural expressions of the new middle class.

In emphasising the relatively homogenised daily life of the overwhelming majority of the population in the public-housing estate and the competition for positional goods as significations of the emerging class structure, we are consciously displacing 'ethnicity' as a variable in our current analysis. This analytical displacement deserves some comment. In raising the class dimension, our intention is precisely to provide an alternative to the conventional, thus dominant and indeed most obvious and convenient, view that Singapore society is divided along ethnic lines, comprising Chinese, Malays and Indians. The prevailing rhetoric of multi-ethnic Singapore argues that each ethnic group is integrated vertically, with the poor and rich of each group bound by a shared 'traditional culture'. Furthermore, this rhetoric argues that the similarity in culture among members of the three ethnic groups is more significant, substantively and analytically, than the possible horizontal integration between

Singaporeans along income divisions across ethnic lines. Singapore society is thus conceptualised as a divided society because of its ethnic/cultural differences. We are thus left with the question of whether there is any cultural basis for constituting Singaporeans as a people.

In examining the culture of different classes, we are contesting precisely the constitution of Singapore society as one which is divided by ethnic cultures. Instead, we want to emphasise the culture that Singaporeans share in their everyday life, namely, a culture that is derived from the logic of capitalist development, in which they reproduce themselves daily, individually and collectively. It is the logic of the capitalist economy, to which every Singaporean is subject, that constitutes them as a people and Singaporean as a social/national category. The same logic also separates them into classes, within their own national boundaries, across ethnic lines. Class differences thus constitute a potential basis for cultural, social and political organisation among Singaporeans, in spite of ethnic differences.

Substantively, when one examines Singapore society even impressionistically several points can be made. First, ethnicity is no longer a defining variable for poverty. It is defined more by family characteristics; when the heads of household are middle-aged, without much formal education and with children who are too young to be wage earners, the family is most likely to be poor. Second, there is ample evidence that Malays count among the ranks of the emerging middle class, alongside Chinese and Indians, largely as a result of the universalisation of education under the same 'national' system. This has occurred despite the fact that some 'elite' and better-endowed schools use Chinese as a first language of instruction along with English, thereby tending to exclude Malay and Indian students. Finally, to the extent that our analysis on the cultural construction of different classes in Singapore is based on the acquisition and display of material necessities and positional goods, ethnicity plays an insignificant part in such constructions. The same jeans are purchased and worn by all youths; the same Mercedes and Lexus cars are driven by all rich; and there are young women and men, of varied origins, guzzling beer and, increasingly, wine in pubs and wine-bars. In all these instances, ethnicity is of minor significance if any, and is definitely exceeded by social class considerations.[3]

Thus, on both conceptual and substantive levels, class constitutes an independent basis for analysing contemporary Singapore society and its cultural constructions by Singaporeans themselves. It is on this basis that this chapter consciously eschews and displaces the use of ethnicity as a given and therefore necessary basis for analysis of differences among Singaporeans. This chapter aims to show another basis of differences among Singaporeans.

A CLASS STRUCTURE IN SINGAPORE

As the cultural identity of a particular class is achieved largely via its expressed differences from other classes, a working delineation of the stratification structure in Singapore is necessary. In addition to statistical information on the nature of economic and material conditions, drawn from official reports and census data, we also consider the assumptions of government policies regarding the consequences of class.

Three decades of sustained economic growth (1965–95) have obliterated any overt poverty in Singapore. However, poverty is unavoidably a matter of contextual relative deprivation. Because of its ideological belief that property ownership gives citizens a stake in the nation's future, the ruling People's Action Party (PAP) government is committed to 100 per cent home-ownership. In this context, poverty – at the household level – may be defined as the inability to own the minimum public-housing flat, for a family of four. Such a definition is indeed the basis of the existing housing policy which provides a cash grant of $30,000 towards the purchase of a three-room public-housing flat to any family of four whose monthly income is less than $1,200.[4] The 1990 census shows that 21.3 per cent of Singapore households are in this category (see Table 5.2). In general, these families have lowly educated parents aged at least in their middle thirties, with low-income earning capacity and with children who are too young to contribute economically to the household. They would constitute the lowest rung of the production structure, often doing unskilled manual work.[5]

Our estimate of the median monthly household income from the 1990 population census is approximately $2,300. To refine divisions among middle income households, a consumption criterion needs to be added to the income measure. Stringent regulations have made car ownership decidedly expensive. A car is a high-status positional good which can be afforded only by those in the middle class or higher, making it the premier cultural icon of the middle class in Singapore. A household expenditure survey of 1987–8 indicates that about one-third of the families within this middle-income range ($2,000–$2,499) are car owners (Dept of Statistics 1989). It follows that households at the upper end of

Table 5.2 Distribution of monthly household income (from all sources), 1990

	Proportion	*Class Structure*
< $1,199	21.3%	Poor
$1,200–$1,999	21.6%	} Working class
$2,000–$2,999	20.1%	
$3,000–$3,999	13.0%	
$4,000–$4,999	8.2%	} Lower middle class
$5,000–$5,999	5.1%	
$6,000–$6,999	3.3%	
$7,000–$7,999	2.1%	
$8,000–$8,999	1.4%	} Upper middle class
$9,000–$9,999	1.0%	
$10,000+	2.9%	
Median (estimate)	$2,320	} Rich

Source: Dept of Statistics (1992: table 13).

this income group can be classified as being in the 'middle' class. By the same token, those between the poverty line and the median may be considered the 'working' class. These are likely to be families of blue-collar workers, some of whom achieve the middle-level income by pooling the earnings of several family members. Approximately one-third of households fall into this category.

Households with incomes between $2,300 and $6,000 constitute the largest group in the population, accounting for more than 45 per cent of the total number of households. As will be shown later, at the lower end of this group families continue to struggle to maintain what would be conventionally labelled a middle-class lifestyle, involving high-quality daily goods and services, annual vacations abroad and car ownership. Only those at the top end, who are likely to be entrepreneurs or tertiary-educated professionals, may be able to enjoy the lifestyle of the middle class comfortably.

Finally, the 3 per cent of total households with monthly incomes of more than $10,000 are clearly the 'rich'. They include the families of capital owners, top civil servants, multinational corporate executives and successful professionals. Here the privilege of wealth, which includes escaping the clutches of the nation-state, are enjoyed.

A substantive point must be noted here. Given that the wealth of Singapore as a whole is of very recent origin, the middle class and a significant portion of the 3 per cent rich are also of recent origin. They constitute the nation's 'new rich' and represent the majority of Singaporeans. The former minority middle class, made up of English-educated, Straits-born colonial civil servants, has either declined or been absorbed into, and become indistinguishable from, the larger new middle class.

This fourfold classification (poor, working class, middle class and rich) provides a framework for examining the differences in cultural expression of the emerging social classes in Singapore. Obviously, the cultural expressions of different classes are blurred at the boundaries. However, those who can be placed squarely within each category will have fairly distinct patterns, which may be abstracted and generalised. For the purpose of bringing these differences into sharp relief, it is the generalisable portrait of each category that will be subject to our analysis.

HOMOGENISED POLITICAL ATTITUDES AND BEHAVIOUR

One of the terrains in which we might expect class differences to be expressed is that of political culture. This, however, appears not to be the case in Singapore.

For its entire thirty-three years as an independent nation, Singapore has been governed by the PAP. Consequently, the country's political culture is largely shaped by the ideology and practices of the PAP. From the start, the PAP government had reined in the civil service to form a new alliance. The bureaucratic and technocratic nature of the civil service was well suited to the task of making good the political promise of economic growth through 'rational administration' and 'pragmatism' (Chan 1975; Khong 1995). As economic plans succeeded in leaps and bounds, it became increasingly difficult to challenge the PAP government on ideological grounds; partly because it is difficult to argue against success, and partly because 'pragmatism' as an ideology precluded a consistent ideological component that could be defined and challenged (Chua 1995: 70). The political culture that developed is one that is defined by the government; it is conservative and is organised consensually through networks of political agents who share relatively uniform perceptions on the shape of the nation. This uninterrupted hegemonic reign of the PAP has as one of its consequences the engendering of political apathy across all social classes, each having different reasons for it acquiescence.

In a 1992 survey by Mak and Leong (1994) on political attitudes and political behaviour of Singaporeans, it was found that differences between middle and working classes are marginal, with the middle class being slightly more 'liberal' in attitude. For example, on the statement that there was a lack of readiness for democracy in Singapore society, the same proportions of both classes agreed with the statement; but, among those who disagreed, a greater proportion came from the middle class. Middle-class respondents were also less likely to believe that a challenge to the government is a threat to social order (see Table 5.3). The overwhelming majority of respondents were shown to be politically inactive and there was little difference between the two classes' propensity to mobilise support and/or campaign for political candidates (see Table 5.4). In spite of this inactivity, respondents from both classes felt rather strongly that government should be concerned with public opinions and that it matters that politics be democratic, even if the government is doing a good job economically, that is they do not uncritically prefer development over democratisation (see Table 5.3).

The absence of significant differences between the middle and working classes renders political attitudes and behaviour ineffective as elements in the delineation of cultural boundaries between different classes. This is not the case with consumption.

BETWEEN GENERATIONS, ACROSS CLASSES: CONSUMING YOUTH

Rapid expansion of education and economic opportunities, along with the changing occupational structure over the past three decades (1965–95), have resulted in very high rates of inter-generational upward social mobility among Singaporeans, which is itself one of the planks of legitimacy of the government. Within the same family, children tend to exceed their middle-age parents in education and income; it is common to find in one household university-educated children with professional occupations and parents with no formal education who are employed in informal sector jobs. One estimate suggests that slightly more than 70 per cent of male individuals have greater educational

Table 5.3 Political attitudes of the middle and working classes

	Agree	*Neither/ No opinion*	*Disagree*	*Total*
Agreement with the statement: 'Singapore society is not yet ready for real democracy.'				
Middle class	33%	29%	38%	100%
Working class	35%	35%	30%	100%
Total	33%	30%	36%	100%
Agreement with the statement: 'Too great a challenge from the public is not a good thing for social order.'				
Middle class	56%	19%	25%	100%
Working class	61%	21%	17%	100%
Total	57%	19%	23%	100%
Agreement with the statement: 'As long as the government can do a good job in the national development whether it is democractic or not becomes less important.'				
Middle class	34%	16%	49%	100%
Working class	40%	12%	48%	100%
Total	35%	16%	49%	100%
Agreement with the statement: 'The central government knows what is best for the nation and should not be bothered by public opinion.'				
Middle class	16%	11%	73%	100%
Working class	20%	10%	71%	100%
Total	17%	11%	73%	100%

Source: Mak and Leong (1994: 107–8, 261–2).

Table 5.4 Political behaviour of the middle and working classes

	Yes	*No*	*Total*
Willing to vote			
Middle class	78%	22%	100%
Working class	72%	28%	100%
Total	77%	23%	100%
Campaign for political candidates			
Middle class	3%	97%	100%
Working class	3%	97%	100%
Total	3%	97%	100%

Source: Mak and Leong (1994: 111–12).

attainment than their fathers (Quah *et al.* 1991: 210). This generalised upward mobility has brought about corresponding changes in consumption patterns across generations.

This is best illustrated by a typical three-generation extended family. Between the grandparents' and parents' generations, Singapore has been transformed physically from a city with a deteriorating and overpopulated urban core, fringed by squatters in impermanent structures, to one with nothing but modern high-rise commercial and residential structures, which follow breathlessly major trends in international architectural design. This physical transformation is itself indicative of the generalised improvements in material life for the entire population in terms of sustained employment, health and social security. If improvements between these two generations had been confined to basic needs and attendant social and psychological stabilities in daily life, further improvements into the third generation transforms Singapore to a palpable consumer society.

This consumer society is played out most explicitly among those who are aged from their mid-teens to their mid-twenties. This is a period in which consumerism as a way of life can be exercised with greatest impunity because one is adult enough to make independent consumer choices, although often with the financial indulgence of parents, but too young for the responsibilities of adulthood, when the anxieties of cars and houses close in. It is indeed a decade-long window of consumption.

The body has become the locus of consumption of this age stratum, with emphasis on clothes and other accessories of self-adornment. This is evident across social classes, each with its own 'style'. Among the lesser-educated twenty-somethings, gold is still the rage: gold watches, gold pens, gold-plated lighters, chunky gold bracelets and rings, and gold-plated hand-phones. In contrast, for tertiary-educated young professionals, understatement to the point of self-efface-ment is the rule; display of 'taste' is largely through prominent designer labels which they wear proudly, giving rise to the colloquial term of 'branded' good. They are the 'walking mannequins' of mass-marketed designer-labelled goods.

Teenagers, extending to university students, are equally inscribed with 'brand' consciousness – Armani jeans, DKNY blouses, Esprit dresses and Dr Marten's shoes. As the group that is least subjected to the need to appear 'respectable', and who are most exposed to international music and television – which consti-tutes an image bank from which they draw – they tend to attempt a sense of being 'funky' through the sartorial language of 'American street fashion'. It is in this apparent mimicry that the cultural-moral criticism of youths is to be located.

In addition to simple moral criticism of being materialistic and spendthrift, teenagers are also criticised, not only by parents but also by the PAP govern-ment, as being 'Westernised', invoking a simplistically and dichotomously constituted cultural-moral discourse of 'decadent West/wholesome East(Asia)'. Thus, the 'aping' of American funk is read as symptomatic of the 'cultural confusion' of youth, who are seen to have lost their cultural bearings and identity as Asians. However, consistent with the postmodernist injunction that identity is configured and expressed through symbolic universe(s) constituted by objects of consumption, the teenagers may be said to be quite clear about their own identity as cohorts. The image bank of internationalised popular music and television from which they draw their dress sense provides a stability of identity as 'youth'; a globalised image of youth is their reference point and not the local practices of their parents. Rather than confused, they are arguably quite focused.

The inter-generational debate regarding 'American street fashion' has more to do with the contest within Singapore's ideological terrain than with what is simplistically labelled as the 'Americanisation' of Singapore's youth. Contemporary Singaporean everyday life is one that is highly administered, where conformity is ideologically promoted within a reinvented 'Asian' tradition. Within and against this ideological space, America is ideologically and iconically transformed by Singaporean youth into the apotheosis of freedom, where individuality and differences are not only permitted full reign but respected, indeed celebrated. 'Freedom' and 'difference', perceived by the teenagers to be grossly lacking in Singapore, are two components, among others, of the concept of 'cool'.

American street fashion is thus consumed by both the teenagers and their parents through two sides of a Singaporean semiotics: by the teenagers to express resistance to local repression and disciplinary practices, and by their parents as the very realisation of the dreaded absence of discipline in the liberal West. This is why American street fashion is politicised in Singapore not only at the familial level but also at the state-ideological level, while the same item of clothing, for example the ubiquitous jeans, will evoke no comments in an American home, let alone from the government.

NEW RICH MIDDLE CLASS: OF CARS AND PRIVATE PROPERTIES

Unlike the extremes of income groups, the numerically largest middle class is amorphously constituted and internally highly differentiated. The status of this class is itself constructed by self-identifying individuals from an aggregate of experiences and sentiments derived from different realms of daily life: work, housing environment, material consumption, recreation and leisure, and family and personal affiliations, with each contributing only partially to this status (Leong 1995: 17). But consumption seems to play a pre-eminent role. It does not matter, for example, how wealth is obtained; as long as one is able to purchase an above-average car, one is deemed to be and can place oneself in the middle class. The nation is filled with apocryphal stories of Mercedes-driving hawkers. Within the list of constitutive elements, housing and car ownership appear to have disproportionate significance as the measures that divide the Singaporean middle class into two almost 'archetypal' groups: the contented and the anxiety-laden (see Table 5.5).

To fulfil a desire not to be part of the overwhelming public-housing majority, many households have acquired low-end private properties as status goods.

Table 5.5 Distribution of resident private household and car owners by type of dwelling, 1990

	Households	Car owners	Proportion of households which are car owners
Landed	7.0%	18.0%	71.9%
Condos and private flats	4.1%	9.0%	61.4%
HDB*	84.6%	67.1%	22.2%
5-room	13.0%	24.4%	52.5%
4-room	27.4%	25.1%	25.6%
3-room	35.4%	15.5%	12.2%
1- and 2-room	8.1%	1.3%	4.5%
Others	0.7%	0.8%	32.0%
Others	4.3%	5.9%	38.4%
Total	100.0%	100.0%	28.0%**

Source: Dept of Statistics (1994: 8, table 8).
Note:
*HDB = Housing and Development Board dwellings.
**Percentage of all households that own cars.

These include 99-year-leasehold high-rise condominiums in suburban areas, which provide very similar conditions to public-housing living – often with reduced living spaces – but cost about three times as much. Others at the low end of private accommodation live in terrace houses-on-the-ground. In an exploratory study of households who live in the lowest rung of private properties, Foo (1995) identifies a pattern of coping with tight budgets.[6] Significantly, just under 50 per cent of these households still express a desire to 'upgrade' their accommodation.

In order to sustain their residential preference and own a car at the same time, the following management strategies are common: (i) not only are both spouses already working, one may take an additional job (see Table 5.6); (ii) compromise on the quality of both residence and car and other consumer items; (iii) forgoing some items of consumption, such as annual family holidays abroad, sometimes to the detriment of the overall quality of family life. In all these instances, households live tightly on the margin of their income or even slightly beyond. The end result is aptly summarised by one journalist, who refers to them as the group of Singaporeans who have 'Ralph Lauren tastes but are on Stockmart budgets (after making car payments and mortgages)' (*Straits Times*, 28 May 1995). The need to compromise is often experienced by many middle-class households as 'status degradation'. For example, as a result of compromise, each subsequent car purchased becomes a lesser car than the one just sold, in terms of size, make, vintage or all three.

These anxiety-laden households, which include newly married professional couples who have yet to acquire the prized possessions of either a private property or a car, live under heavy anxieties concerning their ability to maintain what they perceive as a preferred, or even necessary, lifestyle. Their aspirations have

Table 5.6 Married couples by monthly income from work and working status, 1990*

	Total	Both	Husband only	Wife only
< $1,000	17.8%	0.2%	30.7%	53.6%
$1,000–$1,999	37.3%	29.4%	45.3%	36.6%
$2,000–$2,999	19.3%	28.6%	12.2%	4.3%
$3,000–$3,999	9.4%	14.8%	5.1%	3.0%
$4,000–$4,999	5.2%	8.6%	2.6%	1.8%
$ 5,000 +	10.5%	18.4%	4.18%	0.7%
Average income	$2,257	$3,557	$1,778	$1,171
Estimated median	$1,863	$2,287	$1,168	**

Source: Dept of Statistics (1992: 15, table 16).
Notes:
*For 11.7 % of married couples, neither spouse was working.
**Denotes no median estimate.

aroused significant government attention and led to certain policy changes. First, to satisfy demands for private property, the government has reduced its earlier plan to house 90 per cent of the population in public housing to about 70 per cent. This is to be achieved by auctioning off state land to private developers who not only provide more private housing but are also expected to stabilise property prices, which had seen astronomical inflation in the early 1990s. Second, there has been no more prominent middle-class issue in Singapore since the mid-1980s than the prices of cars. In general, there is agreement among the population that there should be limits on the number of cars in Singapore because traffic congestion is antithetical to economic production and efficiency. A survey among university students shows this general agreement; nevertheless, most students still aspire to own cars (*Straits Times*, 9 March 1996).[7] Consequently, car ownership has become a 'scarce resource' whose allocation has become a major social issue. Public debate and government deliberations led to the institutionalisation of the certificate of entitlement (COE) in 1990. In order to purchase one of the new cars which is to be added to the road each month, aspiring car owners have to bid successfully for a COE in monthly auctions. The cost of the COE is to be added to the approximately 200 per cent tariff that is already imposed on a car's actual market value. By December 1994, within four years of its introduction, the price of a COE for large-sized cars escalated rapidly from $1,000 to $100,000. Subsequent public outcry led to some fine-tuning of the allocation system which brought down the prices. Nevertheless, people have come to accept that COE prices are determined by market demand and the cost of a car would be about four times its price elsewhere.

If life for those who are anxiety-laden seems to be centred on juggling trade-offs around private housing and car, the burden is lifted and contentment found as soon as one decides to live within the not uncomfortable material conditions of the high end of public-housing flats and use the MRT.

A 1993 survey of the aged-forty-something established middle-class population shows that an overwhelming number of the respondents can be
characterised as follows:

> All the basic necessities can be gotten, from the market or the government.
> The middle-class band has become so wide that they feel it is difficult to fall
> from it just as it is difficult to rise above it. There is little point in struggling
> for more. It is better to lavish in what they have achieved. With regard to
> their inner state of being, the middle class is simply contented. The top
> three ideals are maintaining high economic growth, maintaining a stable
> economy, and maintaining order in the country.
>
> Associated with the contentment and security is a lack of interest in
> public affairs. The class is enveloped in an aura of political apathy and fear
> of political retribution. Politics become a passive state of submitting to the
> forces of the government, receiving government guidance, and asking for
> more intervention if policies are not working towards their well-being.
>
> This apathy and political passivity comes from the feeling of not being in
> control of its own destiny in the various realms of life experience. It has
> been overwhelmed by the larger forces that shape its identity. Indeed, most
> are grateful, grateful to the government and the same forces that brought
> them to this situation. So as individuals and a class, it feels powerless. If it
> cannot control the tide the least it wants to do is to go against it. Inwardly, it
> feels contented with the state of well-being which is largely not of its own
> creation.
>
> (Leong 1995: 19)

Significantly, there is no contradiction here between the government-imposed
ethos of 'meritocracy' and a sense of lack of control of one's own destiny
because personal effort as merit is realised only within a larger social and
economic context not of one's choosing; it is doing one's best within a context
beyond one's control.

Contentment comes, either because one had already acquired both private
housing and a car at an earlier time when such possessions were within the reach
of a middle-class salary (although there is always the issue of necessary replace-
ment of the car), or if one resigns oneself to never owning private property and
to living in public housing, preferably with a car, or in private housing without a
car. With their dependency on the state to provide a substantial amount of their
consumer goods and services, this established middle class constitute the loosely
organised mass-support base of the ruling government; with their desire for
stability, they constitute the mass inertia for social change.

The government's long-term worry is mounting difficulty in satisfying the
consumerist demands of the middle-class mass, which, if frustrated, may turn
them against the ruling regime. Attempts to dampen consumerist demands are
mounted through both material and ideological means. Materially, stringent
conditions are imposed by the Monetary Authority of Singapore (MAS) on the

issuing of credit cards and granting of unsecured credits. Advertisements that 'unwittingly' or intentionally encourage 'excessive' consumption are sanctioned by the Ministry of Information and the Arts. Ideologically, the young are exhorted to reduce their material expectations and be 'realistic';[8] negative comparisons of life conditions across class lines are criticised for inciting the 'politics of envy', for which opposition parties are often blamed. However, ideological exhortations aside, the middle-class mass must not readily be allowed to become contented because this could lead to a decline in national competitiveness which the economy can ill afford.

The cultural delineation of new middle-class Singaporeans around the central components of their lifestyle, namely cars and private housing, is strengthened by their preoccupation with acquiring and maintaining these consumer goods.

ASPIRING WORKING CLASS

As with its political attitudes, so with its cultural identity, there is little that is distinctive about the working class; indeed, its members may be said to aspire to join the ranks of the middle class rather than to define themselves against the latter. Their material conditions correspond with the median income position in the class structure, often attained by pooling incomes of spouses; they are not materially deprived like the poor, nor do they struggle to own a car or private house. In housing, they are mostly found in purchased three-room public-housing flats (40.3 per cent), with aspirations to 'upgrade' to larger, preferably five-room flats.[9] A common sarcastic response of working-class individuals to discussions on the rising costs of COEs is that 'I have no problem at all, I am not looking for a car'.

In general, working-class people are appreciative of the tight labour condition which reduces risks of unemployment; indeed, in many instances being laid off by a firm means a windfall of retrenchment pay because another job can be immediately secured, often with the assistance of government agencies or unions. Furthermore, in anticipation of the relocation of low-skill jobs to neighbouring countries, as a result of rising wages in Singapore, opportunities for skills upgrading are increasingly being made available to the unskilled and low-skilled workers, thus raising their wage-earning potential and reducing the likelihood of permanent displacement from the labour force.

On the whole, younger workers still strive for upward social mobility through skills upgrading, while older ones transfer their aspirations for a better life to their children. Opportunities for upward social mobility through education for working-class children remain widely available, although class and family background are beginning to exercise greater determining effect in the very competitive tertiary-education selection. The radical politics of labour of the late 1950s and early 1960s have all but disappeared as the trade unions become increasingly incorporated into partnership with the ruling party/government through the cross appointments of elected politicians in the National Trades Union Congress.

The middle-class status aspirations of the working class are reflected in the one-third of middle income families who have become car owners at the expense of other aspects of daily life. A further anecdotal glimpse of this aspiration can be gained from the consumption pattern of working-class teenagers featured on a Chinese language current affairs programme on state-owned national television (24 June 1995). All the teenagers interviewed expressed the desire and determination to buy high-price, 'brand' name fashion items of self-adornment. In one instance, a mother said that she gives in to demands from her daughter for money for such purchases because otherwise the latter would not speak to her for days. Such brand consciousness appears to be a common feature of youth in Singapore, regardless of class.

Unlike mature capitalist societies where there are strong working-class traditions which enable its members to construct identities in opposition to other classes, it appears that in the newly industrialised economy of Singapore, the aspiration of the working class is one of moving up the economic class structure rather than proudly preserving a distinctive cultural tradition. Nowhere is this more apparent than among the working-class youth. Unlike mature capitalist nations, where working-class youth culture may be interpreted as a counter-culture (Willis 1977), there is no fear of working-class fashion, such as 'punk' clothes in Britain, becoming 'normalised' and appropriated by the middle class (Wilson 1990) in Singapore.

THE RICH: PRIVILEGE OF WEALTH

There is a wide range of Singaporean households in the top 3 per cent income group, including owners of the three private local banks, successful indigenous entrepreneurs of small- and middle-size enterprises, senior corporate managers, successful professionals and top civil servants. At the low end of this range, the household may be a dual-income family with each spouse earning much less than a $10,000 monthly salary. Relative to other Singaporeans, this group is 'rich'.

Financially able to meet all personal and familial needs and obligations, they are not dependent on any state provisions. Financial independence is reinforced by geographical mobility. Well disposed to take up employment or set up business anywhere in the globalised market, work is a movable feast. Location of residence is usually the result of a combination of professional demands, personal preferences and emotional attachments. Like all wealthy individuals in capitalist economies, they are 'transnationalised' individuals.

The relationship between these transnational individuals and the state is one of unequal disadvantage to the state. Because the state needs the rich for economic stability, growth and even tax revenue, the rich are placed in a good position to use the state for their own interests; for example, as a source of financial loans, business partnership and even protection of investments. Thus, in the government's push to regionalise Singapore's economy, local businesses have actively co-operated with government-linked corporations, behind the protective shield of inter-governmental memoranda of understanding.

Despite their business link-up with the government, the rich refrain from involvement in electoral politics. Since at least the mid-1980s, the PAP has found it difficult to recruit these individuals. This is apparent when one looks at the 'third'-generation PAP ministers, who are without exception drawn from the armed forces.[10] Events came to a head when the government, in 1994, raised ministerial salaries to an unprecedented level, in an attempt to attract suitable individuals among the rich into politics; ministerial salaries, averaging $600,000 per annum in 1994, have increased overall by another 30 per cent (Kwok 1995: 301). This was not a politically popular move in view of the increasing public awareness, and explicit expression, of concern over income differences. Furthermore, the new salary scale did not attract the targeted individuals from their privileged space in the business world because there seems to be little incentive for them to step into the limelight of national politics, which does not just shine, but also casts shadows upon those on whom it falls.

Culturally, what is significant about the rich in Singapore, relative to their counterparts in Hong Kong or the Philippines, is their public absence. They are not surrounded by glitter. They do not make public appearances as an excuse to show off their wealth or 'taste'.[11] That they have money is not to be doubted; for example, while emerging middle-class Singaporeans are struggling to maintain their cars, there are enough rich people to make the Mercedes the largest-selling car in Singapore, with prices ranging from a minimum of $200,000 to half a million dollars. Similarly, while the mass-market side of the retail trade on this 'shopping isle' has been in the doldrums since 1991(see *Asia Magazine*, 4 June 1995), the highest end of the rag trade with 'real' designer clothes, is reporting brisk business with more and more designer wares added monthly (*Straits Times*, 1 June 1995).[12]

With the exception of individuals from established business families, and self-made tycoons who are 'known' to everyone by reputation, via the media – such as the families of the Shaw Brothers, the Lee Foundation, bankers like Lien Lin Chow and Wee Chor Yeow, and property developers like Ong Beng Seng and Ng Teng Fong – little is known publicly of the rich, especially those who make their wealth through professional practices. Those who have public profiles tend to be seen as generous supporters of public institutions, such as tertiary-education institutions, clan associations and other civic organisations. Prominent among these is the Shaw Foundation, whose annual contributions are now publicly acknowledged by the National University of Singapore with the opening of The Shaw Foundation Building, the first edifice on the university campus to bear the name of a financial benefactor. This group of individuals and households are known in Singapore for their public spirit and philanthropic generosity, not for the display of their legendary wealth.

It is difficult to provide a definitive explanations for this apparent 'humility' and 'public self-effacement' of the rich in Singapore. One likely contributing factor is that, unlike in Hong Kong and the Philippines, there is the absence of an extensive media (particularly film) industry that provides grist to the mill of glitterati culture, especially a movie industry with its parasitic tabloids and magazines. A second factor is that the ruling PAP may have reinforced the suppression of public display with its own code of 'humility' applied to its ministers, Members of Parliament and party members. The 'uniform' for a national party convention and national day celebration is alike: white shirt and white trousers, no tie. The usual working attire does not include suits, which are reserved for formal meetings with foreign visitors; even this is of relatively recent vintage, crafted to be more appropriate for international consumption. Members of Parliament and junior ministers are known to have given up luxury cars, leaving them for family use, and to have switched to more humble makes. The rich who work closely with the government are thus constrained in their appearance so as not to upstage the politicians.

The public absence of the rich as cultural consumers may have reduced the pressure on the new middle class to engage in possible cycles of imitation. Thus, the new middle class may become culturally self-satisfied without the pressure of having to keep up with or imitate the rich, only to find that the rich have moved on to greater heights or other terrains when they get there. This absence of the rich as possible 'cultural trendsetters' may have helped the new middle class to accept their realisation that it is 'difficult to rise above it' and that there is 'little point to struggle for more' as Leong (1995) observes.

THE POLITICS OF THE LOWEST 20 PER CENT

In contrast to the rest of society, the lowest 20 per cent income group is highly dependent on state provisions of housing, health care, education and public transportation. Here, the use of consumption – which in this context is always about excess rather than necessity – as a basis of class construction, is inappropriate. Instead, the relations of the poor to the new middle class have to be investigated via their dependency on state provisions. State provision of public goods appeared to have been satisfactory to the lower-income electorate until the 1991 general election when, according to the PAP itself, a substantial quantum of low-income people, particularly Chinese, voted against the Party. Their dissatisfaction apparently arose from difficulties in meeting the rising cost of living, which some attributed to government efforts to privatise some public services, such as hospitals. Since then the government has put in place a fund of several billion dollars, targeted for general distribution, to be used in such programmes as Edusave (a scholarship fund for students from poor families) and Medifund (to aid families who are unable to meet their own medical costs, especially the elderly).

The most spectacular welfare increase is in additional housing subsidies for the poor. These include the 'small family scheme' in which the government will help low-income households in rental flats to purchase their own flats.[13] In addition, a cash subsidy of $30,000 is granted to families with less than $1,200 monthly income. Finally, as part of the government's strategy of using the family as the first line of mutual assistance, a sum of $30,000 is granted to families who choose to relocate closer to their parents.[14]

In social services, the government has also become more generous in its grants-in-aid to voluntary welfare agencies with specific client groups (*Straits Times*, 20 March 1996). However, direct relief to the poor remains meagre and stringently means-tested. This is reflected in the low cost of state welfare, which was just above 2 per cent of the annual total government expenditure in 1993, but has been almost doubled in the 1995 budget.

The additional provisions in housing and social services are implemented within the vehement anti-welfare ideology of the PAP government. They are distributed in the following manner: first, all subsidies are effectively transfers between government departments, no direct funds are given to recipients. The latter have no discretion of speeding grants in ways other than for specifically stated purposes. Second, to deflect welfare entitlement claims on the state, grants to voluntary welfare agencies are given to community groups that are committed to providing and operating the agencies. Detached from direct government involvement, public assistance is not deemed as an entitlement of citizens of a welfare state, but as benefits of the generosities of the public channelled through voluntary agencies. According to the government, this eliminates the development of a 'mentality of dependency' (*Straits Times*, 20 March 1996) among the citizens, particularly the poor.

Because the subsidies are obliquely distributed, it is unclear whether the additional expenditures will satisfy the lower-income electorate's complaints against rising costs of living, which the government apparently believes is more perceptual than 'real'. For example, a 1995 survey quoted by the deputy prime minister, Lee Hsien Loong, found that more than 50 per cent of Singaporeans said that their circumstances had not improved for the past five years. Yet in politics, perception is almost everything – of this the PAP government is well aware. Consequently, it uses every opportunity to exhort Singaporeans to lower expectations because, having already achieved a very high level of material life, from here on every little gain can be achieved only with greater difficulty, relative to the past.[15]

Meanwhile, the poor appear to have discovered their own voice, without conscious or formal organisation, in the ballot box. Indeed, as noted above, it was this voice in 1991 that initiated an expansion of subsidies. Furthermore, it is a voice that appears to be multiracial and national in character because ethnicity is no longer a discriminating variable for poverty. Following the apparent success of the 1991 general election, it is a voice that will likely continue to extract concessions from the government with varying measures of success.

Increased subsidies to the poor are potentially a source of class antagonism between the middle class and the lower-income groups. This is because the general tendency in developed capitalist nations is that the taxes raised to finance such subsidies are extracted from the wage-earning middle class rather than from the capitalist class (Offe 1984: 154).[16] Indeed, in Singapore, there have been some complaints from a segment of the new middle class who are living in private housing against the apparent endless public expenditures, presumably using taxpayers' money, in upgrading public-housing estates (*Straits Times*, 25 August 1995). This has led to suggestions, in Parliament and elsewhere, that to maintain equity, the government should also help to upgrade private housing estates (parliamentary debate in March 1996).[17]

To the extent that the national economy, which is still growing annually at very robust rates, translates into incremental improvement of material life for all, the potential class antagonism between the middle class on the one hand and the working class and the poor on the other will not likely manifest in tangible ways that would affect social order and stability.

CONCLUSION

Singapore has been immensely successful economically, under the PAP government. Among the effects of this success is the spawning of a class structure, amidst the vastly improved material life of the entire population. However, this emergent class structure is seldom part of the public discourse because the success has created an ideological aura which makes raising of issues of social inequalities difficult, at both conceptual and empirical levels. Conceptually, as a consequence of its collaboration with communists in the 1950s, the PAP may be said to realise the ideological appeal of class analysis of social inequalities; hence, its ideological vigilance against any suggestions of class, especially within a Marxist framework. Empirically, the relative homogenisation of daily life, as a result of extensive and standardised provision of collective consumption goods to the overwhelming majority of the population, has glossed over class differences, giving the impression that Singapore is 'homogeneously' a middle-class society; an idea which the PAP government itself is promoting.

The government actively attempts to diffuse, rhetorically and administratively, at many sites and layers, the potential politicisation of social inequalities. It promotes 'meritocracy' as the basis of allocation of material rewards, so as to individualise success and failure. It denounces criticisms against social inequalities and suggestions of a more egalitarian distribution of wealth as indulging in the 'politics of envy'; instead, it encourages individuals to compare their present circumstances with their past rather than synchronously across class lines. It promotes a new ideology of 'communitarianism' which elevates the family and the ethnic group to the level of 'primordial' institutions meant to provide successive levels of social support for the socially and economically needy. All these strategies reinforce each other in displacing structural explanations and theorisations of social inequalities.

Nevertheless, social inequalities are intrinsic to capitalist societies, Singapore is not an exception. Furthermore, the cultures of the different classes can be delineated relative to each other; indeed, these different 'cultures' are mutually constitutive. What is significant in the Singapore instance is that contrary to conventional theoretical expectations, the different classes appear to be rather similar in their political attitudes and behaviour, as a consequence of the unbroken political governance by a single political party, the PAP. Other elements that may help to define the class lines are thus necessary.

The central elements of the life of the emerging newly rich middle class are to be found in their desired objects of consumption; namely, the car and private housing. Both items set them apart from the overwhelming majority of the population who live in public-housing flats and are dependent on public transportation. Prohibitive prices have transformed both into status goods which impart to their owners corresponding social esteem. In the pursuit of these objects of desire, many middle-class households, who could only marginally afford both, are forced to forgo other trimmings of the middle-class lifestyle, such as annual vacations.

Prohibitively priced cars and private housing may serve, therefore, as the defining features of the class structure. Fortunately for the new middle class, the thin layer of rich Singaporeans is not conspicuous in its lifestyles and does not serve as a model for material envy and emulation. In short, the rich do not impose any overt pressure on the middle class by setting increasingly demanding standards of achievement. On the other hand, under the social and economic conditions of a newly industrialising nation, where rapid and high rates of upward mobility have been the norm, there is a total absence of any entrenched working-class culture. The working class, on the whole, is oriented towards and aspires to the standards of the new middle class, among whom are likely to be their friends, neighbours and relatives who had lucky breaks. Finally, in the lowest-income group, which may be as much as 20 per cent, individuals are still struggling to keep up with the high costs of living that are in train with a higher standard of material life. Many are able to better their conditions only with additional financial help from the state. Among the bottom 20 per cent of wage earners, the lifestyle of the new middle class does not set the standard, because it is too exacting. Yet for Singapore society as a whole, the newly rich middle class sets the standard for the society, giving credence, at the ideological and perceptual levels, that it is a 'middle-class society'.

Looking to the medium-term future: the rich will continue to enjoy an intentionally highly privatised life, well screened from public view; the present middle class will continue to strive to build a better material life for itself and its progeny; while the poor having tasted some success in obtaining concessions from the government will continue to use their votes to achieve further gains. None of these classes intends to bring about a radical social restructuring, so long as the PAP government is able to keep the economy growing.

Notes

1 Only the bus system is provided by publicly listed companies operating on a profit basis under government-regulated prices and routing.

2 However, it should be noted that reputably the best secondary schools in the nation, the Raffles Institution for boys and the Raffles Girls Secondary School, have no feeder arrangement and draw their students from the top performers in the national school-leaving examinations among each cohort of graduating primary-school students.

3 While the pattern we describe is true for the great majority of Singaporeans, and more particularly for the new rich, it should be noted, for example, that marginalised poorly educated Chinese and Malay youth dress differently and have quite different entertainment patterns. Moreover, they are labelled differently in local popular parlance: the Malay youth as 'Mat Rock' and the Chinese youth as 'Ah Beng'. However, in general, ethnicity in Singapore is a highly privatised phenomenon, or tends to be limited to such activities as the wearing of 'ethnic' clothes on particular festival occasions.

4 In fact the financial assistance is greater than the cash grant. The three-room flats are purchased by the public-housing authority from existing tenants at a market value of $70,000–$100,000 and refurbished for another $30,000 and then sold to the poor households for about $70,000 before the $30,000 cash subsidy. The currency in this chapter is the Singapore dollar, which in 1996 had an exchange rate of approximately US$0.71.

5 More than half (56 per cent) of heads of households in the $1,000–$1,499 income range are between the ages of 35 and 54, inclusive. About 97 per cent of these heads of households have a secondary education or less. Also, in 73 per cent of married-couple households in this income range, only the husband is working because the wives are likely to have no wage-earning skills or are confined to domestic work.

6 The study was conducted as an honours-year undergraduate academic exercise by Foo Sek Min (1995), at the Department of Sociology, National University of Singapore.

7 For now, an irony should be registered; that is, ownership of private property, especially condominiums, may be more easily attained than cars in spite of the former's much higher cost. This is because payments during the long mortgage period can be made directly through one's monthly compulsory social security savings, which amounts to 40 per cent of one's salary, while borrowing for the car is subjected to higher consumer-loan interest rates, shorter repayment periods and cash repayment. Car ownership is particularly onerous because of its prohibitive price as a result of stringent control of the car population which restricts ownership to a small population segment; 28 per cent of households owned cars in 1990 (see Table 5.6).

8 The high expectations of the younger generation, particularly the university-educated, was highlighted in the speech by senior minister Lee Kuan Yew to undergraduates of the two national universities on 14 March 1996.

9 In public housing, kitchen and washing facilities are standard provisions and not added into the room count. For more details of the public-housing system, see Chua (1995: ch. 6).

10 This is in sharp contrast to the recruitment pattern of the second generation that included individuals with proven track records in private enterprises, such as Dr Tony Tan, Mr S. Dhanabalan and Dr Yeo Ning Hong. All three had resigned from ministerial duties by 1994; however, Tony Tan was recalled in 1995 to assume the post of deputy prime minister and Minister of Defence.

11 Following media hype around annual junior-college graduation dances, there was one attempt in the late 1980s to organise a 'debutante' party for the daughters of wealthy families. Those who were left out organised a counter-event. Each then tried to hide the real intentions of these events by both limiting the expenditure permitted to each young girl and using the occasions to raise funds for charity. The 'proms' are no longer newsworthy and the 'coming out' parties were never repeated. In contrast, the social editor of the Hong Kong *Tatler* says, 'Hong Kong people are proud of what

they have achieved; that's why they display it with Rolls Royces and Chanel suits. They don't look at it as showing off. The term "nouveau riche" has no meaning here' (quoted in 'Rich and Righteous', *Asia Magazine*, 19–21 January 1996).

12 For the business practices of boutiques that cater only to women who are 'self-employed or unemployed', see Chua (1990, 1992).

13 In 1994 alone, these schemes had cost the government 160 million Singapore dollars, benefiting 4,000 households (*Straits Times*, 1 March 1994).

14 This scheme has not been widely popular because of the conditions imposed (*Straits Times*, 5 June 1995).

15 It has also institutionalised its position on welfarism by establishing the office of the elected Presidency in 1991. The elected President is empowered to veto any drawing down of the national reserve by an incumbent government. This is meant as a check on any future government's readiness to expand social welfare provisions for reasons of political expediency. More speculatively, senior minister Lee Kuan Yew has suggested that the one-person-one-vote rule may have to be changed in future to some-people-two-votes in favour of the able-bodied, gainfully employed heads of family against an expanding population of retirees, for fear that a future incumbent government may be held to ransom by the retirees and forced to expand social security measures. This fear is, perhaps, obliquely substantiated by a survey finding, in 1994, that Singaporeans who are 45 years of age and above are more inclined than their younger counterparts to see the government as the provider in times of need (*Straits Times*, 18 September 1994).

16 Consequently, in Britain, for example, working individuals who are able to pay for their own consumption needs in transportation and housing are inclined to vote for right-wing candidates who promise reduction of welfare spending (Saunders 1984).

17 To the presumption that the middle class is being taxed for such subsidies, the Minister of Finance pointed out that in fact the level of personal income tax has been declining steadily since the mid-1980s, from a high of 33 per cent to 25 per cent. The subsidies could not possibly be raised from such taxes, he said; rather it is paid for by the non-tax revenues of an efficiently managed economy. On the question of helping to upgrade private housing estates, the government countered that the values of these properties have escalated tremendously through the early 1990s and such asset inflation should enable these privileged residents to pay for the upgrading of their own facilities.

Bibliography

Chan Heng Chee (1975) 'Politics in an Administrative State: Where Has the Politics Gone?', in Seah Chew Meow (ed.), *Trends in Singapore*, Singapore: Singapore University Press, pp. 51–68.

Chua Beng Huat (1990) 'Steps to Becoming a Fashion Consumer in Singapore', *Asian Pacific Journal of Management*, no. 7: 31–48.

——— (1991) 'Not Depoliticised but Ideologically Successful: The Public Housing Programme in Singapore', *International Journal of Urban and Regional Research*, no. 15: 24–41.

——— (1992) 'Shopping for Women's Fashion in Singapore', in R. Shields (ed.), *Lifestyle Shopping: The Subject of Consumption*, London: Routledge, pp. 114–35.

——— (1995) *Communitarian Ideology and Democracy in Singapore*, London: Routledge.

Department of Statistics (1979) *Report on the Household Expenditure Survey 1977/78*, Singapore: Department of Statistics.

——— (1984) *Report on the Household Expenditure Survey 1982/83*, Singapore: Department of Statistics.

—— (1989) *Report on the Household Expenditure Survey 1987/88*, Singapore: Department of Statistics.

—— (1992) *1990 Singapore Census of Population: Households and Housing*, Singapore: Department of Statistics.

—— (1994) *1990 Singapore Census of Population: Transport and Geographic Distribution*, Singapore: Department of Statistics.

Drysdale, J. (1985) *Singapore: Struggle for Success*, Singapore: Times Books International.

Foo Sek Min (1995) *The Paradox of Affluence: Undergraduate Academic Exercise*, Singapore: National University of Singapore, Department of Sociology.

Khong Cho-Onn (1995) 'Singapore: Political Legitimacy through Managing Conformity', in Muriah Alagappa (ed.), *Political Legitimacy in Southeast Asia*, Stanford: Stanford University Press, pp. 108–36.

Kwok Kian Woon (1995) 'Singapore: Consolidating the New Political Economy', *Southeast Asian Affairs 1995*, Singapore: Institute of Southeast Asian Studies, pp. 291–308.

Leong Choon Heng (1995) 'The Construction of a Contented and Cautious Middle Class', unpublished.

Mak Lau Fong and Leong Choon Heng (1994) 'The Singapore Middle Class', unpublished East Asian Middle Class Research Report, Taiwan: Academia Sinica.

Offe, C. (1984) *Contradictions of the Welfare State*, Cambridge, MA: MIT Press.

Quah, Stella, Chiew Seen Kong, Ko Yiu Chung and Sharon Mengchee Lee (1991) *Social Class in Singapore*, Singapore: Times Academic Press.

Rodan, G. (1989) *The Political Economy of Singapore's Industrialisation*, London: Macmillan.

Saunders, P. (1984) 'Beyond Housing Class: The Sociological Significance of Private Property Rights in Means of Consumption', *International Journal of Urban and Regional Research*, no. 8: 202–25.

Tremewan, C. (1994) *The Political Economy of Social Control in Singapore*, London: St Martin's Press.

Willis, P. (1977) *Learning to Labour*, Westmead: Gower Publishing.

Wilson, E. (1990) 'Fashion and Postmodernism', in R. Boyne and A. Rattansi (eds), *Postmodernism and Society*, London: Macmillan, pp. 209–36.

6 The years of living luxuriously
Identity politics of Indonesia's new rich

Ariel Heryanto

Until recently, there were only two quick answers in Indonesia to the question of who constituted the rich. They were unequivocally Westerners and the Chinese. Occasionally one would include top government officials in the list, but at a tier lower than the previous two. Now there can be more diverse answers to the same question, with some hesitation and necessary qualifications. Before 1990 there were more or less fixed stereotypes of Westerners, the Chinese, and top government officials in Indonesian popular culture. Now their public images have undergone significant changes.

What follows is an examination of those changes. Obviously economic factors feature in the multiple causes, and diverse directions of these changes. Some consideration of the economic dimension is imperative. However, the bulk of this discussion is more a cultural analysis of economic power, than an economic analysis of cultures.

This chapter is therefore about cultural constructions of the rich, which may or may not come close to facts about the economically rich. Westerners and Chinese who personify the rich in Indonesian popular knowledge are cultural constructs. They are fictional. But like most fictional figures, they are neither totally misleading, nor fabricated from pure fantasy.[1] Like most fictional works, the popular cultural construction of Westerners and Chinese profiles in Indonesia conveys an important message; and so does the reconstruction of Indonesia's new rich in the 1990s. The qualifier 'new' in the designation of the new rich refers primarily to the first half of the 1990s which is marked by significant prosperity and changes to social identities and relations.

I will focus on lifestyle, including consumerism, as an important site for the contemporary work of culturally constructing, contesting and negotiating identities of the new rich. No social act such as human consumption takes place in a social vacuum. It always operates within specific historical settings and embodies historically specific constructions of time, space and social relations. It involves socially situated persons, relationships, passions, fears, desires and memories. No consumption takes place in a purely natural, biological, ahistorical universe. Eating a McDonald's hamburger in Los Angeles never means the same as eating 'the same thing' at the same moment in one of its counter-outlets in Yogyakarta, supposedly the capital city of High Javanese Culture, or in Mahathir's Kuala Lumpur, or in Ho Chi Minh City.[2]

Consumption always makes a social statement, sometimes more and sometimes less than simply indicating the consumer's purchasing capacity and personal taste. Moreover, the messages that emanate from consumption practices may not have been intended by individual consumers. These messages become more important and complex in contemporary urban settings, where consumption increasingly transforms itself into 'consumerism' (significantly stylised acts of consumption), as a part of lifestyle. The boundary that separates consumption from consumerism is often blurred.

THE OLD RICH

A striking feature of Indonesian public discourse, especially before 1990, is a pervasive hostility towards the rich. This is by no means unique, but it is nonetheless important to recognise. Throughout much of Indonesia's modern history, the rich have almost always been regarded with suspicion. This is not to say that Indonesians are not keen on getting rich. The widespread negative image of the rich is probably an index of the poor's success in outwitting the rich within the cultural battle to establish a dominant narrative of their antagonistic relationship. Until the 1980s, there were as many as, if not more folk tales, anecdotes and modern works of fiction that ridiculed rather than praised the rich. A common theme in Indonesian narrative is the unhappy life of rich characters and the moral superiority of the poor.

It is telling that the popular identification of the rich has been with Westerners and Chinese, leaving aside sex, class, religion or urban–rural differences. To understand the contemporary reconstruction of the rich from 'old' to 'new', it is necessary to look at the main elements that constitute the public image of Westerners and the Chinese. In popular discourse, the effect counts much more than accuracy of facts. In Java, the vernacular word for Westerners is *Landa*, short for *Belanda* (Hollanders), the former colonial masters. All white-skinned persons can be easily referred to as *Landa*, or more casually *Bule*.

There are also the so-called 'Indonesian citizens of Chinese descent'. In Java, the vernacular designation *Cina* refers to all Oriental-looking persons. More recently these have included resident or visiting Japanese and Koreans who, incidentally, are very wealthy. As in most acts of identification, the construction of stereotypes of the rich tells us about the object being identified as much as the identifying persona in a set of binary oppositions.

Unless indicated otherwise, the account below describes the common stereotypes in popular culture evident in everyday conversations in the streets, published cartoons, caricatures, comic strips, jokes, gossip or soap operas. It is a crude reproduction of already familiar cultural constructs. Like all folk tales, there are varied versions of these popular constructs. They are all anonymous and equally legitimate. They are also marked by prejudice and caricaturing.

Westerners are not just rich in the common view. More importantly they are considered to be essentially non-Indonesian, regardless of their actual citizenship. They are uniformly modern, and are seen as carriers of the modernising spirit into Indonesian social life. They are expected to be unable to speak Indonesian properly, despite frequent cases to the contrary, and are believed to be Christians. As the carriers of superior civilisation, high technology and modernity, they are looked up to culturally. The *Landas* who exist in the popular mind are primarily those appearing in Hollywood movies and television soap operas. Their images are reproduced most visibly in advertisements, films and other entertainment industries. Morally, however, they are regarded with suspicion. The *Landa* are notorious for their liberalist, individualist and materialistic dispositions.[3]

Although many Indonesians have seen or heard of poverty-stricken Chinese families, in popular discourse *Cina* generally refers to tycoons such as Liem Sioe Liong, Bob Hasan and Ciputra (McBeth and Hiebert 1996). In New Order Indonesia the existence of this ethnic minority has come to prominence only on badminton courts and in commerce. They may be called fellow citizens, but are seen to constitute a distinct category as 'non-indigenous' Indonesians. The ethnic Chinese are generally known to believe in Confucianism, Buddhism or Christianity, but significantly not Islam which is the faith of the majority of the population. Worse than the Westerners, the Oriental-looking Indonesians are not only morally questionable. They are also seen as ideologically threatening and culturally unattractive.

Sino-Indonesians are indiscriminately considered rich and notoriously industrious, but also cunning and stingy. In the common stereotyped image, they have the worst taste in culture and aesthetics. Socially they may have strong in-group feelings, but politically they seem to have no patriotism. Regarded as being sympathetic towards Communism, they have been deprived of representation in successive state cabinets and formal political activity. Until very recently they never appeared on print media covers, talk shows or popular entertainment, except on rare occasions as minor foils to the protagonists. Periodically these people have been the easy target of public scolding, blackmailing and violence during mass riots.

The elite among New Order government officials may or may not be as rich as Westerners or Chinese Indonesians, but they enjoy the most comfortable position among the country's rich. Despite their extraordinary social and material privileges, these state agents and their families encounter less scrutiny from the general public. Though their wealth does not always escape criticism and hostile comment, they enjoy special exemption by virtue of being indigenous Indonesians and formal representatives of the nation-state. These state agents may be poorly trained professionals, and their rural backgrounds may impede their acquisition of fashionable taste. Nonetheless, the poor majority see these officials as belonging to the same group as themselves and as providing achievable models for their offspring.

In the dominant public discourse, the majority of Indonesians are stereotypically 'indigenous', Muslim, and come from rural backgrounds, but they are also seen as making impressive adjustments in the fast-changing world to which they are subjected. As in many 'developing countries', there is a prolific romanticisation of the 'people' (*rakyat*) in contemporary Indonesia. *Rakyat* represents an affectionate depiction of the innocent, morally superior, economically unprivileged but politically sovereign figures who often suffer from injustice inflicted by the rich and powerful.

While I do not claim these popular stereotypes to be truthful or even accurately represented, neither are they totally wrong, innocently fabricated, nor aimlessly reproduced. Despite their fictional status, such stereotypes illustrate, par excellence, a case of a dominant cultural construction of the rich – a construction that is never totally controlled by the economically powerful elite.

PRESSING AGENDA OF THE NEW RICH

Something fundamental in public life is now being transformed by the recent influx of wealth into the region. A central message in the dominant discourse about Indonesia's economy until the 1980s was that 'the rich are anything but us, Indonesians', and that 'we Indonesians are many things, but not rich'. The rich were non-Asian, or non-indigenous, non-Muslims, and non-*rakyat*.

Since the 1990s things have changed. The motto of the day has become 'it is cool to be rich'. Significant numbers from within the old Indonesian 'self' have improved their economic position. Two social groups that have assumed outstanding status in the public eye, as a consequence of their new wealth, can be called the new middle class and the indigenous Muslim elite. Other social identities, such as urban professional women, made their presence clear. However, their emergence has not reached the high level of significance of the other two categories. Space limitations prevent a special discussion on these newly emerging female groups. Suffice it to say that women play a significant role within the growing identity politics of the middle class and Muslim elite, and we will take into account their role in those non-gendered categories.

For similar reasons, it will not be possible to devote special discussion to the new poor, or the underclass more generally. The recent economic boom in the region has not only enlarged the wealth of nations, it has also widened the gap between the haves and have-nots, and deepened their mutual antagonism. Suffice it to acknowledge here that industrial workers and the urban underemployed have developed into important social groups. From time to time they have contested mainstream discourses of the status quo, the new rich, and economic disparity.[4]

Like most success stories of capitalism in Asia, the new rich in Indonesia encounter a serious problem of lacking moral support from the general public. Industrial capitalism has grown vigorously, but without the supplement of a strong capitalist ideology that renders capitalist social relationships as normal, rational and just. From the beginning, capitalism has been a dirty word. While most Indonesians want to be rich, only a few have attained the desired position and they endure the stigma and discomfort of being regarded with suspicion.

In the 1990s the new rich are under greater pressure than ever before to protect and legitimise private ownership of substantial wealth. Negotiating or reconstructing the already dominant images of wealth, wealth-making and the wealthy becomes a serious project. They must seek ways to secure their dominant position on a long-term basis, and to maintain the broader social order that laid the foundation of their dominance. This security, however, cannot be achieved simply by constant concealment of wealth, denial of wealthiness or incessant retreat from luxurious lifestyles.

Like everyone else in a similar position, the new rich need convenient ways to exercise their economic power and enjoy the material privileges available to them beyond the economic arena. And they must do this in the face of obvious envy and resentment from the poor masses. These problems require confidence, creativity and experimentation. One social space where these experimentations take place is lifestyle. However, in the course of their development, particular lifestyles can move far beyond the rational calculation, modern economic principles or ideology that informed the initial agenda.

Indeed, to speak of contemporary lifestyles among the new rich merely as a necessary route to a higher level of dominance does not go far from political economism. Irrationality is occasionally at work in the desire for pleasure in consumption. It is more socio-psychological than economically motivated or rationally calculated. 'What is the point of being a capitalist, an entrepreneur, a bourgeois', Immanuel Wallerstein reminds us, 'if there is no personal reward?' (1991: 146). He asserts that although the logic of capitalism demands abstemious puritanism, the psycho-logic of capitalism calls for a display of wealth and conspicuous consumption (1991: 148).

Many observers agree that the emergence of a new bourgeoisie in Indonesia is more a product of political patronage than of market competition, successful rational planning or hard work.[5] It is not a surprise, therefore, that a large portion of the abundant fruit of the economic boom goes into excessive consumerism rather than productive investment. What comes easily, goes away easily. The new preoccupation of the emerging Indonesian capitalists is no longer how to get rich and sustain wealth, but how to maximise enjoyment and expand the scope of what money can buy. Among some of the most successful young professionals too, consumption has gone beyond the logic of utility or economy (*Kompas* 1995b).

The rest of this chapter will focus on some of the most salient directions of meanings in contemporary Indonesian consumer culture. We will begin with two distinguishable social clusters: middle-class intellectuals and the new bourgeoisie in their mutually reinforcing effort to build a new bourgeois hegemony through culturalisation.

THE NEW MIDDLE CLASS: TOWARDS A BOURGEOIS HEGEMONY?

The notorious conceptual confusion over the term 'middle class' has been widely recognised and well documented, and permits no easy resolution.[6] Here, the term is used primarily because its Indonesian equivalent, *kelas menengah*, has been central in contemporary discourse, referring to a segment of the new rich. We employ the problematic term in the popular sense, variously referring to the well-educated, economically better-off urbanites, with structural occupations ranging widely from the petty bourgeoisie to intellectuals, artists, middle-ranking bureaucrats and managerial or technical professionals. More often than not, these people use the term *kelas menengah* to identify themselves. Significantly, as elsewhere, the middle class in Indonesia has been described as the main agent of contemporary consumer culture and lifestyle. Such a broad and culturalist description can be seriously problematic, but for our purposes it will suffice.

It is impossible to discuss the growth of the Indonesian new middle class in isolation from those designated with other categories of the country's new rich (Muslims, Chinese or Westerners). Partly this is due to the fact that actual individuals shift between, or belong to more than one of, these categories, and partly to the fact that the formation of one category has implications for the others. Nevertheless, the new middle class is not always reducible to these alternative categories and needs to be considered separately.

One major characteristic of the new middle class that distinguishes this category from other groups identified among the new rich is its highly cosmopolitan outlook and activities. While cosmopolitanism denationalises, de-ethnicises and secularises social categories, in practice it also frequently reinforces class structuration. As Yoon (1991: 128) observes, Indonesia's economic dynamics are revitalising 'a new capitalist class'. Strong cosmopolitanism alone, if not class formation, has made a fundamental impact on the previously entrenched imagination of social groupings in terms of such categories as East/West, Muslim, women or indigenous Indonesians. It is important to stress, however, that while a cosmopolitan consumer culture is of primary significance in this recasting of social imagination, it is more than merely about class politics.[7]

The formation of a new middle-class identity and the parallel establishment of a capitalist hegemony in contemporary Indonesia operate on several fronts. First, through intellectual debates, there is a fairly overt advocacy of liberalism, pro-market sentiment and private property. Secondly, of equal importance, the state has enacted a series of economic measures, both token and sincere, to redress grievances over the alarming economic imbalance in financial assistance, loans and corporate partnerships. Thirdly, and more curiously, is the recently popular and unprecedented trend among top business figures to read poetry and sing popular songs specifically prepared for performance in serious public gatherings.

Yoon (1991) has already recorded a fairly detailed history of the first two of these developments in the period up to 1990. More than updating the continued trend, the following paragraphs indicate the remarkable progress that these campaigns have achieved. A recent event of major significance in the struggle for capitalist hegemony in the economic field is the Jimbaran Declaration, an official accord signed by Indonesia's 96 biggest businessmen in a government-sponsored meeting in Jimbaran, Bali, 24–7 August 1995. The document announces renewed commitments by those business people to assist the less successful in the fight against the wealth gap. Many Indonesian observers, however, commented sceptically that real benefits for the needy were more urgent than promises. Some even demanded a broader and fundamental transformation of the overall economic system.[8]

As mentioned earlier, 'capitalism' has been a dirty word in Indonesia throughout much of the twentieth century. It is used mainly for demonisation by all sections of the population, despite their being bitterly antagonistic to each other on other matters. It was thus remarkable that early in 1995 one of the most respected intellectuals in the country, Kwik Kian Gie, openly applauded the merits of capitalism. In one of his regular columns for the Jakarta-based *Kompas*, Kwik (1995) made this extraordinary remark: [9]

> liberalism as well as capitalism are all fine, by no means do they contradict *Pancasila* and the 1945 Constitution....Therefore, it is okay if we overtly state that the liberalisation we are espousing at present implies liberalism, after all liberalism is in accord with *Pancasila* and the 1945 Constitution. Likewise it is okay to say openly that the triumphant success of the private enterprise today is the materialisation of capitalist doctrines, after all capitalism conforms with *Pancasila* and the 1945 Constitution.[10]

Just a week earlier, Christianto Wibisono (1994), Director of the Centre of Indonesian Business Data, and Kwik's close associate, wrote in the same daily that liberalism 'put into practice the soul and spirit of *Pancasila*'. In this sense, Wibisono adds, 'by conducting a modern reformation of liberalism', Europe, the United States of America and Japan have already become 'true *Pancasilaists* by putting into practice' the major tenets of what is known as P4 (*Pedoman Penghayatan dan Pengamalan Pancasila* – Guidelines for the Comprehension and Implementation of *Pancasila*), a virtual state indoctrination programme.

Both Kwik and Wibisono had already attracted Yoon Hwan-Shin's attention a decade earlier when they spoke mildly in defence of capitalism. Yoon is one of the first scholars to help us recognise the insistent attempts on the part of the urban middle class to create capitalist ideology and culture in post-1980 Indonesia (1991). He noted how non-economic forces emanating from the state and intelligentsia were active in promoting a liberal, market-oriented economic system and ideology. Yoon correctly assessed the impressive success of this politico-cultural effort.[11]

This success would not be possible without a more balanced racial representation of economic dominance in Indonesia, or an appearance of something to that effect. Thus, one can understand the long and steady phasing-out of anti-

Chinese sentiment in official public discourse, and the state's continual withdrawal from the nation's economy as private enterprise moved progressively to
centre stage.[12] Indeed, in the past few years controversies have focused more
consistently on the enormous privileges enjoyed by the President's children and
grandson, for instance in the clove industry, beer levy and first national car-
industry (see McBeth 1996; Schwarz 1994: 133–61). One should neither
overemphasise the change, nor be sure of how long this development will last.
Undoubtedly anti-Chinese sentiments are still alive, and will continue to be in
many years to come.

Nonetheless, it has been remarkable how such sentiments have been toned
down, repressed from public expression, or confined to private communication
and anonymous pamphlets during the last decade or so. There were local incidents involving the expression of anti-Chinese and anti-Christian sentiments in
Central and East Java from late 1995 to the to time of this writing in early 1997.
But the public discussions and media coverage of these events have too often
overemphasised racial and religious aspects.[13] More instructive are the statements made in the hundreds of student demonstrations and publications since
1989. While capitalism has been their longstanding target, in no single instance
have they been reported to have attacked the ethnic Chinese in their banners,
posters or chants, in contrast to previous decades. The workers' demonstration in
Medan in 1994 has often been described as an anti-Chinese riot but, as I have
argued elsewhere, such description is seriously misleading (Heryanto 1994 and
1998).

CULTURALISATION OF THE NEW RICH

Almost without exception, observers of Indonesia have been condescending in
their discussions of consumer culture lifestyles. They all view the practices of the
new rich as simply hedonistic. Although there is some truth in the negative
remarks, the empirical evidence to support this old argument is increasingly
problematic. Some of what will be described below might be said to be universal
of the *nouveaux riches*. Nonetheless, the Indonesian new rich deserve close scrutiny
here, both because of their newness and their particular contexts. Empirical
details are imperative. Below I describe a new preoccupation of some individuals
from the top layers of the new rich.

Poetry reading for the public has always been popular in Indonesia. In the
mid-1980s, for example, it cost a Semarang-based organising committee 10
million rupiah to invite Rendra, the nation's most celebrated dramatist and poet,
to read ten poems at the city stadium.[14] In the 1990s something novel has
happened: segments of the new rich have themselves taken on the joy of public
poetry reading. The 1991 commemoration of Independence Day was probably
a major starting point of this new tradition. The person who was responsible for
this and similar subsequent events was retired Major-General Syaukat
Banjaransari, a former military secretary to President Suharto. In that meeting

the nation's notable poets read their poems on stage, interspersed with readings by the nation's biggest tycoons such as Liem Sioe Liong, William Suryajaya, Ciputra and Mrs Siti Hardijanti Rukmana (the President's oldest daughter). Joining the event were top government officials such as Co-ordinating Minister for Political and Security Affairs, retired Admiral Sudomo, Minister of Education and Culture, Fuad Hassan, and leading figures of the Parliament, such as Vice-Chairman Naro, General Chairman of the ruling party Golkar, would-be Parliamentary Chairman, Wahono, and State Secretary Moerdiono (*Bernas* 1991). Apparently impressed by the event, several print media reprinted photographs of individuals reading poetry from that event in their reporting of other occasions (for example, *Tiara* 1991a, 1991b).

Since then public poetry reading by big business people and state officials has become popular in privately run radio stations, while the print media have invited them to write poems for their publications. On the national Mother's Day, 20 December 1993, another major poetry reading was held, featuring several tycoons, top state officials, Islamic leaders and military elite. Bearing more cultural weight than the 1991 meeting, this public performance took place at Taman Ismail Marzuki, Jakarta's most prestigious arts centre. Ironically, many of the poems composed by the performers themselves were full of sharp criticism of misconduct by the Indonesian new rich. One exception was Minister of Labour, Abdul Latief's poem, 'Tanda Cintaku Padamu Mama' ('Token of My Love to You, Mama'), which recalls his mother's words of wisdom: 'You must get rich/ So that you can help the poor/ The poor cannot possibly help their lot...' (*Panji Masyarakat* 1994).

Feeling pleased with the various experiments in the previous years, Major General Syaukat Banjaransari prepared a similar event for the golden anniversary of the nation's independence in August 1995. As before he invited business people, members of the newly appointed state cabinet, top military officers and accomplished professional poets (*Kompas* 1995g). Another event took place on 17 January 1996 at the Jakarta Arts Hall, where state ministers, businessmen, journalists, movie directors and retired military officers participated (*Kompas* 1996c).

It should be emphasised that these events were intended to be taken very seriously and were prepared specifically to feature members of the new rich.[15] No doubt, some participants took the affairs more seriously than others. The same can be said about those new rich whose prime interests are in music or painting. Rather than simply patronising big concerts or art exhibitions, which they do, new rich individuals commonly take high profiles as newborn artists. Some demonstrate their musical talents in prestigious public or professional settings, while others have participated proudly in a whole new era of painting exhibitions and art criticism (*Kompas* 1995b).[16]

However, these new trends do not go without challenge and cynicism from the general public. In the Jakarta-based news magazine *Forum Keadilan*, a reader from Kalimantan wrote an open letter, welcoming the new poetry-reading tradition, but protesting against the use of certain venues normally devoted to distinguished artists (see Ganie 1995). In Semarang, the capital city of Central

Java, collective poetry reading by known poets, military and police officers, and businessmen provoked polemics in the local daily, *Suara Merdeka* (Utomo 1995; *Suara Merdeka* 1995a; Saparie 1995; Set 1995).

Participants in the new trend are fully aware of the public's mixed reactions. In response to the sceptics, two strategies have been adopted. The first is to reject any attempt to label these activities as mere fads. When Minister of Transmigration, Siswono Yudohusodo organised a poetry reading with his colleagues from the ministry, along with selected artists and politicians, it was necessary to demonstrate a serious engagement with the aesthetic. This was emphasised in a front-page *Kompas* report which opens with a sympathetic sigh on the difficulty of being a bureaucrat. If s/he reads poetry at a time when poetry reading has become trendy, it says, others are quick to doubt their sincerity (Tejo 1995). The second strategy is to write a history of individuals' artistic talent, proving that these various professionals, business people and bureaucrats have already devoted themselves to music or poetry long before the current fashion (see *Tiara* 1991b, 1991c, 1992; *Tiras* 1995b).

Having noted this, it remains necessary to examine contemporary consumer culture beyond any rationally calculated 'logic of late capitalism' or class politics.[17] Consumer culture and the pursuit of luxury certainly complement capitalist production. In the West, the elevation of a luxuriously stylised life involved what Immanuel Wallerstein calls 'aristocratization of the bourgeoisie' (1991: 139). Consumer culture in the life of the Indonesian new middle class implies a public statement to the effect that being rich is now 'cool and necessary'.[18] However, the stylisation of life can take on a life of its own. Featherstone's understanding of the 'new petite bourgeoisie' is highly relevant in examining the urban middle classes in Indonesia, as in many other Asian countries: 'Here it is not a question of...a particular style, but rather...a general interest in style itself, the nostalgia for past styles,...in the latest style,...subject to constant interpretation and reinterpretation' (1991: 91).

After a few years of experiments, several Jakarta-based glossy magazines (*Matra*, *Tiara* and *Jakarta-Jakarta*) found solid ground in the 1990s by devoting themselves exclusively to the newly desired lifestyles. Like all other social constructs, the new identities embedded in these lifestyles must be acquired through an extended learning. With the new trend, one is trained to be 'constantly self-consciously checking, watching and correcting' oneself (Featherstone 1991: 90). The areas and objects of learning are virtually limitless: from ideal body size and shape, to health, sex, eating, drinking, speech, clothing, accessories, technological gadgets and choice of leisure, entertainment and shopping.

ASIANISATION OF ASIA: GOOD BUY, THE WEST[19]

Since colonial times, the West has been a fascinating model for lifestyling and consumer desire in Asia. The West continues to attract Asians during the current years of prosperity, so that consumerism and Westernisation have often been considered one and the same thing. However, we need to make two qualifications about the current 'Western' elements that go with Indonesia's consumer culture in the 1990s.[20]

First, what constitutes the West, the East, and their relationships has become vague, if not meaningless. This is partly a consequence of the second qualification: in devouring things 'Westernised', contemporary Asians reassert and remodify their new selfhood. Both render the common nativism and empiricism in most discussions about consumer culture embarrassingly naive and obsolete. The notion of Asianisation of Asia has become popular in response to this confusing problem. But this popular phrase can be deceitful. There is no Asia, let alone Asianisation without the West and Westernisation. East and West have always constituted each other. In contemporary consumer culture their mutually embedded relationships become glaringly evident. In isolation, East and West become increasingly empty signifiers.

Yao Souchou (1995) notes the paradox in the McDonald's televised advertisement to Singaporeans. The fast-food restaurant that has become 'the most blatant American cultural export' is now transformed into something quite the opposite: Singaporean nationalism.

> One ad begins with the title: 'The Sounds of Singapore', and from the first scene one sees that it is designed to rouse nationalistic sentiments. The bright-eyed [Oriental-looking] school children are outdoors with the school flag being raised under the blue tropical sky. They sing their allegiance to Singapore: 'When the sun shines upon our land.'
>
> (Yao 1995: 00)

During the Muslim fasting month of Ramadan in 1996, Surabaya's McDonald's distributed a complimentary piece of *ketupat* (rice cooked in coconut leaf, traditionally consumed during this fasting month) for every Rp. 1,000 its clients spent (*Jawa Pos* 1996).

Consumption of things Westernised still runs high. What is somewhat new, however, is how new rich Asians aggressively objectify the West in the form of commodities at their disposal. Occasionally one still hears the old anti-Western rhetoric, especially among defensive state bureaucrats in the context of human rights debate. It is now clear that the rhetoric appeals to fewer and fewer young Asians. Instead of continuing to regard the West as a major threat, or simply an object of obsessive idolisation, more and more Asians regard many Western things as pliable resources, and Westerners as equals. One area that illustrates this quite clearly is the (mis-)use of English.

Over the twentieth century, English has been important in Indonesia and most Asian countries. In the 1980s it was fairly common to see Indonesians striving to learn the language, showing off their skills, and materially benefiting from a mastery of the language. Now Indonesian urbanites are more exposed to the language, many through greater access to international travel, and they are more fluent in it. While mastery of the language still engenders some prestige, there is also a new fashion of wordplay, called *plesetan*. *Plesetan* has different variants. One of them involves creating funny names and idiomatic expressions by twisting English words. While Japanese and South Korean never rival English, some *plesetan* makes use of both familiar or non-existent Japanese- and South Korean-sounding words. It is significant that the target of *plesetan* is only those foreign languages belonging to the politically and economically most powerful nations.[21]

Reviewing the details of the new rich's recent ventures in consumer culture can be entertaining. However, such a lengthy account would contribute limited insight to the present study. Thus I will limit myself to one case: the new trend in hosting international pop music stars. Until the late 1970s, Western pop music stars mainly existed, for their Indonesian middle-class fans, through audio recordings, movie screens, posters, news-magazines and fantasies. In the 1990s, however, hardly any Western music stars escaped the more direct embrace of Indonesia's new rich.[22] None could see and appreciate the change better than those in their late forties and over, who still played the oldies in the 1990s and welcomed Cliff Richard in Jakarta on 17 March 1995 to celebrate the launching of the luxurious 'Legend City' real estate.

Clearly tickets to these and other such shows were expensive, even to average middle-class Jakartans.[23] They were largely financed by top government officials, or their children, who competed with each other as hosts for the more prestigious artists. Some even offered more than the standard fee to outdo their rivals. 'As for the ticket sales, they made big business people or their parents' relations purchase the ticket *fait accompli*' (*Forum Keadilan* 1994a). Franz Harry's magic show in October 1992 failed to attract an audience, as a result of a competing David Copperfield show in the city a month earlier. The concert in Jakarta of Bryan Adams in December 1993 did not succeed because it had to compete with others by Julio Iglesias, Andy Williams and Sergio Mendes.

Earlier I noted how Asia's economic growth is becoming more and more self-sufficient, rendering the rest of the world less relevant. Without implying any direct causal relationship, one can see something similar taking place in the area of culture. There is now a growing pride and interest among Asians in their traditional cultural heritage. This extends to an expanding industry devoted to rediscovering, reinventing and manufacturing exotic and traditional ethnic cultures of Asia.[24]

Asianisation of Asia means different things to different people. We have seen Asian state bureaucrats launching xenophobic 'Asian Values' in response to American-led international debates on human rights after the Cold War. Among the young urban new rich in Asia, the aphorism can mean Asian ethnic cuisine, holiday travel to exotic Asian resorts, and air-conditioned Asian houses, decorations and accessories. However, the distinction is not simply bureaucrat *vis-à-vis* yuppy. Recently the local government of Ujung Pandang, South Sulawesi, decided to renovate the old Chinese ghetto and to turn it into a tourist destination, a first ever Chinatown in Indonesia (*Kompas* 1995j).

In any case, the new interest in Asian cultures among Asians cannot be considered natural. Neither can it be seen as a new trend or uniquely Asian. It is not totally separable from the past and present experience of the West's othering of Asians. In fact one is tempted to think that at the bottom of the Asianisation of Asia is a recuperation of Westerners' colonial orientalism. Sociologist Chua Beng Huat described the phenomenon as a process where sections of the Southeast Asian middle class become 'post-colonial', as distinct from their past 'de-colonised' relationship with the West.[25]

This is not a case where rich Asians have had enough of consuming Western cultures, and have rediscovered Asia for want of something new and more exotic beyond Hollywood and Disneyland. Rich and Western-educated Asians who still find the West attractive can easily share interest with the West in exploring – and either intentionally or not, reconstructing – the wonder of Asia's past. Both colonial and post-colonial Westerners are well known for their long and uninterrupted history of discovering and manufacturing the exotic beauty and mysteries of the East. Instead of simply mimicking their former colonial masters from an inferior position, the new rich in Asia have now become new masters of, and on, their own soils. This means both Asianising Asia and Westernising the Asian taste for Asia. The East–West dichotomy comes to an end, although the more complex nuanced differences between the two signifiers continue to appeal to many of us.

RETURN OF THE DRAGON

Several points in the foregoing discussion have indicated social changes that involved Chinese Indonesians. These include the new interest in Asian Values and ethnicities, the participation of Chinese tycoons in poetry reading, the intellectual advocacy of liberalism and the formation of a multiracial capitalist class in the nation's economy. All of these developments help to refurbish the legitimacy of this ethnic minority.

This is evident in three major areas: first, the decline of public hostility towards the Chinese and the easing of restrictions against their activities; secondly, the presentation of certain Chinese individuals as successful Indonesian fellow citizens in areas other than those traditionally allotted to them; thirdly, and most significantly, the reassertion of blatantly Chinese ethnicity into public culture (see Heryanto 1998).

Now, more than a decade has passed in New Order Indonesia since there were any major anti-Chinese riots. By 'major' riots I mean racial/ethnic-based mass violence that lasts for a week or more, and which is linked across a number of towns or cities. There were a number of separate 'minor' riots in East and Central Java in 1995, and there was major unrest in Medan in 1994. These were not just focused on the Chinese. The last major anti-Chinese riot was in 1980. Under the new circumstances it is not difficult to understand the easing of old restrictions against Chinese cultural artefacts. Two examples illustrate the point, one concerning language, the other celebration of the Chinese New Year.

Chinese characters and utterances have been illegal since the birth of New Order Indonesia in 1966; and so have all Chinese schools, mass organisations and mass media. Visitors entering Indonesia are informed on the customs declaration form that Chinese medicine and printed materials in Chinese characters fall in the same category of illegal items as pornography, arms or narcotics. This is probably one of the extremely rare cases in modern history where a major world language is officially proscribed, without protest, by a strong government in a relatively long and stable political climate.[26]

However, the 1990s are witnessing rapid change. Chinese Prime Minister Li Peng visited Indonesia in 1990, following a series of exchange visits by officials from the two governments. Not long afterwards, the two governments founded the Chinese–Indonesian Institute for Economic, Social and Cultural Cooperation. While the bans on the use of Chinese language and characters have not been repealed, in 1994 the Indonesian government sponsored the publication of a Chinese–Indonesian dictionary and allowed hotels and travel agents to publish leaflets and brochures in Chinese characters (*Kompas* 1994a).

The year before Li Peng visited Indonesia, the government banned the staging of a play in the North Sumatra city of Medan on the official pretext that the story originated from a Chinese legend, *Sam Pek Eng Tay*, which was incompatible with the national personality. Unlike similar incidents in the past, the ban angered the general public. In 1993 both the Central Government and the Governor of Central Java reminded the public of the ban on the celebration of Chinese New Year in public places, like vihara (Buddhist temples), and on the performance of the dragon dance. The Governor even banned the sale of a certain Chinese cake, traditionally consumed at New Year. Again, for the first time, critical responses to the restrictions appeared in the mass media (Indrakusuma 1993; Subianto 1993).

On the following Chinese New Year, the largest Indonesian daily, *Kompas*, published large advertisements conveying good wishes for the Chinese Holiday Season. This provoked no one. The issue came into sharper relief in 1996 and again in 1997 when Chinese New Year fell one day before Muslim *Idul Fitri*. Most national media gave equal coverage to the big Holidays despite the Jakarta Governor's reiteration of the ban.[27]

What took place was not a sweeping improvement of inter-ethnic relations; rather the pattern has been contradictory and inconsistent. One may speculate that anti-Chinese sentiments survive like still water that runs deep. But no culture is like nature. What is historically significant is that it is the first time in many decades that the old sentiment has not seriously asserted itself in public.

More important is the elevation of high-profile individuals of Chinese ethnic identity into the arena of popular culture as prominent Indonesian citizens, and the reinsertion of blatantly Chinese cultural artefacts into the same public space. One of Indonesia's most popular novels, a highly rated television show and a highly acclaimed play produced at Jakarta's most prestigious arts centre in 1994 were all based on the Chinese legend *The Lady White Snake*. The banned dragon dance played an important part in all these versions of the narrative. Televised film series based on Chinese legends have not only been screened, but they occasionally outnumber other film series. Comics and novels featuring Chinese legends now occupy a considerable space in all major bookshops. These are only a few examples of the reinsertion of a Chinese presence into the nation's multi-ethnic cultural arena.

If Chineseness appears to be more acceptable in public, it is little wonder more and more accomplished ethnic Chinese now appear in high-profile positions outside the business world and badminton court, without any reference to their ethnic origin. Some names that came to prominence recently include: Nano Riantiarno (theatre), Jaya Suprana (humour, cartoon, piano), the late Prajudi Admodirdjo (clothes design), Kwik Kian Gie (politics), Dede Oetomo (Gay movement and AIDS- awareness campaign), Agus Dermawan T. (art criticism), Andy Siswanto (architecture), Putri Wong Kam Fu (astrology), and most recently Alifuddin El Islamy (Islam proselytising).

Several uncertainties remain. Given past hostilities, we do not know how solid, fragile or long-lasting is this new inter-ethnic friendliness. It is difficult to gauge whether it represents simply the acceptance of an ethnic minority that has undergone a long history of social stigmatisation as a result of its economic dominance, or whether we are witnessing a profoundly new phenomenon. Are we dealing with the attribution of new meanings to ethnicity, ethnicisation and ethnic politics, at a time when a good number within the urban multi-ethnic middle class take a comfortable life for granted? These changes seem to reflect an era characterised by sustained economic growth and political stability, not only in one country but in the whole region.[28] The next section provides an even stronger case of a 'new' identity politics, in which religion features as a central signifier.

'NEW' MUSLIMS

No identity politics in contemporary Indonesia has been as spectacular as that involving the transformation of Islamic communities. The newly established, government-sponsored *Ikatan Cendekiawan Muslim Indonesia* (ICMI – Association of Indonesian Muslim Intellectuals) has taken a lead in the most visible developments, and leading functionaries within ICMI occupy positions in the current state cabinet. However, ICMI is only part of a bigger story in which Islam provides a contemporary inspiration for the lifestyles of the new rich.

Not all prominent Muslim figures and their followers are happy with the establishment of ICMI, yet none doubt Islam's recent dramatic ascendancy. Those within ICMI applaud the development and point out that this is the first time in New Order Indonesia that Islam has been accorded considerable social respect and political clout in the formal political arena (Hefner 1993: 23).[29] The post-1990 rise of Islam to Indonesia's centre stage may continue to be a significant factor in the course of the country's immediate future. Whatever lies ahead, the scope and style of this contemporary 'Islamisation' have now gone far beyond anyone's imagination in the 1980s.

Since 1966 'Communism' has been regularly referred to as a potential threat, and hundreds of thousands of citizens were deprived of civil rights for alleged sympathy with the bygone Indonesian Communist Party. Nevertheless, in the 1970s and 1980s, Islam was the government's primary target of repression and stigmatisation. The notorious Anti-Subversive Law was most frequently used to prosecute individuals the New Order labelled as 'right extremists' (see TAPOL 1987).[30]

Social forces identified with Islam were also the chief targets of the controversial decree of 1985, which demanded that all organisations declare the state ideology *Pancasila* as the sole foundation of their constitutions. The same was true when the government launched the ambitious *Pancasila* indoctrination project, *Pedoman Penghayatan dan Pengamalan Pancasila*.

By mid-1990 the scene was almost the complete reverse. Nothing seemed to rival Islam as a source of 'correct politics' among the elite. President Suharto went on a pilgrimage to Mecca in 1991, just a few months after he officially inaugurated ICMI. In the next few years, courtrooms in Jakarta, Yogyakarta and Salatiga were packed with people watching defendants charged with making public statements disrespectful of Islam. Meanwhile prisoners, previously labelled 'right extremists', were released despite long sentences. The phenomenon was not restricted to politics and law.

A decade ago it was difficult for many ordinary Muslims to identify themselves as such for fear of being labelled 'right extremists'. Today the situation seems to have been reversed: in 1996, rioters attacked non-Muslim communities and buildings of worship. Yet these attacks were condemned by respected Muslim leaders.

At least up to the mid-1990s the rise of Islam had changed the nation's intellectual landscape. ICMI established the Center for Information and Development Studies (CIDES) in early 1993, following the already active Paramadina Foundation. Islamic schools developed not only in size, but also in quality and prestige. Some of them rank as the most expensive schools in Jakarta (*Femina* 1995c). Most bookstores in major cities have special sections on Islam or on various social issues written from an Islamic perspective. The publication of Islamic texts has reportedly boomed (*Berita Buku* 1996). In two years, ICMI's daily, *Republika*, reached a considerable portion of the national readership.

These changes occurred in parallel with developments of the most visible form, namely the construction of mosques and the practice of religious rituals. In 1993 Robert Hefner (1993: 10) noted that the number of mosques in East and Central Java was suddenly almost double the number of twenty years earlier, while the number of Christian churches had increased only minimally.

More interesting than the increased number of mosques is the widespread and growing number of prayer halls in fancy office buildings, shopping centres, hotels and restaurants. Religious discussions take place on the Internet as well as in select homes in the wealthiest districts of Jakarta (*Femina* 1995b). Collective prayers, Ramadan-dining in fancy restaurants and Islamic education among top business executives, state bureaucrats, rock singers, movie stars and other celebrities have become regular cover stories in today's media industry (*Femina* 1996; *Forum Keadilan* 1996b; *Jakarta-Jakarta* 1996; *Sinar* 1996). Several segments of the booming real-estate business have offered 'Islamic real estate' in West Java for the better-off (*Tiras* 1995e). Following the opening of an Islamic Bank, there are now Islamic shopping markets in several cities in Java (*Suara Hidayatullah* 1996).

Islam and fashion find a most celebrated collaboration in the business of female Muslim (*Muslimah*) clothing. This development is even more remarkable when we consider that until 1990 there were strong restrictions against female Muslims wearing the Islamic veil. There were many cases where female students were punished for wearing Islamic costume, especially the veil, instead of the official school uniform. Several private employers discouraged female employees from doing the same. Under these circumstances, wearing the veil in general, and especially to school and work, was a statement of political protest.[31]

Since 1990, however, the first daughter of the President has seldom appeared in public without wearing the veil. While some scattered opposition to the new fashion continues, highly prestigious fashion shows have regularly – at least once a year during the Ramadan month – presented elaborate designs of Islamic women's clothing in five-star hotels.[32]

The intricate qualities of the new Islamic fashion warrant a separate study (see Surtiretna (1995) and *Ummat* (1996a)). Here I simply wish to emphasise three important points. First, this new fashion has engendered a big industry which promises to grow even bigger (see *Kompas* 1996b; Royani 1996). Second, far from being targeted simply as consumers of the new industry, women take a leading role in both the artistic design and commercial aspects (see, for example, *Kompas* 1995a). In the 1994 annual of 'Trends of Islamic Fashion' at Puri Agung Sahid Jaya Hotel, more female designers participated than their male counterparts. Most of these female designers devoted their careers exclusively to Islamic clothing (*Kompas* 1994a). Third, key figures in this new fashion industry repeatedly make unsolicited comments that they draw their design inspirations from international trends (often meaning the West) and not from the Arab world! This suggests an attitude parallel with the trends we discussed earlier about the Javanese *plesetan* and the creative consumption of other Western goods.[33]

Admissions by two designers in the 1996 annual Islamic fashion show in Jakarta are typical. Raizal Rais was proud to acknowledge that his work was inspired by Jackie Onassis, while Dimas Mahendra stated: 'I don't want my designs to look like the clothes of the Arabs, because Islam is not identical to Arab'. Instead he wanted to present an 'empire' (English in original) style (*Kompas* 1996a). Event choreographer Denny Malik made a strikingly similar remark. He adopted elements of ethnic Acehnese and Minangkabau dances, and stressed his attempt to turn away from the Arab: 'Islam doesn't have to be identical to Arabian culture...Islam doesn't have to be stiff and introvert...Islam doesn't have to look shaggy...I want to present something bright' (*Ummat* 1996b).

The same attitude dates back to the first series of the annual 'Trends in Islamic Fashion' in 1994. Then designer Anne Rufaidah explained openly to reporters that Europe had become a major source of inspiration, albeit with local modification. Other cultural sources varied widely from Morocco to China and Pakistan (*Kompas* 1994a). Little wonder that the discourse of this new Islamic fashion is heavily indebted to European jargon. In a four-paragraph text, reporter Santi Hartono had to italicise these words: *siluet* (silhouette), *sexy*, *palazzo*, *bias cut*, *lace*, *crepe*, *viscose*, *royal blue*, *fuchsia*, *terracotta*, *chiffon* and *fashion* (*Tiara* 1994). Similar writing is found in *Femina* (1995a). No paragraph goes without italicised terms: 'tumpuk tiga *pieces*...lengkap dengan *vest*...motif Toraja dibuat dengan teknik *stitching tie-dye*...kerudung dari bahan *chiffon*...Lapis luarnya berupa *vest* panjang...terdiri dari *blazer*.'

Islam and Islamisation have become a great deal more heterogeneous and complex, involving more actors and interests than anyone could have imagined before. Parts of it may be primarily about religious devotion. But other elements go beyond this and, in light of the above developments, it is fair to ask ourselves whether it is apt to describe the emergence of 'new' Muslims. This is not to suggest a new religion. It is to resist the easy temptation to reduce the phenomenon to the simple re-emergence of something old and familiar. This is to go beyond the common practice of labelling Indonesia's contemporary Islamisation no more than 'primordial' or 'sectarian' politics.[34]

Gone are the old and rigid meanings of 'religion' and 'politics', as well as the clear boundaries that separate them from 'lifestyle'. In today's Islam in Indonesia, old familiar images have been replaced by new ones. The associations of Islam with rural poverty, religious dogmatism, the Middle East, anti-Chinese, anti-West sentiments, and with fundamentalists seeking to establish an Islamic state, are juxtaposed with new images. Now Islam is also associated with television talk shows, name cards with PhDs from prominent Western schools, erudite intellectual debates, mobile telephones and consumption of *ketupat* during Ramadan at McDonald's.

THE PAINS OF AGEING

The New Order government can proudly take credit for ushering in the prosperity that the Indonesian new rich enjoy. Ironically the same government has been undermined in the unfolding events it sponsored. After the continuous fall of oil prices in the world market in the 1980s, there was a steady retreat of the New Order government's involvement in the nation's economy. For much of the 1980s it flew the banner of privatisation. Though partly rhetorical, this was followed, in the subsequent years, by policies of deregulation, debureaucratisation, liberalisation and openness. Private (domestic and foreign) investments represented as much as 77 per cent of the state budget for the period of the 6th Five-Year Plan, 1994/5–1998/9 (*Kompas* 1995h). In 1994 Indonesia's 300 biggest conglomerates owned total assets worth nearly 70 per cent of the country's gross domestic product (*Forum Keadilan* 1995a). By 1995 the top 200 of these conglomerates were responsible for 86 per cent of the nation's gross domestic product (*Jawa Pos* 1995), compared with 35 per cent in 1990 (*Kompas* 1995i).[35]

Nothing showed more clearly the declining position of the New Order than the Government Decree No. 20/1994. This decree allows 100 per cent foreign ownership of existing companies or new, locally based investments with only 1 per cent divestment after fifteen years of operation. Foreign investors are also invited to take 95 per cent ownership of enterprises in sensitive areas previously prohibited by the constitution, including ports, electricity, telecommunication, airlines, water, railways and mass media.

The government's retreat has not been confined to the nation's economic activities; similar moves are found in political (see Heryanto 1996b) and cultural areas. In the words of a foreign journalist:

> As the state has progressively loosened its control over the economy, status has come to depend increasingly on wealth and individual ability rather than one's position on the bureaucratic totem pole. The idols of urban society today are executives, while once-coveted careers in the civil service and armed forces now face recruitment problems.
>
> (Vatikiotis 1991: 31)

Nearly 70 per cent of Jakartan middle-class respondents of a survey conducted by *Tiara* bluntly admitted that they wished to be successful businessmen. Half of them were admirers of prominent business people. One state-run high-school student had an ambition to be like 'Uncle Liem' Sioe Liong, the biggest Indonesian tycoon. His admiration was so high that he knew by heart all the names of members of Liem's family (*Tiara* 1991a).

There is little that the ageing New Order regime can do to contain the new public effervescent desire for pleasurable lifestyles. In an attempt to retain some of its old authority, the government launched a series of measures, including the 'Simple Life Pattern' (*Pola Hidup Sederhana*).[36] This campaign began with the Presidential Decree of 22 January 1974, officially aimed at civil servants and members of the armed forces.[37] Nonetheless, the restrictions were widely discussed in public as if to set the prescribed conduct for the whole population, with government officials and military officers acting as role models. Initially the decree was a response to the biggest yet student-led mass protest against economic disparity, and the economic dominance of Sino-Indonesian and foreign investors. As many expected, the campaign failed. It could not quell the wave of consumer culture that the same government was also partly responsible for.

Government invocation of the Simple Life slogan has fluctuated. It was mentioned in the 1983 State Broad Guidelines. It regained popularity in 1986 when the New Order suffered its biggest state budget cut. Its latest comeback was in mid-1993 when Minister for Reform of State Apparatus Major General Taipan Bernhard Silalahi made several public statements to express his concerns about the extravagant lifestyle among the Jakarta elite. When the Simple Life campaign hit a few targets, the victims were always state officials. It was partly for this reason that the general public, including the new rich, never took the programme very seriously. They could always cite contrary cases, such as in the concluding months of 1995, when various local governments planned to spend sizeable amounts of money on office cars and for building an official guest-house and swimming pool.[38] In the most conspicuous practices to run counter to the official campaign, members of the first family appeared in the forefront.

A classic example of these apparent double standards relates to television commercials which were banned on 1 April 1981. The pretext of the ban was the government's paternalistic intention to protect the audience, especially the rural population and urban under-class, from the seduction of a consumer lifestyle advocated by the commercials. Indonesians saw no more television commercials until 1987 when Bambang Triatmodjo, the President's middle son, brought them back on his station, Rajawali Citra Televisi Indonesia, Indonesia's first privately owned television network (see Kitley 1992: 75–8).

Luxury cars have always been in the top list of items targeted by the government's Simple Life policy. And yet proscribed vehicles have continued to be smuggled into the country (*Jakarta-Jakarta* 1993b: 20–1). In 1993, this controversy re-erupted when the President's youngest son, Hutomo ('Tommy') Mandala Putra, was suspected of having been involved in the illegal imports. The charges were denied (*Jakarta-Jakarta* 1993b: 16–17) and the issues were not pursued but suspicions remained. The following year, the media reported that Tommy had bought the famous Italian automobile factory Lamborghini, which produces luxury cars. Using a quote from Tommy as a provocative story title, the daily *Kompas* reported that the deal was conducted 'in order to uplift the nation's image' in the international arena (1994c).

CONCLUSION: THE POLITICS OF LIFESTYLE

Lifestyle and consumer culture have not simply occupied a larger slice of the nation's quantitative spending and public discourse. They have participated, to say the least, in the changing dynamics of the nation's social hierarchy, providing new profiles to the new rich, and modifying or undermining the profiles of others. Lifestyle has become a crucial site for the construction, negotiation and contestation of identity in Indonesia. At the centre of this new identity politics stand the new rich.

This conclusion runs contrary to the common argument among observers who see contemporary changes as having turned young middle-class radicals from political activists into consumer hedonists, or as one journalist dubbed it, 'from protests to parties' (*Asiaweek* 1995: 64–5). The foregoing indicates that, under certain historical circumstances, going to parties, just like shopping or hanging out in shopping malls, can be as political as going to a polling station, engaging in parliamentary debates, wearing fashionable clothes or reading poetry.

Obviously, not all aspects of lifestyle are instructive of or relevant to identity politics. This chapter has selected elements of lifestyle change in contemporary Indonesia from a particular context and with a particular aim in mind. In exploring the political significance of contemporary lifestyles, I could not help but be conscious of the inclination among political analysts to share the main-stream practice of dismissing consumer culture as politically incorrect, or irrelevant. I hope I have not overreacted by giving the impression that identity politics in the cases discussed above is necessarily progressive or libertarian.

Economic changes are real and materially grounded. And so is wealth. However, the value and power of wealth are always socially constructed, recon-structed and deconstructed. And so is the cultural significance of owning wealth. They are never inherently material. They are never stable. The directions, constraints and dynamics that describe the changing value and power of wealth are neither fully random, nor universally law-governed.

Notes

In preparing this chapter, the writer benefited from critical comments and suggestions made by Muhamad AS Hikam, Yoseph Adi Stanley, Alex Irwan, Angela Romano, Ruth McVey, Don Sabdono and Purwadi Budiawan. Michael Pinches and Gotje offered very helpful editorial advice. Any shortcomings remain the writer's sole responsibility.

The exchange rates of Indonesian rupiah between 1990 and 1996 gradually declined roughly from around Rp. 1,900 to Rp. 2,400 against US$1.00.

1 In 1995 Indonesia paid each working expatriate an average monthly salary 30,000 times higher than it did to each of its civil servants and military officers. About half of the 57,000 working expatriates in 1995 were Japanese and South Koreans. On the economic power of expatriates and local reaction, see *Forum Keadilan* (1996a) and Rachbini (1996). Between 70 per cent and 80 per cent of private economic activity is reported to be in the hands of Chinese Indonesians (Mackie 1994; Schwarz 1994). A proponent of economic indigenism suggested in 1994 that 18 of the 25 richest Indonesian conglomerates are of ethnic Chinese origin (Sjahrir 1994; see also Vatikiotis 1993: 50; Suyanto 1994).

2 'In Asia,' wrote a columnist, 'if you own a Mercedes, you are held in awe. In Australia, you're seen as a pretentious peacock' (Amdur 1996). He may be right, but only partially and only at times. The precise meanings of owning a Mercedes are never as fixed and stable as Amdur implies.

3 For a recent analysis of a contemporary recycling of this prejudice in Indonesia, see Keith Foulcher (1990).

4 After years of persistent protests by workers, the government raised workers' minimum wage in 1993, 1995 and again in April 1996. Rather than seeking higher and fairer wage rates, thousands of workers in Java demonstrated over the refusal of employers to pay the official minimum wage. In the 1993/4 fiscal year, the sixth largest tax-paying individual earned 7,185 times the wages his employees were supposed to receive (*Kompas* 1995d). I am thankful to Arief Budiman for bringing this report to my attention.

5 This may be a more common phenomenon world-wide than generally acknowledged, and not uniquely Indonesian.

6 On the conceptual problems of the so-called 'middle classes', see Abercrombie and Urry (1983) and Wright (1989). For a pioneering collection on contemporary East Asia, see Hsiao (1993). The first and only English-language book on the Indonesian middle class is Tanter and Young (1990). The term 'new rich' is not an easy substitute. First, it includes the (new) bourgeoisie which is distinguishable from what has commonly been referred to as the middle classes. Secondly, the term 'new rich' may carry unintended and inappropriate residual connotations of the *nouveaux riches* – characterised by a comfortable life with no 'true luxury and a certain awkwardness of social behaviour' (Wallerstein 1991: 136). Robison and Goodman (1996) do not seem to convey this pejorative residual meaning of *nouveau riche* when speaking of Asia's new rich. But neither do they make an explicit distinction between the 'new rich' and the 'nouveaux riches'.

7 MacCannell and MacCannell (1993) offer one of the best attempts to juggle diverse and conflicting aspects of consumer culture.

8 See cover story of the news-magazine *Tiras* (1995a).

9 One month prior to the publication of Kwik's column, *Kompas* presented an editorial, assuring the population of the harmless nature of liberalisation (1994d). The basis of this argument was presented in the editorial title, 'Liberalisasi Perdagangan Bukan Berarti Liberalisme' ('Trade Liberalisation Does Not Mean Liberalism'), which had previously been disseminated by the country's elite. Even this moderate line of thinking received a rebuke from Rasuanto (1995). A sharper denunciation of Kwik's arguments came from Mubyarto (1995), an eminent Indonesian economics professor.

10 Translations from Indonesian to English here and elsewhere are the author's. On *Pancasila* ideology, see Ramage (1995).

11 In reply to criticism of the government's liberal economic policy from a seminar audience in July 1995, two senior economic ministers, Marie Muhammad and Ginandjar Kartasasmita, declared unequivocally that the Indonesian government would not slow down *konglomerasi* ('conglomerates'), a euphemism for capitalism (see *Kompas* 1995f).

12 In the 1990s the ratio of private/government share of investment has constantly been around 77/23 (*Forum Keadilan* 1995a). The reverse was true in the early years of the New Order's rule.

13 More independent reports suggest a varied, more complex, picture. Some of the riots could be described as inter-ethnic but the ethnic Chinese were not always the target. Some violent confrontations were more class-based, while in others government agents, institutions and properties were the chief targets of mass attacks. In a few cases where Chinese shops and non-Muslim houses of worship were targeted, there were suspicions that the initial perpetrators were not local Muslims but state agents provocateurs from out of the town.

14 In about the same period, operas by Guruh Sukarnoputra's *Swara Mahardhika* and theatrical performances by Nano Riantiarno's *Teater Koma* were two of the most extravagant and commercially successful cases of staged productions in the country. These productions were often mentioned as indicators of the rise of a new middle class in Jakarta (see *Kompas* 1986). In the 1990s they found a rival in the short-lived collaborative project of the social critic-cum-singer Iwan Fals, and 'indigenous' billionaire and rock-music lover, Setiawan Djodi.

15 Not all performances have artistic pretension. President Suharto himself read poetry before a group of the nation's biggest tycoons on 2 October 1995 (*Tiras* 1995c), in a way comparable to American President Clinton's public playing of the saxophone.

16 Some noticed the new trend starting in the 1980s with a sudden huge market demand for contemporary art works (Rizal 1989). The phenomenon received wide media coverage (see *Tiara* 1993a; *Suara Merdeka* 1995). In 1985 Bandung-based painter

Jeihan Sukmantoro sold his works for US$15,000 (*Editor* 1990a). The market was so lucrative that foreign artists from various countries sought to make their fortune (Yusuf 1996; *Tiara* 1993b). In 1993 direct sales during exhibitions ranged from US$50,000 to US$60,000 (*Tiara* 1993b).

17 Culturalisation of economically derived identities is not the sole prerogative of the new rich. Poetry readings and theatrical performances have been equally popular among worker activists in today's Indonesia.

18 This is a rough translation of the Indonesian expression '*enak dan perlu*', a motto of *Tempo*, the biggest news-magazine in Indonesia before the government banned it and two other weeklies on 22 June 1994. *Tempo* was one of several New Order journals that made notable success commercially as well as culturally, because it catered to the aspirations of the emergent urban new rich/middle class. One of its successful strategies was to adopt a more literary style than conventional journalistic writing.

19 Adopted from Nury Vittachi's anecdote 'Good Buy, Democracy', *Far Eastern Economic Review*, 11 January 1996: 28.

20 For the most informative accounts of Indonesia's consumer culture in the 1980s, see Dick (1985) and Crouch (1985). For quantitative data on Indonesia's consumer culture, see *Tempo* (1986), *Editor* (1990b), Vatikiotis (1991) and Duffy (1992). The Jakarta-based glossy magazines *Tiras*, *Matra* and *Jakarta-Jakarta* are devoted specifically to feature trends in Indonesia's metropolitan lifestyle, while the English daily *Jakarta Post* publishes the annual directory of consumer culture for Jakartans (*The Jakarta Post Lifestyle*).

21 Elsewhere, I consider the political culture of *plesetan* that is made of English, Japanese and Korean (Heryanto 1996c). There I make a provisional argument that this language game asserts a new confidence to deal with the cultural constructs of world superpowers, past and present. Although more complex, the cases of *Taglish* (Tagalog English) and *Singlish* (Singaporean English) strike an accord. They all share something fundamental; they signify a new identity marker of assertive urban middle-class Southeast Asians, familiar with English, who domesticate and appropriate the language rather than try to sound like its native speakers. For a more careful political analysis of *Taglish*, see Rafael (1995). For the case of *Singlish*, see Hiebert (1996).

22 Just to mention a few, here are some names and dates of shows in Jakarta: Michael Bolton (March 1994), Bon Jovi (May 1995; see *Kompas* 1995b), Mick Jagger (October 1988), Color Me Badd (1990), Jimmy Page (1990), B. B. King (1992), New Kids on the Block (1992), Whitney Houston (1993), Sting (February 1993), Metallica (April 1993), Air Supply (January 1994), Phil Collins (March 1995), Wet Wet Wet (October 1995).

23 Tickets to Julio Iglesias' show were Rp. 750,000 (US$357); Sting's, Rp. 350,000 (US$167); Bolton's lowest ticket was Rp. 90,000 (US$43). A one-hour charity show of Kenny Rogers with dinner cost Rp. 1 million (US$476) per person. The record for ticket prices still belongs to Diana Ross, who charged Rp. 2 million (US$952) per ticket (*Forum Keadilan* 1994b).

24 In Southeast Asian societies which endure problems of economic dominance by ethnic Chinese, the new interest in Chinese culture can have an immense political impact.

25 Personal communication, 1996.

26 A comparable ban occurred on Catalan under Franco's fascism, 1939–45 (Laitin 1989: 302). The governments of France in 1994 (*Tempo* 1994) and of Vietnam in 1996 (Schwarz 1996) failed in their attempts to restrict the use of all foreign languages. A more common practice world-wide is a limited linguistic ban, such as against English in billboards and names of domestic enterprises in Indonesia today (*Jakarta-Jakarta* 1993c).

27 See a letter to the editor by Subagyo (1996). The ban created a heated debate in the Internet exchanges among Indonesians and Indonesian specialists.

28 Joel Kahn (1993 and forthcoming) articulates this issue in the broader context. The revival of Chineseness outside China, and in association with economic growth, is sporadic but widespread, having become especially evident in Hong Kong, Singapore, Vietnam and Thailand. On Thailand, journalist Michael Vatikiotis wrote: 'Suddenly, it's cool to be Chinese' (1996).

29 According to Aswab Mahasin, a well-respected Muslim intellectual, the growing influence of Muslim institutions has 'made many people who were previously embarrassed about their faith, because it looked backward and unmodern, proud to act like Muslims' (Hefner 1993: 33). See also Amir Santoso's defence of ICMI against accusations that it is responsible for the recuperation of 'sectarian', primordial politics in the country (1995).

30 Apparently there were three times more 'right extremists' jailed in 1989 for political reasons than their 'left' counterparts in the same period (see Heryanto 1996a).

31 Thus the wearing of veils by female Muslims is not always an unambiguous index of disempowerment: during the late 1980s many progressive female activists chose to wear the veil.

32 On the difficulties of wearing women's Islamic clothes, see letters of grievance to the editor of *Tiras* (Apriansyah and Nara 1995; Mulyani 1995), and an interview with a senior female television newsreader (Ramelan 1996).

33 There is an important counter-trend. From the mid-1980s to the mid-1990s, one found many stickers and T-shirts with writing in English praising the glory of Islam (e.g., 'Islam Power', 'We Are Muslims', 'We Love Islam'). The Islamic newsmagazine *Suara Hidayatullah* regularly advertises T-shirts with texts only in English: 'Save the World with Islam', 'YES! Islam Is Our Choice', 'Islam The Wave of The Future', and a windbreaker in three colours with the text 'The Spirit of Islam'. This suggests a recognition of the superior authority or prestige of English over Arabic or Indonesian.

34 No doubt, some elements of 'primordial' or 'sectarian' politics persist in contemporary Indonesia, but this is not the whole story. Joel S. Kahn observes something strikingly similar in today's Malaysia. In his view, cultural identity and identification in Southeast Asia are increasingly 'international or global in orientation, in the sense that they have reference to what many have termed diasporas rather than localised cultural or national groups' (forthcoming).

35 This is not to suggest that the government's interests and those of the private enterprise are fundamentally antagonistic. However, the government's retreat from business indicates its irremediable decline of political prowess. Government attempts to reassert its economic power have been disastrous as illustrated by the Timor national car industry in 1996 and Busang gold-mine scandal in 1997.

36 A complementary government measure is the 'National Discipline Movement' (*Gerakan Disiplin Nasional*) directed at public service and activities like queuing or littering. Another government move attempted to reinvigorate defunct nationalist sentiments. In 1993 and 1995, for example, the names of all buildings, real-estate complexes and corporations were converted to Indonesian. Most new rich complied only superficially with these various programmes.

37 An excerpt of the decree can be found in *Jakarta-Jakarta* (1993a: 19). Among other things, it imposed restrictions on gifts, official hospitality, holiday celebrations, birthdays, weddings, and anniversaries. As early as the 1960s it was illegal for military officers to stay at Hotel Indonesia, the country's first international-class hotel. In 1979, no military office could have an air-conditioner or carpet (*Jakarta-Jakarta* 1993a: 20).

38 The Governor of Central Java proposed to build an official residential complex costing Rp. 7.04 thousand million (US$3.2m). Local government in South Sulawesi intended to purchase 23 cars, each worth Rp. 180 million (US$81,800). The Regent of Bekasi, West Java, was preparing to pay Rp. 1,000 million (US$455,000) to build a

swimming pool within the Regency compound (*Forum Keadilan* 1995b, 1996c; *Tiras* 1995d).

Bibliography

Abdullah, Irwan (1994) 'Market, Consumption and Lifestyle Management', unpublished paper presented to the seminar on Cultural and Social Dimensions of Market Expansion, 3–5 October, Batam.

—— (1995) 'Tubuh; Ekspansi Pasar dan Reproduksi Hubungan Gender', unpublished seminar paper, 29 November, Yogyakarta: Pusat Penelitian Kebudayaan dan Perubahan Sosial, Universitas Gadjah Mada.

Abercrombie, Nicholas and Urry, John (1983) *Capital, Labour, and the Middle Classes*, London: George Allen & Unwin.

Akademika (1995) 'Konsumerisme dan Perlindungan Konsumen', XIII (1): 2–108.

Amdur, Mark A. (1996) 'Heads in the Sand', *Far Eastern Economic Review*, 8 February: 30.

Apriansyah, J. B. and Nara, Hartini (1995) 'Ternyata Kasus Jilbab itu Belum Selesai…!', letter to editor, *Tiras*, I (8), 23 March: 8.

Asiaweek (1995) 'Kids: From Protests to Parties', 15 December: 64–5.

Berita Buku (1996) 'Bisnis buku-buku Islam', a cover story, VIII (58), March–April: 8–33.

Bernas (1991) 'Om Liem akan Baca Puisi', 14 August: 1, 11.

Crouch, Harold (1985) *Economic Change, Social Structure and the Political System in Southeast Asia*, Singapore: Institute of Southeast Asian Studies.

Devan, Janadas (1995) *Sojourn*, 'Special Focus on Post-modernism and Southeast Asian Scholarship', 10 (1), Singapore: Institute of Southeast Asian Studies.

Dick, Howard (1985) 'The Rise of a Middle Class and the Changing Concept of Equity in Indonesia – an Interpretation', *Indonesia*, 39: 71–92.

—— (1990) 'Further Reflections on the Middle Classes', in Richard Tanter and Kenneth Young (eds), *The Politics of Middle-Class Indonesia*, Clayton: Monash University, pp. 63–70.

Duffy, Michael (1992) 'Making It in Jakarta', *The Independent Monthly*, February: 5–7.

Editor (1990a) 'Jeihan Sukmantoro: Seniman Gubug Yang Dikejar Uang', IV (7), 27 October: 43–6.

—— (1990b) 'Kaum Gamang yang Diam', III (49), 18 August: 11–23.

Featherstone, Mike (1991) *Consumer Culture and Postmodernism*, London: Sage.

Femina (1995a) 'Parade Busana Muslim', extra supplement, XXIII (6), 9–15 February.

—— (1995b) 'Menikmati Siraman Rohani', XXIII (8), 23 February–1 March: 10–13.

—— (1995c) 'Pendidikan Anak Muslim Era Globalisasi', a cover story, XXIII (8), 23 February–1 March: 40–8.

—— (1996) 'Buka Puasa di Resto Hotel Berbintang', XXIV (7), 15–28 February: 106–12.

Forum Keadilan (1994a) 'Mengimpor Artis: Laba ataukah Rugi?', III (1), 28 April: 60–1.

—— (1994b) 'Di Balik Panggung Pertunjukan Mewah', III (4), 9 June: 67.

—— (1995a) 'Lahirnya Deklarasi Janji dari Bali', IV (12), 25 September: 85.

—— (1995b) 'Giliran Pejabat Mewah', IV (17), 4 December: 26.

—— (1996a) 'Mahal Karena Asing', IV (23), 26 February: 92–3.

—— (1996b) 'Semaraknya Pengajian Kaum Kosmopolitan', IV (23), 26 February: 12–20.

—— (1996c) 'Jatah Mobil Mewah', IV (25), 25 March: 24.

Foulcher, Keith (1990) 'The Construction of an Indonesian National Culture: Patterns of Hegemony and Resistance', in Arief Budiman (ed.), *State and Civil Society in Indonesia*, Clayton: Centre of Southeast Asian Studies, Monash University, pp. 301–20.

Ganie, Tadjuddin Noor (1995) 'Hormatilah Chairil Anwar', letter to the editor, *Forum Keadilan*, IV (12), 25 September: 10.

Hefner, Robert W. (1993) 'Islam, State, and Civil Society: ICMI and the Struggle for the Indonesian Middle Class', *Indonesia*, 56 (October): 1–35.

Heryanto, A. (1994) 'A Class Act', *Far Eastern Economic Review*, 16 June: 30.

—— (1996a) 'Undang-Undang tentang Subversi', *Kompas*, 17 February: 4.

—— (1996b) 'Indonesian Middle-Class Opposition in the 1990s', in Garry Rodan (ed.), *Political Oppositions in Industrialising Asia*, London: Routledge, pp. 241–71.

—— (1996c) 'Pelecehan dan Kesewenang-wenangan Berbahasa; Plesetan dalam Kajian Bahasa dan Politik di Indonesia', in Bambang K. Purwo (ed.), *PELLBA 9: Pertemuan Linguistik Lembaga Bahasa Atma Jaya Kesembilan*, Yogyakarta: Kanisius, pp. 105–27.

—— (1998) 'Ethnic Identities and Erasure; Chinese Indonesians in Public Culture', in Joel S. Kahn (ed.), *Southeast Asian Identities: Culture and the Politics of Representation in Indonesia, Malaysia, Singapore, and Thailand*, Singapore: Institute of Southeast Asian Studies, pp. 95–114.

Hiebert, Murray (1996) 'War of the Words', *Far Eastern Economic Review*, 21 March: 44.

Hsiao, Hsin-Huang Michael (1993) *Discovery of the Middle Classes in East Asia*, Taipei: Institute of Ethnology, Academia Sinica.

Indrakusuma, Danny (1993) 'Imlek dan Larangan Menjual Kue Ranjang', *Surya*, 25 January.

Jakarta-Jakarta (1993a) 'Hidup Sederhana, Slogan Doang?', cover story, 361, 05–11 June: 11–23.

—— (1993b) 'BMW Selundupan dan Ancaman Tommy Soeharto' and 'Selandap-Selundup Old Story', 362, 12–18 June: 16–21.

—— (1993c) 'Jangan Berbahasa Inggris', 364, 26 June–2 July: 79.

—— (1996) 'Lebaran: Indah, Mulus, dan Seru!', 501, 10–16 February: 57–63.

Jameson, Frederic (1991) *Postmodernism, or, The Cultural Logic of Late Capitalism*, Durham: Duke University Press.

Jawa Pos (1995) 'Pengusaha Besar Kuasai 80 Persen', 28 December: 1, 13.

—— (1996) 'Ketupat Hadiah McDonald's', 8 February: 11.

Kahn, Joel S. (1992) 'Class, Ethnicity and Diversity: Some Remarks on Malay Culture in Malaysia', in Joel S. Kahn and Francis Loh (eds), *Fragmented Vision: Culture and Politics in Contemporary Malaysia*, Sydney: Allen & Unwin, pp. 158–78.

—— (1993) *Constituting the Minangkabau*, Oxford: Berg.

—— (1998) 'Southeast Asian Identities', an introductory chapter in Joel S. Kahn (ed.), *Southeast Asian Identities: Culture and the Politics of Representation in Indonesia, Malaysia, Singapore, and Thailand*, Singapore: Institute of Southeast Asian Studies, pp. 1–27.

Kedaulatan Rakyat (1990) 'Pemda Jateng Larang Kesenian "Lhiang Liong" Dipertontonkan', 28 August: 12.

Kitley, Philip (1992) 'Tahun Bertambah, Zaman Bertambah: Television and Its Audiences in Indonesia', *Review of Indonesian and Malayan Affairs*, 26: 71–109.

Kompas (1986) 'Fadjar Kesenian Kelas Menengah Jakarta', 27 April: 1.

—— (1989) 'Menghindari Promotor Kalkulator', 4 July: 6.

—— (1994a) 'Makin Mempopulerkan Busana Muslim', 30 January: 13.

—— (1994b) 'Rakor Polkam; Hotel-hotel Boleh Cetak Brosur Berhuruf Cina', 3 August: 1, 18.

—— (1994c) 'Pembelian Lamborghini untuk Meningkatkan Citra Bangsa', 8 November: 5.

—— (1994d) 'Liberalisasi Perdagangan Bukan Berarti Liberalisme', editorial, 8 December: 4.

—— (1995a) 'Perancang Busana Muslim: Tinggalkan Karier Politik dan Ingin Berdakwah', 5 February: 14.

—— (1995b) 'Kesenian sebagai Gaya Hidup', 18 February: 1, 18.

—— (1995c) 'Menebak Perilaku Penonton', 2 April: 16.

—— (1995d) 'Eka Tjipta Widjaya Terlambat Masukan SPT', 22 February: 1, 18.

—— (1995e) 'Indikator Ekonomi dan Perilaku Orang Kaya Baru', 13 May: 13.

—— (1995f) 'Pemerintah Tak Akan Rem Konglomerasi', 9 July: 1, 8.

—— (1995g) 'Menteri, Pengusaha, dan Seniman akan baca Puisi Bersama di Monas', 12 August: 8.

—— (1995h) 'Presiden: Sasaran Repelita VI Direvisi', 18 February: 1, 11.

—— (1995i) 'Selembar Deklarasi, Segenggam Janji, Semua Menunggu Bukti', 30 August: 13.

—— (1995j) 'Daerah Pecinan Ujungpandang sebagai Obyek Wisata', 12 October: 4.

—— (1996a) 'Busana Muslim 96 Laris Menyambut Lebaran', 14 January: 13.

—— (1996b) 'Peminat Terus Meningkat', 14 January: 13.

—— (1996c) 'Puisi Bening di Gedung Kesenian Jakarta', 20 January: 9.

Kwik Kian Gie (1995), 'Liberal, Liberalisasi dan Liberalisme', *Kompas*, 2 January: 1.

Laitin, David D. (1989) 'Linguistic Revival: Politics and Culture in Catalonia', *Comparative Studies in Society and History*, 31: 297–317.

Leger, John M. (1995) 'Come Together', *Far Eastern Economic Review*, 12 October: 46–52.

McBeth, John (1996) 'All in the Family', *Far Eastern Economic Review*, 14 March: 50–1.

—— and Hiebert, Murray (1996) 'Try Next Door', *Far Eastern Economic Review*, 7 March: 17.

MacCannell, Dean and MacCannell, Juliet Flower (1993) 'Social Class in Postmodernity: Simulacrum or Return of the Real?', in Chris Rojek and Bryan S. Turner (eds), *Forget Baudrillard?*, London: Routledge, pp. 124–45.

Mackie, Jamie (1994) 'Succession Politics Poses Threat to Chinese', *The Australian*, 15 July: 17.

Mangunwijaya, Y. B. (1996) 'Demo Subversif 1001 Manusia Tanah', *Forum Keadilan*, IV (25), 25 March: 68.

Mubyarto (1995) 'Kapitalisme, Liberalisme, Pancasila dan Undang-Undang Dasar 1945', *Kompas*, 5 January: 5.

Mulyani, Siti (1995) 'Jilbab dan Kesempatan Kerja', letter to editor, *Tiras*, I (29), 17 August: 9.

Panji Masyarakat (1994) 'Puisi Tidak Hanya Lahir dari Penyair', 778, 1–10 January: 73–5.

Piliang, Yasraf Amir (1995) 'Ekonomi Libido dan Masyarakat Ekstasi', *Prisma*, XXIV (9): 21–34.

Rachbini, Didik J. (1996) 'TKA vs Pengangguran', *Forum Keadilan*, IV (23), 26 February: 86.

Rafael, Vicente L. (1995) 'Taglish, or the Phantom Power of the Lingua Franca', *Public Culture*, 8: 101–26.

Ramage, Douglas (1995) *Politics in Indonesia: Democracy, Islam, and the Ideology of Tolerance*, London: Routledge.

Ramelan, Mariana (1996) 'Lebih Tenang dengan Jilbab', *Ummat*, I (16), 5 February: 89.

Rasuanto, Bur (1995) 'Liberal Yes, Liberalism No?', *Kompas*, 2 January: 4.

Rizal, Ray (1989) 'Bisnis Lukisan Melalui Galeri', *Suara Pembaharuan*, 8 December: 8, 9.

Robison, Richard and Goodman, David (1996), 'The New Rich in Asia: Economic Development, Social Status and Political Consciousness', in R. Robison and D. Goodman (eds), *The New Rich in Asia*, London: Routledge, pp. 1–16.

—— and Hadiz, Vedi R. (1993) *Privatization or the Reorganization of Dirigism? Indonesian Economic Policy in the 1990s*', Canadian Journal of Development Studies, *special issue: 13–32*.

Royani, Ida (1996), 'Busana Muslimah', live interview with GM Sudarta in AN-TV network series 'Mutiara Ramadhan', 18 February, 17:30–18:00.

Santoso, Amir (1995) 'ICMI not a Sectarian Group', *Jakarta Post*, 14 December: 1.

Saparie, Gunoto (1995) 'Sandyakalaning Puisi di Jateng', *Suara Merdeka*, 9 September: 7.

Schwarz, Adam (1994) *A Nation in Waiting; Indonesia in the 1990s*, St Leonards: Allen & Unwin.

—— (1996) 'Bonfire of the Vanities', *Far Eastern Economic Review*, 7 March: 14–15.

Set, Bambang (1995) 'Haruskah Pembaca Puisi Seorang Penyair?', *Suara Merdeka*, 16 September: 7.

Sinar (1996) 'Antara Mengaji, Eksklusif, dan Lobi', cover story, 24 February: 84–9.

Sinar Harapan (1978) 'Mendagri Larang Atraksi Leangleong', 5 August: 2.

Sjahrir (1994) 'Pribumi dan Sarasehan Golkar', *TEMPO*, 21 May: 46.

Suara Hidayatullah (1996) 'Pasar Muslim, Pasar Menjanjikan', VIII (10), February: 67–8.

Suara Merdeka (1995a) 'Ketika Puisi Tak Cuma Milik Penyair', 26 August: 7.

—— (1995b) 'Galeri Lukis Berpeluang Bisnis, Pameran Bersama Pemilik Galeri, and Ketika Mereka Go Gallery', 16 September: 8.

Subagyo (1996) 'Larangan Imlek', letter to the editor, *Forum Keadilan*, IV (25), 25 March: 7.

Subianto, Benny (1993) 'Tahun Baru Imlek: Boleh atau Tidak?', *Jakarta-Jakarta*, 344, 30 January–5 February: 24–5.

Surtiretna, Nina *et al.* (1995) *Anggun Berjilbab*, Bandung: al-Bayan.

Suyanto, Dany (1994) 'Ternyata Naga Indonesia Berjumlah 22', *Jawa Pos*, 5 June: 1, 16.

Tan, Mely G. (1991) 'The Social and Cultural Dimensions of the Role of Ethnic Chinese in Indonesian Society', *Indonesia*, special issue, Ithaca: Cornell Southeast Asia Program, pp. 113–25.

Tanter, Richard and Young, Kenneth (eds) (1990) *The Politics of Middle-Class Indonesia*, Clayton: Centre of Southeast Asian Studies, Monash University.

TAPOL (1987) *Indonesia: Muslims on Trial*, London: Tapol.

Tejo, H. Sujiwo (1995) 'Menteri Siswono Berpuisi', *Kompas*, 30 August: 1, 11.

Tempo (1986) 'Sejumlah Angket tentang Kemakmuran', 23 August: 20–4.

—— (1994) 'Oui, Anti Bahasa Asing', 28 May: 74.

Tiara (1991a) 'Perilaku Warga Jakarta, Snob?', no. 29, 23 June: 18–22.

—— (1991b) 'Saya Bisa Dua Belas Jam di Kantor', no. 35, 15 September: 15.

—— (1991c) 'Eksekutif Bernyanyi', no. 36, 29 September: 19–21.

—— (1991d) 'Puisi Para Eksekutif', no. 62, 22 December: 62–6.

—— (1992) 'Orang Bisnis Main Musik', no. 63, 11 November: 9–15.

—— (1993a) 'Bisnis Art Galeri', no. 79, 23 May, no pages indicated.

—— (1993b) 'Melongok Realitas Lukisan-Lukisan Mahal', no. 83, 18 July: 9–11.

—— (1994) 'Trend Busana Muslim 1995', no. 120, 18 December; 8.

Tiras (1995a) a series of seven articles (see especially Agar Tak Terlelap di Terang Bulan, and Aneka Jurus Mendongkrak si Lemah), I (33), 14 September: 18–31.

—— (1995b) 'Tak Cukup Hanya Melukis Laut dan Bulan', I (33) supplement, 14 September: pp. A–H.

—— (1995c) 'Dengan Puisi Memancing Partisipasi', I (37), 12 October: 68.

—— (1995d) 'Parade Unjuk Gigi Sang "Raja Kecil" ', I (45), 7 December: 71.

—— (1995e) 'Rumahku Agamaku', I (45), 7 December: 36.

Ummat (1996a) 'Anggun Berjilbab', a book review, I (16), 5 February: 95.

—— (1996b) 'Gerakan Tari yang Dinamis dan Serasi', interview with Denny Malik, I (16), 5 February: 100.

Utomo, S. Prasetyo (1995) 'Sebuah Tanda Tanya Besar', *Suara Merdeka*, 26 August: 7.

Vatikiotis, Michael (1991) 'Discreet Charms', *Far Eastern Economic Review*, 21 March: 30–2.

—— (1993) *Indonesian Politics under Suharto*, London: Routledge.

—— (1996) 'Sino Chic', *Far Eastern Economic Review*, 11 January: 22–4.

Wallerstein, Immanuel (1991) 'The Bourgeois(ie) as Concept and Reality', in Étienne Balibar and Immanuel Wallerstein (eds), *Race, Nation, Class; Ambiguous Identities*, London: Verso, pp. 135–52.

Wibisono, Christianto (1994) 'Pancasila dan Liberalisme', *Kompas*, 24 December: 12.

Wright, Erik Olin (ed.) (1989) *The Debate on Classes*, London: Verso.

Yao Souchou (1995) 'U.S. Products Help Globalize Nation-State Ideas', *Jakarta Post*, 17 December: 3.

Yoon Hwan-Shin (1991) 'The Role of Elites in Creating Capitalist Hegemony in Post-Oil Boom Indonesia', special edition of the journal *Indonesia*, pp. 127–43.

Yusuf, Merwan (1996) 'Upaya Asing Meraih Dollart (Dollar Art)', *Forum Keadilan*, IV (24), 11 March: 110.

7 The new rich and cultural tensions in rural Indonesia

Hans Antlöv

Studies of contemporary Pacific Asia have often been concerned with the economic and political position of the new rich and the middle class. Within the economic sphere, the focus has been on how the middle class contributes to the development of the burgeoning Asian economies. Within the political sphere, the focus has been on the emergence of a civil society and the middle class as an agent of democratisation. In this literature, members of the middle class are seen as representing a basically new development. Their emergence signifies the breakthrough of modern society, whereby Asia will eventually converge with the West. The modernity and morals of the middle class stand at the centre of analysis, since it is inferred that a similarity in cultural tastes in East and West will bring about the convergence of the two. The economic strategies and political thinking of the middle class mark them off from the 'non-modern' layers of 'traditional' society. Everything new and good is credited to the middle class; what is traditional represents peasant values and must be dissolved. In short, the picture of the middle class is close to mythical: a vague and delightful cliché about the modernity of the new rich, and not much more.

I believe this picture is too condensed, which is not to say that it is false. At first glance, the lifestyles of the Asian rich look very similar to a modular European or American type: mobile telephones, membership in golf clubs, lunches at McDonald's, shopping tours abroad. And the middle class has been imperative in the transition to democracy: in Korea, in the Philippines and in Thailand. It is also the middle classes that have been the promoters and beneficiaries of economic growth in Pacific Asia over the 1970s–1990s period. But this is only part of the picture. 'Modernity' needs to be deconstructed and understood from within. Going to a McDonald's outlet or watching a Michael Jackson video are perhaps global and modern events, but by looking at their internal meaning and cultural logic they say just as much about the local setting of the new rich.

This is nothing new. The old Asian elites also maintained high standards of living, often of European style: one only has to think of the rajas in British India or sultans in Malaya who were often more Anglophile than their masters. Southeast Asian nationalists in the early twentieth century were educated in Europe, they wore European clothes, they adopted European ideologies of liberalism, socialism and nationalism. Many twentieth-century nationalist movements demonstrated their independence through norms, rituals and symbols strikingly similar to those cherished in London, Paris, Washington and Moscow. But this was always done with some local flavour. What has been called the 'New *Priyayi*' (new nobility) in Indonesia refers to the emergence of a Western-educated middle class during the 1930s and 1940s (Frederick 1989). These nationalist intellectuals became leaders of the Indonesian revolution, and the culture-builders of the new nation (that European invention). Some read Dale Carnegie or Karl Marx, and many spoke perfect Dutch. But they marked themselves off from European politicians by talking about resurrecting the grand Majapahit state, and by seeking to find a cultural essence that could unite all Indonesians. And not only in Indonesia. The first sentences in Vietnam's Declaration of Independence in 1945 were direct translations from the American Declaration of Independence and the French Declaration of Man and the Citizen. But President Ho Chi Minh singled himself out by wearing the simple clothes of a Tonkinese peasant. The independence rally was organised in a way bearing striking resemblance to the *Grande Féderation* of Paris in 1790, with the addition of microphones and automobiles, but Ho Chi Minh read out his speech under a parasol reminiscent of the ones which used to shield the Vietnamese emperor's mandarins from excessive sunshine.[1]

All culture-builders, but especially the new rich, must relate not only to their modernity and where they are going to, but also to where they come from and what they carry with them. When we investigate the emergence of the new rich, who can perhaps be described as oriented upwards, outwards and onwards, we must also be sensitive to their history and what they have retained. Many of the new rich we discuss in this volume are 'class travellers' with a background under very different social and cultural conditions. These people, mainly of lower middle-class or upper working-class background, have in the fast-expanding economies found the opportunity to climb their way through the class system. They have made the perilous move away from the peasantry or proletariat into the petty bourgeoisie, displaying lifestyles which they often lack the means or social skills to sustain. The *new* in the 'new rich' thus relates to their social position, more than their wealth. We are witnessing the development of a new and global value system in which social positions are no longer determined by seniority and descent, and morals no longer by position and the maintenance of order. It is this process that I will refer to in this chapter as 'modernity', a transition away from intimacy and community, towards disembeddedness and individualism.

But the new rich cannot adopt a Western way of living without reference to a social and cultural context. Although the new rich sometimes isolate themselves in their fancy mansions, and eagerly display their new values and habits, they do so in a social and cultural community in which modern values are not always normative. The lifestyles of the new rich are often under fire, particularly away from the shopping centres and discothèques of the metropolis. It is a little-noted fact in the globalisation literature that most people still live outside the major cities. Southeast Asia has a relatively low degree of large-city urbanisation, and during the last decade of economic growth, the countryside has to a large extent absorbed the growing population. In the densely populated areas of Java and the central plain of Thailand, I find it difficult to draw a clear distinction between urban and rural communities: at times Java feels like a giant suburb (to Jakarta? Singapore? Tokyo?). Again, this does not mean that everyone is urban and modern. People remain in the countryside, even many of the new rich, and the socio-cultural setting affects the ways they can adopt and present their new morality. Changes are localised, in as much as they take on local shapes and forms that cannot be interpreted simply as a process of global convergence. It is in the local settings that we might find some of the more interesting processes of globalisation occurring. In a sense, the new rich do not conform to our sociological understanding of them.[2] The whole idea of an increasingly homogeneous social class with converging patterns of consumption, cultural tastes and political preferences is put to shame in light of real practices.

Savage *et al.* (1992) distinguish three assets that allow the middle class to establish a separate class identity: property, bureaucracy and culture. Property is the wealth that gives rise to capitalist class formation; bureaucratic assets allow the middle class to control the labour of subordinates and to secure a place for themselves through hierarchical bureaucratic positions; culture becomes exploitative when one's own cultural tastes are made legitimate and other lifestyles are discredited. Mutually antagonistic classes are formed as each group attempts to legitimise its own culture. As we will see, these assets are of varying value in contemporary Indonesia: the cultural assets are relatively speaking less significant, while bureaucratic assets are the most important.

THE RURAL NEW RICH IN THEIR CONTEXT

In the following section I will discuss the positions, assets and tensions that characterise the rural new rich in a Sundanese village in West Java, here called Sariendah, which I have visited regularly since 1986. Sariendah has been integrated into an international market since the early 1930s when textile mills were set up in the neighbouring town of Majalaya. Close to half of Sariendah's population travel daily the seven kilometres to the weaving factories in Majalaya. With its 7,000 people occupying two square kilometres, Sariendah is not your typical closed corporate peasant community. It is rather a good representative of the new semi-urban villages that are emerging in Indonesia (and elsewhere in Asia) with economic and population growth. Peasants in Sariendah have successfully adopted the green revolution and programmes of economic diversification, but villagers still maintain in many ways a moral community based on intimacy and social order.

The people with whom we will be concerned in this chapter make up an expanding group of villagers who have enjoyed radically improved living standards, and who are trying to break away from the intimate social order of their locality. These are the people who have embraced most vigorously a new so-called *moderen* lifestyle. Neighbours call them *orang kaya baru*, or simply OKB, 'the new rich'. These people have successfully taken advantage of the new opportunity provided by the opening up of the economy in the mid-1970s. Since the 1980s they have been able to invest in capital goods, and to expose publicly their new patterns of consumption.

During the last twenty years in Indonesia, there has been a dramatic increase in state intervention in village affairs. Many of the new rich are village-based state clients. Through a strategy of 'civilian patronage' the Indonesian government has recruited nearly all local notables and leaders into state functions. Sariendah has 178 official positions in 18 state-related formal associations (Antlöv 1995: 50–8). These leaders-cum-state-clients are expected to be loyal to the government and to promote extension programmes and state directives faithfully. In exchange, they get privileged access to credit schemes and government programmes, and the ideological support of higher authorities in their search for increased wealth and power. They make up a large share of the new rich.

The rise of the rural OKB and state officials in Indonesia is only secondarily a result of market forces: first and foremost they have been empowered by the New Order to be loyal state representatives and brokers between the local government and higher authorities. Access to the market and wealth have followed naturally from this. The access to property and bureaucracy has allowed certain individuals to carve out a new middle-class identity. In Thailand the middle class is ideologically constructed by its role in the democratisation movement, while in Malaysia it has been as the Malay element within a complex cultural/ethnic mosaic (see Shamsul and Ockey, this volume). The middle class in Indonesia is also culturally constructed: they are the ideological champions of the New Order. Again, this is nothing new. In the 1950s the indigenous middle class was mobilised within the so-called *Benteng* programme to 'Indonesianise' the Chinese-dominated economy. Today, given that the Chinese entrepreneurs have close connections with the government, many of the new rich are dependent on the Chinese for their wealth.

Before 1965 it was difficult for the rich to spend their income on building personal wealth. The two decades 1945–65 were characterised by intense political activity. A myriad of political parties competed for power. Members of village councils were elected by the village population, and local power-holders had to vie for votes and invest in village loyalties. Attempts by the village elite to introduce labour-saving devices and monopolise power were successfully combated by the poor. Landowners could not withdraw from their local responsibilities without running the risk of being socially ostracised.

This political setting changed radically in 1965, when Suharto ascended to power. With a policy that Wertheim (1969) has called 'betting on the strong', Suharto introduced a new trickle-down modernisation programme, in which village-based state clients played a central role. By involving them in agricultural intensification and small-scale industrial development, it was hoped that Indonesia would become a developed nation. Accompanying this opening up of the economy was a closing down of politics. Control of administrative offices, the hierarchical organisation of state-based officials, and restrictions on party politics give the New Order government almost unlimited powers to regulate the activities of both institutions and individuals. Thus, there is only a limited 'civil society' in Indonesia, if one means by this a stratum of people who are not incorporated within the state. This is the fundamental reason why the middle class in Indonesia has not opted for democracy; it is often more profitable to maintain the old structures.

A national administrative network reaches down to the village level in even the most remote parts of the country. Following the national *Pancasila* ideology, politics must operate in a spirit of consensus and mutual assistance.[3] To avoid the cleavages which estranged people from each other under the Old Order, the New Order regime has released the rural population from the restraints of manipulative party political activities, a process that is referred to as the policy of the floating mass. It is said that the conflicts and cleavages of the earlier period prevented the rural people from devoting their full energy to economic development and political stability. Party political activities in the countryside are under heavy restrictions. The New Order policy has been to ban all party-political activities except for a short election campaign preceding the general election every five years.

Who then are the new rich in the village of Sariendah? It is a difficult count, but in one hamlet (out of 12) where I have collected material, 17 out of 147 households were in 1989 classified by neighbours as rich. Ten of them had gained their wealth during the last twenty years, and could thus be considered OKB – an approximate 8 per cent of the population. As has been shown by Edmundson (1994), households in Java pass over time through different wealth standards, depending on life-cycle and luck in enterprise. Thus, we need to look beyond pure monthly income to delimit the new rich. The fluctuation in incomes does not occur randomly. During the New Order it is the politically correct households that have gained the most, as 'political entrepreneurs' using their skills and connections to maximise both market profits and state support. These are the landowners who have benefited from the green revolution and cheap credit, the traders and the entrepreneurs who have taken advantage of the rural demand for services, and the factory workers who combine their work in Majalaya with farming or trading in Sariendah. Three of the new rich in our sample hamlet are farmers; two are contractors in building; two are minibus operators; two are civil servants in Bandung and Majalaya, with low nominal incomes but substantive extra incomes; and the last OKB works as a village official. All have in common the fact that they do not have single sources of income, but combine their primary salaries with money from trading and commissions from various services. And they are loyal clients of the state.

THE AGE OF MONEY

I contest the proposition that it is sufficient in rural Indonesia to have only entrepreneurial skills in order to become rich. Without political connections it is almost impossible to get the permission to establish a small company, to apply for subsidised credit, and to find the correct distributors. In the increasingly outward-oriented New Order world, local control is crucially maintained through the disciplinary powers of registration. People need compulsory letters of recommendation and official endorsement to look for work, enrol in high school, buy land, move, get married, hold a *wayang* show, and so on. It is impossible to survive in modern Indonesia without these endorsements. The key word is *koneksi*, because these letters of endorsement can only be achieved through contacting higher authorities, whether village headman, the local headmaster or a friend working at a government office. Ambitious and upwardly mobile OKB must cultivate good relations with the village headman, the Golkar (ruling party) chairman, the chairman of the Village Community Resilience Board (LKMD) and sub-district officials. Authorities from outside the traditional village structure have become sources of power and prominent actors in village affairs. A lot of money and energy is spent by the elite, and especially the new rich, on lubricating good contacts in village and sub-district offices, thus seeking peer respect. In this process, the OKB draw symbolic (and not so symbolic!) boundaries between themselves and the common villagers. OKB households cultivate relations with other OKBs and officials: by inviting them to ceremonies, by acting as their promoters during elections, by joining their state organisations, by being active in village affairs. This gives them entrance into the official sphere, and access to both the economy and patronage. This again is a case of 'betting on the strong': the OKB tend to mix with their peers, who have the same cultural tastes and share a similar ideology.

Let me give an example. Sunarya is a well-educated and ambitious man in his late thirties. He belongs to one of the settler families, and can claim descent to the first headman in Sariendah (who governed in the 1850s). He is also a distant relative of the present headman. Earlier Sunarya was a hamlet leader, the only one in Sariendah with a programme for hamlet development. In the 1982 national election he was local chairman of one of the opposition parties (PPP), but has since found Golkar to be more true to his personal and political aspirations. Some people say he joined Golkar out of strategic considerations. He also had to end his affiliation with PPP when he became a civil servant in 1983. He works as a lower bureaucrat in the provincial office in Bandung. Sunarya commutes daily, leaving at 7.00 in the morning and, at best, arriving home at 5.00 in the afternoon. He is a very energetic leader who finds Sariendah too small for his future ambitions. He has functioned as Golkar leader only for three years, but has already built a whole new village organisation. The village is divided into a number of geographic sections and each is headed by a community leader who is responsible for recruiting a number of members. In the 1992 election, he enrolled close to all Sariendah residents as Golkar members.

Sunarya is one of the new rich in Sariendah. His wealth comes from his work in Bandung, but also from commissions he receives when helping people to fill in letters and when providing administrative information. Together with his wife, he also runs a shop in the village junction selling foodstuffs and renting out videos. He plans to buy a Daihatsu minibus to ply the route to Majalaya. He lives in a rather fancy house he bought two years after he became Golkar headman: people still wonder how he can afford it. And they also wonder how he manages to work in Bandung, run the shop, and act as Golkar chairman, all at the same time.

To be OKB, or new rich, is not only a matter of income. It is also related to cultural tastes and attitude. The term 'OKB' in itself is somewhat derogatory and tells of a villager who does not really belong to the community or who does not conform to village values. And this is true of many of the new rich. In lifestyle and values, they set themselves off from others. 'OKB' is not used to characterise the traditional elite or those villagers who, over generations or decades, have gained enough income to live a comfortable life. An understanding of the OKB must therefore recognise the way people conceptualise their social character: as frugal, pretentious and secluded (which was exactly what neighbours thought of Sunarya). The OKB are sometimes called the *kaget kaya*, the 'confounded rich', because they do not have the social competence, sensitivity or basic *savoir faire* to manage their riches: sensing, for example, that it is enough with one car, not three, or that one must invite neighbours, and not only peers, to village celebrations.

This is not to say that the values of the OKB and other exponents of modernity are not taking root. People call the times of today *zaman duit*, the Age of Money. Economic ventures are pursued to maximise individual profits. Wealth is accumulated and invested for further profit. Money is needed to pay school fees, to commute to work, to get a sick-leave letter from the hamlet chairman and to get a son or daughter through high school. In the New Order, people must live up to what is expected of them as Indonesian citizens: bring education to their children and health-care to the family. The obligations of a responsible citizen put pressure on people to have a regular income, and to be hard-working, loyal employees. A good description of petty businessmen in Jakarta is provided by Murai, who argues that they are: 'hard put to keep up appearances as modern salary men and to meet the costs of their children's education…the demands of their jobs require that they even…dine in first-class restaurants when necessary to fulfill business and social obligations. But to scrape together the money to do so they eat lunch for 100 rupiah at street stalls' (Murai 1994: 37). This is also the theme of several recent Indonesian films.

If one wants to be a good New Order citizen, one should be self-reliant and competent, escaping the inward-looking 'traditional' lifestyle. Some poor villagers are now embarrassed to ask help from neighbours because they fear that a request will be turned down, and they will consequently 'lose face'. Indeed, some *moderen* households hesitate to offer help to neighbours with the cynical argument that the poor have themselves to blame for their poverty. The social mechanisms that once used to support poor households (such as labour exchanges and public harvests) have all but disappeared in the face of a rapidly growing population and more commercial approaches to work. In a comparative article on agrarian transformation in Thailand and Java, Gillian Hart (1989: 35) argues that social and religious relations of patronage, which might mitigate conflict and resentment against inequality, 'are notably absent in Java'.

In this ideological climate, consumerism has emerged as an alternative way of seeking happiness. Stories of success and wealth take on a new positive quality. Blessed by expanding markets and growing incomes, the rich enthusiastically acquire highly visible symbols of wealth: grand villas, Japanese minibuses, satellite disks. Some young people no longer dream of becoming peasants; they want to *Hidup Diatas Roda Empat*, 'Live on Four Wheels'. They do not want to be tied to land. Rather, they want the ultimate dream: to be mobile, like a *royal*, free of worries, and with enough money to spend on whatever they wish.

The new patterns of consumption carve out new restricted spheres of social interaction: households have television sets and families spend evenings behind closed curtains, with flickering images of faraway places.

To be *moderen* is thus very much associated with a lifestyle that only the new rich can afford to maintain. Without the access to property and bureaucracy, it is difficult, if not impossible, to maintain the cultural taste the new rich strive towards. Many of the new rich are materialistic. Traditional morality plays only a minor role in their cultural construction and self-identity: of most importance to them is the possession of signs that they have accomplished things. With that also comes power to claim submission. This is something new: it is not only the hereditary elite who live in faraway cities and palaces who have the right to display their wealth, but now it is also fellow villagers. In previous times, neighbours and kinsmen were expected to contribute to the welfare of the community, not to put their private consumption first. Nowadays, consumption has become each man's – and indeed each woman's – privilege. There is also a shift away from refinement as a basis of social distinction (as in colonial Java), to money.

Modernity is upheld by both men and women, but in different ways. Many social relations within the village are typically maintained through women, and when a family isolates itself, it will thus affect women the most. Men can establish new relations outside the family and village, but women often have greater problems going beyond the borders of the community, if for no other reason than because their husbands do not allow them to. But I also found it fascinating to talk to a few OKB women who pressed their husbands not to be so generous towards neighbours, and to spend more money on capital goods. Women often have control over the household purse in Java, and if they find a possibility to save on expenses, they will not always hesitate. One important difference from the growth of the middle class in Europe is that relatively few women in Indonesia have left the household economy and become professionals, at least outside the major cities. Although women earn a substantial part of the income, they do not yet have a separate economy, but pool their earnings in the household. Their personal autonomy is thus lower in Indonesia than in Europe, even among the new rich.

Let us present two examples of the lifestyles of the new rich in Sariendah. A first indication of the lifestyle of the elite is reflected in the habits of a 16-year-old high-school student, the daughter of a rich peasant. Euis stands out clearly from the rest of the hamlet girls. She dresses flashily and wears lipstick and perfume bought in Bandung. Like other members of the Sariendah elite, she frequents the Chinese-run fashion shops in Majalaya, with their own (very particular) rural version of *haute couture*. While it might impress her friends, high heels are not very practical on the dirt roads in Sariendah. But Euis does not care. Her long nails are painted red, a sign that she never does any manual work. Together with her like-minded cousin, she goes to a private high school in Majalaya. They travel by public transport every day and her father gives Euis a 2,000-rupiah allowance for her expenses, which in 1991 was more than the daily income of an agricultural labourer. Although Euis and her cousin are still teenagers, they are often away in Majalaya in the evening. Euis always stopped me when I passed by her house, asking about life in Sweden. She says she has a boyfriend in Majalaya who, one day, will take her to Europe. But before that, she claims, she will go to university in Bandung.

Another example is the family of Cep Agus. Just like Sunarya, Cep Agus works as a clerk in the provincial office in Bandung. He commutes the 35 kilometres, Monday to Saturday, in the relative comfort of a minibus. His official monthly income in 1991 was 150.000 rupiah (US$75), which just covers his costs of transport and expenses in Bandung. But his real income must be much higher, given his expensive standard of living. He has a Swiss-style villa, white-washed with two nice Greek pillars at its entrance, and a fence around the house. Cep Agus is 34 years, and his wife Jamaliah is two years older. She is of local descent, and works as a secondary-school teacher in the village. The additional household incomes are gained by performing a brokering role between villagers and the provincial government. Cep Agus and Jamaliah practise the *koneksi* game, and help people to get their letters and contacts. Jamaliah knows the local setting, Cep Agus knows people in Bandung. If a family wants to send a daughter to high school or university, if someone wants to look for a job in Bandung, or have any other out-of-village business, they can ask the Aguses to provide them with the necessary contacts and endorsements. And it is not for free. People who visit the family are those with aspirations, for themselves or their children, to leave the village, and who can afford it. Almost all visitors are of high status. Colleagues and peers from Sariendah and Majalaya would come to seek the advice of the Aguses. I never saw an ordinary resident from Sariendah in their home, not even their neighbours. The Aguses receive quite substantial sums for the assistance provided, money that goes towards maintaining a standard of living much higher than their neighbours'. In 1986, they already had a colour television and video player, one of the very first families in Sariendah to do so. Cep Agus is known to have borrowed a car from his Bandung office and taken his family for a holiday to Pangandaran, a favourite resort on the South Java Sea. Once or twice, I have also joined them at one of the many Kentucky Fried Chicken outlets in Bandung. They have a maid to take care of their two children during working hours.

Among their neighbours, Cep Agus and his family are not popular. The maid, the fence, the holidays are not exactly what one expects of a typical Sundanese villager. People's main criticism is that the Aguses isolate themselves. They do not participate in community life. Jamaliah said that she did not want to fraternise with lower-status neighbours. She could not see why she, as a rich resident, should provide food for neighbours at ritual celebrations, as community norms prescribe. And, as a schoolteacher, she also needs to keep a social distance from the parents of her pupils, or so she claims. It is easier to mix with relatives, she explained, because one does not need to count what is being served and also because status is more easily defined as it is based on kinship. Some of the 'traditional' rich in Sariendah, those who have maintained their position over generations, scorned the attitude of the Agus family. They would rather see the Aguses spend their wealth in more conventional ways: on rituals, buying land, and productive enterprises. But Cep Agus is not alone in his new lifestyle. In 1991 there were a dozen families in Sariendah who maintained a similar attitude towards their wealth: that it was for private, albeit often conspicuous, consumption and that other people should not really bother about it.

To a high degree, these new-rich lifestyles are supported by the ideology of the government. The principle behind the New Order modernisation programme is 'betting on the strong', in which prosperity and modernity are achieved by a middle class whose wealth will eventually trickle down to the poor. When the new rich live their new life, they do so with the tacit (and often not so tacit) approval of state ideology. The self-image of the new rich, even in a small Sundanese village, is that they are the avant-garde who must drag the *masih bodoh*, the uneducated and poor, into the future. Cep Agus and Sunarya are both very aware of this mission. For them, working in Bandung and living modern was more than a question of lifestyle. It was an attitude, indeed a moral obligation, to maintain their present living standards and provide an example for others to follow.

Generally speaking, and this is unlike the situation in Europe, North America and perhaps even upper middle-class Jakarta, cultural distinctions are not very important in the creation of class identity in rural Indonesia. Sariendah is a fairly homogeneous social setting, and differences in lifestyles and tastes are not very great (although they are on the increase). It has been argued that cultural exclusiveness is one of the prime boundary markers in Europe (Bourdieu 1984; Featherstone 1991; Lamont 1992). Likewise, in colonial Java class distinctions between the hereditary elite (*priyayi/menak*) and commoners (*wong cilik/jelma leutik*) were marked by a cultural exclusivity according to which the elite and commoners hardly shared the same imagined community: they literally lived worlds apart. While ascriptive superiority and aesthetic sophistication may once have been the markers of social difference, class distinctions in contemporary Indonesia are made more on the basis of bureaucratic incorporation, patterns of consumption, and wealth.

Cep Agus did not doubt that his lifestyle was the correct way for Indonesia to be transported into the future. And in this, he could successfully associate himself with the state ideology of *pembangunan* ('development').[4] According to President Suharto, *pembangunan* represents an 'all-encompassing change in which the society becomes modern, prosperous, just, peaceful and built upon Pancasila'.[5] In order for Indonesia to become an advanced nation, it is argued, it needs people like Jamaliah, Euis, Sunarya and Cep Agus to pave the road into the future.

The patterns of consumption evident among these people have become a norm, not only among the new rich, but for many layers of society in Indonesia. The struggle to maintain this new standard of living is a common theme in books and films. Consumerism is more or less openly celebrated as proof that Indonesia is a modern and prosperous nation. But it is not a nation of liberalism: consumption can only take place within the norms provided by the authoritarian state. The OKB must be good representatives and display what in Indonesian is called *mono-loyalitas* towards the official ideology. Most of the new rich do not want to be separated from their state protection. They might be agents of social and economic change, but they are not exponents of a procedural democratic development. The rights they talk about – to live in privacy, to spend money as they want – have certain limits and are only for the rich and the powerful. Ordinary people, the *masih bodoh* masses, are seen by the new rich as having different rights: to support the present path of development, to be loyal citizens and to accept the new ways of living.

COMMUNITY SPIRIT AND COUNTER-MODERNITY

Given this account, one might believe that not much is left of local community norms. But we must be cautious here. It is easy to overemphasise the globality and modernity of social change. For most people, especially in the countryside and smaller towns but also in the wards of larger cities, the life of the new rich is neither common nor fully desired. Ordinary people might want the wealth of the new rich, but they do not strive for the latter's morality. In many ways there is a vigorous local 'community spirit' that operates as a counter-image to that of modernity. Seen from below and within, there is another picture of the drastic economic changes taking place over the last decades of the twentieth century. Most of the new rich in Sariendah were born in the village, and they expect to die in the village. They belong to a richly textured community with networks of relatives, friends and neighbours. The new rich might have taken on new moral standards and styles of living, but they must also, in different ways, relate to the local social texture and to community values. For most of the rural OKB, the new lifestyles have been carved out within the confines of the village community. Few of the new rich in Sariendah have left the village. A few have moved in, but these are often families with relatives in the village who wish to settle down during old age, after having lived in Bandung, Sumedang or some other city. The

Sunaryas and Cep Aguses have chosen to remain in the village, and they gave the same reason: the social familiarity.

Social relations are strong in the village community. The bilateral kinship system makes neighbours into kinsmen; there is always some kinship relation to recognise. To some extent, kinship has become more important during the social changes of recent years, when some families have oriented themselves inwards. These more restricted spheres of social interaction take the kin-group as centre. Cognitive descent groups (sometimes called *trah* in Java) have grown stronger. As in most peasant communities, there is a conformist and redistributive ideology in Sariendah. Richer households are expected to assist poorer households with political protection and economic security; in exchange they receive the loyalty and support of subordinates. Concepts such as *hormat* (respect for hierarchy) and *rukun* (harmonious social appearances) are essential, at least on an ideological level.

The village community is maintained by a number of social relations and institutions: by *arisan* (rotating credit associations), by *slametan* (ritual meals), by *tolong menolong* (mutual assistance labour parties), by state-supporting social organisations, by Islamic *ummat* gatherings, and such activities as jointly watching a soccer game or cooking for a celebration. In the late afternoon, young men and women stand in groups and exchange comments about each other. Adult men join in, to learn the latest round of gossip before going home for dinner. This helps to strengthen the affinities that bind the community together. It is important to note that this 'community spirit' is neither a survival of the past, nor a retreat from the modern world. It is rather a reconstruction of everyday practices and beliefs, an identity in which the modern factory work meets the traditional village. Because of the tenacity of this community spirit, we have every reason to believe that it will survive. Although young people perhaps want Cep Agus's wealth, they do not wish to inherit his social position, isolated from the community. The same people who want to live a royal life also wish to be part of the community.

There is another factor at work here. In a certain sense, the state needs a strong community spirit. The community is the arena where development programmes are carried out and where political control is maintained. Since the 1980s, the New Order government has consciously promoted notions of 'familism' (*kekeluargaan*) and 'original democracy' (*demokrasi asli*) in which liberal notions of individual freedom and procedural democracy are less important than consensus, harmony and the maintenance of hierarchy. This is in line with a more general trend in East and Southeast Asia to return to Asian values turning away from Western liberal values of freedom and choice. We can also notice here that the Suharto government has promoted a more refined (*halus*) style of language, art and ritual, if not of everyday lifestyle (Pemberton 1994). According to this ideology, the local community plays a central, but often underrated, role. The community is a critical arena for the government's political control and ideological mobilisation. From the perspective of higher authorities, the strength of the local government, of village celebrations, of notions of a common Indonesian nationality, and of national development, have helped to make the community an important arena in the policy of economic development and political stability. In the local community, authorities can have a high level of control, and can even afford to ignore much of what happens, because communities are so tightly knit that they become 'effectively self-regulating' (Sullivan 1992: 198). This is one of the factors providing high legitimacy to the New Order regime.

In the new global culture, the 'home' has become a celebrated object of nostalgia, a model of the pre-modern past (Hannertz 1990: 248) where one does not have to prove oneself, and where face-to-face relations prevail. So too in Indonesia. 'Tradition' is also an important part of the self-identity of the new rich. Very few would say that they are breaking with the past (although socially they are oriented up- and not downwards). Thus, in the fancy homes of some OKB, one can also find 'traditional' objects, such as the *keris* (Javanese daggers) but now as objects of glorification without any practical meaning. The *keris* has become a part of the national heritage, and can be understood only as such, not as a thing with a local meaning. It is just like the refrigerators the first batch of 1970s OKBs had in their living rooms. While there was no electrical power to which they could be connected, they were still highly valued objects.

There is also another reason why the new rich do not simply embrace a rational, market-oriented, liberal ideology. This has to do with constraints within the Indonesian form of capitalism itself, where it is more profitable (and hence economically rational) to maintain 'traditional' relations. The patronage of sharecropping relations, in which landowners give privileged access to selected sharecroppers, is used as a mechanism by rural capitalists to tie up a loyal clientele. The opening up of the economy has thus, in many cases, led to restricted, eye-to-eye labour relations rather than the expected 'pure' capitalistic employer–employee relationships.

TENSIONS AND RESPONSES

The new rich are therefore not simply agents of change or promoters of modernity. They also reconcile themselves with the community spirit, because it is the main way through which the government can continue to rule, and because in many cases it is more efficient in terms of their own interests. Although the new rich and the elite may wish to evade their local obligations, and although the suppression of political activities has made their position more secure and their new lifestyle more viable, a limitation on their position and local legitimacy is set by community allegiances and state ideology. There is a realm of what could be called community morality, in which the wealth and power of the village elite must be acknowledged by their neighbours. The new rich cannot simply convert their wealth into authority. Cutting across economic and political hierarchies, tradition continues to influence social interaction. If a village-based state client lets his community authority assume the upper hand, he might lose the crucial support of higher authorities. If a community leader lets his administrative authority assume the upper hand, he might lose the support of his neighbours and relatives. Because many new rich in rural Java are state clients, they must also conform to state ideology.

Thus, unlike their fellow urbanites, the rural OKB cannot display their wealth in shopping centres and movies without some sense of discomfort or anxiety. In one sense, there is not much geophysical difference between Java in the 1950s and today, only better houses and better roads. The human geography of the countryside is basically the same; villages have only become more cramped and intense. This lack of space and privacy puts limitations on how the new rich can consume their goods. There is a paradox here: if the OKB want to consume without arousing comment, they must leave the village, and then nobody takes any notice of their wealth! It should also be remembered that we are not talking about the traditional elite who hold a secure social position within the rural community and who, to some extent, are accepted and expected to practise a rich pattern of consumption. It is rather the mixture of class travel and modernity that people have difficulty accepting.

We need here to say something about the social and moral ties between the new rich and the non-OKB. How embedded are the OKB in the village social fabric? From the evidence provided so far, one could conclude that the new rich in Sariendah are spearheading a new development towards what summarily could be called modernity, and that they are under heavy fire for disregarding age-old village norms. Both of these images are valid. The OKB are isolated in the village, but they are also a part of its social fabric, *mau tidak mau*, as one would say in Indonesia, 'whether they wish it or not'. One could thus argue that the OKB are isolated because they are a part of the community. It is never the case that people do not care about what the OKB are doing; neighbours are watched very carefully, especially those who do not conform.

This reveals a number of tensions built into the ideological construction of the new rich, tensions which I believe have always been there, but which, for political reasons, have become more obvious in recent years. The primary field of tension is between privacy and wealth, on the one hand, and loyalty to the community and affinity, on the other; between the 'individualism' of the new rich and the 'community spirit' of the subaltern. The struggle is about ideology and resources: what largesse the new rich should contribute to the community, when and how people can demonstrate their wealth, whether to conserve or reform the community spirit; how, in the end, communities are to be organised. As actors in this struggle, new rich households are very much a part of the village community.

It has been argued that communitarianism and individualism in Java are located in two different spheres: those of ritual and production, respectively (Schweitzer 1989; Hefner 1990). I would add that this distinction is not only about different spheres, but also about class and ideology. Different villagers, depending on economic position, social background and political aspirations, emphasise one set of values over another. For instance, while some members of the new rich maintain that their new wealth is necessary for Indonesia to become modern, others say that it will spoil village life and people will end up like in Bandung and Jakarta, not knowing their neighbours. Many villagers are also disappointed with those members of the village elite whose children have been educated in cosmopolitan Bandung or Jakarta and who now refuse to return to rural Sariendah. To make things more complicated, some subordinates argue that they must break away from the traditional patterns of hierarchy and dependency. Alternatively, some new rich simply do not want to discard existing social relations and the spirit of communality, because traditional authority, patronage and restrictions on conflict work to their advantage.

In short, we cannot in Indonesia find a clear division between the modern and the traditional or between the rich and the poor. Rather we find a mixture of modernity, globality and community that repudiates any such dichotomies. When we hear of 'community' we should not think of tradition only; when we hear of 'global influence' we should not think of modernity only. Both have been remoulded, revised, even blended together in their localised encounter with the Indonesian reality. In curious ways, the result is a mix of old and new, traditional and modern, local and national, community and state. The state has adopted both modernity and community, while the village maintains the community spirit along with its obligations towards the state.

There are in all communities certain norms and manners that people are expected to subscribe to. Not even in the fancy suburbs of Jakarta (or New York) can people live totally separated from such values. A village in Java is sustained through a joint ideology of labour-sharing and intimacy. If a villager does not maintain the appearance of being a good neighbour and kinsman, there are several cultural and ideological mechanisms through which people react. Some of the new rich who have achieved their wealth fast and spend it on personal consumption, or who have isolated themselves from the rest of the community, are put under negative community sanction.

Within a polity of affinity and community spirit, pretension and privacy among peers are strictly condemned. If the wealth of a household suddenly increases, if the family evades rules of generosity, or if people boast and brag, various forms of negative sanction are at hand. One penalising sanction is to withhold the daily gestures of neighbourly respect, to speak rudely, and not to invite the arrogant person to various social events. Another common sanction is to condemn unpopular people for being un-Islamic. The Islamic way of achieving wealth, according to villagers, is to work hard and diligently. Without work, nobody can become rich. But people say that a number of families in Sariendah have become rich without any work. They are allegedly involved in what is called 'black magic' (*ilmu hitam*). To account for their wealth, but also to sanction their uncommunal manners, people say that these OKB families have entered a spiritual treaty with a wild boar. In exchange for prosperity in this life, the new rich family is said to have promised a spirit the regular sacrifice of a child at Mount Ciremay outside Cirebon. When family members die, their souls must be offered to the spirit, and they may themselves become boars. This practice is well known in Indonesia and known as *munjung* among the Sundanese. It is not the practice of *munjung* as such that bothers people, but the new rich's lack of correct appearance and their *moderen* attitude. Only the rich, and especially the newly rich, are accused of *munjung*. Several spiritual teachers and Islamic leaders also visit Ciremay regularly, but no one would ever believe that they sacrifice human beings. But because the new rich do not conform to village ideals, they are subject to these accusations.

One of those who is slandered is Pak Guru (lit. Father Teacher), a local headmaster. He has worked his way up through the hierarchy of rank and wealth, and is now the proud owner of one of the few two-storey houses in Sariendah. Several of his children have passed university, and now work in surrounding villages as bureaucrats and teachers. But something is amiss. People seldom go to his house for advice and never pay him a social visit. They defer to him as they should, according to etiquette, but behind his back they call him names. Neighbours say that the family of Pak Guru does not possess the correct inner (*batin*) qualities. The Gurus feel superior and distance themselves from their neighbours. They make no attempt to conceal their wealth or rank. On the contrary, Pak Guru takes every opportunity to brag about his work at the school and to display his fancy house, his colour television set and video, and the family's three motorbikes. The family keeps to itself and the neighbours reciprocate by avoiding contact with the Gurus. The only time I met Pak Guru at a hamlet council was when a boy in the neighbourhood was accused of slandering the Guru family. The boy had said that one of Pak Guru's sons had stolen a cassette recorder, and Pak Guru vehemently rejected the accusation. Pak Guru dared the boy to file a police report. Knowing that a son of Pak Guru's brother-in-law worked at the Majalaya police station, the boy perhaps did the sensible thing by dropping the case. The Gurus eventually won the case in a community council, but this did not mean that people stopped talking behind their backs. When I asked Pak Guru why he did not participate in hamlet activities, he said that he was too busy with his work. And when I asked why he had not been a candidate in the last Sariendah headman election, he was sincerely surprised and could not really understand the question: why should he, an upwardly mobile headmaster, bother to become a village headman? His aspirations were to become a board member of the private Bandung-based foundation that administered his school.

When Pak Guru's firstborn daughter married, his neighbours boycotted the ceremony. According to community tradition in Java, the size and style of a marriage ceremony should reflect the host's wealth. A richer household should thus hold lavish ceremonies and redistribute some of its wealth to the local community. Neighbours and relatives should be invited without distinction, and the whole community should be involved in the preparation, providing some relaxation as well as extra food. But the Gurus held a typical New Order OKB ceremony: inviting only the people they wished to attend, hiring cooks from Majalaya, and having experts prepare the house. Pak Guru told me that he could not understand why he should have to use people who did not know their jobs if he could afford to hire professionals.

Only 50 out of 150 households in the neighbourhood were invited, out of a total of 1,250 invitations. Pak Guru demonstrated in this way that his nice colleagues and rich friends, from Bandung and elsewhere, were more important than the community in which he lived. So in a fantastic feat of solidarity, none of his low-rank neighbours showed up (although five richer and rather like-minded peer families did, including Cep Agus). Pak Guru and his family are not liked and are commonly criticised behind their backs, yet they accept this price for their seclusion, and have no desire to achieve an exalted position in the community.

The reactions towards the lifestyle of Pak Guru are indicative of the tensions that the New Order village is enduring, and which the new rich must face up to. It is not merely for the new rich to take on a new standard and style of living, and expect that it will be acclaimed by neighbours and friends. Even in the globalised economy of Sariendah, there are social relations and cultural imaginations that balance the forces of modernity.

CONCLUSION

How general are these observations? They are from a single location in Java, but I believe that these trends and tensions can be identified also in larger cities. As to the state support of the new rich, even conglomerate capitalists in Jakarta cannot operate without state support (Raillon 1994). As for the community orientation, it is notable that Jakarta is almost emptied of its Muslim population once a year at Idul Fitri (end of the fasting holiday). Families return to their home village (*pulang kampung*), to seek the blessing of the family elder. I can still vividly remember one man posted as an army sergeant in Jakarta who returned home with his Chinese wife at Idul Fitri. They arrived in a nice new minibus and, to show off their new wealth, they threw 50-rupiah coins on the ground as they walked through the hamlet, a 'traditional' royal custom. Not all of the new rich would be so blatantly pretentious, but it is important for all of them to retain an affinity with their home village. In doing so, they also preserve some of its values. The hope of the army sergeant was to gain status and prestige, as he was planning to return to Sariendah after his posting in Jakarta. But what he demonstrated was that he was a typical class-traveller who could not handle the lifestyle expected of him.

A quite different story might exemplify the resilience of local community spirit. In one of the typical middle-class suburban wards of Yogyakarta, built in the early 1980s, a respected man died in January 1996. It happened at 3.00 in the morning, at the main Yogyakarta hospital, after some time of illness. After only two hours, several men and women from the ward had arrived to assist and bring comfort. The local ward chairman, the *Kepala* RT, even brought 2 million rupiah (appr. US$900) in case the family could not pay the hospital bill (the body is not allowed to be removed unless the bill is paid). When the family returned with the corpse at 7.00 am, hundreds of people had already gathered.

Neighbours brought food and all the necessary ritual cloth and incense needed for the funeral. At 10.00, the family and some neighbours left to make the 6-hour trip to the home village of the deceased. When they returned 24 hours later, a week-long period of mourning began, with neighbours passing by every day with food and a word of comfort.

Deaths are important events in Indonesia, but this show of communion still surprised me. This was a typically suburban ward: none of the people living there had been born there, and people worked in different parts of Yogyakarta. Every house had a fence and people mostly stayed in their homes in the evenings. But this death showed that 'traditional' social practices are not gone: it is exactly on such critical occasions that the community spirit is best displayed. To be sure, visitors got food when they arrived, and some of those who assisted were paid in cash. But these monetary transactions – which no doubt can be attributed to the 'Age of Money' – did not undermine the very real sense of community solidarity.

The parvenus, Pak Guru *et consortes*, seem to live a perfectly well-adjusted modern and global life. They have TVs and cars, they go on holidays to fancy resorts on the South Java Sea, and once in a while they take the one-hour drive into Bandung for a snack at KFC and to watch a movie. But, as we have seen, they are also subject to local restriction. Not all of the new rich are totally free of the places they come from. On one level they might wish to cut off as many social relations as possible, at least those involving social obligations, but on another level they still value village life. When I asked Cep Agus why he continues to live in Sariendah, he says that he relishes the quietness of a small village, and that he does not have the yearning to move to Bandung. Through his contacts outside the village he is not in need of everyday relations with neighbours, and seems rather content with the present situation.

Frans Hüsken has proposed the term 'hesitant capitalist' for those Javanese entrepreneurs who shrink at the prospect of adopting the uncompromising strategies of the free-wheeling capitalist. Rather, they chose to retain some of their local security and, most of all, their state protection (Hüsken 1989: 166). In this spirit, Cep Agus and other new rich in Indonesia might be called the 'hesitant rich' who prefer to maintain some local social ties, rather than taking the unsafe step away from the community. Even though the new rich live secluded in their mansions, they are a part of that community, willingly or unwillingly. The future of the middle class and the new rich in Indonesia is not easy to predict. What we can say, though, is that we are not witnessing a simple transition from an Asian traditionalism to Western modernity. The community-based lifestyles discussed in this chapter can definitely not be understood within such a framework.

The new rich are in many ways placed between the community and the state, operating not only as the political clients of the government, but also as cultural brokers. They take a middleman position with dual responsibilities and dual orientations. Since they are state clients, they must also be credible examples. Elsewhere (Antlöv 1995), I have argued that a successful village leader must achieve a balance between state ideology and community values. To a certain extent this is also true of the new rich, especially since so many of them have gained their wealth from their relations with the state and are seen by the community as representing the state. Disliked leaders arouse criticism, political action and disorder. If tensions continue to grow between the new rich and the broader masses of the population, it might be difficult to take Indonesia further into modernity without at the same time causing social instability. We should thus watch carefully the relationships between the new rich and ordinary people.

POSTSCRIPT

Laying the last hand on this chapter, in February 1998, Indonesia is experiencing the worst economic and political crisis in thirty years. I believe that part of this crisis can be understood as a consequence of the tensions described in this chapter. During recent years, Indonesia has seen an increasingly large gap between state-backed capitalists and those without privileged access to state resources. More recently this has created a lack of confidence that the present system is sustainable, which in turn has led to a political crisis. The scale might be very different from that in Sariendah, but I would argue that some of the mechanisms are the same. Just as in Sariendah, there is a need for social adjustments to be made between state actors and the great majority of the Indonesian population. The cultural tensions discussed for rural Indonesia in this chapter will become increasingly visible arenas of struggle as new political structures are introduced.

Notes

1 For more details on this argument, see Tønnesson and Antlöv (1996). For empirical material, see Tønnesson and Antlöv (forthcoming).
2 For a similar argument for the British middle class, see Savage *et al.* (1992).
3 For more on *Pancasila* see Antlöv (1995: 37–8).
4 See Heryanto (1988).
5 Quoted from President Suharto's 1988 Independence Day speech.

Bibliography

Antlöv, Hans (1995) *Exemplary Centre, Administrative Periphery: Leadership and the New Order in Rural Java*, London: Curzon Press.
Bourdieu, Pierre (1984) *Distinction: A Social Critique of the Judgement of Taste*, Cambridge, MA: Harvard University Press.
Edmundson, Wade C. (1994) 'Do the Rich Get Richer, Do the Poor Get Poorer? East Java, Two Decades, Three Villages, 46 People', *Bulletin of Indonesian Economic Studies*, 30 (2), August: 133–48.
Featherstone, Mike (1991) *Consumer Culture and Postmodernism*, London: Sage Publications.
Frederick, William H. (1989) *Visions and Heat: The Making of the Indonesian Revolution*, Athens: Ohio University Press.

Hannertz, Ulf (1990) 'Cosmopolitans and Locals in World Culture', in Mike Featherstone (ed.), *Global Culture: Nationalism, Globalization and Modernity*, London: Sage Publications.

Hart, Gillian (1989) 'Agrarian Change in the Context of State Patronage', in G. Hart, A. Turton and B. White (eds), *Agrarian Transformations: Local Processes and the State in Southeast Asia*, Berkeley: University of California Press.

Hefner, Robert (1990) *The Political Economy of Mountain Java: An Interpretative History*, Berkeley: University of California Press.

Heryanto, Ariel (1988) 'The Development of "Development"', *Indonesia*, no. 46 (October): 1–24.

Hüsken, Frans (1989) 'Cycles of Commercialization and Accumulation in a Central Javanese Village', in G. Hart, A. Turton and B. White (eds), *Agrarian Transformations: Local Processes and the State in Southeast Asia*, Berkeley: University of California Press.

Lamont, Michèle (1992) *Money, Morals, and Manners: The Culture of the French and American Upper-Middle Class*, Chicago and London: The University of Chicago Press.

Murai, Y. (1994) 'The Authoritarian Bureaucratic Politics of Development: Indonesia under Suharto's New Order', in T. Shiraishi (ed.), *Approaching Suharto's Indonesia from the Margins*, Ithaca: Cornell University Southeast Asia Program.

Pemberton, John (1994) *On the Subject of 'Java'*, Ithaca: Cornell University Press.

Raillon, François (1994) 'Can the Javanese Do Business? The Awakening of Indigenous Capitalists in Indonesia', in Hans Antlöv and Sven Cederroth (eds), *Leadership in Java: Gentle Hints, Authoritarian Rule*, London: Curzon Press.

Savage, Mike, James Barlow, Peter Dickens and Tony Fielding (1992) *Property, Bureaucracy and Culture: Middle-Class Formation in Contemporary Britain*, London and New York: Routledge.

Schweitzer, Thomas (1989) 'Economic Individualism and the Community Spirit: Divergent Orientation Patterns of Javanese Villagers in Rice Production and the Ritual Sphere', *Modern Asian Studies*, 23 (2): 277–312.

Scott, James C. (1985) *Weapons of the Weak: Everyday Forms of Peasant Resistance*, New Haven: Yale University Press.

Sullivan, John (1992) *Local Government and Community in Java: An Urban Case Study*, Singapore: Oxford University Press.

Tjondronegoro, S. M. P. (1984) *Social Organization and Planned Development in Rural Java*, Singapore, Oxford University Press.

Tønnesson, Stein and Antlöv, Hans (1996) 'Asia in Theories of Nationalism and National Identity', in Stein Tønnesson and Hans Antlöv (eds), *Asian Forms of the Nation*, London: Curzon Press.

—— and —— (forthcoming) *Mosaic of Nations: Indonesia, Vietnam and Malaya, 1945–1950*, London: Curzon Press.

Van Niel, Robert (1960) *The Emergence of the Modern Indonesian Elite*, The Hague: W. van Hoeve (reprinted in Dordrecht: Foris Publications, 1984).

Wertheim, W. (1969) 'From Aliran towards Class Struggle in the Countryside of Java', *Pacific Viewpoint*, 10 (2): 1–17.

8   How a revolution becomes a dinner party

Stratification, mobility and the new rich in urban China

Christopher Buckley

INTRODUCTION

Mention of the 'new rich' in urban China is likely to evoke images of ostentatious wealth and fast-talking entrepreneurs; and mention of their 'culture' or of 'cultural constructions' is likely to bring to mind the garish status symbols favoured by the newly wealthy sections of China's urban population – portable telephones, luxury imported cars, nightclubs and expensive restaurants, foreign liquor. But any attempt to explain the cultural dimensions of the emergence of a class of 'new rich' in present-day urban China must attempt to look past familiar images and address the conundrum of the relationship between culture and social change, between the social features of the new wealthy elite and the objects, activities and practices that define their emergent identity. Like a Möbius strip, culture – the attitudes, values and beliefs expressed in material life and social organisation – and changes in society and economy seem to lead to endless loops of mutual causation (Lamont and Lareau 1988). In this chapter, I hope to suggest how we can better disentangle the links between the 'cultural construction' of the new rich and their socio-economic position in urban Chinese society by focusing on the social structures or networks which mediate between broader economic and social changes and the lives of individuals. In attempting to relate cultural processes to social change, we can easily fall into the habit of treating culture either as a homogeneous, unitary thing 'owned' by all members of a class, or as a set of psychological dispositions, such as entrepreneurial values, locked inside the heads of its possessors.

What is missing from such approaches is consideration of the role of intermediary social networks, such as family units and personal social networks, as elements in social life that form bridges between broader social and economic changes and the circumstances that shape individuals' life-chances, values and identities. In this chapter, I hope to show how social networks, especially ties of friends and associates, help us better to understand the cultural identity of urban China's 'new rich' – those people who have acquired considerable wealth and status as a result of the economic reforms initiated by Deng Xiaoping. I will argue that, in many respects, the self-creation of a 'new rich' cultural identity in this setting reflects the personal interactions and exchanges, and the related forms of sociability, that play an important role in wealth attainment and status mobility in urban China. In China, as in many other societies, strategies of entrepreneurialism and wealth attainment rely heavily on personal social networks. But the dynamism and uncertainty of opportunities in urban China make personal ties unusually important, and it is the interplay between personal status and group expectations in these networks that helps to explain many aspects of the cultural life of the new rich in urban China.

This chapter will proceed in three sections. The first will define what we mean by the 'new rich' in a mainland Chinese city; and consider their social origins and status attributes. The second will consider the role of personal networks (social capital), in particular friendship networks, in shaping the social life of the new rich, by establishing boundaries between them and the rest of Chinese society, and by providing sources of support, information and assistance that are crucial to getting ahead in present-day urban China. The final section will examine how the values, lifestyles and consumption patterns of the 'new rich' class are shaped and reproduced through these structures of personal inter-action and exchange. In this way, I hope to show how the 'culture' of the new rich emanates from their social position and social relations. The statistical data used in the following pages was a random stratified household survey of 1,260 households in urban Beijing (excluding, that is, the rural counties in Beijing Municipality) conducted by myself and a Chinese collaborator during May and June 1994. The data that appear here will be restricted to those below the age of 65 at the time of the survey.

MAKING IT IN CONTEMPORARY BEIJING

The first question we must answer is: who are the new rich in urban China? And perhaps the best way to introduce the question of who 'makes it' in a large Chinese city such as Beijing is by way of anecdote. An acquaintance, a mid-ranking cadre in a central government agency, was contacted by an old school friend, a computer-store owner in Beijing's 'silicon valley', Haidian District. He had plans for a housing development on the outskirts of the city and was hoping that the agency could be persuaded to sell him land at a reasonable price in return for a share in the venture (as well as apartments for the leaders of the agency). The cadre agreed to approach his most trusted superior with the scheme, and then to introduce the old school friend to him. To shepherd the scheme through the bureaucracy, close connections would have to be mobilised while avoiding leaking the scheme to potential rivals or spoilers. After several months of meetings, mustering contacts, and persuasion, it appeared that the real-estate venture would go ahead.

This common scene from Beijing suggests some of the main features of acquiring wealth in present-day China. Entrepreneurs and their backers strive to survive in an environment where, as well as individual skills and resources, they often depend on the skills, resources and influence of others – especially access to bureaucratic influence and reliable information. For, the other feature that this anecdote illustrates is the nexus between power and profit in Chinese entrepreneurial activity. Although most recent work on China's newly rich has focused on the role of private business and small firms, on the assumption that 'trade is the classic route of upward mobility for urban Chinese' (Wank 1990: 1), in large, bureaucratic cities like Beijing, navigating the shoals of success often requires a combination of individual entrepreneurship and access to power and influence. In interviews with several successful and not-so-successful business owners, many ruefully commented on the role that personal influence and bureaucratic power can play in deciding who succeeds and who fails. To be sure, the degree to which entrepreneurial wealth is intertwined with bureaucratic power varies considerably across China, especially between the established northern cities and the more heavily commercialised southern coastal provinces. Moreover, the interdependence of commercial success and political power may not be a permanent state of affairs (Nee and Matthews 1996). Nevertheless, studies of entrepreneurial activity in contemporary China indicate that success is often aided by access to political power.[1]

In sum, getting ahead and getting rich in contemporary urban China requires a combination of skills, entrepreneurial ability and access to bureaucratic power, and those who do best should be the people who have the largest quantities of these resources. Using the concepts of class adopted by Pierre Bourdieu, Erik Olin Wright and others, we can conceptualise these resources as different kinds of 'capital', which individuals and families invest in, and pass on across their careers and from one generation to the next (Wright 1985; Western and Wright 1994). The patterns of inequality that distinguish the newly rich in urban Chinese society from other segments of society can be seen arising from unequal access to these different kinds of capital.

First and most obviously, there is financial capital, the property and wealth that traditional Marxism saw as being the hallmark of the bourgeoisie. Clearly, amassing wealth in industrial and business assets is also important in defining the new rich in urban China. But there is more to describing the 'new rich' in China (and, indeed, in any other context) than financial capital. Next, there are the resources that individuals command through their possession of technical skills and talents – what, following the economists, we will call 'human capital' (Wright 1985: 78). Professionals and intellectuals who have generally acquired their skills through higher education and special credentials – to become lawyers, engineers, doctors and artists – have the most valuable forms of human capital; they also form a significant proportion of China's new rich. Although urban China's white-collar professionals have received little scholarly attention, economic growth and diversification have fuelled demand for their skills, rapidly enhancing their status and income.

We have already noted how important access to bureaucratic power is in defining the status hierarchy in China; a resource which can be described as 'organisational capital' (Wright 1985: 80). Organisational capital describes the resources available to individuals through their positions as political decision-makers and as managers. In market economies, organisational capital is largely restricted to managers in firms whose status and income derive from their role in exercising control over workers and employees. But in reforming state socialist societies, such as mainland China, the importance of the state and its officials in controlling social and economic life gives organisational capital a much larger role in social stratification. This is especially so in a city such as Beijing, which is still dominated by state industry and significant administrative control. Organisational positions are a form of 'capital' in that, just as individuals can invest in, and compete for, financial capital, so can they compete for the positions and statuses that give them access to organisational decision-making. In China membership of the Chinese Communist Party (CCP) and occupations as cadres and officials have given people special access to such resources.

In order to show how these forms of social stratification influence urban Chinese society and how they have underpinned the creation of a 'new rich' social group, the following analysis will use an occupational class schema that captures the different kinds of resources or 'capital' that individuals have access to. This schema is shown in Table 8.1.

Historically, the two most prominent social classes in China after 1949 were (i) officials and managers in government offices, Party organisations and workplaces whose jobs involved a high degree of organisational authority – the so-called 'cadre' class of government officials and state enterprise managers; (ii) professionals and experts whose jobs involved technical knowledge (engineers, doctors, teachers, writers, reporters) – the so-called 'intellectuals' (*zhishifenzi*). Other social classes in the table are different types of white-collar workers and blue-collar workers. Finally, there has always been an important social division in China between peasants and urban-dwellers. In the following analysis, we will consider how these occupational class divisions, as well as divisions based on gender, political status and education, have influenced the composition of China's 'new rich'.

Since the early 1980s, China has been steadily transformed, from a heavily bureaucratic and relatively egalitarian society, into a society where economic reforms and opening up have expanded opportunities for people to make money by exploiting their skills and resources in the new market environment. At the same time, the extended and uneven nature of the transition to a market economy has meant that access to bureaucratic power and influence remains an important advantage. Success in this mercantile environment has largely depended on being able to exploit two types of 'capital' – human capital, in the form of entrepreneurial abilities and professional skills, and organisational capital, in the form of access to bureaucratic influence – and converting them into financial wealth.

A first step, then, in understanding who the new rich are and how they got to be newly rich, is to specify and measure who has privileged access to human and organisational capital, and the relative importance of each in contributing to income. Only a tiny minority of Chinese belong to the most privileged and most visible section of the new rich – the wealthiest of entrepreneurs and the offspring of senior government officials or 'party of princelings' who dominate many new

Table 8.1 Occupational class classifications

Class	Title	Features and examples
I	CADRE	Occupations possessing considerable organisational and political responsibilities, e.g. factory managers, business people, senior military officers, government and party cadres of section head (*kezhang*) level and above.
II	PROFESSIONAL	The 'intelligentsia' (*zhishifenzi*). Occupations requiring specialised individual expertise and, typically, tertiary-level educational credentials, e.g. academics, fully qualified doctors and accountants, lawyers and jurists, scientists, researchers and engineers, artists and writers, teachers of senior-secondary level (*gaozhong*) and above.
III	UPPER NON-MANUAL	Non-manual occupations in administration and commerce, typically requiring some training and supervised responsibilities. Often adjunct jobs to managers and experts, e.g. engineering technicians, medical assistants and nurses, unqualified accountants, teachers of junior secondary and below, secretarial and clerical staff, financial and planning clerks, junior government and Party staff (*keyuan*), supervisors of lower service workers.
IV	LOWER NON-MANUAL	Lower-grade and routine non-manual workers, mostly in sales and service enterprises, e.g. shop assistants, lower clerks, cashiers and ticket sellers, routine bookkeepers.
V	PROPRIETOR	Small- and medium-sized proprietors (*geti hu*), e.g. restaurant owners, shopkeepers, guest-house operators, stall operators.
VI	SUPERVISOR & LOWER-GRADE TECHNICIAN	Supervisors of manual workers and shop-floor technical workers. Also includes lower-level union and Party workers in enterprises, e.g. foremen, work-shop supervisors, manufacturing technicians, shop-floor propaganda, Party and union functionaries.
VII	SKILLED MANUAL	Industrial and other workers doing manual tasks requiring considerable training or special skills, often gained through apprenticeship, e.g. electricians, fitters and mechanics, metalworkers, cooks, skilled construction workers, drivers, carpenters, printers.
VIII	SEMI-SKILLED & UNSKILLED MANUAL	Industrial and other workers doing manual tasks requiring little or no training or special skills, e.g. production-line workers, packers, warehouse workers, road and track workers, water-boiler stokers, sewing-machine operators, miners, and unskilled construction workers.
IX	PEASANT	Those engaged in farming and agriculture, e.g. farmers (*nongmin*), fishermen, apiarists and other agricultural workers.

companies and enterprises. Given the relatively small quantitative survey sample used here, their world remains largely invisible to the quantitative researcher. But using survey data has the advantage of allowing us to describe the broader patterns of change occurring in urban Chinese society, and to assess the relative importance of different kinds of capital in getting ahead.

In terms of occupational, educational and income attributes, the respondents in this survey provide a representative sample of the population of China's largest cities. A significant proportion of the population are in administrative and professional jobs (16 per cent and 19 per cent respectively), but most of the population is either in manual and production jobs (39 per cent) or in clerical and other routine non-manual positions (26 per cent).[2] In terms of education, Beijing has a disproportionately large number of tertiary-educated people, with 13 per cent of those surveyed having university degrees, and a further 16 per cent having tertiary-college (*dazhuan*) qualifications. But most people surveyed possessed a secondary-level education (55 per cent). Table 8.2 shows income attainment according to sex, education, occupational class, work unit and political status. There are a number of patterns present in this table which provide some indication of what helps in 'making it' in present-day Beijing. Males earn significantly more than females. Contrary to earlier speculation that economic reform had inverted the relationship between education and income – providing higher incomes to those with lower educations – it is clear, at least as of 1994, that increased education also increased income. Those with university (659 yuan) or graduate education (923) earn significantly more than those with senior-secondary (484) or junior-secondary (434) education.[3] But there are also major disparities between earnings in the new private and individually owned businesses and state-owned work units. Table 8.2 further indicates that in Beijing political resources remain an important social-economic advantage – Party members (620 yuan) earn more than non-Party members (475).

It is also evident from the data that the distribution of income is skewed towards the lower levels: 76 per cent of respondents reported total monthly incomes of 700 yuan or less. At the other end of this scale are the relatively small number of high-income earners who are the focus of this chapter. For the purposes of the following analysis, I classify the 'new rich' as those with reported monthly incomes of 1,000 yuan and above: they constitute 6.5 per cent of those surveyed. Those on 'middle incomes', with between 500 and 999 yuan a month, make up 33.1 per cent of the sample; and those on 'lower incomes', with between zero and 499 yuan a month, make up 60.3 per cent. Although in relative terms 1,000 yuan may not seem a great deal of money, the rationale for selecting those above this income level as 'new rich' is that there are many non-pecuniary benefits attached to urban jobs – inexpensive housing, benefits such as cheap medical care, and possibly, for the lucky few, a car. Thus 1,000 yuan is enough money to assume a lifestyle or status that is significantly different from that of the rest of the population.[4]

This income stratum can be defined as 'new rich' in the context of socialist China, because an 'old rich' largely ceased to exist in China after 1949: although

Table 8.2 Average monthly income by occupational class and other major variables for working respondents (N = 1128)*

Variable	Category	Income – Yuan (standard error)
Sex	Male	551 (346)
	Female	469 (329)
Education	Graduate	923 (771)
	University	659 (384)
	Tertiary college	614 (307)
	Technical secondary	515 (290)
	Senior secondary	484 (362)
	Junior secondary	434 (278)
	Primary	332 (184)
	Illiterate/semi-literate	204 (114)
Class	Cadre	754 (468)
	Professional	592 (343)
	Upper non-manual	570 (317)
	Lower non-manual	454 (269)
	Proprietor	725 (759)
	Supervisor	480 (343)
	Skilled manual	438 (216)
	Unskilled manual	376 (250)
Work unit ownership	State agency	549 (267)
	State enterprise	490 (280)
	Collective	411 (376)
	Private	1173 (708)
	Individual	889 (812)
	Foreign/joint venture	832 (296)
Political status	Party member	620 (317)
	Non-Party member	475 (342)

Note:
*Respondents presently unemployed or out of the workforce have been excluded.

certain status groups, such as government officials, enjoyed considerable political influence and privilege, this did not translate into striking financial or material inequalities. A considerable body of research has shown that during the Maoist era from 1949 to the end of the 1970s, urban Chinese society was extremely egalitarian compared to other societies, even other socialist societies (Parish and Whyte 1984). Thus, understanding the social and cultural identity of the new rich in urban China cannot be based on comparisons with an 'old rich' class; rather, it must be based on comparisons with other, less wealthy groups in Chinese society.

If we compare the social characteristics of the 'new rich' in our survey sample with the rest of the sample, a striking difference emerges: in terms of all resources, they are significantly better endowed than the rest of the population. In this high-income group, 53 per cent have tertiary-level schooling and are highly concentrated in administrative (25 per cent) and professional (32 per cent) jobs. Also a relatively high proportion (37.8 per cent as compared to 38.9 per cent of medium- and 19.2 per cent of lower-income respondents) are members of the Chinese Communist Party. In terms of occupational class, some important tendencies too are evident. Only in the cadre class are a large fraction of members in the 'new rich' category (19.5 per cent). In contrast, 7.6 per cent of professionals count as new rich – most professionals (47.5 per cent) are medium income, as they tend to work in state institutions such as schools and research institutes which pay only relatively low wages. But taken together, cadres and professionals make up just under half of the new rich (45.1 per cent), with a further 22 per cent working in upper non-manual occupations. A smaller, but significant number of the new rich are in lower-status jobs, especially as individual business operators (*getihu*), 14.3 per cent of whom are in the high-income category. Thus, even these simple comparisons make an important point that has perhaps been neglected in recent work which has concentrated on private business as the source of new wealth in urban China: most high-income earners in larger Chinese cities are not household business operators but members of an increasingly visible middle class of cadres and professionals whose organisational and human capital resources, rather than pure entrepreneurial ability, give them an advantaged position in China's commercialising economy.

Factors shaping the values, lifestyle and cultural profile of a status group are to be found not only in the characteristics of the group itself, but also in the background of the people who become members of that group. Thus, the next basic is: what are the social backgrounds of those people who make it into urban China's highest income brackets?

Before looking at the 'new rich' in particular, and in order to provide a context for understanding their special features, I will first examine the social characteristics of urban Beijing as a whole. Table 8.3 is a cross-tabulation of the occupational class of respondents against the occupational class of their fathers – or, if the latter were deceased, mothers – when the respondent was about 18 years old. The inflow percentages represent the proportion of respondents from different class origins in each class destination; the outflow percentages measure the proportion of destination classes for each origin class. Taken together these figures give an overview of patterns of class inheritance and fluidity between generations. It is evident from Table 8.3 that economic development and the sheer expansion of jobs in the most prestigious occupational classes (cadres and professionals) have allowed considerable numbers of people from lower-class backgrounds to move up the class hierarchy. Nevertheless, the table also reveals that there is a great deal of inheritance within these most prestigious (and most highly rewarded) occupational classes. Note, in particular, the extremely high level of inheritance in the professional class (40.2 per cent), and the similar proportion of children of cadre backgrounds who either remained in the cadre class (21.4 per cent) or entered the professional occupational class (24.3 per cent). Thus, despite dramatic political upheavals, such as the Cultural Revolution from 1966 to 1976 when intellectuals and other high-status groups suffered persecution and officially degraded social status, professional families and cadre families remained generally much more successful than the rest of the population in

Table 8.3 Inflow and outflow table of respondents' most recent occupational class (column) by family head's occupational class (row) (%)

Respondent's class	Cadre	Profess-ional	Upper non-manual	Lower non-manual	Prop-rietor	Super-visor	Skilled manual	Unskilled manual	Total (N)
Family head's class	30.3	18.4	17.0	7.6	16.7	3.7	4.8	5.8	140
Cadre	(21.4)	(24.3)	(26.4)	(7.9)	(1.4)	(1.4)	(8.6)	(8.6)	
Professional	11.1	22.2	12.8	4.2	16.7	5.6	2.4	2.4	102
	(10.8)	(40.2)	(27.5)	(5.9)	(2.0)	(2.9)	(5.9)	(4.9)	
Upper non-manual	5.1	8.1	11.0	11.8	8.3	5.6	4.0	6.3	88
	(5.7)	(17.0)	(27.3)	(19.3)	(1.1)	(3.4)	(11.4)	(14.8)	
Lower non-manual	4.0	8.1	6.0	13.2	0.0	14.8	7.6	7.8	94
	(4.3)	(16.0)	(13.8)	(20.2)	(0.0)	(8.5)	(20.2)	(17.0)	
Proprietor	1.0	4.9	2.3	4.9	8.3	5.6	5.6	6.3	53
	(1.9)	(17.0)	(9.4)	(13.2)	(1.9)	(5.7)	(26.4)	(24.5)	
Supervisor	3.0	2.2	4.6	2.1	8.3	5.6	4.8	3.4	43
	(7.0)	(9.3)	(23.3)	(7.0)	(2.3)	(7.0)	(27.9)	(16.3)	
Skilled man.	12.1	11.9	17.9	22.9	33.3	29.6	32.8	26.7	263
	(4.6)	(8.4)	(14.8)	(12.5)	(1.5)	(6.1)	(31.2)	(20.9)	
Unskilled manual	10.1	12.4	16.5	21.5	8.3	14.8	21.6	23.8	212
	(4.7)	(10.8)	(17.0)	(14.6)	(0.5)	(3.8)	(25.5)	(23.1)	
Peasant	23.2	11.9	11.9	11.8	0.0	14.8	16.4	17.5	173
	(13.3)	(12.7)	(15.0)	(9.8)	(0.0)	(4.6)	(23.7)	(20.8)	
Total (N)	99	185	218	144	12	54	250	206	1168

Note:
Outflow percentages are in parentheses.

ensuring the educational, political and occupational success of their children. In other words, the middle class of cadres and professionals which makes up the bulk of the 'new rich' is distinctive not only in terms of its income and other positional characteristics, but also in terms of the social background of most of its members.

Turning to the 'new rich' themselves, it is evident that this group displays certain dominant features but also many differences. Thus the importance of political status varies widely between occupational classes: 71 per cent of 'new rich' cadres are members of the CCP, compared to 50 per cent of professionals and 10 per cent of all other occupational classes in this high-income bracket. Similarly, the importance of education among the 'new rich' also varies considerably: 36 per cent of cadres have university-level qualifications, compared to 73 per cent of professionals and only 5 per cent of other occupations. In sum, the Chinese new rich in this study are a varied group, but in general their composition reflects the contours of power in the relatively orthodox enclave of socialism that is Beijing.

The largest cleavage within the new rich is between those with middle-class occupations, who we have concentrated on so far, and the individual business operators (*getihu*), who make up a smaller but extremely visible proportion of the new rich in urban China. Therefore it is necessary to give more attention to this group of private traders, restaurant and shop proprietors, and small-time manu-facturers, who make up the small-scale private sector in China's cities.

Along their route to wealth, it also seems that access to political power and scarce technical skills, as well as entrepreneurial acumen, are important in deciding who gets ahead. Most private businesses in Beijing have been estab-lished by low-status and less-educated manual and non-manual workers, often unemployed or semi-employed workers from failing state enterprises. Interview and survey information make it evident that most such businesses remain small. Only a small proportion of 'street-level' individual business operators make it into the ranks of the 'new rich'. However, from the late 1980s, increasing numbers of cadres and professionals began to '*xia hai*' ('jump into the sea'): to leave their secure jobs in state enterprises and institutions, and to use their skills and connections in entrepreneurial ventures. A nationwide survey of private and individual businesses conducted in 1992 asked respondents about their previous occupations (Fu *et al.* 1993). It found that most technicians and administrators went into manufacturing and technological businesses, whereas the great majority of those formerly employed in clerical, sales and manual occupations were in service-sector businesses such as restaurants and repair shops (Fu *et al.* 1993: 127).

My own interviews along Haidian Road – the heart of Beijing's large computer and electronics sector – confirmed this general pattern. Many of the proprietors I interviewed were former researchers, academics or, in a few cases, government workers. Many of them had 'jumped into the sea' during the 1980s, especially after 1989, when the Beijing massacre and subsequent political crack-down had either placed their careers under a cloud, or convinced them that the risks of the private sector were more attractive than the bureaucratic encum-brances of work in a government or university office. When asked about their motives for starting up a private business, several emphasised that although the attractions of a high income were important, the freedom and autonomy they enjoyed as individual proprietors was also an important consideration. One said, 'of course, making money is important, but for me it is also important to be making money on my own and not having to worry about anyone telling me what to do'. These impressions are borne out in the same 1992 survey of private and individual businesses mentioned above (Fu *et al.* 1993). Respondents were asked to describe their motives in going into the private sector: whereas most former manual and routine non-manual workers appeared to embrace short-term objectives – scraping together a livelihood or making money – most former technicians and administrators stated a desire to establish an enterprise or under-taking (*shiye*).

To sum up: urban China's new rich remain a heterogeneous and ill-defined group, but members of China's middle class of cadres and professionals make up its core. Contrary to the Chinese version of the log cabin myth, in which private entrepreneurialism is the predominant, even sole, route to riches, people in middle-class occupations in firms, factories and companies form the bulk of China's emerging 'new rich'. Even in private entrepreneurial ventures, it would seem that those from high-status jobs, with valuable skills and managerial experience, enjoy a considerable advantage over lower-status aspirants to success and wealth.[5] A significant number of Beijing's wealthiest inhabitants are taxi drivers, restaurant owners and other small proprietors on the fringes of social respectability, but it is still people in high-status jobs and from high-status backgrounds who form the core of the city's 'new rich'.

CLASS, CONNECTIONS AND MAKING MONEY

Thus far, I have considered the 'new rich' in urban China in terms of a set of inert sociological categories. I have shown that the 'new rich' are a mixed lot; most of them work in high-status middle-class occupations, but a significant number are individual business operators who have benefited from the expanding commercial activities of the 1980s and 1990s. What I want to show in this section is how the patterns of advantage and inequality addressed above infuse the lives of the newly wealthy, shaping their social relations, behaviour and cultural values. In other words, I hope to show how the cultural construction of the 'new rich' is above all a social process rather than – as the word 'construction' may suggest – an individually based subjective or psychological process.

To illustrate what is meant by a social process, it may be useful to start with a quote from an interviewee, a senior cadre in his early sixties whose two sons had both gone into private businesses – one was a wholesale bookseller, the other an electronics exporter. He contrasted the bookselling son's prosperity with the stalled career of his eldest son, also a cadre:

> Since ancient times, not just intellectuals but also officials had both wealth and status. But these days? Look at my eldest son. He's a department-level (*keji*) official and some day might get a promotion…His work is pretty high status, enough to make most people envious. But don't think his family gets much good out of it; I don't think his wife would be worse off if she married a worker…So, now you can see, why I wanted [my second son] to try out going into business. The whole family has benefited…Since he started in business, we've been able to have guests over for dinner whenever we like. His mother doesn't have to just worry about the bare necessities when shopping. He even helped pay for his sister's wedding, and his nephew's school fees…So I guess the whole family is doing well.

What the father did not mention in this interview but what became clear in discussions with his sons was his instrumental role in helping both sons go into private business. For the bookselling son, he used his connections with colleagues to help with the thicket of licences and bureaucratic procedures confronting booksellers in China. He also found his son's company a military unit to act as its sponsor (*guakao danwei*), thereby insulating it from other branches of government. In these ways he was able to give one son a decisive boost in founding his business.

What this example illustrates is the crucial role of social connections (*guanxi*) in shaping and defining routes to success in contemporary urban China (Blau *et al.* 1991; Ruan 1993; Yang 1994), and therefore their crucial role in shaping the social relations and behaviour of the 'new rich'. For, if, as we have seen, wealth, skills, power and influence are the scarce resources that decide who gets ahead in urban Beijing, then people who have access to those resources are also an important ingredient in success. In other words, social connections with people who have access to valuable information, influence and resources are in themselves a kind of 'capital' that can be cultivated, sustained and called up in times of need (Coleman 1988). These connections may be, as in the above example, familial or, as in many other cases I encountered in my fieldwork, based on other relations – work colleagues, old school friends, old army ties, and so on.[6] In this sense, the social structure is not an inert cage deciding people's fates, but rather a possible resource that can be exploited by those in the right position.

In this section, I will examine how social ties, and the resources they contain, are an important factor in determining status attainment in urban Chinese society. The third and final section will examine how the cultural identity of the new rich in urban China – defined in terms of their lifestyle, values and material culture – is in many respects a reflection of that fact. To complement the statistical data, which deal with non-kin ties, I draw on interviews and observation to gauge the importance of kin relations.

Again, before focusing on the new rich as a special category, I will first examine the general role of interperonal relations in urban Chinese life. In the survey, respondents were asked to list the friends with whom they had had significant contact in the previous six months. Table 8.4 is a cross-tabulation of the social class of the friends named by respondents.

These and the corresponding data on education, political status and work-unit status show how individuals' social networks are heavily shaped by the same patterns of social stratification we examined in the first section. Once more, what is most striking is how the personal relations of the cadre and professional occupational classes are extremely homogeneous. Slightly over half of professionals' friendship ties are with other professionals, and nearly two-thirds of cadres' friendship ties are either with other cadres (36.2 per cent) or with professionals (22.7 per cent). Measured in terms of gender, educational status and political status, similar patterns of stratification emerge in personal social networks. These data provide support for what other recent studies in China have found, namely that, as in all modern societies, urban Chinese people's social relations are shaped by the prevailing patterns of stratification and status distinction, and that high-status individuals socialise most among their own status peers (Ruan 1993; Yang 1994). Turning to the survey respondents with

Table 8.4 Distribution of friendship ties by class (%) (N = 1168)

Friend's class	Cadre	Profess-ional	Upper non-manual	Lower non-manual	Prop-rietor	Super-visor	Skilled manual	Unskilled manual
Respondent's class								
Cadre	36.2	22.7	18.1	2.3	2.3	5.8	9.2	3.5
Professional	11.5	50.2	21.1	4.9	1.0	4.7	5.6	1.0
Upper non-manual	12.2	13.6	42.0	9.0	3.2	4.3	10.7	5.1
Lower non-manual	3.6	5.9	26.1	39.5	2.0	4.0	12.3	6.7
Proprietor	5.7	0.0	11.4	14.3	42.9	2.9	17.1	5.7
Supervisor	16.8	13.9	15.8	11.9	5.0	8.9	23.8	4.0
Skilled manual	4.3	6.6	16.0	8.9	3.8	7.4	44.7	8.4
Unskilled manual	1.6	4.9	11.5	14.2	3.8	9.8	25.7	28.4

incomes of over 1,000 yuan a month – our 'new rich' – we find that their friendship networks manifest the same traits, only more so. That is, most of their friendships (65 per cent) are with individuals they described as co-workers (*tongshi*) or as friends in the same business (*tonghang*). This compares with half that figure for middle- and lower-income respondents. This is not surprising given that many new rich spend such long hours at work, and the boundary between work and socialising – at restaurants or clubs, or at home – is extremely blurred.

While interpersonal relations provide many important intangible benefits, such as emotional support and companionship, they may also provide many important forms of instrumental assistance in situations such as finding or changing jobs, solving bureaucratic problems, or getting a child into the right school. For a variety of reasons, this instrumental dimension of personal social relations seems to be unusually (though not uniquely) important in China. First, an emphasis on the importance of maintaining and observing social relations has been an important part of Chinese culture. Hence, the role of social connections in Chinese life is unusually visible and surrounded by many explicit and implicit rules of conduct. Second, the importance of the instrumental uses of social connections has been accentuated by the tremendous social and economic changes urban China has undergone in recent decades. Under Mao, the Chinese economy was placed under a rigid and complex system of central planning: goods, food, housing, jobs, schooling, all came under the control of bureaucracy. Consequently, making sure that you got what you wanted often required cultivating and maintaining personal relations with people who had access to those goods and resources.

Paradoxically, although the economic reforms that Deng Xiaoping has overseen since 1978 have done away with much of the central planning and bureaucratic control of the Maoist period, they have in many ways enhanced the importance of interpersonal connections in the lives of Chinese people. The introduction of market reforms and commerce into China has expanded private opportunities and has removed many controls on social and economic life. But these market forces have evolved unsteadily and they coexist with many of the institutions and rules of Maoist China: often commercial interests also involve political and bureaucratic interests. This makes life in reformed China often uncertain and capricious; especially for business people and entrepreneurs. In these circumstances, the trust and certainty that comes through close personal relationships is in itself an important asset, especially where the people concerned occupy influential or resource-rich positions. In this unstable context, where becoming wealthy is often based on reading the unpredictable currents of market forces and official policy, friends and kin play an important role in 'making it'.

This is clear from both survey and interview data. In interviews, I asked respondents to discuss when and how they turned to family, friends and other personal relations for assistance. Although many expressed reluctance to burden their friends or embarrass themselves by seeking out 'connections', there were many instances where the information or influence of a 'connection' was an important factor in, for example, obtaining a lucrative job or sealing a business deal. At the same time, a number of informants, especially those with higher education or in high-status jobs, expressed unease at drawing too frequently on friends to solve material or instrumental problems, partly out of a sense of self-respect but also, as one respondent described: 'If you go to a friend for help too often, then sooner or later he's going to want you to help him; and if you can't do it, that's just losing face (*diu mianzi*).'

Similarly, in another case, a friend of an informant was able to make a considerable profit (just how much I never found out) by using the professional contacts of the informant to obtain preferential treatment in a real-estate purchase. Shaking his head, my informant said: 'If we weren't such close class-mates from university, I wouldn't have done it. These days, there's too much corruption and pulling connections, but that's how everybody does things.' Another example of the nature of personal social ties comes from a sales representative for the branch office of a Japanese pharmaceutical firm. She originally studied pharmacy at Beijing Medical University and was introduced to her current job by a university class-mate who also worked in the office. As she explained, several other of her university class-mates also found work in the company in a chain-like movement from their former jobs: 'Jobs like this pay well, but there's lots of pressure from the boss. Since we've known each for quite a long time, we know they'll do their job but won't try to show off too much.' On the other hand, it was common for respondents to stress the dangers and irksome responsibilities involved in, for example, finding employees or business help through personal ties: there was always the danger that such an employee would perform badly, reflecting badly on the person in question.

These instances of the power of social connections in urban Chinese society are confirmed, but also qualified, by an analysis of the survey data. In the survey, respondents were asked if they had ever given or received assistance or advice, in a variety of situations, from those they called friends. In another section, respondents were also asked how they had found their present and previous jobs; if through personal ties, they were asked to describe the characteristics of the individuals who had helped them and to describe the nature of their relations with them, in terms of such things as frequency of contact. Using the resultant data, we can develop a better understanding of how social ties shape the life in Chinese cities, and especially of its wealthiest inhabitants.

Table 8.5 shows how these webs of personal assistance vary with different forms of stratified inequality. Respondents were asked whether in the previous six months they had given/received various forms of personal assistance (economic aid, finding a job and so on) to/from the friends they had named. The results indicate that, although instrumental social exchanges between friends occur relatively infrequently, it is the highest-status groups that benefit most from such social relations, but only in quite specific ways. For example, 11.6 per cent of high-income respondents reported that one of their friends had helped them change jobs, and a further 5.8 per cent reported doing so through relatives. The corresponding figures for medium-income respondents were 10.8 per cent and 8.4 per cent; for lower-income respondents, 8.3 per cent and 10.5 per cent. Until recently, all jobs in China were supposed to be filled through state-planned allocations, yet these figures confirm what Bian Yanjie and others have argued: that the most successful – in this case, the wealthiest – sections of urban Chinese society tend to have personal social networks which provide high-status individuals with greater opportunities and resources, because of their wider reach beyond the family (Bian Yanjie 1994, 1997). Also of note here is the fact that just under 8 per cent of high-income respondents reported *both* helping and being helped to find jobs by the friends they named; as against an average of 3 per cent for other income groups. This provides some support for the anecdotal evidence cited above, of the 'new rich' middle class tending to use their personal networks to change jobs in a chain-like process of mutual recruitment into attractive positions. In other words, higher status can reinforce rather than weaken the importance of social ties. The figures in Table 8.5 also indicate, however, that wealthier individuals tend to rely on their friendship ties less for other, non-instrumental assistance such as help at work, for personal disputes, or during illness.

The significance of these general patterns in the social lives of urban China's new rich becomes clearer through some examples from my fieldwork. One of Beijing's new rich – a manager in a large foreign-funded hotel – recounted to me how he succeeded in enrolling his daughter in a prestigious 'key-point' senior middle school, despite her living in the wrong district and having slightly less than sufficient marks. He did this through a friend – someone who had been 'sent down' to the countryside during the early 1970s – who knew a senior official in the district education bureau. After some discussions between all three, the official agreed to use his influence to ensure that the interviewee's daughter made it into the school. No money or goods changed hands, but as he explained:

Table 8.5 Frequency of different forms of personal help in urban Beijing friendship networks (%) (N = 1168)*

Type of help	Admin.	Finding a job	Economic hardship	At work	Domestic	Personal dispute	Illness
Sex							
Male	4.9	9.5	20.1	44.9	9.1	13.4	50.0
Female	3.9	9.5	19.3	35.4	17.6	21.4	55.0
Class							
Cadre	8.9	8.1	13.0	37.4	8.5	14.8	40.4
Professional	4.6	9.0	16.9	36.4	7.4	16.2	43.4
Upper non-manual	6.0	14.7	22.0	47.9	12.4	20.3	53.9
Lower non-manual	3.5	9.2	20.0	39.2	12.7	16.5	58.8
Small proprietor	2.7	2.7	21.6	64.9	13.5	10.8	40.5
Supervisor	1.8	3.7	17.4	39.4	9.2	14.7	58.7
Skilled manual	2.4	8.7	21.6	39.9	17.8	14.9	57.2
Unskilled manual	1.9	6.6	26.1	37.0	21.8	20.9	61.3
High income	4.3	11.6	21.7	31.1	8.5	15.9	32.9
Medium income	6.9	10.8	17.0	45.5	10.3	18.2	49.8
Lower income	2.8	8.3	18.3	38.6	15.3	16.4	56.4

Notes:
Admin.: help or advice with administrative procedures or difficulties
Finding a job: help or advice with finding or changing jobs
Economic hardship: help or advice with economic hardship
At work: help or advice with problems at work
Domestic: help or advice with domestic responsibilities
Personal dispute: help or advice with a personal dispute
Illness: help or advice with illness.
*Respondents provided multiple answers to this question.

> [the senior official's] daughter graduates from technical college in a year or two and then maybe he'd like me to find a place for her here [in the hotel]…That's how it is. We go back a long way, so I'd be happy to help my friend, and his friend too. It's not a who-owes-who sort of deal.

To sum up this section: in China's cities, and more particularly in Beijing, the interpersonal relations of residents not only reflect the patterns of occupational, educational and income stratification; they play an important active role in creating and reproducing those patterns. They do this by giving individuals unequal access to scarce resources and opportunities: friends and acquaintances can be an important source of help in finding a job, changing housing, securing a loan, and so on. As a source of material assistance and information, as well as emotional support, such social ties are a vital element in understanding the behaviour and outlook of China's 'new rich'. Although these *guanxi* relations tend to be represented as involving purely economic transactions, they are more often based on long-standing interpersonal ties based on common experience and social status.

REPUTATION, CONSUMPTION AND GETTING AHEAD IN URBAN CHINA

So far I have described the social characteristics and position of urban Beijing's new rich, as well as the dynamic way in which urban Chinese must cultivate and use their social connections in order to get ahead. But how does this help us to understand the cultural identity of Beijing's 'new rich'? How and why do they create social boundaries based on their lifestyles, values and behaviour, thereby identifying themselves and excluding others? In this final section, I will argue that social networks, and a general concern for personal reputation, help to explain why certain patterns of distinction, based on consumption and status objects, define the cultural identity of urban China's new rich. If cultural markers are thought of as status signals used to locate particular status groups, then we would expect that these cultural markers would be most important in frequent and close interactions with others. For it is in such situations that a person's perceived reputation, influence and trustworthiness matter most. Given the important role that interpersonal ties, in general, play in Chinese social life, we can expect that the markers of status based on culture will be unusually prominent and important.

Clifford Geertz applies a similar line of reasoning to analyse the behaviour of merchants in Morocco's souk market (Geertz 1979). He notes that the market is characterised by general uncertainty and poor information, and this has a decisive effect on the merchants' social organisation and behaviour:

> The level of ignorance about everything from product quality and going prices to market possibilities and production costs is very high, and a great deal of the way in which the bazaar is organised and functions (and within it, the ways its various sorts of participants behave) can be interpreted as either an attempt to reduce such ignorance for someone, increase it for someone, or defend someone against it....The search for information – laborious, uncertain, complex, and irregular – is the central experience of life in the bazaar, an enfolding reality its institutions at once create and respond to. Virtually every aspect of the bazaar economy reflects the fact that the primary problem facing the farmer, artisan, merchant, or consumer is not balancing options but finding out what they are.
>
> (Geertz 1979: 124–5)

In spite of the vastly different setting, Geertz's observations also ring true for creating and keeping wealth under late-Deng market socialism, where, as we have seen, actions such as business deals, changing jobs and finding suitable employees are all, to some extent, at the mercy of market uncertainty and bureaucratic flexibility. This is suggested in the rich variety of norms, affinities and obligations expressed in terms such as 'face' (*mianzi*), 'connection' (*guanxi*) and 'sentiment' (*renqing*) that are found in modern Chinese culture (Yang 1994; Pieke 1995). Much like Geertz's traders, the Beijing residents I interviewed were seeking, in various ways, to overcome uncertainty and risk in a capricious social and economic environment. For them, success and wealth are often dependent on combining individual resources and talents with the opportunities and information that come through relations with others. Hence, developing trust and social reciprocity among close friends, partners and colleagues is an important element in social life. Many of the culturally defined actions and practices of urban China's 'new rich' become clearer when we examine them through this prism of cultivating and consolidating interpersonal affinity and trust.[7] In this final section, I will describe some of these objects and practices.

Anybody who has spent time in a Chinese city like Beijing will be familiar with many of the objects and practices that define the lifestyle of urban China's moneyed elite. Most notable are the emphases on collective sociability in settings such as restaurants, nightclubs and karaoke bars; the highly visible (and expensive) items such as portable telephones and imported cars; and the emphasis given to consuming – and being seen to consume – 'famous brand' (*mingpai'r*) goods. In many cases, tastes for pleasures, such as for Cantonese yum-cha or French brandy, have been diffused from the commercial hubs of Hong Kong and Japan. Set against the self-conscious austerity which characterised Maoist social ethos, and which still provides an important underpinning for many social attitudes, this new ethic of consumption is even more striking.

The unspoken rules and expectations governing the new milieu of calculated extravagance have been well described in Shi Xianmin's study of individual business operators in Beijing. Shi describes how relations between private traders – who are both rivals and allies in the competition for customers – work according to implicit but strict rules (Shi 1993). Above all, aspiring successful business operators must win and maintain the trust and respect of their peers, a requirement reflected in the forms of sociality and consumption that characterise their lifestyle. Solving many of the problems of running a private business in Beijing, such as reducing or avoiding tax and choosing, ordering and pricing goods, needs the assistance of other traders. Shi observes that the kind of social relationship which facilitates this commercial activity:

> is an ethos of mateship (*gemenr yiqi*) based on exchange relations. The usual way to give things, for example, taking along cigarettes…Paying the expenses of these connections has already been incorporated into the business costs, something that has to be factored into market prices…Many interest relations are based on friendship ties; treating someone to a meal, giving presents, even gambling together.
>
> (Shi 1993: 300–1)[8]

Shi quotes one small proprietor who sums up this nexus between reputational concerns, conspicuous consumption and making wealth in an uncertain environment:

I'm happy when I can treat them [officials and commercial connections] to a meal. The more they eat proves that my business is increasingly successful. We're all mates, and its all very low-key (*moqi*). Sometimes they'll even help you without you asking. Like the time when I wanted to lease a market stall and was told I had to get a collective licence [i.e. as a 'collective' not 'private' operator], the market manager helped me to set up a firm…You've got to have a family so you can have kids, create the next generation, and that's the social role of wives and kids. But here is where I am. I'll give the wife and kids whatever they want, take care of their needs. But my life is here. My life is my business and my mates.

(Shi 1993: 301)

Although they did not approach the macho solidarity of Shi Xianmin's informant, my own wealthier informants also felt the importance of reputational concerns and peer expectations in their lives. One businesswoman, formerly an engineer in the People's Liberation Army and now in charge of a bulletproof clothing exporter, described the expensive and tiring process of doing business:

You might think I got the car [a new Mercedes Benz] because I'm stuck up. But you've got to show your stuff (*ba fenr*), or nobody takes you seriously, especially a woman. And if nobody takes you seriously…it hurts business. Sometimes I get sick of buying meals and buying expensive clothes, but that's what capitalism is like, isn't it.

Although perhaps disingenuous, this informant and others expressed a strong belief that their potential success could not be separated from the image of success they wished to project among their peers and rivals. And an essential aspect of this behaviour seems to be soliciting the trust and respect of others.[9] Another interviewee, a lawyer in his late twenties, explained: 'I don't believe in *guanxi*; that's for Hong Kong people. Who you need above all is good friends. So if I have problems [at work], I can go and find my old classmates. I know they'd stand by me because we've got feeling (*renqing*) as well.' This desire for respectability and trustworthiness is reflected not only in individual-level exchanges, but also in the involvement of several individual business owners I interviewed in charitable works, especially Project Hope (*Xiwang gongcheng*). While they all knew that they were 'expected' to make a contribution, all but one said they would have done so anyway. The one interviewed at greatest length, a taxi driver who made well over 3,000 yuan a month, claimed that: 'I'm not trying to pretend I'm more virtuous than anybody else, but it feels good to show people that I deserve some respect (*zunzhong*).'

As Alan Smart has observed, the instrumental dimensions of social ties should not be confused with a view that such ties are purely instrumental:

Clearly *guanxi* can be used for instrumental purposes, and this usage is recognised by the members of the society. However, it is referred to as the art of *guanxi*, because the style of exchange and the appropriateness of the performance are critical to its effectiveness. The style and manner of gift exchange is not optional; rather it is fundamental to its operation. Although a relationship may be cultivated with instrumental goals foremost in mind, the forms must be followed if the goals are to be achieved. The relationship must be presented as primary and the exchanges, useful though they may be, treated only as secondary.

(Smart 1993: 399)

It is against the backdrop of these prevailing practices and expectations, about how business should be conducted and how wealth should be accumulated, that the importance of various forms of sociable consumption in the life of China's 'new rich' becomes intelligible. Karaoke sessions, banquets, even the ubiquitous exchange of name cards, all provide contexts in which interpersonal trust and standing can be established and renewed, and the coexistence of 'instrumental' and primary or affective relations confirmed.

Though superficial impressions might suggest otherwise, the material culture and social interactions of China's new rich – with the emphasis placed on visible wealth and consumption – is not entirely an instance of Veblen's (1979) conspicuous consumption. Rather, the lifestyle of China's 'new rich' is better understood as a product of conspicuous conformity in that it shows an underlying impulse to demonstrate a person's belonging to a certain status group, a new moneyed elite, that is still unsure of its social boundaries and its relations with the rest of Chinese society. Through their lifestyle practices, aspiring members of the new rich seek to demonstrate, to their peers, colleagues and rivals, their possession of resources and personal qualities befitting an elite position in Chinese society (Lamont and Fournier 1992).

CONCLUSION

The rapid growth of China's economy during the 1980s and 1990s, and the concomitant rise of a new wealthy class in China's cities, has inspired, among other things, a flood of reportage about newly rich entrepreneurs and business people. In much of this reportage, such as Xie Dehua's lurid *Money, the Crazed Beast*, China's new rich are depicted as possessed by the wealth they have created for themselves (Xie 1988). In various forms, this image of exorbitant consumption, combined with dubious morality and taste, also colours Western descriptions of China's new wealthy elite; and with some good reason – the disparities between the rich and the poor in a country like China make the extravagance and conspicuousness of the new culture of wealth all the more jarring. But what I have attempted to show in this chapter is that the culture of the 'new rich' is neither simply wasteful, nor a symptom of psychological insecurity. The cultural identity of the 'new rich' in Beijing is an emanation of their none-too-secure position in a society which, until very recently, was dominated by Maoist economics and a Maoist social ethos. The culture of these 'new rich' is the product of a rapidly changing and unpredictable economic environment, in which personal trust and reputation are valuable resources in themselves. Opulence, visibility and connectedness are thus *de rigueur* if one hopes to be invited to the dinner party after the revolution.

Notes

1 For a review of the literature see Nee and Matthews (1996) and Walder (1996).
2 For other recent discussions of social stratification and mobility in China, see Cheng and Dai (1995), and Li (1993).
3 In 1994, 100 yuan was equal to approximately US$8.5.
4 Another consideration is more practical: if the group selected was restricted to the very rich, the size of the sample would not allow for valid statistical comparisons.
5 For more detailed consideration of the role of different resources in income attainment in China, see Nee (1989 and 1991).
6 For an overview of the role of connections in urban Chinese social life, see Yang (1994).
7 For other sociological reviews on the consequences of trust and distrust, see Gambetta (1988 and 1993).
8 My translations of Chinese text.
9 For more on the role of trust and moral judgement forming cultural distinctions, see Lamont (1992).

Bibliography

Bian Yanjie (1994) *Work and Inequality in Urban China*, Albany: State University of New York.
—— (1997) 'Bringing Strong Ties Back In: Indirect Ties, Network Bridges, and Job Searches in China', *American Sociological Review*, 62: 366–85.
Blau, Peter, Ruan, Danching and Ardelt, Monika (1991) 'Interpersonal Choice and Networks in China', *Social Forces*, 69 (4), June: 1037–62.
Buckley, Christopher (1997) 'Social Mobility and Stratification in Urban China from Maoism through Reform', Ph.D. thesis, Australian National University, Canberra.
Cheng Yuan and Dai Jianzhong (1995) 'Intergenerational Mobility in Modern China', *European Sociological Review*, 11 (1): 17–35.
Coleman, James S. (1988) 'Social Capital in the Creation of Human Capital', *American Journal of Sociology*, 94, supplement: S95–S120.
Fu Xuedong and Dai Jianzhong (eds) (1993), *Zhongguo geti siying jingji diaocha* (A Survey of China's Individual and Private Economy), Beijing: Zhongguo shehui kexue chubanshe.
Gambetta, D. (ed.) (1988), *Trust: Making and Breaking Cooperative Relations*, Oxford: Basil Blackwell.
—— (1993), *The Sicilian Mafia: The Business of Private Protection*, Cambridge, MA: Harvard University Press.
Geertz, Clifford (1979) 'Suq: The Bazaar Economy in Sefrou', in Clifford Geertz, Hildred Geertz and Rosen Lawrence, *Meaning and Order in Moroccan Society*, New York: Cambridge University Press, pp. 123–244.

Lamont, Michèle (1992), *Money, Morals, and Manners: The Culture of the French and American Upper-Middle Class*, Chicago: University of Chicago Press.

—— and Fournier, Marcel (1988) 'Cultural Capital: Allusions, Gaps and Glissandos in Recent Theoretical Developments', *Sociological Theory*, 6 (2), Fall: 153–68.

—— and —— (1992) 'Introduction', in Michèle Lamont and Marcel Fournier (eds), *Cultivating Differences: Symbolic Boundaries and the Making of Inequality*, Chicago: University of Chicago Press, pp. 1–17.

—— and Lareau, A. (1988), 'Cultural Capital: Allusions, Gaps and Glissandos in Recent Theoretical Developments', *Sociological Theory*, 6 (2): 153–68.

Li Qiang (1993) *Dangdai Zhongguo shehui fenceng yu liudong* (Social Stratification and Mobility in Contemporary China), Beijing: Zhongguo jingji chubanshe.

Nee, Victor (1989) 'A Theory of Market Transition: From Redistribution to Markets in State Socialism', *American Sociological Review*, 54 (5): 663–81.

Nee, Victor (1991) 'Social Inequalities in Reforming State Socialism: Between Redistribution and Markets in China', *American Sociological Review*, 56 (3): 267–82.

—— and Matthews, Rebecca (1996) 'Market Transition and Societal Transformation in Reforming State Socialism', *Annual Review of Sociology*, 22: 401–35.

Parish, William L. and Whyte, Martin K. (1984) *Urban Life in Contemporary China*, Chicago: University of Chicago Press.

Pieke, Frank N. (1995) 'Bureaucracy, Friends, and Money: The Growth of Capital Socialism in China', *Comparative Studies in Society and History*, 37 (3), July: 494–518.

Ruan, Danching (1993) 'Interpersonal Networks and Workplace Controls in Urban China', *Australian Journal of Chinese Affairs*, no. 29, January: 89–105.

Shi, Xianmin (1993) *Tizhi de tupo: Beijing shi Xicheng getihu yanjiu* (Breaking through the System: A Study of Individual Businesses in Beijing's Western District), Beijing: Zhongguo shehui kexue chubanshe.

Smart, Alan (1993) 'Gifts, Bribes, Guanxi: A Reconsideration of Bourdieu's Social Capital', *Cultural Anthropology*, 8 (3), August: 388–408.

Veblen, T. (1979) *The Theory of the Leisure Class*, New York: Penguin.

Walder, Andrew G. (1996), 'Markets and Inequality in Transitional Economies: Toward Testable Theories', *American Journal of Sociology*, 101, January: 1060–73.

Wank, David L. (1990) 'Private Commerce as a Vocation: Social Mobility and the Wholesale Trade in Urban China', *China News Analysis*, no. 1424, 15 December.

Western, Mark and Wright, Erik Olin (1994) 'The Permeability of Class Boundaries to Intergenerational Mobility among Men in the United States, Canada, Norway and Sweden', *American Sociological Review*, 59, August: 606–29.

Wright, Erik Olin (1985) *Classes*, London: Verso.

Xie Dehua (1988) *Qian: Fengkuang de guaiwu*, Chansha: Hunan yishu chubanshe.

Yang, Mayfair Mei-hui (1994) *Gifts, Favors, and Banquets: The Art of Social Relationships in China*, Ithaca: Cornell University Press.

9 Creating the Thai middle class

Jim Ockey

The new rich in Thailand have invariably been described as a new middle class. That this new rich middle class was responsible for the democratic uprising of 1992 goes virtually unquestioned.[1] Yet, there has been surprisingly little debate on just what constitutes the middle class in Thailand. Rather, the middle class is left undefined, as if somehow everyone knows just what it is and all that is left is to determine how it functions. In fact, the Thai word for middle class is a direct translation from English, literally meaning 'people of the middle level', which has only recently spread beyond the academic community, and is still unknown to many Thais. In this chapter, I discuss the new rich in reference to variable constructions of the Thai middle class. I will describe some of the ways the middle class is being constructed to include the new rich. I will also examine the role of the middle class in politics, particularly since the rise of the new rich.

Academic literature on the development of middle classes can, for my purposes, be divided into structural approaches and historical approaches. In structural approaches, the middle class is described according to its position in the social structure, with the appropriate structural criteria a matter of considerable debate. For Marx, the criterion was the relationship to the means of production.[2] For Mills (1956), it was necessary to distinguish between the old middle class, made up of independent farmers and small entrepreneurs, and the 'new' or white-collar middle class, made up of salaried professionals. For Weber (1946), the criteria included lifestyle and status. For Giddens (1980), there were qualifications. Each of these writers constructs a different 'middle class', and while there may be considerable overlap between them, we might thus expect each of these differently defined groups to act somewhat differently. In the Thai case, this is particularly important as many traditionally high-status occupations do not allow, either morally or materially, for a lifestyle of high consumption, while many traditionally low-status occupations do. This results in an unusually high level of fragmentation among the various structurally defined middle classes.

The historical approach to class formation is best exemplified in E. P. Thompson's description of the English working class. Thompson (1968) argued that classes create themselves. This type of approach has been applied to the middle class by Frykman and Lofgren (1987). According to Frykman and

Lofgren, the middle class constructs a distinct lifestyle in order to set itself apart from both the aristocracy and the lower classes. The middle class then claims superiority for its lifestyle and attempts to impose it on other classes. Several problems are clear in this approach. First, a middle class cannot construct itself out of nothing – middle-class elements must exist before they can construct a lifestyle. In other words, neglecting the structural basis of class is as problematic as neglecting the historical process through which it forms itself. Second, this approach downplays the constraints that limit the ways the middle class can construct a distinct lifestyle (Ellin 1991: 821).[3] Classes are not only cultural constructs, they are structured by the capitalist system, and by external actors, but the balance of these sources of identity clearly varies. For example, media constructions of the middle class are constrained by the needs for profit. On the other hand, there might be fewer, or at least different, constraints on academic constructions of the middle class.

In describing the making of the English working classes, Thompson stressed the formation of working-class organisations and culture. Similarly Frykman and Lofgren emphasise the development of middle-class culture. Yet, the middle class, however it might be defined, is better suited to construct itself and its culture(s) in ways not readily available to the working class: discursively. Segments within it are responsible for writing and editing newspapers and magazines, for radio and television programming, for writing textbooks and teaching students, and for writing advertising copy. In this way, the middle class is able to construct itself academically, ideologically and culturally. To understand the way the middle class is being constructed, then, I will discuss the way it has developed structurally, within the context of the way it is constructed discursively. By examining both academic discourse and media representations, it is possible to highlight the contrasts inherent in the different mix of educational and monetary constraints.

DISCOVERING THE MIDDLE CLASS IN THAI HISTORY

In her 1992 dissertation, Jiraporn Witayasakpan wrote that by the end of the nineteenth century commercial theatre became viable as a result of the rise of 'the middle class'. This she attributed to 'expansion of trade, western education, and the bureaucracy' (p. 39).[4] 'The middle class which emerged…encompassed merchants, bureaucrats, and intellectuals with western-style education and distinct tastes towards western elements' (p. 43). The late nineteenth century seems to be the earliest date offered for the appearance of 'the middle class', although Jiraporn is not unique in pointing to this time period.[5]

Although not new, this middle class grew rapidly at the turn of the century. While the number of merchants had been increasing since the Bowring Treaty of 1855, the semi-hereditary bureaucracy was transformed into a salaried civil service and expanded dramatically during the 1890s. Siffin (1966) estimates that 'the salaried bureaucracy more than doubled in size between 1892 and 1899'. By

1900, he estimates a bureaucracy of some 25,000, growing to about 80,000 officials by the year 1918 (1966: 94). The structurally defined middle class of the
period was made up, then, largely of traders, independent farmers and civil
servants, including academics. There was also a sprinkling of journalists.

Descriptions of the middle class of this period focus on the salaried intellectuals and bureaucrats. According to several influential analyses, this salaried
middle class was responsible for the 1932 overthrow of the absolute monarchy.
Thawatt Mokarapong (1972: 86–7, 77–8) argued that 'with the spread of education...a new class – the intelligentsia – began to emerge...[This]...dissatisfied
intelligentsia...became the principal supporters of the revolution'. Although here
Thawatt defines the group according to education, in his description of the
leaders he invokes socio-economic criteria. Thus he refers to: Pridi Phanomyong
who was born 'of a typical lower middle-class family'; Pibul Songgram who 'was
a son of a simple farmer of considerable means'; Tua Laphanukrom who was
born to 'a middle-class family'; and so on (1972: 5f.). Benjamin Batson (1974)
argued that the 1932 coup resulted from the introduction of a salary tax.
According to Batson: 'The tax affected mainly middle-class government officials
and employees of Western-style firms" (1974: 75). According to Virginia
Thompson (1941: 61): 'groups of European-trained junior officials, largely
drawn from the middle class, were the theorists behind the revolt'. On the left,
Udom Sisuwan argued in 1950 that, following the 1932 overthrow, power 'fell
into the hands of the petty capitalist class, mid-level capitalists, and the Land-
Lord class' (1950, cited in Reynolds and Hong, 1983: 81–2).

Recent analyses of Thai scholars have assigned a greater role to the extra-
bureaucratic middle class. Chanwit Kasetsiri (1992: 37) writes that the period
since the reforms at the turn of the century 'saw the development of a new
class...the "middle class" with one part in military and civilian government
service...and the other part outside government service, perhaps as writers or
journalists, including entrepreneurs and traders. "New leaders" of the middle
class spearheaded the change of government.' Nakharin Mektrairat (1992:
85–90) refers to a 'middle class' made up of those with 'independent occupations'. This middle class, he argued, developed during the period 1857–1927,
though it had existed even earlier (1992: 85). Nakharin then reclaims the 1932
'revolution' from mid-level soldiers and bureaucrats for a wider middle class:

> The middle class outside government service did not play a role in seizing
> power...That task fell to the mid-level civil servants and soldiers. However,
> the act of seizing power took place in circumstances where the middle class
> outside government service had already helped to destroy the legitimacy of
> the upper class to govern...almost completely (1992: 105).[6]

When the military and the bureaucracy acted on the side of democracy or popular
upheaval, they were middle-class. Later, when the military acted against democratic
rule in 1992, they were defined as outside of the middle class. According to the
1990s constructions, the middle class must always act on the side of democracy.

DISCARDING THE MIDDLE CLASS

For the above period of Thai history, the academic literature recognises a middle class conceptualised as a combination of independent entrepreneurs and white-collar bureaucrats. Yet this middle class is disaggregated, and then eliminated, in academic literature describing the 1950s and 1960s. This was done in a two-part process. In the 1950s, G. William Skinner (1957a, 1957b) analysed Chinese communities in Thailand. He argued:

> There are what appear to be two middle classes, or at least two major middle-class groupings – the Chinese and the Thai. They overlap for the most part in stratification, but the mean status of the Chinese middle class is appreciably higher. The latter consists of most ethnic Chinese in occupations of highest and mid-high status, i.e., occupations of relatively high income which involve no manual labor…The Thai middle class consisting mainly of those in mid-high status occupations (government employees, small entrepreneurs, teachers, newspapermen, clerks, secretaries, and so on), is strongly white collar in flavor.
>
> (1957a: 307–8)

Skinner here makes the primary division ethnicity, rather than class, and then ties that ethnic division to 'old' and 'white-collar' middle classes. Thus we have an old middle class of independent entrepreneurs, the Chinese, and a white-collar middle class, the Thais. That the Chinese described by Skinner might more accurately be called Sino-Thai becomes lost in the constant reference to 'the Chinese'. That there are entrepreneurs who are Thai, and bureaucrats who are Sino-Thai, is also obscured. And the shared middle-class culture described in Jiraporn's analysis of theatre disappears from the analysis.

While Skinner had turned 'the old middle class' into 'the Chinese', it remained for Fred Riggs (1966) and William Siffin (1966) to turn the (Thai) white-collar middle class into the bureaucracy. Wrote Siffin (1966: 134): 'the emerging middle class was a bureaucratic class'. Riggs and Siffin thus made the conceptual shift from white-collar middle class to 'the (Thai) bureaucracy'. There remained but one minor problem, that of the large number of Sino-Thai in the bureaucracy. This long-ignored problem was addressed by Chai-anan Samudavanija (1991), who argued that due to the socialisation process of the bureaucracy 'a son of a Chinese immigrant will remain Chinese if he chooses to be a businessman, but once he enters the bureaucracy his ethnic identity disappears and he becomes a *kharatchakan* or civil servant' (1991: 65).

The elimination of the middle class from academic discourse is central to the analysis of David Wilson (1962), who explained the apparent stability of Thai society by pointing to the absence of a middle class. He argued that: 'the society of the Thai is characterized by a gross two-class structure,…in which the classes are physically as well as economically separated and differential status is satisfactorily justified…[This structure consists] of an extremely large agrarian segment and a small ruling segment' (1962: 274–5).[7] As for the roles generally played by middle classes, Wilson had this to say:

'The more intimate economic relationship concerned in transfer of goods and services between town and country takes place through Chinese traders. These people as aliens are easily contained politically' (1962: 275).

Meanwhile in 1958, debate on the left was suppressed by the new military government and Udom's work (see above) was censored. Thus by the late 1960s, scholarly discourse argued that there was no middle class, and as a result, the Thai political system was extremely stable.[8] Writing the middle class out of academic discourse ensured that the middle class could not make itself, or develop into a coherent social class. It also ensured that when 'the middle class' returned to the discourse in the 1970s, it was considered new.

'NEW' MIDDLE CLASSES: THE RISE OF THE NEW RICH

During this period when academics were defining the middle class out of existence, the middle classes (defined structurally) began to undergo another rapid expansion. Much of the growth was in services and sales, with education and media sectors also expanding dramatically. The occupational distribution of Thai workers for 1960, 1970, 1980 and 1990 is summarized in Table 9.1. The white-collar middle class are found in categories A, B, C, D and I; these categories have grown more rapidly than the total workforce in every decade since 1960. These five categories have grown from 9.85 per cent of the total workforce in 1960 to 20.2% by 1990. These new rich, concentrated in the sales, technical and services sectors of the economy, have overtaken a structural middle class formerly made up largely of small traders, intellectuals and bureaucrats.

As the new rich multiplied, the higher-education system was expanded to meet their needs. Enrolment in universities climbed from less than 25,000 in 1950 to well over 600,000 by 1990. There was a concomitant growth in the number and size of universities, and in the number of academics. More Thais were being socialised in the higher educational system, and more were acquiring educational credentials that, in many eyes, accorded them middle-class standing. While structural position and educational credentials are two ways in which this expanding middle class came to be understood, there were other ways as well: in terms of occupational status, spending power and political action.

While the growing number of academics – the teachers of the new rich – enjoyed high occupational status (see Table 9.2), their income was not congruent with this status. Many struggled to afford the new rich lifestyle that was developing around them. Along with academics, a growing number of writers and journalists have come to play a key role in discursive constructions of the middle class. They too commonly have only moderate incomes, but unlike academics, rank quite low in occupational status, so on these counts might be excluded from the middle class. Conversely, while the lowest-status occupation, a euphemism for prostitution, may clearly fall below one conception of middle class, some in

Table 9.1 Occupational groups in Thailand age 11 and up, 1960, 1970, 1980, 1990*

Occupation	1960 total	1970 total (% increase)	1980 total (% increase)	1990 total (% increase)
A. Professional, technical and related workers	173, 960	284,104 (63.3%)	665,255 (134.2%)	1,397,100 (110%)
B. Administrative, executive managerial workers and government officials	26,191	246,591 (841.5%)	434,682 (76.3%)	864,000 (98.8%)
C. Clerical and related workers	154,303	190,238 (23.3%)	389,226 (104.6%)	763,000 (96%)
D. Sales workers	735,457	833,607 (13.3%)	1,591,268 (90.9%)	2,472,400 (55.4%)
E. Agricultural, animal husbandry, fishers, forestry workers and hunters	11,332,489	13,217,416 (16.6%)	16,838,477 (27.4%)	21,096,500 (25.3%)
F. Miners, quarrymen, well drillers and related workers	26,255	42,605 (62.3%)	59,405 (39.4%)	24,600 (-58.6%)
G. Transport equipment operators and related workers	146,610	225,204 (55.7%)	369,207 (63.9%)	606,600 (64.3%)
H. Craftsmen, production workers and labourers	806,205	1,109,943 (37.7%)	2,232,356 (101.1%)	3,514,000 (57.4%)
I. Service workers	273,375	471,999 (72.7%)	663,386 (40.4%)	924,200 (39.3%)
J. Workers not classifiable by occupation or unknown	99,259	30,560 (-69.2%)	38,180 (24.9%)	61,300 (60.6%)
K. New entrants	64,880	197,869 (205.0%)	**	**
L. All workers	13,836,984	16,850,13 (21.8%)	23,281,442 (38.2%)	31,724,300 (36.3%)

Source: Population and Housing Census 1960, 1970, 1980, 1990.
Notes:
*Census data for 1990 is for workers age 13 or older.
**This category was eliminated in the 1980 and 1990 censuses.

this category earn incomes well above those of academics and can afford lifestyles popularly associated with the middle class. In short, there is no neat coincidence in Thailand between 'middle-class' structural positions, such as those defined by educational credentials, occupational status and income levels. Yet most academics and journalists write as if there is a single, clearly defined middle class. The prostitute, the university professor, the bank manager, the independent farmer, the owner of a Chinese traditional medicine shop, the police officer and the soldier are all 'middle class' under various definitions, yet they have little in common.

As we have seen, 'the middle class', defined structurally, is not truly new;

Table 9.2 Occupations ranked by status

Rank	Occupation	Points
1	Doctor, veterinarian, pharmacist	82.9
2	Cabinet minister	81.8
3	Ambassador	79.7
4	Military officer – general	76.4
5	Provincial governor or equivalent	75.0
6	Architect, engineer	74.1
7	University professor	72.6
8	Nurse	71.5
9	Senator, MP	70.0
10	Physical sciences	68.7
11	Lawyer, judge, prosecutor	68.5
12	Military officer – lieutenant, colonel	67.2
13	Airport/port officials, e.g. pilot, navigator	66.7
14	Manager, entrepreneur	66.4
15	Police officer – general (rank)	65.8
16	Natural sciences	65.4
17	Teacher	64.4
18	Shop owner	63.8
19	District officer and similar	63.3
20	Economist/accountant	63.3
21	Statistician and similar	61.6
22	Restaurant/hotel manager	61.0
23	Police – lieutenant, colonel	59.5
24	Social sciences	57.9
25	Social worker	57.5
26	Foreman	56.8
27	Priest or minister	56.8
28	Farm manager	56.3
29	Manager – marketing	55.6
30	Mid-level civil servant	55.3
31	Large-scale farmer	54.3
35	Soldier – NCO	51.2
38	Heir	50.1
39	Medium-scale farmer	49.6
40	Writer	49.4
41	Journalist	48.4
43	Village and tambon leaders	47.5
47	Police officers – NCOs	42.7
60	Sales representative	39.6
89	Service woman, e.g. masseuse, 'partner'	17.6

Source: Adapted from Suphawong (1991: tables 4, 5, ranked by urban response).

rather, it was defined out of existence during the 1950s and 1960s. The emergence of the new rich was so striking that later writers could no longer ignore what they now saw as 'the middle class'. Since this growth occurred during a period of political change, it was rather simple to attribute all the change to this 'new' group, despite the analytical dubiousness of conflating the various constructs noted above. Nevertheless, descriptions of 'the middle class', and the identification of times when it has 'acted' politically, have become the basis for the dominant discursive construction of the middle class: as a force for democratic change.

CONSTRUCTING THE POLITICAL MIDDLE CLASS

The first of political 'action' of the newly identified middle class, attributed to it in retrospect, was the 1973 uprising that overthrew the military dictatorship and installed democratic rule. The uprising was student-led, but soon came to include people of all classes. The events of 1973 demonstrated that concerted action could overthrow an unpopular government. New leaders emerged, leaders willing to work to induce change. This group has become the conscience of the 'political middle class', and has contributed heavily to its construction.

That the 1973 uprising has been identified in academic discourse as the beginning of middle-class political activity does not mean that it actually was a middle-class uprising. Only in retrospect was this construction of events gradually created. Originally, the demonstrations were credited to the public in general, and students in particular. 'Through the leadership of the country's youth, a mighty force had congealed and made itself evident – people power' (Theh Chongkhadikij, *Bangkok Post*, cited in Zimmerman 1974: 515). Scholars followed this characterisation, attributing the uprising to students and 'the people', 'people from all walks of life' and 'members of the public' (Withayakan 1993: 77; Heinze 1974: 498; Race 1974: 198).

Among the first to describe the 1973 uprising in middle-class terms was Benedict Anderson (1977). Anderson began by describing the changes in class structure that resulted from the expansion of the economy in the 1960s. This created a 'new petty bourgeoisie', the new rich, responsible for the success of the uprising:

> There is no doubt the new bourgeois strata contributed decisively to the huge new crowds that came out in support of students' and intellectuals' demands…Indeed, it can be argued that these strata ensured the *success* of the demonstrations – had the crowds been composed of slum-dwellers rather than generally well-dressed urbanites, the dictators might have won fuller support for their repression.
>
> (1977: 18)

Likhit Dhiravegin (1985) of Thammasat University wrote a similar article, describing the development of 'the middle class' during the 1960s, and attributing the events of the 1970s to its new-found participation in politics. This argument is still dominant in Thai intellectual discourse.

Other scholarship, while attributing the primary role to students, has re-emphasised the role of older intellectuals and academics in the uprising (Withayakan 1993: ch. 5; Khamhaeng 1994; Flood 1975: 61). It might thus be argued that the 1973 uprising was instigated by the educated 'middle class'. This is reminiscent of Lipset (1959), who argued that education would lead to democracy. In the Thai case, scholars seem to have made the connection in reverse, noting the democracy, then searching out a middle class that must have created it. This also led to a re-examination of the 1932 event, to discover if a middle class was present at that time, or alternatively if it had not been a democratic revolution after all.[9]

In 1976, this connection of middle class and democracy was undermined as student demonstrations again erupted in violence. Support for the students failed to materialise and, on 6 October, many were massacred as the military returned to power in a coup. Although these events were initially characterised as 'left' against 'right', analysis soon turned to the role of 'the middle class'. The massacre demonstrated that there was no single unified middle class with a clear awareness of its interests. There were members of middle classes on both sides. Many of the educated middle class were again calling for a more just society. But, as Anderson points out, many new rich turned against them:

> We are to visualize then a very insecure, suddenly created bourgeois strata...faced by strained economic circumstances and the menace of worse troubles still to come...haunted by the fear that...their ascent from backstreet dust would end where it had begun...Such, I think, is the explanation of why many of the same people who sincerely supported the mass demonstrations of October 1973 welcomed the return to dictatorship three years later.
>
> (1977: 19)

Anderson is perceptive in emphasising how the insecurity of the new rich, and their support for a return to authoritarian government, was rooted in the very newness of their riches. Yet, Anderson is reluctant to recognise that the 'middle class' was divided by the event. The students who were massacred are not described as 'middle-class'. Similarly, Wyatt writes of the same event:

> Judging only by its members' behavior, one might conclude that the growth of a middle class has strengthened a traditionalistic sort of Thai political conservatism...While they would support the overthrow of the Thanom-Praphas regime in 1973, they also would join the right-wing reaction against the political chaos of 1976.
>
> (1982: 296)

Again the middle class is depicted as singular, and opposed to the uprising.

The 1976 massacre was constructed by the martial law regime as a victory over Communism. Not until the mid-1980s, after the Communist Party of Thailand had been destroyed, and the economy had taken off under parliamentary rule, could a reconstruction take place. In that reconstruction, the events were described as a massacre of the same students who had fought for democracy and won in 1973. The extent of that reconstruction became evident during an election campaign in 1988, when Bangkok governor Chamlong Simuang, who would later lead the 1992 uprising, was accused of supporting the 'right wing' in the 1976 events. Chamlong vehemently denied any role in what was described in the press at the time as 'the incident in which scores of students were killed by frenzied right-wing mobs' (*Bangkok Post*, 7 October 1988: 3). In this reconstruction, the middle class is still portrayed as singular, although it has switched sides.

The reconstruction of the events of 1973 and 1976 can be seen most clearly in the retrospective work of a leader of the 1973 uprising, Thirayut Bunmi (1994). Thirayut never mentions the middle class, and writes instead of the 14 October 1973 'generation' (*run*). On closer examination, the 'generation' is not an age cohort. But by describing the group as a 'generation' Thirayut, in effect, constructs a 'new' middle class, based on the initial rise of the new rich, distinct from those who might share a similar class position, yet did not share in the experiences of 1973, 1976 and 1992. Thirayut expands the generation to include anyone from the age group 30– 50, then ascribes to it three essential characteristics. Most importantly, members of this 'generation' experienced the events of October 1973, October 1976 and May 1992 as a sort of (ideological) touchstone. Membership of the 'generation' does not depend on being physically present, but on belief in the goals espoused. Secondly, Thirayut makes it clear that he means something very like a middle class, defining the new 'generation' in terms of lifestyle. The lifestyle he describes is one that accepts Western culture, Elvis, the Beatles, long hair and jeans. The new 'generation' are those who wear Bally shoes, eat at McDonald's, use the newest computers, live in luxurious town houses and stay in mountain and seaside resorts (1994: 14–15). Thirdly, Thirayut outlines the occupations of his 'generation', again in middle class terms: 'People of this generation are usually technocrats, experts "professional" [this word is in English]...but there are a few who are owners of enterprises, usually new businesses...such as the hotel industry, newspapers, computers, and electronics, but these are still a minority' (1994: 23).[10] He also points out that his 'generation' is active in parliamentary politics and Non-Governmental Organisations (NGOs), and supports environmentalism and culture.

Thirayut's article exemplifies another aspect of the role the leadership in the 1973 and 1976 uprisings played in the construction of the middle class. Thirayut mentions that his 'generation' is active in the newspapers, and indeed his article first appeared in Thai in *Sayam Post*, then in English in the *Bangkok Post*. As columnists and reporters, those of Thirayut's 'generation' are in key positions to construct the middle class. Thirayut failed to mention several other occupations in which leaders of the 1973 and 1976 uprisings are found. Thirayut is also a professor at Thammasat University. Seksan Prasertkul, another 1973 student leader, was a columnist for *Phujatkan* newspaper, a prolific author, and Dean of Political Science at Thammasat. The most notable success in the media has been Somkiat Onwimon, a university lecturer who signed the petition calling for a new constitution in the lead up to the 1973 uprising. Somkiat went on to become a prime-time news anchor, and is credited with popularising the news through bringing in techniques such as investigative reporting and advocacy.[11] From these positions, leaders of the 1973 uprising consciously and unconsciously construct the middle class, while providing a visible reminder of the uprisings that have become the touchstone of middle-class consciousness.

CAPITALISM AND THE CONSTRUCTION OF THE MIDDLE CLASS

If attempts are being made to construct the Thai middle class in terms of political practice and ideology, it has also became impossible to ignore the generation of a new 'middle-class' lifestyle based on the growth of consumer capitalism. We can get an idea of the scope of this influence through an examination of the growth of the media, of advertising, and of market research.

The size and the persuasiveness of the media have grown tremendously over the last forty years. The clearest example is television. In 1955, there was only one black and white channel, available only in Bangkok and the surrounding area. By the end of 1994, there were 4 regular channels, 2 cable television packages, an educational channel, and plans under way for at least 2 UHF channels (Vivat 1994). By the early 1990s, there were over 8.5 million television sets in use (*Thailand in Figures* 1994), and nearly everyone had access to television in the home or somewhere in the local community. Television has helped to construct a middle-class lifestyle, with virtually all programming – from soap operas with 'middle-class' settings to game shows with 'middle-class' contestants and prizes, to commercials aiming at middle-class consumers – depicting ideal 'middle-class' people, products and ways of life. Other media have expanded rapidly as well. This is evident in the rise in advertising expenditures (see Table 9.3).

Advertising expenditures also demonstrate the growth of advertising agencies which have been highly influential in constructing the middle class in terms of consumer lifestyle. Of the 18 advertising agencies listed in *Thailand Company Information 1990–91*, 2 were established in the 1960s, 6 in the 1970s, and 10 in the 1980s. Advertising expenditures by category indicate that the images being constructed are largely middle-class (see Table 9.4). Most housing estates are aimed at the consumer middle class. Office machines and equipment are aimed at the manager, the purchasing agent or the private entrepreneur. Department stores and shopping malls, the epitome of middle-class consumerism, are the replacements for traditional markets, all under one roof. These shopping malls provide a showcase of middle-class consumer culture, where those who aspire to this status can see the types of furniture they should own, the clothes they should wear, and the places at which they should dine. Furthermore, the workers in these modern capitalist markets often belong to the structurally defined middle class. Passenger cars and petroleum products are also middle-class goods. Only shampoos/conditioners (ranked 4), cosmetics (9) and dairy products (10) aim at a

Table 9.3 Advertising expenditures in million baht, 1979–1993

Year	Newspapers	Television	Radio	Total
1979	267.0	667.0	450	1,557
1980	325.0	951.0	500	2,017
1981	437.0	1,162.0	575	2,433
1982	501.0	1,358.0	603	2,712
1983	758.0	1,767.0	732	3,542
1984	971.6	2,443.5	900	4,716
1985	1,097.2	2,729.6	1,017	5,348
1986	1,199.3	2,612.3	1,050	5,578
1987	1,386.5	3,023.5	1,100	6,403
1988	1,802.2	3,853.7	1,200	8,078
1989	2,650.1	4,957.9	1,300	10,415
1990	3,620.9	6,502.1	n/a	13,514
1991	4,607.4	8,180.2	n/a	16,900
1992	5,449.2	10,119.3	n/a	20,664
1993	7,547.2	13,082.7	3,100	27,519
1994		17,500.0		35,000

Source: *Thailand in Figures*, *Bangkok Post*, 3 January 1995: 22 (figures for radio and for 1994 are estimates).

wider audience, and cosmetics have only recently spread beyond the consumer middle class. Finally, the media is marketing itself quite heavily.

The companies that spent the most on advertising in 1992 in Thailand (to November) were mainly foreign, including Lever Brothers, Nestlé, Procter and Gamble, Colgate-Palmolive, National, and Toyota. Only four Thai companies ranked in the top ten; two developers of housing projects, one pharmaceutical company and the franchisee for Coca-Cola in Thailand (*Khukhaeng Thurakit*, 7–13 December 1992: 22). Of the top ten advertising agencies (by 1994 billings), only one, Spa, was wholly Thai-owned; it ranked tenth, and had the lowest rate of

Table 9.4 Advertising expenditures by category, 1994

Rank	Category	Billings mil. baht	% Increase from 1993
1	Housing projects/real estate	5,647	55.5
2	Office machines/equipment	1,560	56.2
3	Dept. stores/trade centers	1,217	34.5
4	Shampoos/conditioners	1,179	19.0
5	Media	1,027	84.4
6	Passenger cars	967	27.4
7	Alcoholic beverages	928	11.5
8	Petroleum products	857	31.2
9	Cosmetics	824	27.4
10	Milk and dairy	763	64.1

Source: *Bangkok Post*, 3 January 1995: 19.

growth (*Bangkok Post*, 3 January 1995: 22). The others all had a significant foreign-ownership component. Thus advertising agencies are dominated by Western companies and the leading advertisers are Western. It is not surprising, then, that the middle-class lifestyle constructed through advertising is not too dissimilar from that familiar to those in the west. Nor is it surprising that Thirayut and his readers think of the middle class in terms of Bally shoes, jeans and McDonald's.[12]

While it is not possible to outline in detail the middle-class lifestyle constructed through advertising in Thailand, it is important to point out the differences in the middle class constructed by consumer capitalism and that constructed around the political events of 1973, 1976 and 1992. One example should suffice. The middle class constructed by the uprisings is one that de-emphasises differences of ethnicity and gender by focusing on large crowds of people with the primary similarity being that of class.[13] The implication is that women and men act similarly and equally. While this assumption is questionable, it is true that many NGOs, which attract some of the most idealistic of the participants of 1973 and 1976, are led by women. The Thai women's movement is led mainly by this same group. The construction of gender roles in adver-tising's representations of the consumer middle class is quite different. In this rendering, women worry about clean houses and clothes, and about becoming more beautiful; men impress beautiful women by buying expensive imported whiskey and fancy cars.

'New rich' consumerism also created an entirely new industry – market research – which rushed in to survey and measure. Market researchers assumed the existence of 'the middle class', then set about trying to determine its lifestyle. From such firms, we learn that 72 per cent of 'middle-class' Thai women like to shop in department stores, that 60 per cent like to eat out on weekends, that 68 per cent like to watch television, and that 89 per cent of 'middle-class' families own their own home (Laifsatai 1987; 'Chiwit khwampenyu' 1986). These surveys often appear in newspapers and magazines, telling 'the middle class' how it should act, then measuring again how it does act in a self-perpetuating process.

In the press and on television the consumer constructions of advertisers mix freely with political ideological constructions of academics and journalists. Alongside the advertising images are newspaper columns written by academics, and popular television talk shows mediated by academics. This blending of polit-ical and consumer constructions of the middle class is also apparent in the writings of Thirayut and in the way the popular uprising of 1992 was conceptu-alised.

THE MOBILE TELEPHONE MOB AND THE 1992 UPRISING

That the media and others were busily constructing a middle class, and connecting it with democracy, had a profound effect on the way the 1992 uprising was interpreted. The media soon designated the protesters as 'the mobile telephone mob' and 'the automobile mob'. Print journalists made explicit comparisons to the 1973 uprising, seeking to tie together the new rich, the protests and the earlier political touchstones of middle-classness. The Social Science Association of Thailand went so far as to produce a survey 'proving' that the protestors were predominantly middle-class.[14] Thus from the beginning, the uprising of 1992 was constructed as a middle-class event.

Academe followed in this path with relatively little questioning. According to Thirayut: 'it has never happened that a mob anywhere has been so full of automobiles, mobile phones, hand-held radios, and workers of the "white-collar" type'. It was, said Thirayut, a 'yuppie' revolution (*Sayamrat Sapda Wichan*, 14 June 1992: 12). Likhit Dhiravegin argued that the event was of the same order as the 1973 and 1976 uprisings, connecting the new rich to democracy, and even to the 1976 demonstrations that many of them had opposed (Likhit 1992). Anek Laothamathas (1993) wrote articles for various journals, rewrote them in popular form in the weekly *Matichon Sutsapda*, and then published them as a book titled *Mob Mu Thu* (or Mobile Telephone Mob). Anek, a student leader in 1976, attributed the uprising to the 'middle class', and to 'entrepreneurs'. Anek reconstructs the earlier uprisings as well, calling the students a 'proxy' for the middle class in those earlier events (1993: 61).

Not long after the 1992 uprising, the Political Economy Center of Chulalongkorn University organised a conference in 'an attempt to come to grips with the phenomenon of the "middle class" in the protests of May 1992' (Sungsidh and Pasuk 1993: 27). Aimed at an academic audience, the analysis is more sophisticated than that which appeared in the press, and several of the authors attempt to determine the structural position of 'the middle class'. There is no agreement on definitions, yet there is a general assumption that there is a middle class, and only one middle class. The introduction sets the tenor for much of the book:

> Many protestors arrived at the demonstration site in their large cars, carrying their hand phones...Local newspaper [sic] reported that the majority of the demonstrators were 'middle-class'. They included business executives, stockbrokers, civil servants, owners of small and medium businesses, civil servants, academics, other white-collar workers, and educated persons. Students and political activists were present, but formed a small minority of the crowd...The typical member of the 'mob' was a well-off, well-educated, white-collar worker.
>
> (Sungsidh and Pasuk 1993a: 27–8).[15]

Aimed at an academic audience, the publication resulting from the conference (Sungsidh and Pasuk 1993b) presents a more sophisticated analysis than that which appeared in the press, and several of the authors attempt to determine the structural position of 'the middle class'. Some of the papers in the collection do tentatively question the role of the middle class in the uprising, yet the focus remains on 'the middle class'. Sungsidh (1993), for example, writes of the reasons why unionised labour did not join the uprising, before writing briefly of the role of slum dwellers. Voravidh (1993: 139) points out that many of the dead and injured were not middle-class, but concludes: 'The victory of democratic forces is not possible if it lacks the support and the combat that comes from the middle class'. Nithi (1993) reminds us that the middle class does not necessarily believe in either democracy or equality, as Anderson and others had pointed out after the 1976 massacre, a point recent constructions of the middle class have largely ignored. Perhaps most intriguing is the article by Teeranat (1993), who points out that by most definitions, including those of family background and income, the military who fired on the demonstrators are also middle class. Yet, ultimately even the more sophisticated analyses in this book credit 'the middle class' with the uprising of 1992.

In the construction of the events of 1992, we see coming together all the strands of the analysis presented here. The 1992 uprising is the first popular uprising in Thailand where an awareness of the middle class had already developed, and thus the first time an uprising was attributed to it from the outset. The uprising was associated constantly with the earlier uprisings, seen by scholars as the ideological touchstone for determining membership of the middle class. The military, despite its arguably middle-class status or structural position, was not considered part of the middle class, since it took the wrong side in the conflict. Yet retired military officer Lt.-Gen. Chamlong Simuang, who led the protestors, was considered middle-class. In contrast to previous uprisings, the middle class associated with the events of 1992 was also identified in terms of lifestyle and consumer goods, particularly the automobile and the mobile phone, in an attempt to connect the new rich to the political ideological preferences of those in academe and the media. Finally, in the academic and media constructions of events, the 'middle class' becomes so dominant that the role of others in the 1992 uprising disappears, and they are denied any credit.

The middle class did play an important role in the 1992 uprising by providing leadership, yet when fighting erupted, they were not in the forefront.[16] The occupational backgrounds of those killed and those injured have been documented in *100 Wan Wirachon Prachathipatai* (1992: 3–5, 8). On the basis of the information available, only one of the 38 dead was a business person, one a government employee, one a teacher, and one an engineer. At least 20 belonged to lower classes, 4 more were vendors and 10 were students. Even more telling: of the 34 about whom information is available, not one had graduated from a university. Of the 176 injured about whom information is available, only 23 clearly belonged, in socio-economic terms, to the middle or upper classes, though some of the others may, by some definitions, have belonged to a lower middle class. Yet most constructions of the uprising, with the notable exception of Nithi's (above), ignore these figures, referring instead to an earlier survey that identified 52 per cent of demonstrators as having a degree.

Despite the many books and articles that describe the 1992 uprising as a middle-class victory, middle-class Thais are not unaware that the great majority among them went home when the shooting started, while others from the less celebrated classes fought on. Various accounts, encouraged by those who supported the military government, claim that Chamlong led the people to their deaths. The implications of this argument are twofold. First, it shifts some of the blame for the killing from the military to Chamlong, who might otherwise be seen as the hero of the uprising. Second, it implies that the demonstrations would have succeeded without violence, if only Chamlong had not provoked the troops, in the process absolving 'the middle class' for going home when the shooting began. While this construction of the events is outside the mainstream, it is widely known, and may account for the fact that Chamlong's party actually lost seats in Bangkok in the ensuing election.

CONCLUSION

It should be clear that it is at best analytically dubious to speak of a single middle class in Thailand. There are instead diverse fragments and diverse constructions that have not yet been conflated into a single social class. As Giddens (1980) pointed out, in order for a middle class to become consolidated into a social class, a closure of mobility is necessary. In Thailand, not only has there been no closure, but rather the middle class continues to expand, adding more new rich to the mixture.

The differences in the middle-class fragments are most clear between the consumer middle class, many of them new rich, and the occupational (status) middle class, many of them in the media and academe. Despite considerable overlap, these two groups are fairly distinct in terms of income and education. Many in the consumer middle class are relatively well off, but not highly educated. The owners of medium- and small-size enterprises often fit into this category. By way of contrast, academics, teachers and social workers are well educated and enjoy high occupational status, but have incomes at the low end of the middle class. Not surprisingly, this difference manifests itself in the two strands of construction of the middle class. The occupational middle class – with its high levels of education and its positions in universities, the media and NGOs – has constructed a middle class based on an ideology associated with the uprisings of 1973, 1976 and 1992, an ideology of democracy. High occupational status groups thus compensate for their lower income through influence over political ideology. The consumer middle-class construction is based instead on the prestige and lifestyles that come with owning cars and mobile phones, and on making money. The 1992 uprising demonstrates the discursive attempts to draw these two strands together.

Thai middle-class culture is still fragmentary in the age of the new rich, and subject to varied active processes of construction; this has not prevented middle-class cultural imperialism. It is not openly malicious in intent and often goes unnoticed. In the main, it has amounted to an attempt by reformists to promote democracy by associating it with a middle class that is not only fragmented but has shown only limited and sporadic support for democratic practice. The unfortunate side-effect of these attempts has been to consolidate a conviction among the middle classes that democracy belongs to the middle class, and that the lower classes are incapable of effective participation in a democratic system. The middle-class frustration with the common practice of vote-buying is the most dramatic indication of this attitude: frequently it is the poor who are blamed, rather than those doing the buying. Denying the role of lower classes in the popular uprisings that brought about democracy is a necessary part of the conclusion that the poor are unworthy of participation in the democratic system.

The current frenzied efforts to construct a cultural identity for the middle class reflect the latter's fragmentary and largely indeterminate social character. Reformist academics seek to associate the middle class, particularly the new rich, with democracy, while advertisers aim at consumption and an associated need for a high growth economy. When economic downturn was associated with democracy in the 1970s, the new rich turned on the students and academics and supported a coup. This legacy is one reason why academics were so pleased when the new rich supported democracy in 1992. Academics sought to consolidate that limited support, which came only after high economic growth was associated with democracy during the 1980s. Ultimately, despite the differences in the various fragments, it may be the overlap that is most important. Out of this overlap, and the discursive power of intellectuals, may eventually emerge a coherent social middle class. As middle-class cultural identity becomes more intricate, more clearly defined, and moves towards greater consensus, the fragmented middle classes will tend to conflate, perhaps even without closure of mobility. In the meantime, it seems safe to conclude that there is no 'middle class' in Thailand. Rather, there are different fragments in the process of becoming.

Notes

1 See, for example, the cover story of *Far Eastern Economic Review*, 21 March 1992.
2 For a good summary of Marx's views on the middle classes, see Val Burris (1986).
3 See Anderson (1980: ch. 2) for a further critique of Thompson.
4 I have not distinguished clearly between contemporary and retrospective work as, oddly enough, they seem to follow the same general pattern outlined here. See also note 7.
5 Akin (1969: 162) pushes this date back: 'By 1850 the Chinese had gained almost complete control of the interregional trade of Thailand...It seems therefore, that besides the two classes of *phrai* [commoners] and *nai* [nobility], there was perhaps another class, an entrepreneurial class of Chinese traders in the middle.'
6 These recent attempts to reclaim the 1932 event for 'the middle class' should be seen in historical context. Both works were published in 1992 for the sixtieth anniversary of the revolution, just one year after a military coup had ended the latest attempt at parliamentary rule. By 1992, the perceived enemies of democracy were the military and the bureaucracy, which had formerly been getting the credit.
7 Wilson's work appeared before that of Riggs and Siffin, indicating that the pieces were already in place for this elimination of the middle class by the early 1960s. Wilson was perhaps thinking of Thai society as a whole, and meant that the rural

area so dominated the urban area that the urban middle class was insignificant. Riggs and Siffin argued that the relevant polity was the bureaucracy, so the rural areas could be safely ignored.

8 This elimination of the middle class from academic discourse during the 1950s and 1960s occurs in both the writings of the time and retrospective writings. Thompson (1941) writes of the middle class, and Udom (1950, cited in Reynolds and Lysa 1938: 81–2) of the petty capitalist class. Blanchard (1957: 411–14) claims that some 70 per cent of the population of Bangkok was 'middle-class', before quoting Skinner almost verbatim. Ten years later there were only 'the Chinese' and 'the bureaucracy', and references to the middle class disappeared. Retrospective writings are remarkably similar with, for example, Jiraporn (1992) discovering a middle class at the turn of the century, while other writers claim that the development of the middle class took place in the 1960s (see below). This leads to the odd situation in Keyes (1989), where the 'new middle class' is credited with the 1932 event (p. 63), yet just 14 pages later (p. 77) Keyes discusses 'the rise of a middle class' during the Sarit era (beginning in 1957). This may also reflect a tendency to see the middle class not as a class but as a genera-tion (*run*) as Thirayut (1994) does.

9 See Reynolds and Hong (1983) and the special issue of *Pajarayasan*, 8 (June–July 1981).

10 Contrast this to what is surely a more accurate description of the non-student partici-pants in the 1973 uprising: 'government servants, shopkeepers, samlor drivers, workers, and the dispossessed of the city' (Flood 1975: 61).

11 Somkiat gained considerable popularity in the 1980s. In 1992, he sided with the mili-tary government against the uprising and lost his popularity among the demonstrators.

12 The success of advertising in shaping opinion has been aptly described by Dr Boonrak Boonyaketmala, Dean of the Faculty of Journalism and Mass Communications at Thammasat University: 'After TV our society has turned into an oral society, whereby a common culture is born. Consumerism is the common denominator, everyone feels he has to consume. Look, farmers now are wearing jeans and University of Chicago T-shirts. They see that in television [sic]. People now have similar frames of reference, the same views, the same tastes' (*Bangkok Post*, 4 August 1989: 7).

13 Given especially the ethnicising of the middle class prior to 1973, it may have been necessary to de-emphasise these differences in order to construct a class conscious-ness. With the middle class constructed, it then becomes possible to break it down by gender and ethnicity. One fascinating example of the way that ethnicity, gender and the middle class come together, is the rise of the cult of the goddess Kuan Yin (see *Bangkok Post*, 9 January 1995: 31f.). For an example of breaking the middle class back down ethnically, see Kasian (1994).

14 This survey is discussed in Sungsidh and Pasuk (1993b: *passim*. According to the survey some 52 per cent of demonstrators claimed an income of over 10,000 baht (US$400). This statistic is cited regularly. I have yet to see anyone write that some 48 per cent of the demonstrators made less than 10,000 baht. Nor does there seem to be any logical reason to select a cut-off point of 10,000 baht for the middle class.

15 Note the elements of the new rich that are excluded here: sales workers, taxi drivers, prostitutes, those without an education.

16 Leadership was provided by political parties and NGO leaders. Kanjana (1993) conflates the NGOs and the middle class: 'A handful of Non-Governmental Organizations (NGOs)…were leading and organizing the fight for democracy. The May NGO-university lecturers, doctors, lawyers and company workers. Those were the people who represented the so-called "middle-class" of the Thai society.'

Bibliography

Akin Rabhibhadana (1969) *The Organization of Thai Society in the Early Bangkok Period, 1782–1873*, Ithaca, NY: Cornell University Southeast Asia Program.

Anderson, Benedict O'G. (1977) 'Withdrawal Symptoms: Social and Cultural Aspects of the October 6 Coup', *Bulletin of Concerned Asian Scholars*, 9, July–September: 13–30.

Anderson, Perry (1980) *Arguments within English Marxism*, London: New Left Books.

Anek Laothamathas (1993) *Mob Mu Thu* (The Mobile Telephone Mob), Bangkok: Matichon.

Batson, Benjamin (1974) *Siam's Political Future: Documents from the End of the Absolute Monarchy*, Ithaca, NY: Cornell University Southeast Asia Program.

Blanchard, Wendell (1957) *Thailand: Its People, its Society, its Culture*, New Haven: HRAF Press.

Burris, V. (1986) 'The Discovery of the New Middle Class', *Theory and Society*, 15: 317–49.

Chai-anan Samudavanija (1991) 'State-Identity Creation, State-Building and Civil Society', in Craig J. Reynolds, *National Identity and its Defenders*, Clayton, Vic.: Centre of Southeast Asian Studies, Monash University.

Chanwit Kasetsiri (1992) *Kanpatiwat khong Sayam* (The Revolution of Siam), Bangkok: Praphansan.

'Chiwit khwampenyu lae laifasatai khon chan klang nai Krungthep' (Livelihood and Lifestyle of the Middle Class in Bangkok) (1986) *Khukhaeng*, 7, October: 119–32; 7, November: 72–6.

Ellin, Nan (1991) 'Constructing the Middle Class', *History of European Ideas*, 13 (6): 817–24.

Flood, Thadeus (1975) 'The Thai Left Wing in Historical Context', *Bulletin of Concerned Asian Scholars*, 7 (2): 55–67.

Frykman, Jonas and Lofgren, Orvar (1987) *Culture Builders: A Historical Anthropology of Middle-Class Life*, trans. Alan Crozier, New Brunswick, NJ: Rutgers University.

Giddens, Anthony (1980) *The Class Structure of the Advanced Societies*, London: Hutchinson.

Heinze, Ruth-Inge (1974) 'Ten Days in October – Students vs. the Military', *Asian Survey*, 14 June: 491–508.

International Advertising Expenditures (1963), New York: International Advertising Association.

Jiraporn Witayasakpan (1992) 'Nationalism and the Transformation of Aesthetic Concepts: Theatre in Thailand during the Phibun Period', Ph.D. dissertation, Cornell University.

Kanjana Spindler (1993) 'May 1992: When the Tide Finally Turned', *Bangkok Post*, 19 May.

Kasian Tejaphira (1994) *Jintanakam chat thi mai pen chumchon: khon chan klang luk jin kap chat niyom doi rat khong Thai* (Imagined Uncommunity: Lookjin Middle Class and Thai Official Nationalism), Bangkok: Phujatkan.

Keyes, Charles (1989) *Thailand: Buddhist Kingdom as Modern Nation-State*, Bangkok: Duang Kamol.

Khamhaeng Pharitanon (1994) *14 Tula: ratthathamanun si luad* (14 October: Blood Red Constitution), Bangkok: Bangluang.

'Laifsatai' (Lifestyle) (1987) *Khlang samong*, 5 July: 48–52.

Likhit Dhiravegin (1985) 'Social Change and Contemporary Thai Politics: An Analysis of the Inter-Relationship between the Society and the Polity', in Likhit Dhiravegin, *Thai Politics: Selected Aspects of Development and Change*, Bangkok: Tri-Sciences Publishing House.

Likhit Thirawegin [Dhiravegin] (1992) 'Kanchuangching amnat rawang thahan kap chon chan klang' (Contesting Power between Soldiers and the Middle Class), *Decade*, no. 2, May: 61–6.

Lipset, Seymour M. (1959) 'Some Social Requisites of Democracy: Economic Development and Political Legitimacy', *American Political Science Review*, 53, March: 69–105.

Mills, C. Wright (1956) *White Collar: The American Middle Classes*, New York: Oxford University Press.

Nakharin Mektrairat (1992) *Kanpatiwat Sayam pho. so. 2475* (The Siamese Revolution of 1932), Bangkok: Munnithi khrongkan tamra sangkhomsat lae manutsayasat.

Nithi Aewsriwong (1993), 'The Cultural Dimensions of the Thai Middle Class', in Sungsidh and Pasuk (1993b: 49–66).

Population and Housing Census 1960, 1970, 1980, 1990 (n.d.), Bangkok: National Statistical Office, Office of the Prime Minister.

Race, Jeffrey (1974) 'Thailand 1973: We Certainly Have Been Ravaged by Something', *Asian Survey*, no. 14, February: 192–203.

Reynolds, Craig and Hong, Lysa (1983) 'Marxism in Thai Historical Studies', *Journal of Asian Studies*, no. 43, November: 77–104.

Riggs, F. (1966) *Thailand: The Modernisation of a Bureaucratic Polity*, Honolulu: East-West Center Press.

Siffin, William (1966) *The Thai Bureaucracy: Institutional Change and Development*, Honolulu: East-West Center Press.

Skinner, G. William (1957a) *Chinese Society in Thailand: An Analytical History*, Ithaca, NY: Cornell University.

—— (1957b) *Leadership and Power in the Chinese Community of Thailand*, Ithaca, NY: Cornell University.

Sungsidh Piriyarangsan (1993), 'The Workers, the Urban Poor and May 1992), in Sungsidh and Pasuk (1993b: 321–41).

—— and Pasuk Phongpaichit (1993a), 'Introduction: The Middle Class and Democracy in Thailand', in Sungsidh and Pasuk (1993b: 26–39).

—— and —— (eds) (1993b) *Chon chan klang bon krasae prachathipatai Thai* (The Middle Class on the Path of Thai Democracy), Bangkok: The Political Economy Center, Chulalongkorn University and Friedrich Ebert Stiftung.

Suphawong Janthawanit (1991) *Kanjat chuang chan thang sangkhom: Kiattiphum khong achip tang tang nai sangkhom Thai* (Organising Social Structure: Status of Various Occupations in Thai Society), Bangkok: Chulalongkorn University.

Teeranat Karnjana-uksorn (1993), 'The Military and Business', in Sungsidh and Pasuk (1993b: 279–306).

Thailand Company Information 1990–91 (1991), Bangkok: A. R. Business Consultant.

Thailand in Figures (annual), Bangkok: Tera International.

Thawatt Mokarapong (1972) *History of the Thai Revolution*, Bangkok: Chalermnit.

Thirayut Bunmi (1994) *Suan nung khong khwamsongjam 20 pi 14 Tula* (One Part of Memory 20 Years 14 October), Bangkok: Winyuchon.

Thompson, E. P. (1968) *The Making of the English Working Class*, Harmondsworth: Penguin.

Thompson, Virginia (1941) *Thailand: The New Siam*, New York: Macmillan.

Vivat Prateepchaikul (1994) 'An Alternative Vision of the World', *Bangkok Post Year End Economic Review 1994*, 30 December: 74–6.

Voravidh Charoenlert (1993), 'The Middle Class and May 1992'), in Sungsidh and Pasuk (1993b: 117–54).

Weber, M. (1946) 'Class, Status, Party', in H. H. Gerth and C. Wright Mills (eds and translators), *From Max Weber: Essays in Sociology*, New York: Oxford University Press.

Wilson, David A. (1962) *Politics in Thailand*, Ithaca, NY: Cornell University.

Withayakan Chiangkun (1993) *Khabuankan naksuksa Thai chak 2475 thung 14 Tulakhom 2516* (The Thai Student Movement from 1932 to 14 October 1973), Bangkok: Grammy Publishing House.

Wyatt, David (1982) *Thailand: A Short History*, New Haven: Yale University.

Zimmerman, Robert (1974) 'Student Revolution in Thailand: The End of the Bureaucratic Polity?', *Asian Survey*, no. 14, June: 509–29.

100 wan wirachon prachathipatai (100 Days of the Heroes of Democracy) (1992), Bangkok: Thammasat University.

10 The state, globalisation and Indian middle-class identity

Salim Lakha

The celebration of the Indian middle class in recent years symbolises its dominant presence in the economy. To foreign investors and government officials, the middle class is a potential market and a testimony to the country's economic progress. Whereas in the 1960s and 1970s India's image was synonymous with poverty, in the 1980s and 1990s international attention has increasingly focused on the process of economic liberalisation and globalisation. The burgeoning middle class, which gained a new lease of life under a liberalised economic environment (post-1985), has emerged as a selling point for the country in international forums. Subsequent to India's further economic liberalisation in July 1991, a report in *Fortune* magazine announced that the country's attempt to enter the global economy offered ample 'opportunities', especially 'the chance to sell to India's huge middle class' whose expansion, it claimed, was more rapid than that of other sections of the population (Jacob 1992: 20). Similarly, at a business forum in Melbourne, India's Minister of State for External Affairs strongly promoted India as an alternative to China by highlighting his country's strengths, including an estimated middle class of over 250 million people (Caruana 1995: 61).

Viewing the middle class in terms of consumption or a consumer goods market is a common feature of many reports on economic liberalisation in India. The affluence of the middle class in India in recent years is closely associated with the process of economic deregulation at the domestic level and the opening up of the economy to global forces, both of which are intrinsic features of the liberalisation process. One report stated that the middle classes 'claim the economic reforms as their own', and that they have gained 'in terms of a greater variety of produce and greater purchasing power' (Uren 1995: 78). Another report confirmed such an assessment by quoting a middle-class employee of Indian Airlines who stated: 'I support liberalization. Globalization has led to an improvement in the quality of goods and a wider buyers' choice' (Chakravarti 1995: 91). By most accounts the middle class is expressing an insatiable propensity to consume as a consequence of rising incomes and a greater variety of goods offered through an increased exposure to global forces.

Whilst many reports highlight the rapidly growing size of the middle class and its predilection for consumerism, there is insufficient recognition of its transnational character and identity. The underlying assumption in this chapter is that the definition of the Indian middle class is not necessarily limited by space or political boundaries. In the context of globalisation, a rigid distinction between diasporic Indians and locally based Indians is not particularly meaningful.[1] Also, the emigration of Indian professionals through temporary employment contracts has contributed to a substantial circulation of people between India and other parts of the world. For example, the movement of Indian computer professionals (Lakha 1992) between India and countries such as Australia, the UK and the USA, amongst others, is an important trend in recent years and emphasises India's integration into the global information technology sector (Lakha 1994).[2] This integration has been facilitated by the global revolution in communications and transport which has intensified the world-wide flow of capital, commodities, information and people, and contributed to 'time–space compression' by reducing spatial and temporal distances (see Harvey 1989: 147 and 240).[3]

In India economic liberalisation has also accelerated flows of capital, technology and information by lowering the barriers to foreign investment and promoting the modernisation of telecommunications. Consequently, through these developments the articulation between middle-class diasporic Indians and their counterparts in India is assuming greater significance. The combination of economic liberalisation, diasporic Indians and short-term circular migration is contributing to a globalisation of the economy and lifestyles at a rapid pace, especially of the middle class in the metropolitan centres of India. Even prior to the substantial liberalisation of 1991, the influence of diasporic Indians was noted right across the cultural spectrum (Ghosh 1989). According to Ghosh: 'The culture of the diaspora is also increasingly a factor within the culture of the Indian subcontinent. This is self-evidently true of its material culture, which now sets the standards for all that is desirable in the metropolitan cities (1989: 73). Ghosh's observation is pertinent in the context of this chapter which argues that middle-class consumption in India is increasingly globalised, though not entirely at the exclusion of local style and cultural sensibilities. However, as this discussion reveals, the globalisation of consumption is not necessarily a reflection of cosmopolitan identities. Instead cultural identity is built around a tension between globalisation and local affiliations, including those of caste and religion.

This chapter focuses on the middle class because the way in which India's new rich are being represented in much of the literature is in terms of the 'middle class' (or 'middle classes'). This tendency arises because the middle class is growing in size and reflects the structural transformation under way in the Indian economy and society. As revealed in section three below, the discussions on the middle class in India encompass diverse socio-economic groups which some refer to as the new rich.

The chapter is divided into three sections, and begins with a discussion of the role of the state in the structural transformation that has contributed to the growth of the middle class in India. The next section considers the growth of middle-class consumerism in India and how middle-class identity is constructed through consumption. Section three takes into account some of the problems associated with definitions of the middle class, particularly in the context of journalistic representations, and the role of caste and religion in shaping the cultural identity of middle-class Indians.

THE STATE, ECONOMIC LIBERALISATION AND THE NEW RICH

In social and cultural terms, the role of the state has been most significant because it has allowed people who were outside the boundaries of the old rich to experience economic mobility and join the ranks of the new rich.[4] In the process it has fostered new social forces and cultural identities. However, the limits of state-sponsored development paved the way for India's economic liberalisation which, combined with the earlier emigration of professionals, has contributed in major ways to the globalisation of the Indian middle class. The middle class is a major beneficiary of liberalisation.

After independence in 1947, the state assumed a dominant role in industrial development and the promotion of higher education on which industrialisation relied. As Stern aptly states, 'India's industrial revolution was to be engineered from the top' by a state over which the English-speaking middle classes had a substantial influence (1993: 209–10). The beneficiaries of state-driven development included various socio-economic groups such as sections of the peasantry, the so-called labour aristocracy, the professionals, and both small and large businessmen and industrialists.

The state's involvement in industrial development is partly explained by the relative weakness of the indigenous bourgeoisie who, during colonial rule, remained subordinated to the interests of metropolitan capital and the colonial state. Even though the indigenous bourgeoisie managed to expand its economic base during the inter-war period, the lack of economic development at the time of independence generated hostility among the middle class who attributed the country's economic woes to the indigenous bourgeoisie (Khanna 1987: 48). Consequently, the middle class favoured economic planning by the state and encouraged state development beyond the mere provision of infrastructure facilities (Khanna 1987: 49).

The emphasis on industrial development in the first three five-year plans (FYP) (Hardgrave 1980: 80) beginning in 1951, privileged the role of the state in the country's economic development. During the period 1950–65, which encompassed the first three FYPs, the dominant economic objectives included 'self-sustaining growth in industry, transport, and energy' (Bhagavan 1987: 59). The country embarked upon a strategy of heavy industrial development in which the 'state planned, financed, built and controlled' a major part of capital goods and substantial sections of intermediate goods (Bhagavan 1987: 59–60).

Under Prime Minister Jawaharlal Nehru's version of socialist development, the state sector of the economy was viewed as the 'dynamic entrepreneur' creating technical and administrative-managerial positions for the middle class (Khanna 1987: 49). Stern confirms this claim by arguing that the middle classes acted as the 'planners, adjudicators and regulators, technical experts and managers' of India's industrial growth (1993: 210).

Whilst substantial sectors of the economy were owned or controlled by the state, private capital was not entirely excluded from industry and trade, and importantly, agricultural land remained under private ownership. Also, the small-scale sector was regarded as a means of broadening the 'entrepreneurial base' and counteracting the concentration of wealth and resources (Khanna 1987: 49). The considerable growth in small-scale industries has fulfilled the government's objective of expanding entrepreneurial activity and at the same time given rise to the 'new bourgeoisie' (Khanna 1987: 50–3).[5]

The expansion of small-scale enterprises is a significant social phenomenon which has transformed India's cultural, social and political landscape. It has created the new rich or a 'new bourgeoisie' whose social origins are diverse compared to the old bourgeoisie that existed in the pre-independence period when indigenous capitalists were confined to a relatively narrow social base.[6] For example, many of the indigenous industrialists then were Parsis, Jains and those from the traditional Hindu mercantile castes referred to as the *banias*. The regional origins of these industrialists were mainly Gujarat and Rajasthan (for example the Marwaris, and Gujarat (for example, the Parsis who migrated to Bombay).

In the post-independence period those who have risen through the ranks of small-scale industries belong to more diverse religious and caste groups. Their regional background is considerably varied, indicating a geographical expansion of capitalism in the post-colonial period. Those who have entered the ranks of small businessmen and industrialists (and progressed beyond in some cases) also reflect great diversity of educational and occupational backgrounds. They range from those belonging to the traditional artisan castes, to the highly qualified professionals from varied castes and religious backgrounds, though more likely of upper caste origins.[7] Politically, their allegiance is also varied depending upon their caste, religious and regional loyalties. However, there is some evidence to indicate that at least in urban north India the political proclivities of some amongst them are inclined towards the Bharatiya Janata Party (BJP), the right-wing, Hindu nationalist organisation. A similar political tendency is prevalent amongst sections of the professional middle class in the north as discussed below in section three.

Apart from the development of small-scale businesses and industries, the creation of an educational infrastructure by the state also broadened the ranks of the new rich, and created a major avenue for social and economic mobility. The development of the education system in India has been biased in favour of higher education leading to the creation of a vast pool of university graduates, whilst overall literacy has remained relatively low. The Indian system has churned out large numbers of graduates (Dedrick and Kraemer 1993: 470; Rudolph and Rudolph 1987: 298), but the relatively slow rate of growth of the economy has in the past failed to generate jobs at a rate commensurate with this outflow. Moreover, the limited range of employment opportunities and comparatively inferior working conditions lured many graduates of India's elite universities and institutes to Western countries, and other parts of the world, where better employment opportunities have been more readily available. It is these and other diasporic Indians who in various ways have been one of the important forces contributing to India's globalisation.

The state in India succeeded in expanding the industrial base and educational facilities, especially at the tertiary level, but the limits of state-sponsored development were evident at least since the 1960s (see Bhagavan 1987: 61–2; Khanna 1987: 49). The economic crisis experienced towards the end of the third FYP (1961/2–65/6), demonstrated that whilst the state had succeeded in promoting industrialisation, it had not realised the goals it had set for agriculture, employment and poverty alleviation (Bhagavan 1987: 61). According to Frankel, from an economic perspective the crisis experienced during the third FYP provided a strong case for a shift in favour of private capital (1978: 216), especially considering the limitations upon the state's ability to generate substantial resources for investments in industrial and technological development.

To attribute the crisis solely to an inherent weakness associated with state-sponsored development runs the risk of an oversimplification of the political-economic forces at work. The ability of the state to continue to play its former role in industrial development was constrained also by the prevailing coalition of dominant class interests, especially those of the rural elite, the industrial bourgeoisie and professionals in the state sector (Harriss 1989). Subsequently, with the first phase of economic liberalisation (or deregulation) in 1985, private capital increasingly gained access to the public sector, and the state gradually began to relinquish its hold over the 'commanding heights of the economy' (Bhagavan 1987: 72).

The benefits of liberalisation from the mid-1980s were realised mainly by sections of small and large business, the professional middle class and foreign capital. For example, the reforms initiated by the Budget in 1985 included lower taxes for corporations, individuals and owners of wealth; reduction in import duties for capital goods; tax incentives for exporters; and delicensing of twenty-five industries (Harriss 1989: 89). Foreign capital benefited mainly through more liberal investment incentives, especially for investors in export-oriented industries and through easing of import restrictions.

Increased liberalisation since July 1991 has accelerated the process of globalisation and privatisation of the Indian economy, further benefiting sections of the middle class, the local bourgeoisie and foreign capital. Policies have developed entailing a substantial reduction of state regulation over the economy, and a major commitment to privatisation of state-owned industrial and non-industrial ventures. Some of the important changes include: concessions to foreign capital which allow 51 per cent equity ownership; substantial reductions in import duties and licensing requirements; granting permission to Indian businesses to access capital from stock markets overseas; lowering of taxes; and gradual privatisation of public sector enterprises.[8]

By creating more space for private capital and initiative, liberalisation has heightened the interest of diasporic Indians in India's economy, which is reflected in the influx of professionals intending to settle in the country. Many of them are previous graduates of Indian tertiary institutes, motivated to return by a combination of factors including business opportunities, improved employment prospects, cultural ties and 'a sense of belonging' (Kuttappan and Shenoy 1995: 173–6). Whilst some of these overseas settled Indians experienced economic amelioration in their countries of adoption, they continued to feel culturally displaced. The influx and circulation of businessmen and middle-class professionals between India and the advanced countries is leading to a globalisation of technology, business practices and leisure habits. For example, some Indian computer and engineering professionals returning to India from the USA are setting up hi-tech enterprises in India involving substantial transfer of technology and business practices acquired through work experience abroad (Kuttappan and Shenoy 1995: 173–6).

A prime example of hi-tech development was the role of Sam Pitroda (an engineer and entrepreneur formerly resident in the USA) who returned to India to promote the modernisation of telecommunications during the 1980s (Raman 1987; Srinivas and Mathews 1996). Pitroda and the late Prime Minister Rajiv Gandhi, whose patronage Pitroda enjoyed, were both significantly responsible for sponsoring the 'computer revolution' in India. They symbolised the aspirations of India's middle class through their identification with modern technological development. Recently, Pitroda was appointed to serve on a committee advising the Gujarat state government on economic development in that state (*The Times of India* 1996). The profound impact of a diasporic Indian like Pitroda on technological modernisation in India cannot be underestimated and serves to illustrate the convergence of interests and identity between overseas Indians and the local middle class.

Economic liberalisation has also paved the way for an unprecedented exposure to global economic and cultural influences through substantial influx of foreign investments in industry and the opening up of media to satellite and cable television. Though foreign television companies cannot broadcast their programmes within India, they are not barred from doing so through satellite television which has transcended geographical and political barriers. The state television network Doordarshan, which until 1991 enjoyed a monopoly, now faces competition from satellite and cable television companies which has allowed Indian viewers a choice of numerous channels (*Asia Week* 1995a: 37). Consumer goods carrying foreign brand names are also rapidly spreading through the retail sector as a result of lower taxes and higher incomes for some among the middle class. Exposure to lifestyles of the affluent foreign countries through media advertising and television programmes is fuelling rampant consumption of semi-luxury and luxury items.

MIDDLE-CLASS CONSUMERISM: GLOBAL COMMODITIES AND LOCAL CONTEXTS

Since economic liberalisation, Western/global influences in business, entertainment, food, fashion and housing have intensified. Their impact on the middle class is greater because the middle class, through modernisation, Western education and family links with Western countries, is more exposed to these influences. Moreover, it is those in the middle class who can afford the relatively high-priced status symbols that are associated with globalised consumption. It is these status symbols, combined with education, that distinguishes them culturally from the lower classes. The distinction is vividly illustrated by visits to Lacoste and Benetton shops, or posh departmental stores like Ebony in Delhi, where the clientele is predominantly affluent.

In addition to liberalisation, the process of Western-oriented consumerism has also been aided by the transnational character of the Indian middle class. The middle-class diasporic Indians through their lifestyles and circulation of gifts have acted as a window to Western consumerism. According to one informant, those families who have connections with diasporic families always have different possessions that distinguish them from others. These possessions, she stated, were their status markers. An Indian sociologist from the prosperous state of Gujarat claimed that Indian immigrants in Britain and the USA are 'the reference group of the middle class in Gujarat' (Shah 1987: AN-163). One could broaden this claim to argue that generally diasporic Indians in affluent countries are regarded as a reference point by many middle-class people throughout India.

Since liberalisation, consumerism has permeated most sections of Indian society, albeit with uneven intensity and qualitative differences. An important indicator of the growth of the consumer goods market during the earlier phase of liberalisation in the 1980s was the rise in yearly sales of packaged consumer items (besides goods like unpacked food and garments) which increased to 220 per cent to reach US$2.2 billion in the period 1984–9 (Kulkarni 1993: 45). The 1980s experienced a substantial growth in sales of items such as TV sets, refrigerators, motor scooters and mopeds. For example, during 1981–90, TV sets increased from only 2 million to 23.4 million. In the following 2–3 years their sales were 6 million sets annually (Kulkarni 1993: 45). The growth of the consumer goods market has not eluded the attention of foreign investors and the United Nations World Investment Report predicts a likely 'boom' in foreign direct investment in the consumer goods sector in India (Shenoy 1995: 3).

However, the purchases of more expensive commodities, especially refrigerators, motor scooters and mopeds is concentrated amongst the middle class. According to one report, the share of relatively low-income households (less than Rs 18,000 per year in 1992–3; representing 58.5 per cent of the population) was smaller for more valuable and expensive consumer durables such as TVs, VCRs, geysers, sewing machines, vacuum cleaners, refrigerators, motor scooters, mopeds and washing machines (Rao and Natarajan 1994: 14 and 16).

The exclusion of lower-income earners from wider ownership of more expensive commodities is highly significant in terms of identity. According to McCarthy (1994: 121), for example, the ownership of a motor-scooter symbolises mobility from lower-class status to middle-class status. I would argue that with the progression of liberalisation and incomes, the motor car is increasingly overtaking the scooter as the marker of middle-class status, at least in the major metropolitan centres.[9] Whilst lower-class people aspire to the ownership of middle-class status symbol consumer goods, and a better education for their children, they find it difficult to engage in middle-class consumption because it stretches their relatively small resources, and the 'ultimate symbol of distinction' amongst the middle class, which is overseas travel, is well beyond their means (McCarthy 1994: 120–2). The former are, therefore, confined to emulating middle-class consumption through the consumption of inferior copies (McCarthy 1994: 46).

Access to good education, which is a most important channel for economic mobility and entree to global opportunities, is certainly beyond the means of the lower classes. Entry to prestigious schools and universities is highly sought after by the middle class, and stories of big donations to top schools to secure a place for children from middle-class families are common knowledge. Middle-class parents send their children to public schools or convent/mission schools where the medium of instruction is English, whereas others who cannot afford to pay the high fees resort to government schools where students are instructed in the vernacular.[10] An overseas university education for those who either do not manage to secure a place at a prestigious Indian university or prefer a foreign degree, is increasingly popular. The demand from Indian students for postgraduate business and information technology courses at, for example, Australian universities is rising. By seeking overseas education, especially in Western countries, Indian students are also cultivating an international professional identity which provides them with access to business and professional opportunities globally. Those who secure overseas professional employment and residency further enhance their status amongst the middle class at home because they are now more 'marketable' marriage partners, as is evident from matrimonial advertisements which boast possession of a green card (US residency) or, in some instances, solicit partners who have already acquired one. Like the motor car and other global commodities, a foreign education and residency are prime markers of identity.[11] In a culture where family bonds are still strong, those who have acquired foreign residency and an overseas job (especially in the USA or elsewhere in the West) are engaged in a process of economic and social mobility not only for themselves but also for their families in India.

The intense competition for jobs in an expanding labour force has also put a premium on the acquisition of higher education in middle-class families. Consequently, gaining multiple degrees is an additional advantage. In many cases the proliferation and professionalisation of occupations has increased the need for qualifications and higher education. Socially, amongst the middle class, education has now become an important requirement for a boy to find an educated partner, and for a girl to seek a professional husband. Utilitarian considerations have, to some extent, displaced the intellectual value associated with further education.

Through the influence of diasporic Indians, middle-class housing is assuming a distinctive image, style and status. This is particularly evident in urban housing. For example, the inflow of diasporic Indians, together with liberalisation of government policies relating to property investment, is contributing to a globalisation of the urban landscape as property development companies gear themselves to cater for their material comforts and aesthetic tastes. One report claims that an American-based company, NRI Resources Ltd, will embark on a housing project near Delhi's international airport which will offer 'luxurious' accommodation for 'select' non-resident Indians (NRIs) who require housing that is 'built and maintained according to the international standards of design, quality, landuse and property management' (*Business Line (The Hindu)* 1995: 4).[12] The project is not an exception and other residential constructions, for example condominiums, have sprouted in major cities of India to satisfy the tastes of both affluent local Indians and NRIs. Even the names of some of the housing estates and settlements possess a global resonance: Manhattan Apartments, Seawoods Estate, Xanadu, and Trinity Meadows which is 'designed' to replicate rural England (Raina 1995: 70–1)!

A perusal of the advertisements for such housing projects indicates that what they offer is not just the material comforts, but a distinct lifestyle and identity affordable only by the more affluent amongst the middle class. Thus La Gardenia Apartments near Delhi offer a dedicated amphitheatre, health centre and swimming pool, and the apartments and penthouses which are part of Adarsh Residency in Bangalore advertise a clubhouse amongst other amenities. These self-contained enclaves are distinguished both by their high prices and exclusivity, and it is the latter feature which is increasingly a mark of distinction.

Besides housing, external influences are also penetrating leisure and recreation in India, sometimes through the efforts of diasporic Indians employed by foreign companies. An Indian settled in Australia, for example, returned to India to set up Timezone leisure centres on behalf of the company that employed him. Similarly, another Indian from Australia was involved in the promotion of the construction of golf courses in India. The growth throughout India of holiday resorts that offer recreational facilities similar to resorts in the West is a response to middle-class demand for global leisure styles.

A major feature of middle-class consumption, therefore, is its predilection for global icons of consumerism such as television sets, cable television, videocassette players, personal computers, motor cars, a myriad of household items, fashion goods, leisure and recreation facilities, and exclusive accommodation and address for those who can afford it. Even magazines, both foreign and local, such as *India Today, Business India,* and others specialising in fashion and lifestyle, are a mark of middle-class status. Consumption of Western-style consumer goods and chic commodities is perceived as a distinctive feature of middle-class identity. A journalist friend from Mumbai (Bombay) lamented that middle-class children did not even consume local ice cream but only consumed Baskin-Robbins ice cream because they were so hooked on Western consumerism. This Westernisation is also observed with reference to language since the command of younger middle-class people over Hindi (a language common to north India) is weak compared to the older generation's. The tendency of some amongst them to mix English words when speaking Hindi is derisively referred to as 'Hinglish' by critics of Westernisation. Whereas the old bourgeoisie grew up with a sense of nationalism and was inclined to value the icons of Indian culture, the middle class or new rich today are less acquainted with traditional literature. The former were well versed in both the vernacular and English, but the latter are less fluent with the vernacular languages.

Because of its consumerism, the middle class is widely characterised as being excessively materialistic. Middle-class people are viewed as being money-conscious and only interested in someone if they have money. An expatriate Indian middle-class academic friend from Calcutta once remarked that the concept of service to society, associated with his father's generation, had given way with the new generation who were more individualistic. Certainly, the ideal of self-sacrifice and service set by Mahatma Gandhi is now confined to only small sections of the population. One informant observed that since liberalisation consumerism had risen dramatically with some among the middle class flaunting their new-found wealth without reservation.[13] Another claimed that liberalisation had benefited *banias* or businessmen and it had led to '*bania raj*'. It had, he said, promoted '*taraju raj*' (*taraju* in Hindi means scales), which was meant as a metaphor for the primacy accorded to economic/monetary considerations. An extreme and perverse manifestation of such materialism was noted in reports relating to sectarian/religious violence in Surat in December 1992 and January 1993 after the demolition of the mosque in Ayodhya in early December 1992 by Hindu extremists. It is claimed that some middle-class Hindus participated in the looting of Muslim shops during the riots in Surat and that these people were seen driving away with various items of clothing, footwear and jewellery in their Maruti cars (a distinctive status symbol of the middle class) (Chandra 1996: 85). Such incidents are certainly not a generalised reflection of the middle class, and the actual numbers involved may have been small, but they serve to illustrate a kind of acquisitive middle-class behaviour which is unprecedented during such sectarian conflicts.

Whilst global consumer icons and Western-style consumerism are on the rise, it would be simplistic to view their spread as representing the homogenisation of culture in India. Middle-class consumption of commodities is shaped by local contexts, and local cultural/social conditions continue to exert their influence in the face of global commodities and global media images and themes. Thus McCarthy in his study of middle-class families notes that status symbols like microwaves and vacuum cleaners acquired by some middle-class households remained unused because their domestic helpers viewed them as a threat to their skills and labour and thus resented their use (1994: 123).[14] He explains that despite middle-class complaints about less deferential attitudes of their domestic helpers, they are too reliant on them to impose their own preference for the use of these gadgets.

Displacement of local culture through foreign influence is not entirely confirmed, even though such concerns are often expressed by critics of liberalisation and globalisation. Undeniably, the spread of Western-style consumer goods, discos, pubs and Western television programmes is an ongoing feature of liberalisation. These influences, however, have not completely appropriated the local cultural domain, and in some cases there is adaptation to local tastes and even resistance. Western television programmes offered by Murdoch's Star TV, for example, did not manage to sustain their initial popularity, and the launch of Indian-language channels, such as Zee TV, has proved extremely popular (Karp 1994: 56–7). Though Zee TV and EL TV are joint ventures with Murdoch's Star TV, the former have adapted their programmes to local themes with modern content, and made them more relevant to the cultural context of middle-class Indians. When Murdoch was questioned in India about charges of cultural invasion levelled against his Star TV, he claimed that Star would localise its content by offering Hindi and other Indian-language programmes (Chengappa 1994: 50). It appears globalisation is, to some extent, bound by the demands of local culture. As in the case of television programmes, certain foreign-brand consumer goods have failed to make the expected inroads into the local market because they misjudged either Indian tastes or price competitiveness of local products (Bromby 1995: 9).

In some instances, however, the power of local television productions is sufficiently overwhelming to capture the imagination of both local and global audiences. Thus, the series based on the Hindu epics *Ramayana* and *Mahabharata* were avidly followed by the local audiences and, on video, by diasporic Indians in various parts of the world. Interestingly, they were appreciated by Hindu viewers as well as Muslim audiences, and to my knowledge by some Muslims in the West as well as in Pakistan. The different meanings attached to these epics by Hindu and Muslim viewers need to be further explored considering claims by some that the showing of the *Ramayana* may have contributed to a heightened sense of Hindu identity amongst the Hindus, especially in connection with the dispute over Ayodhya (Farmer 1996: 102–3; van der Veer 1994: 178). According to van der Veer (1994: 8–9), the televised series contributed in a major way to popularise 'a standard version of the epic' to middle-class audiences. As with the Hindu epics, the consumption of Indian films and videos of popular music and dance is not only locally based but is also common among diasporic Indians of all classes throughout the world. To that extent, it is a global phenomenon. Indeed, Indian films and popular songs have attracted even some non-Indian fans in parts of the world where diasporic Indians have settled.

Local cultural influences are particularly strong where food habits are concerned. Thus McDonald's, in deference to the cultural sensibilities of the majority Hindu population, does not offer beef hamburgers but instead uses mutton as a substitute. More importantly, to suit local vegetarian tastes, it offers a vegetable burger. The continuing popularity of Indian food amongst both local and diasporic middle-class Indians, and the adherence to vegetarian food, especially by many Hindu women both in India and overseas, attests to the dominance of local cultural identities and preferences over global/Western influences.[15]

Similarly, local dress codes continue to prevail, incorporating new chic variations to appeal to middle-class taste. Thus middle-class women still purchase expensive saris and stylish *salvar kameez* (trousers and long shirt), which are worn for everyday use and important traditional functions as well as Western celebrations such as New Year's Eve parties at five-star hotels and other venues. Brand names are an important consideration and these may not necessarily be Western brands but also good local brand names that offer a fusion of Western and Indian styles in clothing, such as *salvar, kameez* (or *kurtas*), saris, blouses and skirts. Such styles, designed by Indian fashion designers trained in the West and using local artisans, are important status markers amongst middle-class women. Subtle shifts in the mode of dress have been observed in the last few years in the wearing of the *dupatta* (scarf), which traditionally accompanies *salvar kameez*. Whereas in the past it was worn by women over the head as a mark of modesty, over time many women came to wear it only around the neck. In more recent years the *dupatta* has either got shorter in length, or is worn over the shoulder in a manner that middle-class women regard as stylish. In some cases it has been discarded altogether.

Significantly, chic *salvar kameez* are now even popular with middle-class diasporic Indian women from relatively Westernised communities that were initially settled in East Africa but which later emigrated to countries such as Canada. During the 1960s and 1970s in East Africa many of the younger women from these communities preferred Western dress, both for everyday wear and social functions, but now in Canada these same women have adopted stylish *salvar kameez* for parties and various celebratory functions. Thus amongst some diasporic middle-class women, stylish Indian dress has become as much a status symbol as chic Western dress.

The local sartorial preferences, however, do not detract from the appeal of Western clothes such as jeans, and the attempt by fashion houses to promote Western styles. For example, in India's most cosmopolitan city, Mumbai, an Indian fashion designer, Shahab Durazi, who is domestically regarded as the 'king of Western fashion' and who is inspired by the Italian designer Giorgio Armani, staged a fashion show aimed at shifting Indian executive women's attire from the traditional sari to 'smart', Western corporate wear like power dresses (Hariani 1995: 7). A few younger middle-class women in more cosmopolitan cities like Delhi, Mumbai and Bangalore have even taken to wearing shorts. This is part of a trend, amongst some in the middle class, for displaying the body in ways which in the past would have been regarded as taboo. Notwithstanding such trends, indigenous modes of dressing incorporating both chic local and foreign designs are more widely prevalent.[16]

Among middle-class Muslim women in India, the Muslim dress code is still widely followed, either through community pressure or individual preference.[17] Even when families or individuals emigrate to Western countries, there may be little or no concession to the dominant Western culture in matters of dress.

Needless to say Muslim women do not necessarily refrain from the consumption of other global commodities.

Whilst the appeal of Western fashion against traditional (or modern-cum-traditional) Indian fashion designs may still be limited, in other spheres, such as communications, the corporate imperatives exert stronger pressures to adopt Western/global practices. The spread of fax machines and mobile phones in major cities is gradually expanding. As in the advanced countries the mobile phone is a combination of status symbol, useful communications gadget and public nuisance (Chandra and Agarwal 1996: 94–5).

In the context of India's multicultural milieu, homogenised descriptions or explanations of middle-class consumption are unsatisfactory. Through liberalisation and associated globalisation, consumerism and the flow of global commodities are spreading rapidly in India, but middle-class consumption is mediated through local culture. Culturally the middle class is distinguished from the lower classes by the consumption of expensive, global commodities which serve as powerful status markers, but such consumption also defers to local conditions. The impact of globalisation on consumption is aptly summed up by one report which claimed: 'The new lifestyles – and the accompanying music, art and clothes – are all decidedly international, but with a distinctive Indian touch' (*Asia Week* 1995b: 40).

CONSTRUCTIONS OF MIDDLE-CLASS STATUS AND MIDDLE-CLASS IDENTITY

Consumerism and the consumption of global commodities are important in defining the cultural identity of the middle class. However, the existence of caste, religious and regional differentiation cautions against any homogenising attempts to characterise Indian middle-class identity in reference to consumption. The tendency by foreign and Indian media, as well as official experts, to define the middle class in terms of economic criteria and psychological motivations is also of limited analytical value as explained below. However, a discussion of these definitions is of some value in revealing how the middle class is constructed and portrayed in India and overseas.

Economic constructions of the middle class are most evident in journalistic and government reports, both in India and overseas. Sheridan (1995), in his report on India, delineates the middle class on the basis of discretionary income available from annual earnings. Similarly, an Indian-government-funded organisation, The National Council for Applied Economic Research (NCAER), estimated the size of the middle class based on the level of income (Kulkarni 1993: 46).[18] The argument in favour of income-based assessment is justified on the grounds that the diverse character of the middle class, which includes 'small businessmen, executives, professionals, white- and blue-collar workers and land-owning farmers', makes it difficult to define it on the bases of consumption and lifestyle (Kulkarni 1993: 45). The wide range of socio-economic groups encompassed in the above definition overlaps with those groups that are loosely labelled by some as the new rich. Such economic criteria beg the question of whether the diverse groups included under this middle-class label share the same opportunities and class interests.

For others, the middle class is more than an economic phenomenon and represents an attitudinal change. According to one advertising executive in India, 'The middle class is not just an economic phenomenon anymore. Driven by liberalization, the single biggest factor, it is an attitude towards life and straddles various economic groups' (Chakravarti 1995: 89). For this explanation, the pertinent factor is rising aspirations for more possessions across different income groups (Chakravarti 1995: 90). The Director-General of NCAER, who is an economist, concurs with the above view and prefers to label 'middle-income groups' as 'middle mass' rather than 'middle class'. He argues that since such attitudinal change has permeated most income groups, the middle class consists of almost 80 per cent of the population (Chakravarti 1995: 93)! Growing material aspirations amongst a cross-section of the population is not an entirely new phenomenon and for some commentators has been evident in the rise of the so-called 'new middle class' at least since the mid-1980s (Ninan 1990: 326–7). According to Ninan (1990: 327) the 'new middle class' includes the rich farmers, labour-elite, small businessmen-entrepreneurs, professionals, overseas workers in the Gulf region, and the salariat from diverse occupational backgrounds. Needless to say, the high-status global consumer goods that are popularly seen as the distinguishing markers of the middle class cannot be afforded by all the groups included above, and even less so by the majority of the population referred to as the 'middle mass'. The social elasticity of concepts such as 'middle mass' and 'new middle class' raises questions about their value for purposes of social and cultural analyses. In the definition of the 'new middle class' provided above, rich farmers are lumped together with professionals, labour elite and overseas workers. The differences in property ownership, incomes, life-chances, education and labour hierarchy between the various groups are significant enough to undermine or strain the possibility of shared interests and cultural identity.

Similarly, Marxist definitions of the middle class include varied socio-economic groups, but they are singled out on the basis of their relationship to the means of production. Thus one Indian sociologist, following a Marxist approach, refers to the middle class as 'a class between labour and capital which neither owns the means of production…nor does it, by its own labour, produce the surplus' (Shah 1987: AN-155). From this vantage point, the middle class is a class comprising the petty bourgeoisie and white-collar workers. This definition includes a variety of groups between capital and labour which are engaged in occupations that involve some 'formal education', but are otherwise distinguished by significant differences in income and cultural outlook as, for example, may be the case between highly qualified doctors and low-grade office workers.

Economic definitions of the middle class based upon income levels and 'rising aspirations' are inclined towards statistical exercises as demonstrated by various journalistic and government reports. Such exercises indicate that there are as many different estimates of the size of the middle class as there are estimators.[19] Studies of this ilk have provided statistics on the production and consumption of various consumer goods without illuminating much on the distribution of these goods or the cultural meanings attached to them by different sections of society.

A more rounded definition is one which combines incomes with lifestyle and occupation. Such an approach is evident in an Australian government report which estimates the Indian middle class at 120 million people, or approximately 14 per cent of the country's population. Those included in this category had enough 'disposable income to rent or own their residence, hold bank or credit card accounts, engage in holiday travel, own their own means of transportation, afford restaurant meals, and work in white-collar, increasingly service-oriented, jobs' (EAAU 1994: 32). Another estimate suggested more than 150 million people enjoyed middle-class status which was based on high educational attainment and an annual family income of over US$4,000 'in local purchasing power' (*The Economist* 1994: 78). These two definitions combine income, occupation and lifestyle criteria, and entail considerations that are comparable to those applicable to middle-class existence globally.

While these various attempts to position and quantify the Indian middle class offer some analytical or descriptive insight, they do not adequately consider the cultural processes and relations embedded in the construction of Indian middle-class identity. And, as shown earlier, contemporary Indian middle-class identity, particularly that of the influential new-rich elements, is largely constructed through lifestyle practices and media representations centred on the consumption of expensive global commodities. Associated with this, but having longer historical roots, is the acquisition of an English-language-based education. These are the major status markers of today's Indian middle class. And they are not accessible to all the social groups commonly included under the label 'middle class'. Neither are they characteristic of all who have money. For example, the rural rich, despite their substantial wealth, are commonly seen in the cities as lacking the cultural sophistication and taste codes associated with a globalised consumer middle class. These attributes are associated mainly with the urban middle-class professionals, who are in managerial positions in both the private and state sectors. Also sharing these attributes are the new entrepreneurs, some of whom are of urban professional background.

Yet, there is more to the cultural identity of the Indian middle class than consumerism. There is also caste and religious differentiation. One of the most noticeable features of the new-rich elements within the wider middle class is that they come disproportionately from the upper castes. A high proportion of urban middle-class professionals are from the upper castes as are many new entrepreneurs, although amongst the new entrepreneurs there has been a broadening of the social base in certain parts of the country to include those who have middle-caste origins. Some Muslims and other non-Hindus are also represented in these groups. Nevertheless, the upper castes tend to be dominant. The upper-caste presence among the professionals reflects both the historical nature of India's caste structure and colonial experience. Initially, the Indian middle class(es) was a creation of British colonial administration which promoted English education amongst Indians in order to create a cadre of administrators (Frankel 1988: 225; see also Misra 1961). Consequently, in the British period the middle class(es) included significant numbers of civil servants and professionals. Further, many of the educated Indians under colonial rule were of upper-caste origin, especially the Brahmans who constituted the literati of pre-modern India. Under the caste system, caste affiliation is ascribed by birth and corresponds to ritual status which is hierarchically ordered with the brahmins at the apex of the hierarchy (Dumont 1972: 70 and 106). British colonial rule largely worked through and consolidated this structure and its broad correspondence to class differentiation.

However, during the post-colonial period, a wider spread of education has resulted in many people of low- and middle-caste origins acquiring qualifications. The wider middle class in India, therefore, has socially expanded, but the proportionate representation, especially of the low castes, in the upper echelons of government administration and private corporate management is relatively small. Nevertheless, caste divisions and conflict have fragmented the broad middle class. Competition for university places and jobs is intense, particularly as economic opportunities have not kept pace with the expansion of the labour force. Under relatively slow economic expansion, the government policy of reserving a certain percentage of university places and civil service jobs for the middle and low castes has heightened inter-caste competition and tensions. In Gujarat, for example, agitations against the government's reservation policy pitted upper- and middle-caste groups against the low-caste new 'entrants' to the ranks of the middle class (Shah 1987).[20] Caste hostilities arising from economic competition and the reservation policy intensified in north India during the late 1980s and have persisted in the 1990s with varying degrees of intensity in different parts of the country. In the Indian context, therefore, a certain degree of tension exists between the two social categories of caste and class. Yet one line of disparity seems to be between, on the one hand, the new-rich component of the middle class who occupy more powerful, well-remunerated positions, largely in the private sector, and who are disproportionately upper-caste, and, on the other, a broader, less wealthy middle-class population who come from a cross-section of castes.

In the context of reservation (or affirmative action), the resistance of the upper castes has assumed the form not only of overt political action but also the articulation of an ideology that privileges the concept of merit. Thus it is commonly argued that preferential treatment on the basis of caste rather than qualifications is undermining the principle of merit which in turn has lowered the standard of administration and thus diminished the country's development prospects. Such claims are common amongst upper-caste, middle-class people opposed to the reservation policy, and even train accidents and other problems are blamed upon the filling of government positions with those allegedly lacking sound qualifications and merit. Significantly, these discussions and debates are not confined to Indians in India. Participants in the debates also include diasporic Indians who express their views at different forums, including on the internet. One may add that meritocracy is now an important dimension of the discourse of the globally oriented upper-caste middle class.

The situation is further complicated by religious antipathy between some Hindus and Muslims. Like caste, religion is an important dimension of middle-class identity. This has been highlighted particularly since the religious and sectarian tensions and violence associated with the demolition of the mosque in Ayodhya in December 1992, and the rise of the BJP as a political force, especially in north India, from around the late 1980s. The BJP, whose ideology and agenda are associated with militant Hindu nationalism, is notable for the support it has attracted from upper-caste, middle-class Hindus in rural and urban areas (Basu *et al.* 1993: 80, 88–9, 92; Desai 1996: 81–2; Chandra 1996: 85).[21] The support for the BJP in north India is explained by a variety of factors which include the party's origins in the north; its projection as a party of unity, set against the divisions and corruption in some other major parties; the party's criticism of Western economic and cultural domination through globalisation;[22] and its ideology of Hindutva, emphasising unity of Hindus and the nation at a time when upper-caste dominance is challenged by low- and middle-caste groups.

Hindutva, which regards religious and national identities as synonymous, is an important dimension of upper-caste, middle-class identity. Importantly, the appeal of Hindutva is transnational. Many diasporic Hindus are also influenced by Hindu nationalism through the activities of the BJP and its associate organisations, such as the Vishwa Hindu Parishad (VHP) (World Hindu Council) and Rashtriya Swyamsewak Sangh which are engaged in cultural and religious dissemination overseas (Basu *et al.* 1993: 78; Radhakrishnan 1996: xxix). The transnational character of ethnic and religious identities, however, is not confined to the Hindus. Sikhs and Muslims residing overseas have been similarly influenced by their respective religious and political organisations (van der Veer 1994: 114–15, 128–30). In the case of diasporic Hindus, many were clearly involved in the dispute over the mosque in Ayodhya. For example, donations were collected from local and diasporic Hindus from 1984 onwards for the bricks required to construct a temple on the site of the mosque in Ayodhya (Davis 1996: 40–1), and verbal and other support was extended by diasporic Hindus to aid the movement of religious nationalism in India after the demolition of the mosque in 1992. For the foundation of the temple at Ayodhya, the stones contributed by diasporic Hindus were most conspicuously displayed in order to highlight the transnational bases of Hindu nationalism (van der Veer 1994: 4).

A distinctive feature of the contemporary Indian middle class, therefore, is its growing inclination to cultural chauvinism. In large part, this unites new rich, upper-caste Hindus with some elements in the wider Hindu middle class, but marginalises the Muslims. In contrast to the pre-independence anti-colonial nationalism of some of the old bourgeoisie and middle class, substantial sections of the post-colonial middle class are increasingly characterised by religious nationalism.

Ironically, perhaps this shift is reinforced by the experience of globalisation among diasporic Indians. In the West, globalisation has led to greater ethnic diversity and, according to some commentators, an attempt by metropolitan peoples to come to terms with, or 'tolerate', the cultural differences within their countries (Featherstone 1993: 174). The perception of diasporic peoples of such tolerance may, however, vary considerably. Experiences of middle-class Indians in the West are replete with examples of covert and overt discrimination, and a sense of cultural displacement arising from their representations as Other in their countries of adoption. Thus cultural differences in the metropolitan countries often contribute to cultural and religious nationalism amongst sections of the migrant population whose transnational identities in turn impact upon the politics of both their adopted and home countries. Middle-class and non-middle-class diasporic Indians (Hindus, Muslims, Sikhs and others) are prone to appeals of cultural and religious nationalism. Thus Salman Rushdie's *Satanic Verses* created a political furore and agitated some Muslims not only in Britain but also on the Indian subcontinent. In India it stirred political controversy which led the government to ban the book there against the opinion of those in the country who believed that the ban breached the principles of secularism. Others, notably Hindu nationalists, interpreted the ban as an indication of the appeasement of minorities, namely the Muslims. Globalisation in this instance is implicated in the process of cultural and political fragmentation rather than homogenisation.

However, the experiences of the Indian middle class, both in India and overseas, are in some ways contradictory and do not necessarily lead to cultural chauvinism or religious nationalism. Support for the BJP and Hindutva is by no means unanimous among the middle-class Hindus. Indeed, the allegiance of the middle class is being contested by both the religious nationalists and secular-minded organisations. Thus secular-minded middle-class Hindus and Muslims in India, and elsewhere, have actively attempted to promote secular views and heal the sectarian rift. This is so in Australia, Canada, and the USA (Radhakrishnan 1996: 212), and probably in some other countries too. Middle-class identity, therefore, is strongly contested as are other cultural spheres in India (Appadurai and Breckenridge 1995: 6–7).

CONCLUSION

The growth of the middle class in India is integral to state-sponsored development. Through the provision of higher public education, and positions in the administrative services and state-owned enterprises, the Indian state has opened up major channels for social mobility and the growth of the middle class. Through support for small-scale industries, the state has also played a major role in giving rise to a class of new entrepreneurs. The limits of state-sponsored development, however, paved the way for economic liberalisation and globalisation. The deregulation of the economy, combined with the greater influx of foreign capital, technology, people (overseas Indians) and media influences, has contributed to a globalisation, not only of the economy, but also of lifestyles, especially among the urban professional middle class and new urban entrepreneurs. The state, therefore, has played a crucial role in economic development, as well as in the emergence of new social forces manifested in the growth of the middle class and new entrepreneurs. To the extent that these social forces have acquired a distinctive cultural identity through globalisation, the state is also implicated in the process of cultural transformation. This issue is worth emphasising since the development of cultural identity cannot be viewed in isolation from the political-economic processes associated with the role of the state in economic development.

In the Indian case, migration is a major consideration in globalisation and the construction of cultural identity, particularly among middle-class professionals and entrepreneurs. In addition to the flows of capital, technology and media images generated by foreign corporations, the transnational links promoted through migration have provided an important conduit for the diffusion of global and Western cultural influences. These are nowhere more evident than among the new-rich middle class. Through their lifestyles and investments, diasporic Indians are playing a particularly important role in influencing the material culture and consumption of the middle class in India.

Apart from consumption, middle-class diasporic Indians, through their transnational links, are also complicit in the spread of religious nationalism. By incorporating diasporic Indians within its fold, religious nationalism in India has come to transcend geographical and political boundaries. In short, transnational links have promoted transnational identities. Combined with technologies of communication and transport, migration has contributed to a transnationalism which entails, in the words of Basch *et al.* (1994: 52), 'the living of personal and political lives across geographical boundaries'. Tied to the imperatives of capitalist accumulation, the transnational identity of the Indian professional and entrepreneurial middle class represents an aspect of globalisation which in its broadest sense involves 'ever-intensifying networks of cross-border human interaction' (Hoogvelt 1997: 114). The implications of this process for culture and identity are complex, and deny any trend towards the homogenisation of culture across the globe; instead 'there are global cultures in the plural' (Featherstone 1990: 10).

Through increased interaction with global forces, professional and entrepreneurial middle-class Indians are developing lifestyles through the consumption of high-status global commodities. In doing so they are constructing a distinctive cultural identity, distinguishing them from the lower classes, the non-urban population, and even substantial segments among the wider middle class, all of whom either lack the financial means or the cultural attributes to emulate them. Consumption of global commodities does not, however, entail cultural homogeneity. The example of McDonald's is instructive because it is compelled to defer to local cultural sensibilities. Similarly, there is a preference for local television programmes with modern themes rather than a wholesale acceptance of foreign programmes. This accords with Appadurai's observation that: 'the central problem of today's global interactions is the tension between cultural homogenization and cultural heterogenization' (1994: 328). As Appadurai argues, rather than external influences from metropolitan countries leading to homogenisation, they are indigenised into local cultural forms (1994: 328). The fusion of Indian fashion with Western fashion in women's clothing underlines such indigenisation. Conversely, the spread of Hindu religious nationalism beyond India, through the agency of the middle-class Indian diaspora suggests, to some degree, a globalisation of the indigenous.

What I have argued in this chapter is that the new rich in India are to be found in the professional and entrepreneurial middle class, and that this is a global middle class. In part, its cultural identity is to be found in a lifestyle built around an English education and the consumption of high-status global commodities. But it is also constructed through particular caste and religious proclivities.

Notes

I am grateful to Professor Gyan Pandey (Delhi University) for his most helpful comments on this chapter. I would also like to thank Reena and Deepak Verma (La Trobe University) for their considered views on the new rich in Delhi and the surrounding areas.

  1 For Lavie and Swedenburg, the term 'diaspora' includes migrants, exiles and refugees who have 'dual loyalty', that is, on the one hand, their links to the places they live in and, on the other, the ongoing 'involvement' with their countries of origin (1996: 14). In this discussion the term 'diasporic Indians' includes non-resident Indians as well as earlier Indian immigrants who have settled for generations outside India. The latter, as in the case of many East African Gujaratis, have maintained their links with India either through marriage or business or both.
  2 The ramifications of this integration for communication between overseas-based Indians and their contacts in India are potentially immense as underlined by the example of an Indian computer professional working in Melbourne on a short assignment. He informed me that he regularly communicated with his family and friends through electronic mail (e-mail) which had made it possible to reduce his reliance on the less frequent and more expensive link through the telephone. Even middle-class professionals lacking e-mail links maintain regular communication through fax and telephone connections.
  3 'Time–space compression' refers to the acceleration in the 'pace of life' that has accompanied the development of capitalism and changes in communications and transport (Harvey 1989: 240). The onset of the Renaissance in Europe transformed perceptions of space and time by objectifying them. It thus paved the way for the control of space for purposes of power and profit. The process of 'time–space compression' has intensified with the shift from mass production associated with Fordism to flexible accumulation. This shift has witnessed shorter 'turnover times' of production which have altered the organisation of production and space, and brought changes in the spheres of consumption and culture. These changes are viewed as representing the postmodern condition (Harvey 1989: 240–59 and 284–307).

4 In the context of the argument of this chapter, the label 'new rich' is mainly applicable to the upper echelons of the professional middle class (especially in managerial positions) and the new entrepreneurs who have risen in the post-Independence period.

5 Small units are defined on basis of the capital invested in plant and machinery up to the limit of Rs. 35 *lakh* (*lakh* equals 100,000), that is, Rs. 3,500,000 (Mathai and Radhakrishnan 1990: 340).

6 Khanna's definition of the new bourgeoisie is wide-ranging and includes professionals who have entered business and industry; the ex-bureaucrats and their families and the families of politicians; non-resident Indian investors; entrepreneurs with links to trade involved in diversification; and members of the previous aristocratic, zamindar (landlord), banking and trading families (1987: 56–9). The last group are part of the old rich, though some may have experienced declining fortunes before moving into new business lines.

7 The upper castes are equated with the 'twice-born' *varnas* which comprise the *brahmins*, *Kshatriyas* and *Vaishyas*. At the other end of the caste spectrum are the untouchables (*avarna*) or the low castes, and located in between the two are the *Sudra* or the middle castes (Frankel 1988: 228).

8 For a business-oriented view of reforms see Butterworth (1995: 46–7). An Australian government perspective is provided by EAAU (1994: pp 65–82). For critics of liberalisation refer to Patnaik (1994) and Lakha (1994/95).

9 Apart from an increasing number of cars on the road in the big cities, the growing investment and intensifying competition (Bromby 1998: 10) between the car manufacturers are an indicator of this trend.

10 In the British tradition they are referred to as public schools but they are privately owned.

11 A degree from an average Western university, however, will carry less weight in the job market against a qualification from one of the prestigious Indian institutes of engineering, management and science. For those who do not gain entry to premier tertiary institutions in India, a foreign degree is still highly regarded.

12 The term 'non-resident Indian' (NRI) refers to Indian citizens who choose to live overseas for reasons connected with work and which indicates residence for an uncertain period.

13 An observation of one of the 20 Indian professionals in Melbourne who were interviewed as part of a pilot survey undertaken in 1995 to solicit their views on changes in India since economic liberalisation. All had visited India since the liberalisation of 1991.

14 McCarthy's sample of middle class includes individuals and families involved in entrepreneurial activities.

15 Some changes in the pattern of food consumption cannot be denied, for example greater consciousness of health considerations leading to consumption of vegetable oil as against ghee; spread of packaged foods and Chinese noodles; and the trend amongst some middle-class families to feed their children non-vegetarian foods.

16 Refer to Greenough for an interesting discussion of the incorporation of traditional crafts and craft designs into the furnishing styles and local fashion of the affluent in India (1995: 216–48).

17 A female informant in Gujarat related her observation of a Muslim academic colleague who would arrive for work wearing the *burka* or long gown worn by Muslim women but changed out of it before going in to conduct classes. Similarly, informants from Delhi observed that young Muslim female students came to college wearing *burkas* but left them in a common room before going to classes.

18 One report calculates the annual household income range for the lower middle class as Rs 18,001–36,000; middle middle class as Rs 36,001–56,000; and upper middle

class as Rs 56,001–78,000 (Chakravarti 1995: 91). The value of the Australian dollar in mid-November 1995 was approximately Rs. 26.

19 According to an Australian government report, estimates of the size of the middle class range from 100 million people to 250 million people (EAAU 1994: 32). Some reports claim even higher figures of around 300 million people.

20 The agitations occurred in 1981 and 1985 (Shah 1987: AN 163 and AN 167).

21 Though the BJP draws its support across the caste spectrum, it is the upper castes who are less equivocal in their backing for the party in comparison to the middle and low castes.

22 This criticism is welcome to sections of business and industry who fear that reducing tariffs as part of liberalisation will swamp the Indian market with foreign goods and squeeze out the local producers. Others are motivated by considerations of cultural nationalism and feel that the influx of Western cultural influences through television and other channels will undermine 'traditional values' amongst the youth and people generally.

Bibliography

Appadurai, Arjun (1994) 'Disjuncture and Difference in the Global Cultural Economy', in Patrick Williams and Laura Chrisman (eds), *Colonial Discourse and Post-Colonial Theory: A Reader*, London: Harvester Wheatsheaf.

—— and Breckenridge, Carol A. (1995) 'Public Modernity in India', in Carol A. Breckenridge (ed.), *Consuming Modernity: Public Culture in a South Asian World*, Minneapolis: University of Minnesota Press.

Asia Week (1995a) 'An Entertainment Bazaar', 19 May.

Asia Week (1995b) 'The New Indians', 14 April.

Basch, Linda, Schiller, Nina Glick and Blanc, Cristina Szanton (1994) *Nations Unbound: Transnational Projects, Postcolonial Predicaments, and Deterritorialized Nation-States*, Amsterdam: Gordon & Breach Publishers.

Basu, Tapan, Datta, P., Sarkar, S., Sarkar, T. and Sen, S. (1993) *Khaki Shorts and Saffron Flags: A Critique of the Hindu Right*, New Delhi: Orient Longman Limited.

Bhagavan, M. R. (1987) 'A Critique of India's Economic Policies and Strategies', *Monthly Review*, July–August: 56–79.

Bromby, Robin (1995) 'Middle-Class Market Offers Uphill Battle', *The Australian* (The Australian Special Survey: India), 25 January.

—— (1998) 'Industry Seeks a Middle Class', *The Australian* (India: Country Survey), 23 January.

Business Line (The Hindu) (New Delhi) (1995) 'US Firm to Build Villas for NRIs', 16 December.

Butterworth, Ley (1995) 'Investors Urged to Consider the "New" India', *Asian Business Review*, February: 46–7.

Caruana, Lou (1995) 'Call for Direct, Equity Investment In India', *The Australian* (Business and Finance), 20 June.

Chakravarti, Sudeep (1995) 'The Middle Class: Hurt but Hopeful', *India Today*, 12 April.

Chandra, Anupama and Agarwal, Amit (1996) 'Upwardly Mobile', *India Today*, 11 January.

Chandra, Sudhir (1996) 'Of Communal Consciousness and Communal Violence: Impressions from Post-Riot Surat', in John McGuire, Peter Reeves and Howard Brasted (eds), *Politics of Violence: From Ayodhya to Behrampada*, New Delhi: Sage.

Chengappa, Raj (1994) 'I am an Opportunist', *India Today*, 28 February.

Clifford, Mark (1995) 'Let There Be Cash', *Far Eastern Economic Review*, 6 April.

Davis, Richard H. (1996) 'The Iconography of Rama's Chariot', in David Ludden (ed.), *Making India Hindu: Religion, Community, and the Politics of Democracy in India*, Delhi: Oxford University Press.

Dedrick, Jason and Kraemer, Kenneth L. (1993) 'Information Technology in India: The Quest for Self-Reliance', *Asian Survey*, XXXIII (5), May: 463–92 .

Desai, Rashmi (1996) 'Witnessing Ayodhya', in John McGuire, Peter Reeves and Howard Brasted (eds), *Politics of Violence: From Ayodhya to Behrampada*, New Delhi: Sage.

Dumont, Louis (1972) *Homo Hierarchicus*, London: Paladin.

EAAU (East Asia Analytical Unit) (1994) *India's Economy at the Midnight Hour: Australia's India Strategy*, Canberra: AGPS.

The Economist (1994) 'Blinking in the Sunlight', 9 April.

Farmer, Victoria L. (1996) 'Mass Media: Images, Mobilization, and Communalism', in David Ludden (ed.), *Making India Hindu: Religion, Community, and the Politics of Democracy in India*, Delhi: Oxford University Press.

Featherstone, Mike (1990) 'Global Culture: An Introduction', in Mike Featherstone (ed.), *Global Culture: Nationalism, Globalization and Modernity*, London: Sage.

—— (1993) 'Global and Local Cultures', in Jon Bird, B. Curtis, T. Putnam, G. Robertson and L. Tickner (eds), *Mapping the Futures: Local Cultures, Global Change*, London: Routledge.

Frankel, Francine R. (1978) *India's Political Economy 1947–1977: The Gradual Revolution*, Princeton: Princeton University Press.

—— (1988) 'Middle Classes and Castes in India's Politics: Prospects for Political Accommodation', in Atul Kohli (ed.), *India's Democracy: An Analysis of Changing State–Society Relations*, Princeton: Princeton University Press.

Ghosh, Amitav (1989) 'The Diaspora in Indian Culture', *Public Culture*, 2 (1), Fall: 73–8.

Greenough, Paul (1995) 'Nation, Economy and Tradition Displayed: The Crafts Museum, New Delhi', in Carol A. Breckenridge (ed.), *Consuming Modernity: Public Culture in a South Asian World*, Minneapolis: University of Minnesota Press.

Hardgrave Jr, Robert L. (1980) *India: Government and Politics in a Developing Nation*, New York: Harcourt Brace Jovanovich, 3rd edn.

Hariani, Milika (1995) 'India's Armani Power-Dresses the Corporate Smart', *The Times of India* (New Delhi), 13 December.

Harriss, John (1989) 'Indian Industrialization and the State', in Hamza Alavi and John Harriss (eds), *Sociology of Developing "Societies": South Asia*, London: Macmillan.

Harvey, David (1989) *The Condition of Postmodernity*, Oxford: Basil Blackwell.

Hiro, Dilip (1976) *Inside India Today*, London: Routledge & Kegan Paul.

Hoogvelt, Ankie (1997) *Globalisation and the Postcolonial World: The New Political Economy of Development*, London: Macmillan.

Jacob, Rahul (1992) 'India: Open for Business', *Fortune*, August 10.

Karp, Jonathan (1994) 'TV Times', *Far Eastern Economic Review*, 15 December.

Khanna, Sushil (1987) 'The New Business Class, Ideology and State: The Making of a "New Consensus"', *South Asia* (New Series), 10 (2), December: 47–60.

Kulkarni, V. G. (1993) 'The Middle-Class Bulge', *Far Eastern Economic Review*, 14 January.

Kuttappan, Latha and Shenoy, Meera (1995) 'Return of the Techies', *Business India*, 4–17 December: 173–6.

Lakha, Salim (1992) 'The Internationalisation of Indian Computer Professionals', *South Asia* (New Series), XV (2), 93–113.

—— (1994) 'The New International Division of Labour and the Computer Software Industry in India', *Modern Asian Studies*, 28 (2), 381–408.

—— (1994/95) 'Resisting Globalization: The Alternative Discourse in India', *Arena Journal* (New Series), no. 4: 41–50.

Lavie, Smadar and Swedenburg, Ted (1996) *Displacement, Diaspora, and Geographies of Identity*, Durham: Duke University Press.

McCarthy, Paul (1994) *Postmodern Desire: Learning from India*, New Delhi: Promilla and Co. Publishers.

Mathai, Palakunnathu G. and Radhakrishnan, N. (1990) 'Small is Bountiful', in Robin Jeffrey (ed.), *India: Rebellion to Republic. Selected Writings 1857–1990*, New Delhi: Sterling.

Misra, B. (1961) *The Indian Middle Classes: Their Growth in Modern Times*, London: Oxford University Press.

Ninan, T. N. (1990) 'Rise of the Middle Class', in Robin Jeffrey (ed.), *India: Rebellion to Republic. Selected Writings 1857–1990* New Delhi: Sterling.

Patnaik, Prabhat (1994) 'International Capital and National Economic Policy: A Critique of India's Economic Reforms', *Economic and Political Weekly*, XXIX (12): 683–9.

Radhakrishnan, R. (1996) *Diasporic Mediations: Between Home and Location*, Minneapolis: University of Minnesota Press.

Raina, Monika (1995) 'Come Home to Luxury', *India Today*, 14 May.

Raman, P. (1987) 'The Hi-Tech Gift of Sam Pitroda', *Business World*, 14–27 September: 30–41.

Rao, S. L. and Natarajan, I. (1994) *Markets for Consumer Products in India*, New Delhi: National Centre for Applied Economic Research.

Rudolph, Lloyd I. and Rudolph, Susanne Hoeber (1987) *In Pursuit of Lakshmi: The Political Economy of the Indian State*, Chicago: The University of Chicago.

Shah, Ghanshyam (1987) 'Middle-Class Politics: Case of Anti-Reservation Agitations in Gujarat', *Economic and Political Weekly*, XXII (19, 20, 21), Annual Number, May: AN-155–AN-172.

Shenoy, Sujatha (1995) 'Higher Foreign Investment in Consumer Goods Predicted', *Business Standard*, (New Delhi), 16 December.

Sheridan, Greg (1995) 'Economic Reform Transforms a Giant', *The Australian* (The Australian Special Survey: India), 25 January.

Srinivas, A. and Mathews, J. (1996) 'The Man in Room 213', *Tycoon*, December: 24–8.

Stern, Robert W. (1993) *Changing India*, Cambridge: Cambridge University Press.

The Times of India (Ahmedabad) (1996) 'Pitroda to Co-ordinate Work of Development Panels', 26 December.

Uren, David (1995) 'Doing Business in the New India', *Business Review Weekly*, 20 March: 76–80.

Van der Veer, Peter (1994) *Religious Nationalism: Hindus and Muslims in India*, Berkeley and Los Angeles: University of California Press.

11 Entrepreneurship, consumption, ethnicity and national identity in the making of the Philippines' new rich

Michael Pinches

INTRODUCTION: A NEW ERA?

> Better times have come to the Philippines. After years of poverty and misrule, Asia's favorite basket case is proving that democracy isn't the enemy of development....A new era has clearly dawned.
>
> (*Time*, 15 May 1995)

When the article containing this statement appeared in the cover story of *Time* magazine, it aroused much celebration among government officials and sections of the elite and middle classes in the Philippines, in a similar way to *Time*'s cover story on President Corazon Aquino and the restoration of democracy several years earlier. Outside recognition that the Philippines appeared to be following in the footsteps of its more celebrated neighbours along the path of economic development and widening prosperity also came from other sources, and contributed to a growing sense of confidence among the privileged sectors of Philippine society.[1]

Even as the regional currency crisis of 1997 saw a downturn in economic growth, the Philippines was buoyed by the imminent conclusion to decades of dependence on the International Monetary Fund, just at a time when other, once faster-growing, countries in the region were having to negotiate assistance from the lending body. Public recognition from internationally respected media sources like *Time* magazine is held in high regard in the Philippines, underlining not only the ongoing influence of the American colonial and neo-colonial experience, but also the extent to which most Filipinos have increasingly come to identify themselves and their nation in relation to the success stories of their Southeast Asian neighbours. In a region of Tigers and Dragons, the Philippines has almost universally been portrayed as the exceptional failure, and has had to endure the label 'sick man of Asia' as well as the condescending advice of regional leaders like Lee Kuan Yew (*Far Eastern Economic Review*, 10 December 1992: 4, 29). Just as many Filipinos speak of their involvement in the popular overthrow of the Marcos regime as a moment of personal and national pride following a long period of shame, so more recently have many become animated with the confidence that at last they too belonged to a nation that is heading down the road to dragonhood.

This position has been most widely expressed in government and business circles, and among those with newly acquired wealth. Within the middle and upper layers of Philippine society, there is clearly a new optimism, and considerable consensus around the Ramos regime's Philippines 2000 platform, which has the nation achieving Newly Industrialising Country status by the year 2000. The rhetoric of national development is hardly new, and it is not as if the Philippines has not experienced earlier periods of comparatively rapid growth. Nevertheless, it is significant that while the developmental rhetoric of the Marcos years was closely orchestrated by the state, in recent years it has been coming from a range of sources, most notably from within the growing bourgeoisie and middle classes (Pinches 1996). Since 1986 there has been a proliferation not only of daily newspapers, but also of local business and society journals with titles such as *Manila Inc.*, *Philippine Business* and *Asia Lifestyle*. They regularly speak with optimism about 'economic take-off', entrepreneurial success stories and growing prosperity. Some of their commentators speak of the Philippines' 'leapfrogging from an agricultural stage to the post-industrial stage' (Talisayon 1994: 27).[2] In the influential *Philippine Business*, for example, the Rizal Commercial Banking Corporation runs a regular page called 'Dragon Forecast'. In one issue, it describes the future of the Philippines with confidence:

> The trek to dragonhood will take many small steps, from one day to another, not one giant leap....That's how big dragon Japan and the new dragons like Singapore got to be where they are today. And that's how we ourselves are going to find our way to dragonhood....Just like what happened in Japan, mini-booms in regional growth centers will create ripple effects, spreading progress to the outer rims in concentric circles.
>
> (1994, 1(3): 27)

There are some who are deeply sceptical about the claim that the Philippines has entered a new era of growing prosperity. Critics rightly point to the massive poverty that persists both in the countryside and cities, and one only has to talk to factory or department store workers to discover that many Filipinos are missing out on the benefits that are said to come with increased national economic growth figures. Yet even critics acknowledge that growth is taking place, and that there are increasingly visible layers of people who are prospering. The optimism and developmental rhetoric that is to be found in the Philippines today may not accurately represent the state of the nation, but nor is it complete fantasy. It is most indicative of the experience and ideology of the country's new rich.

While economic growth figures give some insight into the transformation that has been taking place in the Philippines, a clearer indication of the increase in private wealth among a growing minority of Filipinos is to be seen in the changing landscapes of the major cities.[3] In Manila and Cebu City, the two largest urban centres, there has been a marked surge in the construction of expensive residential subdivisions, town houses and condominiums with such names as North Olympus and Richville Mansion. Residential property values have soared. More and more land is being devoted to expensive golf courses and there has been a dramatic increase in the numbers of shopping malls and restaurants. Manila now has at least twenty major shopping malls and many smaller ones. Cebu City's mayor boasts that one of the city's new malls is the fourth largest in the world, and that the Megamall in Manila is the third largest. While, in part, the malls simply cater to a growing urban population and reflect a world-wide shift in the spatial organisation of shopping and leisure, they are also associated with heightened spending power in the Philippines. In addition to their cheap mass-market commodities, they are noteworthy for a wide range of luxury goods, designer-label boutiques, expensive gift and specialist novelty shops, coffee lounges, restaurants and fitness clubs. Finally, the clogging of Manila's and Cebu City's roadways has rapidly deteriorated as a direct consequence of the huge increase in late model private cars and taxis. According to one market researcher, about half of the cars in Manila are less than two years old.

In this chapter I focus on the main layers of people who are commonly equated with this growth: the new rich. In particular, I consider the contradictory ways in which they are represented in reference to the country's old elite, to whom they pose a considerable cultural challenge.

THE RISE OF THE PHILIPPINE NEW RICH

Over the past decade and a half, most commentators have represented the Philippines as a society that has undergone little substantial change since the 1960s, except for the interlude of a plundering dictator and his popular overthrow. As I have argued elsewhere, there are major deficiencies in this characterisation (Pinches 1996, 1997). Despite the lack of spectacular or sustained economic growth over this period, the Philippines has undergone continuing capitalist transformation in ways structurally similar to what has been taking place in most other countries in the region. As has been the case elsewhere, this transformation has seen the emergence of peoples who can be described as newly rich (Pinches 1996).

While this chapter concentrates mainly on those new rich who have risen to prominence since the overthrow of the Marcos regime in 1986, it should be noted that there have been earlier generations of new rich whose presence has contributed to the social and cultural dynamics of the contemporary era. At the time of independence in 1946, the Philippines was predominated over by a landed oligarchy whose wealth and power centred primarily on agricultural production and access to political office. In large part, the families who made up this oligarchy behaved as feudal aristocrats, and most were better known for their high living and political prowess than for their economic acumen. During the 1950s and 1960s, some sections of the landed oligarchy became urban capitalists through investments in manufacture, banking, real estate and agribusiness. The growth of home-market manufacture during this era also saw the emergence of a new layer of capitalists from backgrounds in petty trade and middle-class employment. Other layers of new capitalists emerged during the authoritarian Marcos era (1972–86): some through substantial political patronage across a range of economic activities; others, more or less independently, mainly through the growth of export manufacture. Though many capitalists have failed or left the country, most notably during the economic crisis at the end of the Marcos era, each of the above layers is represented in today's class of Filipino capitalists.[4]

Many of the most prosperous new rich capitalists in the Philippines started out in these earlier periods, but have greatly multiplied their wealth and economic activities in the post-Marcos era. Some of them now have business empires and family fortunes which surpass those of many old elite families. While members of the old elite continue to dominate much of the Philippine economy, they have done so only by reorienting themselves to the changing economic environment. Those who have relied solely on old forms and areas of wealth accumulation have generally suffered downward social mobility.

Since 1986, many new capitalist enterprises have been spawned through growth in retail trade, manufacture, banking, real estate development and an expanding range of specialist services like accounting, advertising, computing and market research. Fostered by government policies of liberalisation and deregulation, the development of these new enterprises has been oriented both to the export and domestic markets, and has entailed increasingly diverse sources of foreign investment and variable subcontracting, franchise and service relationships, with a noticeable expansion of ties connecting the Philippines to other countries in East and Southeast Asia.[5] A substantial stimulus for many capitalists, small and large, new and old, has been the growth of the domestic consumer market around the repatriated earnings of the 4 million-odd Filipinos who have left the country for overseas contract work.[6]

Much more numerous than the owners of large business empires are the new capitalist entrepreneurs in medium- and small-scale enterprises, many of them subcontractors or franchise holders, others more independent operators in retail, business services, construction and recreation. Little systematic research has been done on the growth of these businesses, and on the backgrounds of those who own or run them. The material that is available, including my own interviews, indicates that many of these new capitalists are women, former salaried professionals, middle-class Filipinos returning from periods of residence in North America or Europe, and people with a background in even smaller businesses.[7] Only a small minority appear to have been overseas contract workers. The most visible of these new capitalist entrepreneurs are to be found in the many new shopping malls, as the owners of boutiques, restaurants, food outlets and gift shops, in some cases linked to small factories or workshops located elsewhere.

Since independence, other Filipinos have experienced new wealth by becoming part of the educated urban middle class, both through state employment and salaried positions in capitalist enterprise. However, middle-class incomes are generally low in comparison with other countries in the region (Crouch 1985: 32; *FEER*, 28 August 1997: 56). This has prompted large numbers of highly qualified Filipinos to find work overseas, both in salaried middle-class occupations, but also in domestic labour and other manual positions. Nevertheless, middle-class incomes are also highly varied, and over the past decade, in particular, new layers of salaried managers and professionals have risen to positions of prosperity. These relatively highly paid positions have multiplied on the strength of an expansion in corporate capital, both foreign and local, and, in the latter case especially, on the basis of the increased professionalisation of company management. They have also multiplied through the growth of smaller companies in such areas as computer services and advertising. The incomes and social standing of the new-rich middle class rest heavily on their educational credentials and the prestige of the universities they attended. Those who have studied overseas, or at one of the select local universities, gravitate much more easily to the most senior, well-remunerated positions. The high disposable income of many salaried managers and professionals today is partly a consequence of them marrying late, marrying each other and having few children.

An important feature of the new rich in the Philippines is the absence of a clear divide between the salaried new middle class and the new capitalist entrepreneurs. Increasing numbers of salaried professionals have established highly successful businesses. In some cases they have left their salaried positions behind; in other cases, for instance among a number of academics and architects I am familiar with, they have successfully maintained both activities. Many women have built up prosperous small- or medium-sized businesses in partnership with their salaried husbands, some of whom join their wives if the business becomes the more lucrative income source.

How have the above changes been represented in the Philippines; what cultural dynamics have they entailed; and in what ways have the new rich challenged the hegemony of the old? The principal reference point for the cultural construction of the new rich has been the identity and reputation of those described as the old elite or landed oligarchy. Notwithstanding the above-mentioned shifts that have taken place among those who have descended from this elite, they have continued to be identified – by themselves and by others – in much the same way as were their ancestors, that is as a quasi-nobility. This elite emerged from the Spanish era as a powerful class of landlords and educated intellectuals (*ilustrados*) (Wickberg 1964; Constantino 1978: 115–28). During the American colonial period in the first half of the twentieth century, they consolidated their privileged standing, and widened it into the formal political sphere. A number of intersecting ideological principles are entailed in the identity that grew around this elite. While some members are identified as the descendants of Malay Filipinos who made up the early native *principalia* (Spanish colonial bureaucracy), the elite, as a whole, is more generally identified as being *mestizo*.[8] A small minority are identified as Spanish-Filipino.

The *mestizos* came into being as a distinctive social and legal entity during the Spanish era, having come from mixed Malay, Chinese and, to a lesser extent, Spanish ancestries. The *mestizo* identity came to be associated not only with propertied wealth, but also with a lifestyle and outlook that was successively hispanised and americanised, in the tradition of both colonial rulers (Wickberg 1964; Constantino 1978: 115–28; McCoy 1981; Tan 1985: 53–4). The *mestizos* generally came to embody ideas of worldliness, sophistication, refinement and high culture, cultivated, in large part, through a privileged formal education, and defined in counter-distinction to indigenous Malay Filipino villagers and urban workers. And, in contrast to the latter, the *mestizos* came to associate themselves with the qualities of natural beauty and intelligence.[9] As landlords, clergy, politicians and intellectuals, the idealised vision of the *mestizo* and Spanish-Filipino elite saw them as generous, caring patrons and philanthropists. From their clients, and from the broader populace, they came to expect service, respect and ritual deference. The most prominent among the elite assumed the Spanish appellations *Don* and *Doña*, titles that are still used in some quarters.

While these various constructions together defined the broad cultural boundaries of the elite, they did not always coincide. Many individuals identified as *mestizo*, for instance, were not wealthy landlords and lived more modest lives. Nevertheless, the elite was identified within these loose boundaries. At its core, it came to be known through a series of named and interconnected family dynasties, commonly associated with particular regionally based ethno-linguistic groups.[10] In the regions in which they are most powerful, and in large urban settings, the mere utterance of these family names generally evokes most of the above cultural connotations. Despite a good deal of change in the activities, livelihood and social organisation of these families, the aura of cultural eminence outlined here continues to surround the present generation of descendants who, in various ways, endeavour to protect their privileged standing.

Nevertheless, the cultural eminence of the old elite has long been challenged from a number of sources, through popular secular and religio-political movements, as well as through the 'everyday' practices and discourses of peasants and workers.[11] With the growth of a middle-class intelligentsia, less beholden to the oligarchy than their *ilustrado* forebears, there has also developed an influential nationalist ideology which has been particularly critical of the old elite for their 'colonial consciousness' and lack of commitment to national development.[12] Not only was the landed oligarchy represented as an enemy by the two major post-independence communist movements; it was also singled out by President Marcos as the principal reason for the Philippines' economic backwardness (Marcos 1978: 17–22), and hence as a justification for the New Society that was supposed to be heralded in by the declaration of martial law in 1972. Though some of the oligarchic families, partially disinherited and disempowered by the

Marcoses, have again become prominent, the Aquino and, to a greater extent, the Ramos governments have also promoted a rhetoric of national development which questions the exclusive economic privileges and leisured lifestyles associated both with the old elite and with Marcos's crony capitalists. In this case it has been a largely economic rhetoric about hard work and liberalisation. According to one of President Ramos's chief advisers and former fellow military officers:

> Despite our well-known political volatility, our basic problem may really be excessive stability – the continuance over several centuries of a political-economic system that has enabled a small elite to control social wealth, not through its possession of capital or skill at entrepreneurship, its industry or its superior intelligence, but through its monopoly of political power.
>
> (Almonte 1990: 2)

But more than the liberal economic policies and political rhetoric that have come with the post-Marcos era, the major challenge to the privileged social and cultural standing of the old elite has come from the new rich. This challenge and the response to it have been played out through the alternate cultural constructions of the new rich as meritorious entrepreneurs and as conspicuous consumers, one elevating the new rich, the other degrading them. Of central importance to each of these constructions are three others: Filipino national identity, Filipino-Chinese ethnicity and the generational idea of a 'new breed'.

'BUILDING A NATION OF ENTREPRENEURS'[13]

The closest Filipino expression to 'new rich' is the pejorative *biglang yaman* (suddenly rich), which implies that the person so labelled has acquired wealth in an underhand way, rather than through talent or hard work. Among the working classes and peasantry this still appears to be the dominant characterisation of people who are newly rich.[14] It is often said of such people that they will fall as quickly as they have risen (*biglang taas, biglang bagsak*). The pejorative characterisation is also used among the middle classes and elite, and forms part of the negative discourse on corruption that gained ground in response to the practices of cronyism under Marcos.[15] However, though the rich are probably more closely scrutinised than ever, the negative characterisation of the new rich among the privileged classes is increasingly giving way to their representation as meritorious entrepreneurs.[16]

A key element to current developmental rhetoric in the Philippines is the idea that national advancement is taking place primarily through private initiative, rather than the heavy-handed directives of an authoritarian state, or the corrupt, inefficient practices of Marcos-era crony capitalism.[17] Privatisation, liberalisation and level playing fields have become important tenets of the Ramos administration's language of progress, and, to the extent that state-corporate assets have been privatised, tariff barriers reduced and monopolised sectors of the economy opened to competition, there has been wide, if not unanimous, support among business people and the broad middle classes.[18]

The ethos of private enterprise that has become so popular in the middle and upper reaches of Philippine society, finds clearest expression in the rhetoric of entrepreneurship that has become associated with the Philippines' new rich. Entrepreneurial behaviour, and the upward social mobility of those who are seen to have practised it, are celebrated in numerous tales of people who have made good through hard work and business acumen. These narratives constitute much of the subject-matter of the local business magazines *Say*, *Filipino Entrepreneur*, *Manila Inc.*, *Philippine Business* and *Young Taipan*, and are also regularly presented in daily newspapers, television programmes, speeches at civic functions and business training courses. Invariably they emphasise initiative, vision, diligence, resourcefulness and perseverance in the face of setbacks and risks; in short, the qualities that one finds listed in many textbooks on entrepreneurial behaviour.

For the new rich themselves, as well as for those who admire them, the experience of success seems proof enough that these qualities will win out if given free rein. According to one academic who teaches business administration at one of Manila's premier universities, the principal ambition of students had long been to become a professional manager in a large corporation, but since the late 1980s, she says, most graduates leave university in the hope of setting up their own businesses. The celebration and rhetoric of entrepreneurship turn private success into the idea of national advancement. They give new status and respectability to the successful, and help to open the way for some of them to a social, as well as economic, position alongside members of the old elite.

In part, the appeal of entrepreneurship and unencumbered private enterprise among the middle and upper echelons of Philippine society, lies in the country's long exposure to the American ideas of economic liberalism and electoral democracy. These ideas continue to be cultivated among scores of wealthy Filipinos who study in North America and other liberal democratic societies. The appeal of these ideas also arises out of the unpopularity and economic calamity of authoritarian rule under Marcos.

But perhaps more than anything else, the celebration of these ideas needs to be understood as part of the attempt to elevate the status of Philippine national identity in the context of the shifting geopolitical environment of Southeast and East Asia. At the same time as the power of the United States in the Philippines and the Pacific has been receding, the influence of neighbouring countries with booming economies and authoritarian regimes has been growing. Not only has the Philippines been left behind economically by these countries, but in the process its elite has been humiliated and its national reputation demeaned. Some elite and middle-class Filipinos travelling to Hong Kong, Singapore and Malaysia, as well as to parts of Europe, have been appalled to find that Filipino nationals are often thought of, in general, as domestic servants. Increasingly, those in the privileged classes have come to see the often racist mistreatment of Filipino overseas contract workers as an attack on their own national and personal identities. Thus, the popular outrage that was vented against

Singaporian authorities for their execution of Filipino maid Flor Contemplacion in 1995, was as much a response to what was regarded as a national insult as it was an expression of concern about the treatment of Filipino workers (Pinches n.d.). Much of this outrage crystallised around a contrast between draconian Singapore and democratic Philippines.

The idea of democracy, dramatically celebrated and reasserted with the overthrow of the Marcoses in 1986, has thus become a national symbol around which many Filipinos have come to distinguish and elevate themselves and their future dragonhood, in relation to their neighbours. Two businessmen I spoke to expressly claimed that because of the Philippines' democratic and free enterprise traditions, Filipino executives had a greater capacity for initiative and flexibility, and thus had a distinct advantage over their counterparts in countries like Singapore. This, they believed, would be one of the country's assets in its push for national prosperity.[19] According to Gloria Tan-Climaco, one of the new guard of young corporate chief executive officers:

> I do not wish for the Philippines to become just a tiger....[W]e want to be better. I wish for the Philippines to become an eagle. Lightning-fast, aggressive, fierce...but also graceful, stately, caring. There is no more time to lose. For the past twenty years, we have seen our neighbor nations rise...to overtake us in the development race. We pride ourselves in having a trove of natural resources, an abundance of skills. Yet, we are left behind, simply because even now, after the cathartic experience of the People Power Revolution which freed us from the shackles of authoritarianism, we remain bound by the chains of selfishness. We must learn to work together, revive the *bayahihan* spirit for which we were known in the ancient world, and carry the burdens of our problems on our collective shoulders.
>
> (1994: 30).[20]

More than any other group, new-rich entrepreneurs have come to embody and exemplify the new hope attached to a national identity built around the ideas of economic development, freedom and democracy. While the rhetoric of entrepreneurship has been developed in relation to the new rich in general, it has particularly been focused on the Filipino-Chinese. To the question 'Who are the new rich?', most non-Chinese-Filipinos respond that they are the Chinese. Many Filipino-Chinese say the same (c.f. See and Chua 1988: vi). Several names in particular are commonly singled out in discussions of capitalists who have now joined the ranks of the nation's corporate billionaires. They are nicknamed the *Taipans*.[21] Seizing upon the shift in national fortunes which these men seemed to embody, President Ramos recruited six of them to form 'Asia's Emerging Dragon Corporation' to contribute to the government's Philippines 2000 programme (*Business World* 1994: 104–33; Gonzaga 1994).[22] While these very rich Filipino-Chinese capitalists are the best known, there are many others who have established newly prosperous business enterprises, and who are seen as indicative of the ethnic Chinese capacity for accumulating wealth through adherence to the values of diligence and thrift. Indeed, this has long been part of the stereotype of the Filipino-Chinese among non-Chinese Filipinos. It is also a common image the Filipino-Chinese hold of themselves (See 1988; Chua 1988a; See 1990: 86–93), as distinct from Filipinos whom some see as stereotypically lazy, poor, dependent and wasteful (Chua and Herrin 1988: 91; Chua 1988b: 108; Pacho 1986: 88).

Today the values of diligence and thrift, and their association with the Chinese, are celebrated and deferred to in ways that appear quite unprecedented. A number of non-Chinese businesspeople, academics, journalists and officials I talked with spoke of the Chinese entrepreneur as offering a role model that Filipinos should follow in order to bring about national prosperity.[23] Some explicitly invoked the culture of Confucianism and linked this to the success of Chinese capitalists elsewhere in the region (see also dela Cruz 1994). According to one rising entrepreneur:

> The Chinese scrimp and save, and live frugally until they have a lot of wealth, whereas we Filipinos have a tendency to conspicuous consumption. We could do better in the Philippines if we saved and deferred consumption, that is if the entrepreneurial class lived like the Chinese.

Clearly the stereotype of the Filipino-Chinese as successful new-rich business-people in possession of some intrinsic ethnic quality that enables them to accumulate wealth ignores the many Chinese who are materially unsuccessful or who perform a range of other occupations (See 1990: 26–30; von Brevern 1988), including a growing number which might be described as new middle class. Indeed, it is ironic that at the same time as Chinese entrepreneurship is being most reified and celebrated, increasing numbers of young Filipino-Chinese are leaving family businesses to become salaried professionals. The stereotype also ignores the historical role that racism has played in containing many Chinese in commerce, as well as fostering among them relations of mutual trust, which are often seen as central to their economic success (Omohundro 1983). Nevertheless, according to one Filipino-Chinese author: 'Many Filipinos harbour the false notion that the success of the Chinese must be due to something mysterious and/or mystical in their culture, hence, they send their children to Chinese schools' (See 1990: 5). Adopting an apparently more cynical stance, one non-Chinese Filipino business family is reputed to have taken on a Chinese name because they say it is better for business.

The popular representation of the new rich as Chinese evidences complex changes that are taking place in Philippine society and the Asian region. Rather than reflecting immutable cultural distinctions between Chinese and non-Chinese Filipinos, the argument that the new rich are Chinese reflects more the fact that the ethnic and national identities of Filipinos are themselves changing. The Filipino-Chinese, and the ethnic identity they carry, are becoming enmeshed in Philippine society in more complex ways than in the past. For most of Philippine history, the Filipino-Chinese have been seen as having lived a more or less enclave existence, concentrated in the *parian* or Chinatown areas of the major cities, in commerce, artisan work and manual labour, speaking mainly *Hokkien*, sustained by their own schools, theatres, hospitals and other community services, and engaging in domestic politics primarily through monetary support of non-Chinese Filipino politicians. The main departure from this pattern had come with the emergence of the Chinese *mestizos* in the nineteenth century, but their rise was premised on them becoming a distinct social and cultural entity aligned with Spain and the United States. While many individuals with ethnic Chinese backgrounds mixed freely with non-Chinese, the ideas of cultural sepa-ration and distinction remained relatively unchanged until the 1950s and 1960s when many former traders and labourers from the Chinese community became successful manufacturers. Indeed, it is in this way, and in this period, that most of the *Taipans* first became newly rich. However, the most significant change came in the 1980s and 1990s as the *Taipans* made substantial inroads into areas formerly controlled by the old Spanish or *mestizo* elite, and established conglom-erates which surpassed those of some of the old rich. A major factor making this and related developments possible was the opening up of citizenship to Filipino-Chinese in 1975. Increasingly, the *Taipans* also employed more educated middle-class non-Chinese, as they professionalised their corporations. In these ways, Filipino-Chinese were imposing their presence on the lives of elite and middle-class Filipinos in ways most had not previously experienced. Most impor-tantly, they were doing so at a time when these classes were losing status in Asia because of the Philippines' poor record of economic development, and at a time when Chinese ethnicity was being pronounced elsewhere as the source of East Asia's economic miracle.[24]

While these shifts publicly emphasised and strengthened the Chinese ethnic identity of the *Taipans*, that identity was simultaneously becoming less insular and more Filipinised (See 1990, 1995). The younger generations of Philippines-born Chinese are increasingly speaking *Tagalog* and other Filipino languages in preference to *Hokkien*; many of them are entering prestigious schools and univer-sities which had formerly been the almost exclusive domain of non-Chinese, particularly *mestizo* Filipinos; and large numbers have been moving out of the old Chinatowns into more ethnically mixed middle-class and elite suburbs. Some Filipino-Chinese are even said to be having cosmetic surgery to make their appearance more acceptable to the wider population. At the same time, influen-tial Filipino-Chinese civic organisations have been founded upon a stated commitment to Philippine national development. One of these, Kaisa Para Sa Kaularan (United for Progress), proclaims the credo: 'Our blood may be Chinese but our roots grow deep into Philippine soil, our bonds are with the Filipino people' (See 1990: i).[25] Another organisation, the Anvil Executive Club, founded in 1991 by a group of young Filipino-Chinese entrepreneurs and professionals, claims to be 'promoting traditional Confucian values and work ethic, dynamic entrepreneurship and civic consciousness...to the cause of Philippine economic, social and cultural progress' (Coyiuto 1995: 147). One Filipino-Chinese family runs a publishing company named Mahal Kong

Pilipinas (My Beloved Philippines) Incorporated. For several years until the mid-1990s, it published a regular document entitled *VIPs of the Philippines*, as well as a magazine (*Say*), both of which featured hundreds of biographical profiles of wealthy business families, executives, entrepreneurs and professionals, many of them hierarchically categorised by income, but not by ethnic identity. The names include members of the old *mestizo* and Spanish elite, as well as new rich Chinese and Malay Filipinos. Although these publications included some people in apparently anomalous categories like 'bartenders' and 'fashion models', they were for the most part explicitly concerned with identifying, ranking and honouring the country's wealthy capitalists and new middle class, regardless of ethnicity.

While these changes herald the positive incorporation of Filipino-Chinese identity into Philippine bourgeois and national identities, tensions nonetheless continue. Although many business people and politicians see the Filipino-Chinese as national role models, in some other quarters old racist antipathies remain, even if they are waning. It is still often claimed that the Filipino-Chinese have little loyalty to the Philippines and there has been some resentment along these lines as some of the *Taipans* have been investing in China, Singapore, Taiwan and Hong Kong. During the 1990s, many wealthy Chinese families have been singled out by kidnapping syndicates who see them as easier targets than other wealthy people. For this reason *Mahal Kong Pilipinas* stopped publishing its business profiles, and many wealthy Chinese have reasserted the secrecy for which they are well known.[26]

Although Chinese ethnicity is commonly used to identify the new rich, many of the stories of upwardly mobile entrepreneurs that appear in the media, and that are told verbally, feature women and men who are represented as indigenous Malay Filipinos rather than Filipino-Chinese. One informant also pointed to the new family names, normally associated with the working class or peasantry, that were now appearing in elite business circles. As with Chinese ethnicity, recent attempts have been made to conceptualise a distinctive form of Filipino entrepreneurship rooted in traditional indigenous values.[27] Much of the impetus for this came with a movement for cultural revitalisation in the wake of the overthrow of the Marcos regime. A popular view circulating in political and intellectual circles was that the Philippines had a heritage of emphasising negative values, which helped account for the country's dictatorship as well as for its economic backwardness, and that it was necessary to overturn these in favour of positive indigenous values which had remained largely dormant and untapped.[28]

Out of this came the Aquino and Ramos governments' Moral Recovery Programme (Schwenk 1989) which, in turn, fostered a number of attempts to promote and explain indigenous Filipino entrepreneurship. On the one hand, the Rizal Commercial Banking Corporation launched what it called the 'dragon campaign' which, in part, sought to 'reorient Filipino values' by identifying cultural traits that it saw as contrary to the cause of national development (Villegas 1995). On the other, the Development Bank of the Philippines ran advertisements in local business journals presenting a series of Tagalog language concepts which were seen to embody the qualities of the successful entrepreneur: *pagsasarili* (self-reliance), *lakas-loob* (courage), *sipag* (diligence), *pagpapakumbaba* (humility, patience), *pagkamatulungin* (helpfulness), *mapagtuklas* (inquisitiveness) and *saya* (happiness).[29] One business journal's cover story argues similarly that 'Filipino culture is replete with values promoting [entrepreneurship]', and again identifies a series of key Tagalog concepts which are supposed to demonstrate this (UP-ISSI 1994).[30]

While some of the capitalists and professionals I spoke with also referred positively to such values as part of the indigenous tradition and, in some cases, claimed particular cultural advantages for specific regionally based ethno-linguistic groups, entrepreneurial prowess is not inscribed as assertively or singularly into Malay-Filipino identity as it is into Filipino-Chinese identity. Nevertheless, whether it be understood in terms of ethnic makeup or more universalist criteria, the idea of entrepreneurship has been elevated over the past decade, both as a key ingredient of national development and as a defining quality of the new rich. In this sense, the underlying contrast is not so much between ethnic identities as between the new rich and old rich. As one professional and businesswoman commented: 'The new rich are more entrepreneurial, aggressive and risk-taking, whereas the old rich were not brought up to work hard and their inheritance is dwindling. Their sons are treated like precious jewels. But there is change in the new generation.'

Although today's entrepreneurial reading of wealth accumulation in the Philippines is at odds with the more well-worn portrait of the Philippines' rich as idle feudal lords and plundering rent-seekers, it can also be construed as part of the same ideological movement, to the extent that the former is a positive portrait and the latter a negative one, each dependent on the veracity of the other. To the extent that the new rich are being celebrated as entrepreneurs, and the heroes of national development, they have stolen much of the ideological leadership away from the old elite, whose members are now pressured to adopt an ethos of industry and dynamism. Increasingly, members of the old Philippine elite are attempting to reconstruct themselves as innovative, hard-working managers and entrepreneurs. In part, this has been a matter of practical necessity, as is evident, for instance, in the opening of the telecommunications industry to competition. Suddenly the Philippine Long Distance Telephone Company, which formerly enjoyed a monopoly, acted to reduce its backlog of applications for telephones and started to put in place a communications network that would advantage it ahead of new competitors.

But much of the new behaviour of the old rich is also symbolic. For example, 'rolling up the sleeves' and the 'hands-on' approach are often invoked as representing the new attitude of Filipino businesspeople. Indeed, following the lead of President Ramos, businessmen from old elite families now commonly roll up the sleeves, not only of their 'Western' business shirts, but also of their once stiff and stately Barong Tagalog shirts. According to one informant, these businessmen now prefer the new polyester variety of Barong Tagalog because, when soiled, it can more easily be washed and dried than could the old *pinya* (pineapple fibre) or cotton variety. Many businessmen also let it be known that they arrive at their offices early in the morning and do not leave until late in the evening. Long nights of entertaining, eating and drinking are said to have given way to business lunches and a strictly limited one or two hours of relaxation after work at a fitness club or celebrity bar. And golf, the increasingly popular sport of the well-to-do, is commonly described as an occasion for networking and negotiating business deals, rather than leisurely relaxation. Conversely, just as the cronyist style of enrichment – characteristic of the Marcos era – is the subject of widespread derision, so too is the indolence associated with the old elite. Billig (1994: 667–8), for example, reports that several Negros sugar plantation owners 'have lost the esteem of their peers because they continue to live the old style life of leisure', and that even the children of the Negrense elite were embarrassed by their families.

While much social prestige continues to be attached to an ancestry of landed wealth, aristocratic breeding and old elite family name, increasing normative weight is being placed on the ideas of industry, achievement and merit, as more new rich join the old as the owners of wealth and property. The reconstruction of the old rich in terms of this ideology centres not only on changed business practices and the display of a commitment to the work ethic, but also on the idea of a generational break. In addition to the common references currently made in Manila business circles to entrepreneurship, or to the money-making prowess of the Chinese, or the largely untapped positive value reserves of indigenous Malay Filipinos, there is also much reference in conversation and the mass media to the coming of a 'new breed' of business leaders.

The potency of this construct rests on the ambiguous way in which it represents change and continuity, embracing, on the one hand, the new rich and the entrepreneurial meritocratic ethos associated with them, and, on the other, the old rich, through their younger generation, who are also held to exemplify this ethos. Thus, the stories one now commonly hears and reads about the younger generation of executives from old elite families is that they have come to occupy their present positions having earned high educational credentials in top universities and, despite their ancestry, that they have had to demonstrate their talent and industry by working their way up the family corporation. For example, in a special report which attempts to identify 'the new breed', articles dealing with young executives from three of the country's oldest and wealthiest elite Spanish-*mestizo* families are headed: 'The job did not come with the silver spoon: The Aboitiz children relate how they worked their way to the top'; 'The hardworking Soriano brothers'; and 'A former newsboy's future' (*Business World* 1995: 5, 83, 100). Most of the articles dealing with executives or entrepreneurs from families who have risen to prosperity only over the past forty years have more innocuous headings.

In large part, the idea of a 'new breed' represents a push to relegitimise the still powerful sections of the old elite by appropriating for them the language of entrepreneurship, and by placing them in the same group as the most successful of the new rich, above the broader Philippine populace, including the majority of entrepreneurial capitalists and new middle class. Despite these efforts, the new generation of the old elite continues to be tainted, as well as blessed, by their ancestry.

It may be that as capitalist development proceeds, and as some members of the new rich become ensconced in the bourgeoisie, the opportunities for entrepreneurial mobility will decline and with them the rhetoric of entrepreneurship, but the elevation of the ideas of achievement and merit over that of ascription could well continue. For, though the rhetoric I have been discussing here fosuses most directly on the entrepreneurial capitalist, more generally it is also invoked in relation to the successful salaried professionals who exercise increasing influence in the world of corporate capital in the Philippines. The rhetoric of entrepreneurship, and more widely of meritocracy, represent a shift, not only in terms of national identity and elite or middle-class identity; increasingly they have become part of a totalising explanation of the Philippine social order. The idea that this order is constituted by the principle of meritocracy has long been embedded in the American-based system of public education and is evident as well in the labour market, but it has always coexisted with other ascriptive ideas according to which such factors as ethnic identity and family determine one's social position. The current structural reordering and celebration of entrepreneurship have intensified further the idea that success comes to those who are talented and diligent. The hegemonic significance of this is the corollary that those who do not rise to the top do not deserve to. The power of this rhetoric lies in the fact that it contains an element of experiential truth. But at the same time, its concentration on individual agency tends to conceal the structural differences that face those who seek wealth and respectability.

A 'nation of entrepreneurs', in the sense that entrepreneurship is today being celebrated in the Philippines, is simply an impossibility. While the new rich may be characterised by the success of their free-wheeling ambitions and hard work, that success is dependent on the subversion of the ambitions and hard work of a great many more who have to labour on their behalf, or who, in other ways, are denied the opportunities for substantial new wealth. For many such people, the derogatory characterisation of the new rich as *biglang yaman* still seems more fitting than that of meritorious entrepreneur. Neither are many within the old elite and intelligentsia prepared to move aside for the new rich. The principal way in which the new rich demonstrate their new-found power and privilege, and their separation from most of those around them, is through conspicuous consumption. This is also the arena in which members of the old elite are best equipped to assert their cultural authority.

'LET THE GOOD TIMES ROLL'[31]

The mood that has prevailed through much of Manila and Cebu City in the mid-1990s is that the Philippines is entering a new era of prosperity, on a par with its Southeast Asian neighours. Heightened levels of material consumption that can be witnessed in many parts of the country provide the most tangible evidence that many people have suddenly increased their spending power. There has always been an elite and upper middle-class consumer market, but in the past it was much more contained. Now many of the goods and services that were once exclusive to a tiny minority are on open display to all, and while most cannot afford them, an increasing number can. Today the practice of conspicuous consumption, once associated principally with the elite, has widened and intensified through the combined effect of increased social mobility and the globalisation of consumer culture. Not only are those with new money spending it, but in doing so they are also reconstructing their collective and individual identities and social standing.

Today Filipinos are confronted with a vastly expanded array and quantity of consumer items. Newspapers, magazines and television broadcasts are filled with advertisements for mobile phones, luxury condominiums, cosmetic surgery, designer clothes, fashion accessories, washing machines, spa baths, golfing equipment, new cars and overseas holidays. Growing numbers of people from provincial cities and towns are going on shopping expeditions to the malls of Manila and Cebu City. Whole planes and hotel floors are regularly occupied by other Filipino shoppers travelling to Hong Kong, while increasing numbers of very wealthy shoppers venture to London, Paris and New York. Meanwhile, many thousands of Filipino overseas workers return home laden with goods purchased in Europe, the Middle East, Japan and the United States. Even for those remaining in the Philippines, there is a growing sense of becoming a consumer of international fashion by shopping at boutiques, clothing and food stores with such names as The Best of New York, Washington, Italiana, La Donna, Le Cœur de France and the French Baker, and of being able to purchase a widening variety of international brand names.

At the same time as those with heightened incomes increase their consumption of foreign fashion insignia, so too is there more self-conscious promotion and consumption of goods that are identified as Filipino. Though McDonald's and KFC have become popular eating places, even more popular is the local fast-food outlet Jollibee, which many consumers proudly regard as Filipino. While Italian, Thai and other similarly identified new foreign-food outlets are to be found in Manila's major shopping malls, some of the most popular new eateries feature or specialise in particular regional cuisines. Two of the most popular upmarket restaurant chains – Barrio Fiesta and Kamayan (eating with hands) – invoke peasant village traditions as emblems of national identity. So too does the newly popular youth fashion store Sari Sari, named after the small mixed-goods stores that are to be found in villages and towns throughout the country. Similarly, among middle-income and well-to-do households, there appears to be a significant upsurge in the consumption and display of 'tribal' Filipino artefacts, and patronage of a movement to develop a distinctly Filipino architectural style (c.f. Javellana *et al.* 1997). Not only is there a substantially increased capacity for consumption among many Filipinos, but the patterns of consumption also suggest both the desire for participation and recognition in a world of international fashion, as well as a declaration of national identity that is self-consciously Filipino.

While increased levels of consumption have come to stand for a growing sense of national achievement, consumption is also highly stratified and constitutes a major vehicle through which differences in social standing and prestige are asserted and perceived. Though the growth of shopping malls, for instance, reflects an overall increase in spending power, particular malls also tend to be oriented to different income groups. To varying degrees, such distinctions are also evident in the interior spatial configuration of shops and leisure areas. Furthermore, particular malls, and the spaces and shops within them, have commonly become associated with different status identities. What is new in this is not the fact of social differentiation, but rather the multiple layering of consumption between those who are considered rich and poor. The testimony to this, and to the importance of consumption in popular consciousness, is the fact that the alphabetical categories (A–E), which had their origins in market research, are now widely used in Manila and other urban centres as the main language for designating status and class division. Although 'middle class' is also increasingly used as a term of social identification, many people in the middle and upper echelons of Philippine society, in particular, identify themselves and others by using the alphabetical labels. Not only are specific shops, restaurants and fashion stores commonly labelled with these letters, but so too are their customers. And while the largest malls still attract a cross-section of people, some shoppers claim that they are able to differentiate others into the five alphabetical categories simply by looking at their attire, their purchases, the company they keep and the way they carry themselves.

These distinguishing practices have also developed in reference to the variety of new housing estates and condominiums that have mushroomed around Manila and Cebu City, and in relation to the upwardly mobile, who demonstrate their new-found social respectability by changing house and residential suburb. Until a decade ago, the most common language of social stratification simply distinguished between rich and poor, or *burgis* (bourgeois) and *masa* (masses), with only limited reference to a middle class (see Turner 1995). As the emergence of an alphabetical status language indicates, there is now a popular perception, in urban areas at least, that there are new and substantial layers of people in between, that their collective existence is becoming more important, and that their identities are to be discovered primarily in their consumer practices and capacities.[32] And, along with these observations, there is also the perception of new opportunities for social mobility.

Though many of the people in these middle categories might be described as newly rich relative to their own backgrounds, those I spoke to in the upper echelons reserved that term for people they believed had entered the A or B 'classes'. A number also saw the new rich as being defined by the acquisition of key positional goods. One businessman and academic, whose views typified this perspective, suggested that in order to gain recognition as having 'made it', one had to have a BMW or Volvo, a condominium, a cellular phone, an American Express Gold card and membership of a golf club. He added that these possessions were like having sergeant's stripes. Others I spoke to included annual overseas holidays and ownership of a country house. Even though the incomes of most salaried professionals fell well short of the mark, many were able to enjoy a lifestyle that included these sorts of items because of access to credit and a range of company perks. Some measure of the kind of change that is taking place in the Philippines is that no one I talked to about these matters included the ownership of extensive agricultural land, which was seen as the hallmark of old elite privilege.

As a measure of status relations, consumption in the Philippines tends to work along two related axes. According to one, which is more universally accepted, status accrues quantifiably in terms of positional goods, like those listed above. By this measure, the new rich have elevated themselves above their former peers and the broad majority of the population, and some are accorded the same status as those identified with the old elite. According to the second axis, which is more culturally variegated, status is accrued through qualitative judgements concerning the manner and style of consumption. To some extent, one can distinguish between separate aesthetic communities, but there is also a strong sense in which the established intelligentsia and old elite have been able to impose on Philippine society a set of cultural standards, according to which they and their judgements are pre-eminent.[33] Under this regime, the great majority of Filipinos – the peasantry and working class – have long been characterised as *bakya* or *badoy*, that is as common, tasteless and unrefined.[34]

The new rich are typically seen in the same way except that they have more money. But with them, there is perhaps greater intensity to such stereotyping because they are seen to pose a threat to the hegemony of the old elite. Under the Marcos regime, the rise of what Francisco and Arriola called the *nouveau burgis*, 'with their lavish easy-come easy-go affluence and their questionable tastes' aroused widespread ridicule and contempt among intellectuals and old elite families, much of it concentrated on Imelda Marcos, 'the sometime provincial beauty queen and aspiring singer' (1987: 174–5). It also centred on such places as Manila's Corinthian Gardens, a fortified housing estate of newly built neo-classical mansions inhabited by Marcos's millionaire generals. Today, it is often the Filipino-Chinese who are singled out for ridicule. The Chinese have long been demeaned for their alleged lack of refinement; today many non-Chinese simply see this assuming a more grandiose form. While the older generation of Filipino-Chinese are widely known for their frugality, the younger generation of those who have become wealthy are usually portrayed as conspicuous consumers. Among the old elite and intelligentsia, various stories circulate about them. One tells of the plastic grass found outside the penthouse apartment belonging to the sons of one prominent Filipino-Chinese tycoon; another concerns the musical notes which decorate the security grills in a mansion belonging to a Chinese family whose daughter is studying music. As one highly educated professional said of the Filipino-Chinese new rich:

'Money can't buy taste. They're still ill-mannered like they were in Binondo [Chinatown]. They still wear slippers in public. But they know how to spend money on fast cars and cellular phones.' However, many people I spoke to talked in general about the new rich, regardless of ethnic identity. Indeed, this was a subject about which a number were quite expansive:

> The new rich don't have taste yet. They don't have culture... [whereas]...the old rich have been able to travel, to have access to books, to talk to people. And they're related to each other....[The old rich]...have to protect what they have, whereas the new rich want more. The way the new rich move is not co-ordinated. They have no Spanish, no pedigree....They can be seen. They jar. They don't fit into the landscape. They not only buy a good car; they buy a flashy car. They not only build a comfortable house; they build a huge house. They go overboard; to the extreme. People laugh at them. Even the poor laugh at them, because they know that to be reserved is what brings respect. One status symbol for the old rich is a country house; the new rich have them too, but they don't know where it's chic to have one. They're trying to get the trappings of old money and they don't deserve it....When an upstart claims it, he's laughed at or slapped down. Jewellers sneer at the new rich because they come in wanting large flashy diamonds, rather than high-quality ones. But we try to educate them to develop their taste.
>
> (Fourth-generation jeweller, antique dealer and art connoisseur)

> The new rich want to show that they have arrived through big houses, new cars...; whereas the old rich don't have to. They're more concerned with propriety and manners. It's their breeding. The new rich are garish and loud, but they haven't had time to catch up with refinements. Even the old not-so-rich have this refinement.
>
> (Wealthy property developer with professional background)

> If you have been given a good breeding, you don't act flashy like the new rich. Professionals are also amused by the new rich. But some are really nice – they want to show off because they're bursting with happiness. In the long run they will mellow and become like the old rich.
>
> (Newspaper owner from wealthy provincial family)

> The new rich have great respect for the old rich: they want to be invited to their homes.
>
> (Academic and rising entrepreneur)

> The new rich are over-eager, always seeking publicity....They like to flaunt their wealth, but they are tacky...they buy fake antiques and keep plastic over their furniture...The old rich don't seek fame. They're more into environmental responsibility and public service. They're possessed with a sense

of *noblesse oblige*. They're appalled by the new rich, but they are also envious of their money.

(Social pages journalist)

The new rich want to be identified with the old rich and therefore imitate their ways. But the old rich are snobbish to the new rich and protect their clannish circles.

(Highly educated public servant)

Two major points stand out in these statements. The first is that the new rich and old rich are constructed as cultural opposites, one in deprecatory terms, the other, often only by implication, in terms that are complementary. While the old rich are reserved, refined and constrained, the new rich are ostentatious, vulgar and insatiable. While the old rich have family pedigree, the new rich have none. While the new rich are self-seeking instrumentalists, the old rich display paternal care and social responsibility. In the case of the Chinese new rich, an additional opposition is sometimes drawn between the old elite who are represented as implicitly synonymous with Philippine national identity, and the Chinese who are aliens with loyalties that lie elsewhere. The second point is that the new rich are presented as wanting to be like the old rich: they recognise the latter's superior possessions, lifestyle and respectability and want a share in them. Thus the new rich are seen as posing a threat to the exclusive social standing of the old rich, but also to the world of high culture and dynastic family traditions that only the old rich and established intelligentsia understand, and know how to maintain. Particular derision is reserved for those new rich whose efforts to emulate old wealth have gone as far as assuming the quasi-noble appellations Don and Doña for themselves or their ancestors.

In short, the new rich and old rich are ideal hegemonic constructs that are self-serving to most of those who invoke them: principally the people who identify with the old rich or the established intelligentsia.[35] They are constructs that are mobilised to legitimise and preserve old privilege, just at that moment when it is most under threat from new layers of people with as much, if not more, material wealth and a reputation for entrepreneurial prowess to go with it. But some of the above quotations also posit the existence of an elite culture into which the new rich may be incorporated with time and training. Already people who come from educated, professional backgrounds, and whose circumstances can be described as newly rich, are often excepted, or except themselves, from the new-rich caricature above. Some others are described as taking the necessary steps to respectability by undergoing etiquette training, by surrounding themselves with cultivated professionals, or by sending their children to prestigious schools and universities associated with the old elite. Academics I spoke to in Manila's most exclusive university, Ateneo, noted, for example, that there had been a substantial increase in Filipino-Chinese students, and that many of them were now studying arts and humanities, as distinct from the engineering and economics courses with which they were most often identified. And, like the leading families from the old elite, a number of the *Taipans* have set up their own philanthropic foundations whose reach extends across ethnic boundaries. It also appears that there are increasing numbers of second-generation newly rich marrying into old rich families, though not, in some cases, without serious ruction. Notwithstanding the entrance of some elements of the new rich into the social and cultural domain of the old, many more, especially those of more limited means, continue to be excluded through such means as gossip and ostracism, some of which is communicated in the social pages of the daily newspapers.[36]

While all of this might suggest a cultural victory for the old elite, that would be misleading. Many new rich reject or only conditionally accept the high cultural authority of the old elite. Indeed, like the younger generation of that elite, they are also subject to global fashion trends whose main arbiters are located outside the Philippines. When I asked one Filipino-Chinese how the owners of the plastic grass would respond to the ridicule it aroused among some Filipino intellectuals, she responded that they probably would not care. Indeed, for many Filipino-Chinese, the high cultural authority of the old *mestizo* and Spanish elite is to some degree rivalled or diminished by a deference to the idea of Chinese civilisation. And while some new-rich Chinese houses may be regarded as kitsch in reference to the architectural standards of the old elite in the Philippines, it may be that their aesthetic logic rests in this rival cultural tradition. Furthermore, criticisms of ostentation and conspicuous consumption levelled against the younger generation of Filipino-Chinese have been framed not only in terms of old-rich sensibilities. Over much of the 1980s and 1990s an austerity campaign was waged within the Filipino-Chinese community calling for a return to the ethos of frugality and diligence associated with successes of first-generation Chinese migrants (Chua 1988a; See 1990: 84–93).

The fundamental weakness in the high-culture claims of the old elite is their association with economic backwardness and national humiliation. Moreover, not only have many of the old elite family names been tainted by this association, but the public listing of many old family companies on the stock exchange, as well as their increased professionalisation through the employment of non-family members, may further undermine the capacities of these families to command symbolic pride of place in the refashioned elite. While sections of the established intelligentsia and artistic community are vocal in their denunciation of the tastes and lifestyle of the new rich, some young business people and professionals with backgrounds in the old elite, are more interested in embracing the government's liberal developmental ideology, and the work ethic and entrepreneurial spirit which they associate with the new rich.[37] But some also distinguish between those new rich they believe can be described in these terms, and others they dismiss as simply being, in the words of one businessman, like *ampaw* (puffed rice).

CONCLUSION

The emergence of the new rich in the Philippines is testimony to the country's continued capitalist transformation. That transformation has undoubted economic and structural qualities, which tie the Philippines to the region and to the movements of global capital, and which largely explain the positional character of the new rich as capitalists and new middle class. However, there is much to this transformation in the Philippines that is profoundly cultural. As I have argued here, the emergence of the Philippine new rich is rooted not only in the movements of capital, but also in changing identities and ideologies. In particular, the new rich have been variously constructed in terms of entrepreneurship, ethnicity, generation, consumption and national identity. At the heart of the relationship between these constructions are two areas of contention: one between the new rich and old elite; the other involving the shifting regional reputation of the Philippines in the competition for capitalist prosperity.

Increased prosperity in the Philippines during the mid-1990s has been a subject of significant national pride among the privileged classes. Prompted by decades in which the country was denigrated as the exception to the 'Asian Miracle', much of this pride has found form in positively distinguishing the Philippines as a nation of democracy and free enterprise in a region otherwise marked by authoritarianism. In turn, this has found expression in the ideology of entrepreneurship which is seen to explain the success and describe the character of the new rich. This representation poses a major challenge to those associated with the old elite which has come to stand for the opposing qualities of birthright privilege, indolence and economic backwardness.

However, there are significant tensions in this progression. Although some attempt has been made to construct entrepreneurship in terms of indigenous Malay-Filipino ethnicity, the more pervasive ethnic construction of the new rich and entrepreneurship is in terms of Filipino-Chinese identity, which has long been denigrated as non-Filipino. Symbolic efforts from within the Filipino-Chinese community and from the state to establish the nationalist credentials of the Filipino-Chinese have been only partially successful. Those identified with the old elite have attempted to counter the challenge of the new rich in two ways. First, they have attempted to reconstruct themselves as a new generation or 'new breed' indistinguishable from the most prominent new rich entrepreneurs. Secondly, they have attempted to assert their cultural authority in the area of consumption where the new rich, while elevating themselves in spending power beyond the reach of most Filipinos, are denigrated beside the old elite, as ostentatious and tasteless. Just as there has been a selective attempt to identify the old rich with the entrepreneurship of the most prominent new rich, so are more privileged and powerful sections of the new rich being accepted for incorporation into the high cultural domain of the old elite. However, these moves too have been only partially successful as the stigmas of old elite indolence and new rich tastelessness continue to haunt both groups as they set about building or rebuilding class hegemony.

Notes

Most of the research for this chapter was carried out in Metro Manila and Cebu City in 1994–5, and was funded by the Asia Research Centre, Murdoch University, Perth, Australia. My thanks to the many people who generously assisted during my fieldwork, in particular Lorraine Salazar, Chuchi Aguba and Manuel Velmonte. For convenience, I use Manila in preference to Metro Manila, one subdivision of which goes under the same name.

1　See, for example, the cover stories in the *Asian Business Review*, July 1995 ('From Cot-Case to Serious Regional Contender'), and *The Economist*, 11 May 1996. In 1997, the OECD declared its approval of the Philippines by describing it as a 'dynamic non-member economy' (*FEER*, 20 March 1997: 20).

2　This quote from the Assistant Director-General of the National Security Council is repeated almost verbatim by Jaime Zobel de Ayala, CEO of the giant Ayala Corporation (*Philippine Business* 1994, 1 (2): 38).

3　In the years immediately after the overthrow of the Marcos regime, GNP growth increased markedly; it declined in the early 1990s; then steadily increased, and for most of the period 1996–7 stayed above 6 per cent (*FEER* 1997 Yearbook: 194; *Asian Business Review*, September 1997: 19). While economic growth is obvious in Manila, even more remarkable are the higher growth rates in a number of provincial cities, notably Cebu City and General Santos City in the central and southern Philippines.

4　For a fuller treatment of this history, see Pinches (1996).

5　As is the case elsewhere in the region, Filipinos have been drawn into production processes, capital flows, labour markets and consumption practices that are increasingly dynamic and transnational. At one level these changes have involved the proliferation of small- and medium-sized businesses; at another, they have seen the continued dominance of large corporations and conglomerates, the two interlinked by increasingly complex subcontracting, franchise and service relationships (see Harvey 1989: 141–72).

6　For this estimate, see Ball (1996: 70) and *FEER* (30 March 1995: 43). Relative to their past employment in the Philippines, as well as to their peers and friends, the great majority of overseas contract workers can also be described as new rich. I do not focus on them in this chapter because, for the most part, they remain a part of the working class and are looked upon as such by those who identify with the elite and middle classes. But see Pinches 1992a and n.d.

7　Though little systematic research has been done, in the 1990s business magazines and newspapers have published numerous profiles of new capitalist entrepreneurs (see below).

8　There were also regional distinctions: the *mestizo* sugar barons of Negros developed a distinctive ethnic identity as *Negrense* (Lopez-Gonzaga 1991).

9　Though, for nationalists, there has always been some ambivalence over self-identification as *mestizo*. Just before his execution by the Spanish, national hero Jose Rizal, referred to by most historians as *mestizo*, rejected this label, insisting that he was '*indio puro*' (pure indigenous Malay Filipino) (Fernandez-Armesto 1996: 58).

10　These dynasties are variously known and celebrated through public religious ritual, political events, the social pages of magazines and newspapers, and the philanthropic or public service organisations a number of them have set up. Many have commissioned and published detailed family histories for limited circulation. On the political and economic character of some of these families see Koike (1993), Hutchcroft (1991) and McCoy (1994).

11　See Ileto (1979); Kerkvliet (1990); Pinches (1992a, 1992b).

12 Since independence, the most influential polemicist along these lines has been Renato Constantino (1975, 1978).

13 Development Bank of the Philippines advertisement in *Philippine Business*, 1994, 1 (2): 41.

14 I am basing this principally on my own research among workers and peasants in Manila and Leyte. Talent and hard work may be acknowledged as the source of new wealth, but generally only when the details of a case are known.

15 See, for example, Manapat (1991) and the regular series *Smart File*, both of which attempt to record the corrupt practices of businesspeople and politicians.

16 This is not to deny that many continue to distinguish between the two characterisations, while some recognise their frequent coincidence.

17 For some nationalist intellectuals this has entailed a major shift from the former orthodoxy of protectionism. See, for example, Magno (1994).

18 Strong support for this position has come from the Makati Business Club which represents the country's largest corporations.

19 I should add, though, that a minority of businesspeople I spoke to thought some form of authoritarianism was necessary for national development.

20 The allusion here appears to be to the national bird – the Philippine eagle. *Bayanihan* – co-operative labour.

21 According to Tiglao (1990: 68), this is Cantonese for 'big boss'.

22 The first project of the Dragon Corporation was to be the building of a new international airport, though there has been little progress on this.

23 Such views are circulated, for instance, at Manila's regionally influential Asian Institute of Management (see, for example, Limlingan 1986). See also Billig (1994: 668–70).

24 See Pinches, Chapter One, this volume.

25 Two of the various attempts to find a suitable label for the Filipino-Chinese which reflect these combined attachments are *sinpino* and *chinoy*, though neither of them is widely used.

26 In general, I had more difficulty organising interviews with Filipino-Chinese than with other Filipinos. Some businesspeople I did interview, and who were identified as Chinese by non-Chinese informants, did not identify themselves this way with me, though they did speak of others as Chinese. In these cases the issue seemed less one of secrecy than of the ambiguity and situational character of ethnic identity, as it concerns many Filipinos. Despite the ideological power of ethnic categories, the social and interpersonal boundaries constituted in terms of Malay, Chinese, *mestizo* and Spanish identities are contentious and blurry.

27 Though it is argued by Ordonez (1982) and Mendoza (1991) that Filipinos and Chinese belong to a broader Asian cultural tradition of business and management which they describe as paternalism.

28 Central to much of this discussion was an article by American journalist James Fallows (1987) which attributed the lack of economic development in the Philippines to its 'damaged culture'. The characterisation and analysis of Philippine society in terms of cultural values has a long heritage in the social sciences, both local and foreign (see Church 1986 and Enriquez 1989). Indeed, one local writer in management theory, Tomas Andres, has generated a virtual publishing industry in this area with his numerous books (for example, 1981) and periodical, *Values Digest*.

29 The advertisement used here appeared in *The Filipino Entrepreneur*, 1991, II (8): 2 (my glosses).

30 Over this century a number of writers, beginning with Rizal (Schumacher 1973: 202), have defended Filipinos against claims of indolence or lack of business acumen (see also de la Costa 1977; and Billig 1994).

31 From a Mitsubishi advertisement that appeared on television and in newspapers in the mid-1990s, and which began: 'the Philippines is already a tiger…'.

32 The main body conducting social surveys, the Social Weather Station, uses these alphabetical categories as the basis for measuring a range of practices and attitudes, including voting intentions.

33 For theoretical elaboration in reference to the work of Bourdieu (1984), see Pinches, chapter one, this volume.

34 The original meaning of *bakya* is 'wooden shoe', once worn by villagers. See Lacaba (1977), Pinches (1992a, 1992b).

35 While many intellectuals are critical of the political and economic practices of the old elite, considerably less criticism is levelled at their aesthetic authority.

36 These pages which cover gala openings and other such events, regularly single out the names of the old elite families in their efforts to highlight 'who's who'. In some cases they also make reference to the 'faces that didn't belong' (*Daily Inquirer*, November 1994: C4).

37 This tension seems to reflect the distinction which Bourdieu (1984) makes between cultural capital and economic capital. See Pinches, Chapter One, this volume.

Bibliography

Almonte, J. (1990) 'The Filipino Elite Must Listen to its Conscience', *Daily Globe*, 1 April (reprinted by Malaya Books, Quezon City).

Andres, T. (1981) *Understanding Filipino Values: A Management Approach*, Quezon City: New Day.

Ball, R. (1996) 'Nation Building: The Globalization of Nursing – The Case of the Philippines', *Pilipinas*, no. 27: 67–91.

Billig, M. (1994) 'The Death and Rebirth of Entrepreneurism on Negros Island, Philippines: A Critique of Cultural Theories of Enterprise' *Journal of Economic Issues*, XXVIII (3): 659–78.

Bourdieu, P. (1984) *Distinction*, Cambridge, MA: Harvard University Press.

Business World (1994) *Philippines Inc.* New Manila: Philippine Press Institute.

—— (1995) *Philippines Inc: The Next Generation*, New Manila: Philippine Press Institute.

Chua, L. (1988a) 'On Austerity and Extravagance', in T. See and L. Chua (eds), *Crossroads: Short Essays on the Chinese Filipinos*, Manila: Kaisa Para Sa Kaunlaran, Inc.

—— (1988b) 'The Difficulty of Being Rich', in T. See and L. Chua (eds), *Crossroads: Short Essays on the Chinese Filipinos*, Manila: Kaisa Para Sa Kaunlaran, Inc.

—— and Herrin, N. (1988) 'Filipino-Chinese Marriages', in T. See and L. Chua (eds), *Crossroads: Short Essays on the Chinese Filipinos*, Manila: Kaisa Para Sa Kaunlaran, Inc.

Church, A. (1986) *Filipino Personality: A Review of Research and Writings*, Manila: De La Salle University Press.

Constantino, R. (1975) *The Philippines: A Past Revisited*, Quezon City: Tala.

—— (1978) *Neocolonial Identity and Counter Consciousness*, London: Merlin.

Coyiuto, E. (1995) 'The Role of Young Chinese Entrepreneurs in the Philippine Economy: Renewing Tradition, Facing New Challenges and Opportunities', in E. Palanca (ed.), *China, Taiwan, and the Ethnic Chinese in the Philippine Economy*, Quezon City: Philippine Association for Chinese Studies.

Crouch, H. (1985) *Economic Change, Social Structure and the Political System in Southeast Asia: Philippine Development Compared with Other ASEAN Countries*, Singapore: Institute of Southeast Asian Studies.

De la Costa, H. (1977) 'Myths of the Filipino Businessman', in C. Lumbera and T. Maceda (eds), *Rediscovery: Essays on Philippine Life and Culture*, Metro Manila: National Book Store.

dela Cruz, P. (1994) 'The Confucian Principle Personified', in Business World, *Philippines Inc*, New Manila: Philippine Press Institute.

Enriquez, V. (1989) *Indigenous Psychology and National Consciousness*, Tokyo: Institute for the Study of Languages and Cultures of Asia and Africa.

Fallows, J. (1987) 'A Damaged Culture', *The Atlantic Monthly*, 260 (5): 49–58.

Fernandez-Armesto, F. (1996) 'Renaissances: Asian and Other', in Rajaretnam, M. (ed.), *Jose Rizal and the Asian Renaissance*, Manila: Solidaridad.

Francisco, M. and Arriola, F. (1987) *The History of the Burgis*, Quezon City: GCF Books.

Gonzaga, L (1994) 'The Taipans', *Manila Inc*, 3 (3): 24–8.

Harvey, D. (1989) *The Condition of Postmodernity*, Oxford: Blackwell.

Hutchcroft, P. (1991) 'Oligarchs and Cronies in the Philippine State: The Politics of Plunder', *World Politics*, 43 (3): 414–50.

Ileto, R. (1979) *Pasyon and Revolution*, Quezon City: Ateneo de Manila University Press.

Javellana, R., Zialcita, F. and Reyes, E. (1997) *Filipino Style*, Singapore: Archipelago Press.

Kerkvliet, B. (1990) *Everyday Politics in the Philippines*, Berkeley: University of California Press.

Koike, K. (1993) 'The Ayala Group During the Aquino Period: Diversification along with a Changing Ownership and Management Structure', *The Developing Economies*, XXXI (4): 442–64.

Lacaba, J. (1977) 'Notes on "Bakya"', in C. Lumbera and T. Maceda (eds), *Essays in Philippine Life and Culture*, Quezon City: National Bookstore.

Limlingan, V. S. (1986) *The Overseas Chinese in Asean: Business Strategies and Management Practices*, Manila: De La Salle University Press.

Lopez-Gonzaga, V. (1991) *The Negrense: A Social History of an Elite Class*, Bacolod: Institute for Research and Development, University of St La Salle.

McCoy, A. (1981) 'The Philippines: Independence without Decolonization', in R. Jeffrey (ed.), *Asia: The Winning of Independence*, New York: St Martins Press.

—— (ed.) (1994) *An Anarchy of Families*, Quezon City: Ateneo de Manila University Press.

Magno, A. (1994) 'Towards a Paradigm Shift', *Kasarinlan*, 10 (2): 4–6.

Manapat, R. (1991) *Some are Smarter than Others: The history of Marcos' Crony Capitalism*, New York: Aletheia.

Marcos, F. (1978) *Revolution from the Centre*, Hong Kong: Raya Books.

Mendoza, G. (1991) *Management: The Asian Way*, Makati: Asian Institute of Management.

Omohundro, J. (1983) 'Social Networks and Business Success for the Philippine Chinese', in L. Lim and A. P. Gosling (eds), *The Chinese in Southeast Asia*, Singapore: Maruzen Press.

Ordonez, R. (1982) *The Behavioural Skills of the AEAN Manager*, Makati: Asian Institute of Management.

Pacho, A. (1986) 'The Chinese Community in the Philippines', *Sojourn*, 1 (1): 76–91.

Pinches, M. (1992a) 'Proletarian Ritual: Class Degradation and the Dialectics of Resistance in Manila', *Pilipinas*, no. 19, Fall: 67–92.

—— (1992b) 'The Working Class Experience of Shame, Inequality and People Power in Tatalon, Manila', in B. Kerkvliet and R. Mojares (eds), *From Marcos to Aquino: Local Perspectives on Political Transition in the Philippines*, Honolulu: University of Hawaii Press.

—— (1996) 'The Philippines' New Rich: Capitalist Transformation Amidst Economic Gloom', in R. Robison and D. Goodman (eds), *The New Rich in Asia*, London: Routledge.

—— (1997) 'Elite Democracy, Development and People Power: Contending Ideologies and Changing Practices in Philippine Politics', *Asian Studies Review*, 21 (2–3): 104–20.

—— (n.d.) 'Class, Ethnicity and Nation: Ambiguous Experiences and Identities among Filipino Migrant Workers', in J. Hutchison and A. Brown (eds), *Organising Labour Globalising Asia*, London: Routledge.

Say, M. *et al.* (1991) *VIP's of the Philippines 1991*, Pasig: Mahal Kong Pilipinas Inc.

—— (1994) *VIP's of the Philippines 1993–1994*, Ermita: Mahal Kong Pilipinas Inc.

Schumacher, J. (1973) *The Propaganda Movement: 1880–1895*, Manila: Solidaridad.

Schwenk, R. (ed.) (1989) *Moral Recovery and the Democratic Vision in Philippine Context*, Manila: Seed Center.

See, C. (1988) 'Revive Our Spirit of Hard Work', in T. See and L. Chua (eds), *Crossroads: Short Essays on the Chinese Filipinos*, Manila: Kaisa Para sa Kaunlaran, Inc.

See, T. (1990) *The Chinese in the Philippines*, Manila: Kaisa Para sa Kaunlaran, Inc.

—— (1995) 'The Chinese in the Philippines: Continuity and Change', in L. Suryadinata (ed.), *Southeast Asian Chinese: The Socio-Cultural Dimension*, Singapore: Times Academic Press.

—— and Chua, L. (1988) 'Introduction', in T. See and L. Chua (eds), *Crossroads: Short Essays on the Chinese Filipinos*, Manila: Kaisa Para Sa Kaunlaran, Inc.

Talisayon, S. (1994) 'Smart Moves to Post Industrial Philippines', *The Filipino Entrepreneur* January–February: 27–8.

Tan, A. (1985) 'Chinese Mestizos and the Formation of Filipino Nationality', in T. Carino (ed.), *Chinese in the Philippines*, Manila: De La Salle University Press.

Tan-Climaco, G. (1994) 'Take Wing and Soar', *Philippine Business*, 1 (3): 30.

Tiglao, R. (1990) 'Gung-ho in Manila', *Far Eastern Economic Review*, 15 February: 68–72.

Turner, M. (1995) 'Imagining the Middle Class in the Philippines', *Pilipinas*, no. 25: 87–101.

UP-ISSI (1994) 'Enterprise and Filipino Values', *The Filipino Entrepreneur*, January–February: 16–18.

Villegas, P. (1995) 'The Lady behind the Dragon Campaign', in Business World, *Philippines Inc: The Next Generation*, New Manila: Philippine Press Institute.

Von Brevern, M. (1988) *'Once a Chinese, Always a Chinese': The Chinese of Manila – Tradition and Change*, Manila: Lyceum Press.

Wickberg, E. (1964) 'The Chinese Mestizo in Philippine History', *Journal of Southeast Asian History*, 5 (1): 62–100.

Index

Abdul Kahar Bador 89, 91
Abdullah Munshi 94
Abercrombie, N. 8
Acciaioli, G. 30
Adibah Amin 105
advertising: Thailand 240–2
Agarwal, A. 263
Agus family (case study) 196–7,198, 205
Al-Hadi, Sheikh 94, 96
Alatas, S.H. 89
Almonte, J. 281
Anek Laothamathas 243
Anthias, F. 9
Antlöv, H. xiv, 10, 24, 40, 41, 42, 90, 92, 188–206
Anvil Executive Club 285
Anwar Ibrahim 77
Appadurai, A. 29, 268, 270
Ariffin, Omar 94
Armstrong, M. 127
Arriola, F. 292
artistic communities 36–7
Asianisation 170–1
Askew, M. 30
Association of Indonesian Intellectuals (ICMI) 173, 174
Austin-Broos, D. 5

Baker, C. 13, 20, 28, 30, 38
Banjaransari, S. 166, 167
Barker, F. 3
Barnet, R 28
Barth, F. 9
Basch, L. 269
Basu, T. 267
Batson, B. 232
Berger, P. 16, 17
Bergère, M. 10
Betz, H. 26

Bhabha, H. 3
Bhagavan, M.R. 253, 255
Bian Yanjie 222
Billig, M. 288
black magic 115, 202–3
Blau, P. 219
Bocock, R. 8, 26
Boulanger, C.L. 120
Bourdieu, P. 5, 9, 26, 28, 33–6, 39, 67, 75, 76, 197, 210
bourgeoisie, as a term 42, 43, 88–9
Breckenridge, C.A. 268
Brennan, M. 89
Brenner, S. 11
Bromby, R. 261
Brown, A. 14
Buckley, C. xiv, 10, 39, 208–28
bureaucracy 12–13
bureaucratic power, access to 210–11
Burris, V. 25

capitalist transformation 3
car ownership 32; Indonesia 178; Singapore 140, 145, 146, 147, 149, 150, 151, 155
Caruana, L. 251
caste system, India 254, 265–7
Castells, M. 56, 57, 76, 78
Cavanagh, J. 28
Chai-anan Samudavanija 233
Chakravarti, S. 251, 264
Chamlong Simuang 239, 244, 245
Chan Heng Chee 142
Chan, K. 19
Chandra, A. 263
Chandra Muzaffar 88, 89
Chandra, S. 260, 267
Chaney, D. 4
Chanwit Kasetsiri 232

Chengappa, R. 261
Cheong Mei Sui 105
Chew, C. 124
China xiv, 63–4, 208–28; Communist
    Party membership 215, 216;
    consumption practices xiv, 225, 227;
    education 213, 214, 216; gift-exchange
    rituals xiv, 40, 227; incomes 213, 214;
    lifestyles 225, 227; occupational class
    211, 212, 214, 215, 216, 220;
    reputation xiv, 224, 225, 226, 228;
    social class 211; social networks 40,
    208–9, 218–27; the state in 211;
    tributary relations 12; trust xiv, 224,
    225, 226, 228
Chinese ethnicity xii, 16–24, 57–8, 60–6;
    and employment in Japanese firms
    18–19; in Indonesia xiii, 13, 21, 22,
    160,161, 165–6, 171–3, 191; in
    Malaysia xii, 13, 21, 118–19; in the
    Philippines xv, 13, 20, 283–6, 292–3,
    294–5, 296; in Singapore 61–6; in
    Thailand 19–20
Chow, R. 66
Chua Beng Huat xiii, 10, 17, 19, 23, 31,
    33, 40–1, 65, 68, 70, 72, 137–55, 171–2
Chua, L. 283, 284, 295
Clammer, J. 66, 69, 71
class xi, 6–16, 22, 23, 24, 26, 34, 67–9;
    Indonesia 197; Malaysia 112;
    occupational and social
China 211–18, 220; Singapore 139–41,
    142, 143, 154–5, *see also* middle class;
    working class
class consciousness 7
class theory 3–4, 7–8, 230–1
Clegg, S. 16, 17
Cobb, R. 25
Cohen, A. 9
Cohen, M.L. 64, 65
colonialism 12–13, 14; Malaysia 94–7
Communism, Indonesia 174
Communist Party, China 215, 216
community spirit, Indonesia 198–200, 201,
    202, 204–5
Confucianism 1, 16–24
Constantino, R. 279, 280
consumer goods, production of 25–6
consumption practices xii, 24–41,56–7;
    China xiv, 225, 227; and identity
    formation 56–7, 67–74, 77, 78; India
    251, 252, 256, 257–63, 265, 269;
    Indonesia xiv, 159–60, 163, 168–71,
    198; Malaysia 112, 114–15; nationalist

forms 30–1, 290–1; Philippines xv,
    290–4; Singapore xiii, 144–52, 155;
    Thailand 240–2
Contemplacion, F. 283
corruption 15
Coyiuto, E. 285
Crompton, R. 26
Crouch, H. 279
cultural capital 33–5, 39
cultural studies 5
culture, concept of 4–5, 6

Dakwa movement 21, 102–3
Davis, R.H. 267
Dedrick, J. 254
de la Cruz, P. 284
Deng Xiaoping 20
Desai, R. 267
Deyo, F. 13, 14, 15
diasporic Indians xv, 20, 252, 255, 256,
    257, 259, 268, 269, 270
Dirks, B. 4, 5
Doeppers, D. 12
Drysdale, J. 137
Dumont, L. 11, 266
During, S. 5

economy: India 251, 253–6, 268–9;
    Indonesia 164, 165, 176–7; Malaysia
    21, 95–100, 103, 111,113–14;
    Philippines 281–2
Edmundson, W.C. 192
education 12, 13, 25, 36, 59; China 213,
    214, 216; India 254,258–9, 264, 266;
    Malaysia 101, 105–6; Philippines 279;
    Singapore 138, 142, 144, 149;
    Thailand 234
Elegant, S. 67, 68, 77
Ellin, N. 231
employment: lifetime 116, 132; *see also*
    occupational class/status
entrepreneuriship, ideology of, Philippines
    281–9, 296
envy 41
ethnicity 9, 16–24, 44; Malaysia 112, 113,
    114, 126–8; Singapore 138–9; *see also*
    Chinese ethnicity
ethno-nationalism 13–14, 19–20, 21–2, 24
Euis (case study) 196
Evans, G. 11

Faarland, J. 97
Fairbank, J. 11, 13

Farmer, V.L. 261
fashion: India 262–3, 270; Islamic 175–6
Featherstone, M. 4, 7, 25, 26, 28, 168, 197,
    268, 269
Federation of Malaya Agreement (1948)
    94
Femina 175, 176
Feraru, A. 5, 6
Finkelstein, J. 26, 67
Fischer, M. 5
Fiske, J. 26
Fitzgerald, J. 64
Flood, T. 237
Foo Sek Min 146
Forney, M. 63
Fournier, M. 9, 227
Francisco, M. 292
Frankel, F.R. 255, 266
Frederick, W.H. 189
Friedman, J. 29, 72, 74, 76–7
Frykman, J. 9, 230–1
Fu Xuedong 217

Gandhi, R. 256
Ganie, T.N. 167
Geertz, C. 11, 224
gender 9
Genovese, E. 8
Gerth, H. 8
Ghosh, A. 252
Giddens, A. 56, 63, 74–5, 76, 77, 230, 245
gift-exchange rituals, China xiv, 40, 227
Gilley, B. 62, 63
globalisation 28, 44, 59, 104–5; India 251,
    252, 255, 256, 257, 258–60, 268–9
Goh Beng Lan 74, 75
Gomez, E.T. 89, 90, 100, 101
Gonzaga, L. 283
Goodman, D. 6, 8, 14, 59, 86, 88, 89, 90,
    92, 93
Gosling, L. 18
Govers, C. 9
Gramsci, A. 8
Granovetter, M. 106
Grossberg, L. 5, 7
Guldin, G. 62
Guru family 203–4

haj (pilgrimage to Mecca) 21, 122–3, 132
Hall, S. 5, 8, 19
Hannerz, U. 4, 5, 6, 200
Hariani, M. 262
Harriss, J. 255

Harry, F. 170
Hart, G. 195
Hartono, S. 176
Harvey, D. 3, 14, 69, 252
Hefner, R. 77, 173, 174, 201
Heinze, Ruth-Inge 237
Herrin, N. 284
Heryanto, A. xiii–xiv, 13, 18, 20, 21, 26,
    30, 31, 38, 42, 57, 77, 159–79
Hewison, K. 13, 15, 57, 69
Hicks, G. 62
Hiebert, M. 161
Higgott, R. 59
Hindu nationalism 20, 267, 268
Hing, A.Y. 115
Hirschman, C. 89, 93
Ho Chi Minh 189
Hong Kong 63, 66
Hong, L. 232
honours system, Malaysia 91
Hoogvelt, A. 269
Horsman, M. 78
housing/home ownership 71; India 259;
    Indonesia 71, 74, 75–6; Philippines
    291; Singapore 140, 145–7, 149,
    152–3, 154, 155
Hsiao, H. 16
human capital 211
Husin Ali, S. 89, 95
Hüsken, F. 205
Hutchison, J. 14

identity formation: and consumption 56–7,
    67–74, 77; and lifestyle 74–6, 77, 78
Idrus, F.K. 88
incomes: China 213, 214; India 263,
    264–5; Indonesia 179n; Philippines
    279; Singapore 140-1, 147; Thailand
    234, 235, *see also* wages
India xv, 251–70; caste system 254, 265–7;
    consumption practices 251, 252,
    256–63, 265, 269; diaspora xv, 20, 252,
    255, 256, 257, 259, 268, 269, 270;
    economy 251, 253–6, 8–9; education
    254, 258–9, 264, 265, 266; fashion
    262–3, 270; and globalisation 251, 252,
    255, 256, 257, 258–60, 268–9;
    housing/home ownership 259; incomes
    263, 2644–5; industrialisation 253, 255;
    language 260; lifestyles 257–63, 265,
    269; mass media 256; meritocracy
    266–7; privatisation 255–6; religion
    254, 265, 267–8, 270; the state in

253–6, 268–9; traditional cultural influences 252, 260–2, 269–70; women in 262–3

Indonesia xiii-xiv, 13, 15, 20, 21, 22, 38, 42, 58, 59, 159–79, 188–206; car ownership 178; Chinese ethnicity in xiii, 13, 21, 22, 160, 161, 165–6, 171–3, 191; class 197; community spirit 198–200, 201, 202, 204-5; consumption practices xiv, 159–60, 163, 168–71, 177–9, 198; economy 164, 165, 176–7; housing/home ownership 71, 74, 75–6; incomes 179n; Islam 20, 22, 173–6; language 169–70, 172; lifestyles 163, 168–71, 177–9, 194, 195–8; old elite 160–1; *Pancasila* ideology xiv, 165, 174, 192; poetry reading tradition 166–8; rural xiv, 188-206; Simple Life campaign 177–8; the state in 191, 199–200, 205–6; women 195–6

industrialisation 3, 58–9; India 253, 255; Malaysia 111, 113–17

intellectual communities 36–7

Iroha (M) xiii, 112, 115, 117–25

Islam 12; in Indonesia 20, 22, 173-6; in Malaysia xii, 20, 21, 102–3, 111, 115, 122–3, 127, 128, 129,130; *see also* Muslims

Jacob, R. 251

Janelli, R. 23

Japan 29; management systems 115- 17, 132

Japanese firms in Malaysia xiii, 111, 112, 115, 117–33

Javellana, R. 290

Jay, M. 7

Jenks, C. 4, 5

Jesudason, J. 89, 99

Jimbaran Declaration (1995) 165

Jiraporn Witayasakpan 231

Jomo, K.S. 89

Kahn, J. 4, 21, 30, 37, 39, 59, 77, 86, 88, 88–9, 90

Kaisa Para Sa Kaularan 285

Keesing, R. 4, 5

Kessler, C. 88

Khamhaeng Pharitanon 237

Khanna, S. 253, 254, 255

Khasnor, J. 89

Khoo Boo Teik 94, 96, 103

Kitley, P. 178

Kompas 167, 170, 172, 175, 176

Kraemer, K.L. 254

Kua Kia Soong 89

Kulkarni, V.G. 257, 263

Kurtz, D. 5, 8

Kuttappan, L. 256

Kwik Kian Gie 165

Kwok Kian Woon 61, 63, 64, 65, 66, 77, 151

Lakha, S. xv, 10, 11, 12, 20, 23, 28, 29, 30, 36, 251–70

Lamont, M. 9, 35, 197, 208, 227

language: India 260; Indonesia 169–70, 172; Malaysia 105–6; Singapore 65

Laothamatas, A. 57

Lareau, A. 208

Larrain, J. 7

Latief, A. 167

Lee, D. 4

Lee, E. 89

Lee, G.B. 58, 62, 66

Lee, K.H. 89

Lee Kuan Yew 61, 62

Lee Oon Hean 90

Legge, J. 12

Leong Choon Heng 142, 145, 148, 152

Licuanan, V. 18

Liem Sioe Liong 177

lifestyles 7, 56, 57, 188, 189–90, 231; China 225, 227; and identity formation 74–6, 77, 78; India 257–63, 265, 269; Indonesia 163, 168–71, 194, 195-8; Malaysia 112, 126, 1–2; Philippines xv, 290–3; Thailand 239, 240–2

Likhit Dhiravegin 237, 243

Lim Boon keng 61

Lim, L. 17, 19

Lim, L. Y.-C. 57

Lim Mah Hui 89

Lim, W. 30

Lingle, C. 19

Li Peng 172

Lipset, S.M. 238

local cultural influences *see* traditional cultural influences

Lofgren, O. 9, 230–1

Logan, W. 30

Loh, Francis Kok Wah 59, 77

Lopez-Gonzaga, V. 12

MacAndrews, C. 89

McBeth, J. 161, 166
MacCannell, D. and MacCannell, J. 8, 26
McCarthy, P. 258, 260
McCoy, A. 280
McDonald's 169, 261
Mackie, J.A.C. 17, 61, 62
McLaren, A. 65
McVey, R. 14, 17, 57, 60
magical practices 115, 202–3
Mahathir, Dr Mohamed 21, 94, 96, 99,
    105, 111, 122
Mahendra, D. 175
Mak Lau Fong 142
Malaysia xii-xiii, 21, 23–4, 29, 32, 37, 40,
    42, 58, 59, 86–106, 191; British
    colonial rule in 94–7; Chinese in xii, 13,
    21, 118–19; class 112; consumerism
    112, 114–15; Dakwa movement 21,
    102–3; economy 21, 95–100, 103, 111,
    113–14; education 101, 105–6;
    employment in Japanese firms xiii, 111,
    112, 115, 117–33; ethnicity 112, 113,
    114, 126–8; honours system 91;
    Industrial Coordination Act (ICA) 1974
    114; industrialisation 111, 113–17;
    Islam xii, 20, 21, 102–3, 111, 115,
    122–3, 127, 128, 129, 130; language
    105–6; lifestyles 112, 126, 131–2; Look
    East Policy (LEP) 111, 112, 122;
    meritocracy 23–4; nationalist
    movement xii, 93–100, 103–4; New
    Economic Policy (NEP) 21, 99–100,
    103, 111, 113–14; patronage 126–7,
    129, 132, 133; rural development
    programmes 97-8
Malaysian Chinese Association (MCA) 94
Malaysian Indian Congress (MIC) 94
Malik, D. 175
Marcos, F. 280
Marcus, G. 5
Marcuse, H. 7
market research, Thailand 242
Marshall, A. 78
Marx, K. 230
Marxism 7, 8
mass media 69; India 256, 261; Thailand
    240, 242
Mathews, J. 256
Matthews, R. 210
Maznah Mohamad 90
Mecca, pligrimage to (*haj*) 32, 122–3, 132
Mennell, S. 67
merchants 11–12
meritocracy 25, 44; India 266–7; Malaysia

23–4; Philippines 289; Singapore xiii,
    148
middle class, as a term 41–2, 43, 88–9
Miller, D. 29
Mills, C. 8, 9
Mills, C. Wright 230
Milner, A. 93, 94, 95
Mintz, S. 67, 72
Misra, B. 12, 266
modernisation theory 3, 4
Mohd. Eunos Abdullah 94
Mohd. Fauzi Yaacob 89, 99, 102
Mohd. Nor Nawawi 90
Mokhzani, B.A.R. 89
monopoly capital 15
Mouffe, C. 8
Muang Thong Thani 71
Murai, Y. 194
Murphy, R. 5
Muslims: India 267, 268; *see also* Islam

Nagata, J. 89
Naisbit, J. 17, 61, 62
Nakharin Mektrairat 232
Natarajan, I. 257
national development 14, 15
national identity 37–8, 44
nationalism 9, 13–14, 19–20, 21–2, 24;
    and consumption 30–1, 290-1; Hindu
    20, 267, 268, 269, 270; Malaysia xii,
    93–100, 103–4
The Nation 67
Neale, R. 13, 25
Nee, V. 210
Nelson, C. 4, 7
Ninan, T.N. 264
Nithi Aewsriwong 244
Nordin Selat 89

occupational class/status: China 211, 212,
    214, 215, 216, 220; Thailand 234, 235,
    236, 245
Ockey, J. xv, 32, 38, 41, 42, 191, 230–46
Offe, C. 153
O'Hanlon, R. 5, 8
Ohmae, K. 78
old elite/rich 31–2, 37, 38, 188-9;
    Indonesia 160–1; Philippines 279–81,
    287–9, 294, 295, 296
Omohundro, J. 284
Ong, A. 88, 115, 128
organisational capital 210–11
Oriental culture 1

Osborne, M. 11, 13

Pacho, A. 284
Pakulski, J. 4
Palmier, L. 11
Papenoe, O. 89, 101
Parish, W.L. 214
Pasuk, P. 13, 20, 28, 30, 38, 243
paternalism 23, 40
patronage, Malaysia 126–7, 129, 132, 133
peasant culture 37–8, 39
Peletz, M. 89
Pemberton, J. 199
Philippines xv-xvi, 12, 13, 15, 20, 22, 36, 38, 275–96; consumption practices xv, 290-4; economy 281–2; education 279; ideology of entrepreneurship 281–9, 296; Filipino-Chinese in xv, 13, 20, 283–6, 292–3, 294–5, 296; housing/home ownership 291; incomes 279; lifestyles xv, 290-3; meritocracy 289; old elite 279–81, 287–9, 294, 295, 296
Pieke, F.N. 224
Pilbeam, P. 13, 25, 42
Pinches, M. 1–45, 275–96
Pitroda, A. 256
poetry reading tradition, Indonesia 166–8
political culture, Singapore 141-2, 143
political economy 5–6
political participation, Thailand xv, 237–40, 242–5
poverty, Singapore 140, 153
power 5; access to 210–11
privatisation: India 254–5; Indonesia 176–7; Philippines281–2
Putra, Hutomo 'Tommy' 178
Pye, L. 3, 40

Race, J. 237
Radhakrishnan, R. 267, 268
Rahman (case study) 121–3, 133
Raillon, F. 204
Raina, M. 259
Rais, R. 175
Ramage, D. 77
Raman, P. 256
Rao, S.L. 257
Rebel, H. 8
Redding, R. 16, 17
Reich, R. 59
religion 44; India 254, 265, 267-8, 270; Malaysia 113; *see also* Islam

reputation: China xiv, 224, 225, 226, 228
resentment 41
Reynolds, C. 232
Ridzuan (case study) 123–5, 130
Riggs, F. 11, 13, 233
Robison, R. 6, 8, 14, 59, 86, 88, 89, 90, 92, 93
Rodan, G. 57, 137
Roff, W. 94, 95
Rosaldo, R. 4
Roseberry, W. 5
Royani, I. 175
Ruan, Danching 219
Rudner, M. 89
Rudolph, L.I. and Rudolph, S. Hoeber 254
Rufaidah, A. 176
rural communities: Indonesia xiv, 188–206
Rushdie, S. 268
Rustam A. Sani 92

Said, E. 3
Sanusi (case study) 119–21, 127, 133
Saparie, G. 168
Sassen, S. 3
Saunders, P. 70
Savage, M. 190
Savavanamuttu, J. 90
Schwarz, A. 166
Schweitzer, T. 201
Schwenk, R. 286
Scott, J. 89, 92
See, C. 284
See, T. 283, 284, 285
Seek, N.H. 70
Seksan Prasertkul 239
Sennett, R. 25
service industries 15
Shah, G. 257, 264
Shaharuddin Maaruf 94, 96, 100
Shamsul, A.B. xii, 10, 11, 12, 13, 21, 23, 40, 42, 57, 86–106, 113,128, 191
Shang, A.E.L. 89
Shaw Foundation 151
Shenoy, M. 256
Shenoy, S. 257
Sheridan, G. 263
Shi Xianmin 225–6
Shields, R. 70, 71, 73
Shiro, H. 29
shopping malls xii, 36, 69–74, 240; Philippines 277, 291
Shotam, N.P. 65
Shui-shen Liu 17

Sider, G. 5
Siffin, W. 231–2, 233
Sikhs 267
Simmel, G. 72
Simone, V. 5, 6
Singapore xiii, 15, 20, 23, 32–3, 39, 40–1,
    58, 59, 137–55; car ownership 140,
    145, 146, 147, 149, 150, 151, 155;
    Chinese identity in 61–6; class 139–41,
    142, 143, 154–5; Confucianism in
    18–19; consumption practices xiii,
    144–52, 155; education 138, 142, 144,
    149; ethnicity 138–9; housing/home-
    ownership 140, 145–7, 149, 152–3,
    154, 155; incomes 140–1, 147;
    language 65; meritocracy xiii, 148;
    national
identity 19–20; political culture 141–2,
    143; poverty 140, 153; social welfare
    152–4;
unionism 149; working class 149-50
Siti Zaharah Sulaiman 101
Sivaraksa, S. 70
Skinner, G. 11, 12, 233
Slater, D. 25, 26
Smart, A. 226–7
Smith, A. 4, 17
Smith, W.A. xii-xiii, 10, 13, 24, 29, 32, 39,
    40, 57, 111–33
Sobary, M. 75, 76
social class *see* class
social networks 39–40; China 40, 208–9,
    218–27
social welfare, Singapore 152–4
Somkiat Onwimon 239–40
Song Ong Siang 61
Srinivas, A. 256
state 15, 58, 59; in China 211; in India
    253–6, 268–9; in Indonesia 191,
    199–200, 205–6; *see also* social welfare
status xi, xii, 8–16; attribution of 25,
    26; contestation of 27- 41; occupational
    (China) 211, 212, 214, 215, 216, 220;
    occupational (Thailand) 234, 235, 236,
    245; Philippines 291–2
Steinberg, D. 11
Stern, R.W. 253, 254
Stivens, M. 88, 90, 115
Strange, S. 78
Strauch, J. 89
style: acquisition of 36
Sudjic, D. 71
Suharto, President 174, 191, 198
Sullivan, J. 67, 200

Sunarya (case study) 193–4
Sungsidh Piriarangsan 243, 244
Surtiretna, N. 175
Sweeney, A. 91
Swift, M. 89
symbolic boundaries 9

Tai Hung-chao 1, 16, 17, 22, 30
Taiwan 63
Talisayon, S. 276
Tan, A. 280
Tan Joo Ean xiii, 10, 19, 23, 31, 33, 40–1,
    137–55
Tan Leok Ee 89
Tan-Climaco, G. 283
Tanaka, S. 86
Tanter, R. 67
TAPOL 174
taste 33, 34, 36, 37, 39
technological modernisation: India 256
Teeranat Karnjana-uksorn 244
Tejo, H.S. 168
television: India 256, 261
Thailand xv, 12–13, 19–20, 32, 41-2, 58,
    59, 191, 230–46; advertising 240–2;
    Chinese ethnicity 19–20; consumption
    practices 240–2; education 234;
    incomes 234, 235; lifestyles 239, 240–2;
    market research 242; mass media 240,
    242; occupational groups 234–6;
    occupational status 234, 235, 236, 245;
    political participation xv, 237–40, 242-
    5; women 242
Tham Seong Chee 65, 89
Thawatt Mokarapong 232
Theh Chongkhadikjj 237
Thirayut Bunmi 239, 243
Thompson, E.P. 8, 230, 231
Thompson, V. 232
Tiara 167
Tomlinson, A. 25
Tong, C. 19
traditional cultural influences 37–8, 39, 44,
    170–1, 199, 200, 202; India 252,
    260–2, 269–70; Philippines 290–1
transnational corporations 14
Tremewan, C. 65, 66, 137
tribal culture 37–8, 39
tributary systems 11–12
trust, China xiv, 224, 225, 226, 228
Turner, B. 4, 8
Turner, G. 5
Turner, M. 66, 291

Ulin, R. 5
Ummat 175
Ungku Aziz 89, 96
unionism: enterprise 116; Singapore 149
United Malays National Organisation
    (UMNO) 94, 97, 101, 102, 103
Uren, D. 251
Urry, J. 8
Utomo, S.P. 168

Van Der Kroef, J. 87, 90
Van der Veer, P. 261, 267
Vatikiotis, M. 177
Veblen, T. 7, 28, 32, 33, 35, 227
Vermeulen, H. 9
Villegas, P. 286
von Brevern, M. 284
Voravidh Charoenlert 244

wages: seniority principle in 116, 132; *see
    also* incomes
Wakao, F. 29
Wallerstein, I. 25, 42, 163, 168
Wang Gungwu 57, 61
Wank, David L. 210
Waters, M. 4
Wazir Karim 88
wealth production 16–24
Weber, M. 8, 17, 230
Wertheim, W. 191
Western, M. 210

Whyte, M.K. 214
Wibisono, C. 165
Wickberg, E. 11, 13, 279, 280
Williams, R. 4, 7, 42
Willios, P. 150
Wilson, D. 233–4
Wilson, E. 150
window-shopping 69
Withayakan Chiangkun 237
women: as consumers 26; India 262-3;
    Indonesia 195–6; Thailand 242
work ethics, Malaysia 122, 128–30
working class, Singapore 149–50
World Hindu Council 267
Wright, E. Olin 210
Wyatt, D. 238

Xie Dehua 227

Yang Mayfair Mei-hui 219, 224
Yao 33, 39
Yao Souchou 169
Yoon Hwan-Shin 164, 165
Young, K. xii, 10, 19, 28, 29, 36, 39, 56–78
Yudohusodo, S. 168
Yuval-Davies, N. 9

Za'aba, Sheikh 94, 96
Zainah Anwar 89
Zimmerman, R. 237